Bookkeeping

ALL-IN-ONE

FOR

DUMMIES®

A Wiley Brand

Bookkeeping
ALL-IN-ONE
FOR DUMMIES
A Wiley Brand

by Lita Epstein and John A. Tracy

FOR DUMMIES
A Wiley Brand

Bookkeeping For Dummies® All-In-One

Published by
John Wiley & Sons, Inc.,
111 River Street,
Hoboken, NJ 07030-5774

www.wiley.com

For general information on our other products and services, please contact our Customer Care Department within the U.S. at 877-762-2974, outside the U.S. at 317-572-3993, or fax 317-572-4002.

For technical support, please visit www.wiley.com/techsupport.

Wiley publishes in a variety of print and electronic formats and by print-on-demand. Some material included with standard print versions of this book may not be included in e-books or in print-on-demand. If this book refers to media such as a CD or DVD that is not included in the version you purchased, you may download this material at http://booksupport.wiley.com. For more information about Wiley products, visit www.wiley.com.

Library of Congress Control Number: 2015945390

ISBN: 97-811-1909421-0

ISBN 97-811-1909395-4 (ePub); ISBN 97-811-1909417-3 (ePDF)

Manufactured in the United States of America

C10002459_071818

Contents at a Glance

Table of Contents

Introduction

Welcome to *Bookkeeping All-In-One For Dummies!* This book is a compendium of great Dummies content covering soup to nuts on bookkeeping with a good portion of accounting coverage as well.

The term *bookkeeper* may generate images of a mild-mannered person quietly, or even meekly, poring over columns of figures under a green banker's lamp somewhere in a corner. In reality, the bookkeeper is vitally important and wields a tremendous amount of power within a company. Information tracked in the books helps business owners make key decisions involving sales planning and product offerings — and enables them to manage many other financial aspects of their business.

If it weren't for the hard work of bookkeepers, companies wouldn't have a clue about what happens with their financial transactions. Without accurate financial accounting, a company owner wouldn't know how many sales were made, how much cash was collected, or how much cash was paid for the products sold to customers during the year. He or she also wouldn't know how much cash was paid to employees or how much cash was spent on other business needs throughout the year. In other words, yes, clueless.

The creation and maintenance of financial records is also important, especially to those who work with the business, such as investors, financial institutions, and employees. People both inside (managers, owners, and employees) and outside the business (investors, lenders, and government agencies) all depend on the bookkeeper's accurate recording of financial transactions.

Bookkeepers must be detailed-oriented, enjoy working with numbers, and be meticulous about accurately entering those numbers in the books. They must be vigilant about keeping a paper trail and filing all needed backup information about the financial transactions entered into the books. And they must be knowledgeable about all aspects of money as it percolates through a business and how to organize and present that information so that it's useful to everyone involved in the business, including outside interests and, yes, the IRS.

That's where this book comes in.

About This Book

Within this book, you may note that some web addresses break across two lines of text. If you're reading this book in print and want to visit one of these web pages, simply key in the web address exactly as it's noted in the text, pretending as though the line break doesn't exist. If you're reading this as an e-book, you've got it easy – just tap the web address to be taken directly to the web page.

Some figures herein use QuickBooks Pro. Because it's the most popular financial accounting software, some chapters show you some of its advanced features where appropriate.

Foolish Assumptions

The book makes some key assumptions about who you are and why you've picked up this book. Much of the book assumes you are:

- ✔ A business owner or manager who wants to know the ins and outs of how to do the books and what's contained in financial records. You have a good understanding of business and its terminology but little or no knowledge of bookkeeping and accounting.

- ✔ A person who does bookkeeping or plans to do bookkeeping for a small business and needs to know more about how to set up and keep the books. You have some basic knowledge of business terminology but don't know much about bookkeeping or accounting, or how to create and maintain financial records.

- ✔ A staff person in a small business who's just been asked to take over the company's bookkeeping duties. You need to know more about how transactions are entered into the books, how to prove out transactions to be sure you're making entries correctly and accurately, and how to prepare financial reports using the data you collect.

Icons Used in This Book

For Dummies books use little pictures called *icons* to flag certain chunks of text that either you shouldn't want to miss or you're free to skip. Here are the icons used in this book and what they mean:

Look to this icon for ideas on how to improve your bookkeeping processes and use the information in the books to manage your business.

This icon marks anything you would do well to recall about bookkeeping after you're finished reading this book.

This icon points out any aspect of bookkeeping that comes with dangers or perils that may hurt the accuracy of your entries or the way in which you use your financial information in the future. I also use this icon to mark certain things that can get you into trouble with the government, your lenders, your vendors, your employees, or your investors.

This points out material that may be interesting if you really want to know a little more, but which isn't crucial to understanding the concept at hand. You can safely skip material with this icon if you like.

When you see this icon, you have the chance to put your new-found knowledge to use. Practice your bookkeeping skills with real-world questions and story problems.

Beyond the Book

In addition to the material in the print or e-book you're reading right now, this book also comes with some access-anywhere goodies on the Web. Check out the free Cheat Sheet at www.dummies.com/cheatsheet/ bookkeepingaio for some handy bite-sized bookkeeping info, including the three elements of bookkeeping that must be kept in balance, definitions of the balance sheet and income statement, and the differences between the four types of business structures.

This book includes some extras that wouldn't fit between the covers, kind of like the Bonus Content on a DVD. Check out http://www.dummies.com/ extras/bookkeepingaio to read articles on the most important accounts bookkeepers keep, ways to manage cash using your books, tips on reading financial reports, and signs that a company is in trouble.

Where to Go From Here

Feel free to start anywhere you like. You can use the table of contents or index to zoom in on any topic you're particularly interested in.

If you need the basics or if you're a little rusty and want to refresh your knowledge of bookkeeping, start with Book I. For the nuts and bolts of accounting and financial reports, drop into Book II. If you already know the basics and terminology of bookkeeping and are ready for some practical advice on day-to-day activities, you might start with Book III. If you're heading toward the end of the year and need to start wrapping things up, check out Book IV. If you're a manager, Book V was written with you in mind.

Wherever you begin, best of luck on your bookkeeping journey!

Book I
Keeping the Books

Visit www.dummies.com for great Dummies content online.

In this book . . .

- ✔ Learn the basics of bookkeeping, from keeping business records to managing daily finances
- ✔ Explore the Chart of Accounts that keeps a business financially organized
- ✔ Understand the ins and outs of the General Ledger and learn how to develop and post entries
- ✔ Discover how to simplify the journal process through your computer
- ✔ Control your records and protect your business's cash in the process
- ✔ Find the right accounting software for you and your business
- ✔ Review the three key financial statements and understand the difference between profit and cash flow

Chapter 1

Basic Bookkeeping

. . . .

In This Chapter

▶ Introducing bookkeeping

▶ Managing daily business finances

▶ Keeping business records

▶ Navigating the accounting cycle

▶ Choosing between cash-basis and accrual accounting

▶ Deciphering double-entry bookkeeping

. . . .

*T*his chapter provides an overview of a bookkeeper's work. If you're just starting a business, you may be your own bookkeeper for a while until you can afford to hire one, so think of this chapter as your to-do list.

All businesses need to keep track of their financial transactions — that's why bookkeeping and bookkeepers are so important. Without accurate records, how can you tell whether your business is making a profit or taking a loss? This chapter also covers the key parts of bookkeeping by introducing you to the language of bookkeeping, familiarizing you with how bookkeepers manage the accounting cycle, and showing you how to understand the most difficult type of bookkeeping — double-entry bookkeeping.

Bookkeeping, the methodical way in which businesses track their financial transactions, is rooted in accounting. *Accounting* is the total structure of records and procedures used to record, classify, and report information about a business's financial transactions. Bookkeeping involves the recording of that financial information into the accounting system while maintaining adherence to solid accounting principles.

Bookkeepers: The Record Keepers of the Business World

Bookkeepers are the ones who toil day in and day out to ensure that transactions are accurately recorded. Bookkeepers need to be very detail oriented and love to work with numbers because numbers and the accounts they go into are just about all these people see all day. A bookkeeper is not required to be a certified public accountant (CPA).

Many small business people who are just starting up their businesses initially serve as their own bookkeepers until the business is large enough to hire someone dedicated to keeping the books. Few small businesses have accountants on staff to check the books and prepare official financial reports; instead, they have bookkeepers on staff who serve as the outside accountants' eyes and ears. Most businesses do seek an accountant with a CPA certification.

In many small businesses today, a bookkeeper enters the business transactions on a daily basis while working inside the company. At the end of each month or quarter, the bookkeeper sends summary reports to the accountant who then checks the transactions for accuracy and prepares financial statements.

In most cases, the accounting system is initially set up with the help of an accountant in order to be sure it uses solid accounting principles. That accountant periodically stops by the office and reviews the system to be sure transactions are being handled properly.

Accurate financial reports are the only way you can know how your business is doing. These reports are developed using the information you, as the bookkeeper, enter into your accounting system. If that information isn't accurate, your financial reports are meaningless. As the old adage goes, "Garbage in, garbage out."

Delving into Bookkeeping Basics

If you don't carefully plan your bookkeeping operation and figure out exactly how and what financial detail you want to track, you'll have absolutely no way to measure the success (or failure, unfortunately) of your business efforts.

Bookkeeping, when done properly, gives you an excellent gauge of how well you're doing financially. It also provides you with lots of information throughout the year so you can test the financial success of your business strategies and make course corrections early in the year if necessary to ensure that you reach your year-end profit goals.

Bookkeeping can become your best friend for managing your financial assets and testing your business strategies, so don't shortchange it. Take the time to develop your bookkeeping system with your accountant before you even open your business's doors and make your first sale.

Picking your accounting method: Cash basis Versus accrual

You can't keep books unless you know how you want to go about doing so. The two basic accounting methods you have to choose from are *cash-basis accounting* and *accrual accounting*. The key difference between these two accounting methods is the point at which you record sales and purchases in your books. If you choose cash-basis accounting, you only record transactions when cash changes hands. If you use accrual accounting, you record a transaction when it's completed, even if cash doesn't change hands.

For example, suppose your company buys products to sell from a vendor but doesn't actually pay for those products for 30 days. If you're using cash-basis accounting, you don't record the purchase until you actually lay out the cash to the vendor. If you're using accrual accounting, you record the purchase when you receive the products, and you also record the future debt in an account called Accounts Payable.

Understanding assets, liabilities, and equity

Every business has three key financial parts that must be kept in balance: assets, liabilities, and equity. *Assets* include everything the company owns, such as cash, inventory, buildings, equipment, and vehicles. *Liabilities* include everything the company owes to others, such as vendor bills, credit card balances, and bank loans. *Equity* includes the claims owners have on the assets based on their portion of ownership in the company.

The formula for keeping your books in balance involves these three elements:

Assets = Liabilities + Equity

Much of bookkeeping involves keeping your books in balance.

Introducing debits and credits

To keep the books, you need to revise your thinking about two common financial terms: debits and credits. Most nonbookkeepers and nonaccountants think of debits as subtractions from their bank accounts. The opposite is true with credits — people usually see these as additions to their accounts, in most cases in the form of refunds or corrections in favor of the account holders.

Well, forget all you thought you knew about debits and credits. Debits and credits are totally different animals in the world of bookkeeping. Because keeping the books involves a method called *double-entry bookkeeping,* you have to make at least two entries — a debit and a credit — into your bookkeeping system for every transaction. Whether that debit or credit adds or subtracts from an account depends solely upon the type of account.

Don't worry. All this debit, credit, and double-entry stuff may sound confusing, but it will become much clearer as you work through this chapter.

Charting your bookkeeping course

You can't just enter transactions in the books willy-nilly. You need to know where exactly those transactions fit into the larger bookkeeping system. That's where your Chart of Accounts comes in; it's essentially a list of all the accounts your business has and what types of transactions go into each one. Book I Chapter 2 talks more about the Chart of Accounts.

Recognizing the Importance of an Accurate Paper Trail

Keeping the books is all about creating an accurate paper trail. You want to track all of your company's financial transactions so if a question comes up at a later date, you can turn to the books to figure out what went wrong.

An accurate paper trail is the only way to track your financial successes and review your financial failures, a task that's vitally important in order to grow your business. You need to know what works successfully so you can repeat it in the future and build on your success. On the other hand, you need to know what failed so you can correct it and avoid making the same mistake again.

All your business's financial transactions are summarized in the General Ledger, and journals keep track of the tiniest details of each transaction. You can make your information gathering more effective by using a computerized accounting system, which gives you access to your financial information in many different formats. Controlling who enters this financial information into your books and who can access it afterwards is smart business and involves critical planning on your part.

Maintaining a ledger

The granddaddy of your bookkeeping system is the General Ledger. In this ledger, you keep a summary of all your accounts and the financial activities that took place involving those accounts throughout the year.

You draw upon the General Ledger's account summaries to develop your financial reports on a monthly, quarterly, or annual basis. You can also use these account summaries to develop internal reports that help you make key business decisions. Book I Chapter 3 talks more about developing and maintaining the General Ledger.

Keeping journals

Small companies conduct hundreds, if not thousands, of transactions each year. If every transaction were kept in the General Ledger, that record would become unwieldy and difficult to use. Instead, most companies keep a series of journals that detail activity in their most active accounts.

For example, almost every company has a Cash Receipts Journal in which to keep the detail for all incoming cash and a Cash Disbursements Journal in which to keep the detail for all outgoing cash. Other journals can detail sales, purchases, customer accounts, vendor accounts, and any other key accounts that see significant activity.

You decide which accounts you want to create journals for based on your business operation and your need for information about key financial transactions. Book I Chapter 4 talks more about journals and the accounts commonly journalized.

Instituting internal controls

Every business owner needs to be concerned with keeping tight controls on company cash and how it's used. One way to institute this control is by placing internal restrictions on who has access to enter information into your books and who has access necessary to use that information.

You also need to carefully control who has the ability to accept cash receipts and who has the ability to disburse your business's cash. Separating duties appropriately helps you protect your business's assets from error, theft, and fraud. Book I Chapter 5 covers controlling your cash and protecting your financial records.

Computerizing

Most companies today use computerized accounting systems to keep their books. You should consider using one of these systems rather than trying to keep your books on paper. You'll find your bookkeeping takes less time and is probably more accurate with a computerized system.

 In addition to increasing accuracy and cutting the time it takes to do your bookkeeping, computerized accounting also makes designing reports easier. These reports can then be used to help make business decisions. Your computerized accounting system stores detailed information about every transaction, so you can group that detail in any way that may assist your decision making. Book I Chapter 6 talks more about computerized accounting systems.

Using Bookkeeping's Tools to Manage Daily Finances

After you set up your business's books and put in place your internal controls, you're ready to use the systems you established to manage the day-to-day operations of your business. You'll quickly see how a well-designed bookkeeping system can make your job of managing your business's finances much easier.

Maintaining inventory

If your company keeps inventory on hand or in warehouses, tracking the costs of the products you plan to sell is critical for managing your profit potential. If you see inventory costs trending upward, you may need to adjust your own prices in order to maintain your profit margin. You certainly don't want to wait until the end of the year to find out how much your inventory cost you.

You also must keep careful watch on how much inventory you have on hand and how much was sold. Inventory can get damaged, discarded, or stolen, meaning that your physical inventory counts may differ from the counts you have in your books. Do a physical count periodically — at least monthly for most businesses and possibly daily for active retail stores.

In addition to watching for signs of theft or poor handling of inventory, make sure you have enough inventory on hand to satisfy your customers' needs. Book III Chapter 1 discusses how to use your bookkeeping system to manage inventory.

Book I

Keeping the Books

Tracking sales

Everyone wants to know how well sales are doing. If you keep your books up-to-date and accurate, you can get those numbers very easily on a daily basis. You can also watch sales trends as often as you think necessary, whether that's daily, weekly, or monthly.

Use the information collected by your bookkeeping system to monitor sales, review discounts offered to customers, and track the return of products. All three elements are critical to gauging the success of the sales of your products.

If you find you need to offer discounts more frequently in order to encourage sales, you may need to review your pricing, and you definitely need to research market conditions to determine the cause of this sales weakness. The cause may be new activities by an aggressive competitor or simply a slow market period. Either way, you need to understand the weakness and figure out how to maintain your profit goals in spite of any obstacles.

While sales tracking reveals an increase in the number of your products being returned, you need to research the issue and find the reason for the increase. Perhaps the quality of the product you're selling is declining, and you need to find a new supplier. Whatever the reason, an increased number of product returns is usually a sign of a problem that needs to be researched and corrected.

Book III Chapter 2 goes over how to use the bookkeeping system for tracking sales, discounts, and returns.

Handling payroll

Payroll can be a huge nightmare for many companies. Payroll requires you to comply with a lot of government regulation and fill out a lot of government paperwork. You also have to worry about collecting payroll taxes and paying employer taxes. And if you pay employee benefits, you have yet another layer of record keeping to deal with. Book III Chapter 3 is about managing payroll and government requirements.

Running Tests for Accuracy

All the time it takes to track your transactions isn't worth it if you don't periodically test to be sure you've entered those transactions accurately. If the numbers you put into your bookkeeping system are garbage, the reports you develop from those numbers will be garbage as well.

Proving out your cash

The first step in testing out your books includes proving that your cash transactions are accurately recorded. This process involves checking a number of different transactions and elements, including the cash taken in on a daily basis by your cashiers and the accuracy of your checking account. Book IV Chapter 3 covers all the steps necessary to take to prove out your cash.

Testing your balance

After you prove out your cash, you can check that you've recorded everything else in your books just as precisely. Review the accounts for any glaring errors and then test whether or not they're in balance by doing a trial balance. You can find out more about trial balances in Book IV Chapter 5.

Doing bookkeeping corrections

You may not find your books in balance the first time you do a trial balance, but don't worry. It's rare to find your books in balance on the first try. Book IV Chapter 6 explains common adjustments that may be needed as you prove out your books at the end of an accounting period. It also explains how to make the necessary corrections.

Finally Showing Off Your Financial Success

Proving out your books and ensuring they're balanced means you finally get to show what your company has accomplished financially by developing reports to present to others. It's almost like putting your business on a stage and taking a bow — well . . . at least you hope you've done well enough to take a bow.

If you've taken advantage of your bookkeeping information and reviewed and consulted it throughout the year, you should have a good idea of how well your business is doing. You also should have taken any course corrections to ensure that your end-of-the-year reports look great.

Preparing financial reports

Most businesses prepare at least two key financial reports, the balance sheet and the income statement, which it can show to company outsiders, including the financial institutions from which the company borrows money and the company's investors.

The balance sheet is a snapshot of your business's financial health as of a particular date. The balance sheet should show that your company's assets are equal to the value of your liabilities and your equity. It's called a *balance sheet* because it's based on a balanced formula:

Assets = Liabilities + Equity

The income statement summarizes your company's financial transactions for a particular time period, such as a month, quarter, or year. This financial statement starts with your revenues, subtracts the costs of goods sold, and then subtracts any expenses incurred in operating the business. The bottom line of the income statement shows how much profit your company made during the accounting period. If you haven't done well, the income statement shows how much you've lost.

Book II Chapter 4 covers preparing a balance sheet, Book II Chapter 5 talks about developing an income statement.

Paying taxes

Most small businesses don't have to pay taxes. Instead, their profits are reported on the personal tax returns of the company owners, whether that's one person (a *sole proprietorship*) or two or more people (a *partnership*). Only companies that have incorporated — become a separate legal entity in which investors buy stock — must file and pay taxes. (Partnerships and LLCs do not pay taxes unless they filed a special form to be taxed as a corporation, but they do have to file information returns, which detail how much the company made and how much profit each owner earned plus any costs and expenses incurred.) Book V Chapter 4 covers how business structures are taxed, and Book II Chapter 3 goes into more detail on business structures.

Wading through Bookkeeping Lingo

Before you can take on bookkeeping and start keeping the books, the first things you must get a handle on are key accounting terms. This section contains a list of terms that all bookkeepers use on a daily basis. This is just an overview, to get you more familiar with the lingo. Rest assured, all of this is covered in lots more detail throughout the book.

Accounts for the balance sheet

Here are a few terms you'll want to know:

- **Balance sheet:** The financial statement that presents a snapshot of the company's financial position (assets, liabilities, and equity) as of a particular date in time. It's called a balance sheet because the things owned by the company (assets) must equal the claims against those assets (liabilities and equity).

  On an ideal balance sheet, the total assets should equal the total liabilities plus the total equity. If your numbers fit this formula, the company's books are in balance.

- **Assets:** All the things a company owns in order to successfully run its business, such as cash, buildings, land, tools, equipment, vehicles, and furniture.

- **Liabilities:** All the debts the company owes, such as bonds, loans, and unpaid bills.

- **Equity:** All the money invested in the company by its owners. In a small business owned by one person or a group of people, the owner's equity is shown in a Capital account. In a larger business that's incorporated, owner's equity is shown in shares of stock. Another key Equity account is Retained Earnings, which tracks all company profits that have been reinvested in the company rather than paid out to the company's owners. Small, unincorporated businesses track money paid out to owners in a Drawing account, whereas incorporated businesses dole out money to owners by paying *dividends* (a portion of the company's profits paid by share of common stock for the quarter or year).

Accounts for the income statement

Here are a few terms related to the income statement that you'll want to know:

- **Income statement:** The financial statement that presents a summary of the company's financial activity over a certain period of time, such as a month, quarter, or year. The statement starts with Revenue earned, subtracts out the Costs of Goods Sold and the Expenses, and ends with the bottom line — Net Profit or Loss.

- **Revenue:** All money collected in the process of selling the company's goods and services. Some companies also collect revenue through other means, such as selling assets the business no longer needs or earning interest by offering short-term loans to employees or other businesses.

- **Costs of goods sold:** All money spent to purchase or make the products or services a company plans to sell to its customers.

- **Expenses:** All money spent to operate the company that's not directly related to the sale of individual goods or services.

Other common terms

Some other common terms include the following:

- **Accounting period:** The time for which financial information is being tracked. Most businesses track their financial results on a monthly basis, so each accounting period equals one month. Some businesses choose to do financial reports on a quarterly basis, so the accounting periods are three months. Other businesses only look at their results on a yearly basis, so their accounting periods are 12 months. Businesses that track their financial activities monthly usually also create quarterly and *annual reports* (a year-end summary of the company's activities and financial results) based on the information they gather.

- **Accounts Receivable:** The account used to track all customer sales that are made by store credit. *Store credit* refers not to credit-card sales but rather to sales for which the customer is given credit directly by the store and the store needs to collect payment from the customer at a later date.

- **Accounts Payable:** The account used to track all outstanding bills from vendors, contractors, consultants, and any other companies or individuals from whom the company buys goods or services

✔ **Depreciation:** An accounting method used to track the aging and use of assets. For example, if you own a car, you know that each year you use the car its value is reduced (unless you own one of those classic cars that goes up in value). Every major asset a business owns ages and eventually needs replacement, including buildings, factories, equipment, and other key assets.

✔ **General Ledger:** Where all the company's accounts are summarized. The General Ledger is the granddaddy of the bookkeeping system.

✔ **Interest:** The money a company needs to pay if it borrows money from a bank or other company. For example, when you buy a car using a car loan, you must pay not only the amount you borrowed but also additional money, or interest, based on a percentage of the amount you borrowed.

✔ **Inventory:** The account that tracks all products that will be sold to customers.

✔ **Journals:** Where bookkeepers keep records (in chronological order) of daily company transactions. Each of the most active accounts, including cash, Accounts Payable, Accounts Receivable, has its own journal.

✔ **Payroll:** The way a company pays its employees. Managing payroll is a key function of the bookkeeper and involves reporting many aspects of payroll to the government, including taxes to be paid on behalf of the employee, unemployment taxes, and workers' compensation.

✔ **Trial balance:** How you test to be sure the books are in balance before pulling together information for the financial reports and closing the books for the accounting period.

Pedaling through the Accounting Cycle

As a bookkeeper, you complete your work by completing the tasks of the accounting cycle. It's called a *cycle* because the workflow is circular: entering transactions, controlling the transactions through the accounting cycle, closing the books at the end of the accounting period, and then starting the entire cycle again for the next accounting period.

The accounting cycle has eight basic steps, which you can see in Figure 1-1.

1. **Transactions:** Financial transactions start the process. Transactions can include the sale or return of a product, the purchase of supplies for business activities, or any other financial activity that involves the

exchange of the company's assets, the establishment or payoff of a debt, or the deposit from or payout of money to the company's owners. All sales and expenses are transactions that must be recorded. The basics of documenting business activities involve recording sales, purchases, and assets, taking on new debt, or paying off debt.

2. **Journal entries:** The transaction is listed in the appropriate journal, maintaining the journal's chronological order of transactions. (The journal is also known as the "book of original entry" and is the first place a transaction is listed.)

3. **Posting:** The transactions are posted to the account that it impacts. These accounts are part of the General Ledger, where you can find a summary of all the business's accounts.

4. **Trial balance:** At the end of the accounting period (which may be a month, quarter, or year depending on your business's practices), you calculate a trial balance.

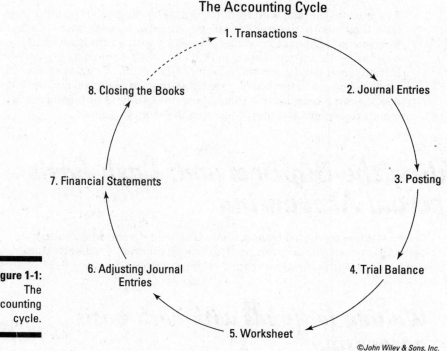

The Accounting Cycle

1. Transactions
2. Journal Entries
3. Posting
4. Trial Balance
5. Worksheet
6. Adjusting Journal Entries
7. Financial Statements
8. Closing the Books

©John Wiley & Sons, Inc.

Figure 1-1:
The accounting cycle.

5. **Worksheet:** Unfortunately, many times your first calculation of the trial balance shows that the books aren't in balance. If that's the case, you look for errors and make corrections called *adjustments,* which are tracked on a worksheet. Adjustments are also made to account for the depreciation of assets and to adjust for one-time payments (such as insurance) that should be allocated on a monthly basis to more accurately match monthly expenses with monthly revenues. After you make and record adjustments, you take another trial balance to be sure the accounts are in balance.

6. **Adjusting journal entries:** Post any necessary corrections after the adjustments are made to the accounts. You don't need to make adjusting entries until the trial balance process is completed and all needed corrections and adjustments have been identified.

7. **Financial statements:** You prepare the balance sheet and income statement using the corrected account balances.

8. **Closing:** You close the books for the revenue and expense accounts and begin the entire cycle again with zero balances in those accounts.

As a businessperson, you want to be able to gauge your profit or loss on month by month, quarter by quarter, and year by year bases. To do that, Revenue and Expense accounts must start with a zero balance at the beginning of each accounting period. In contrast, you carry over Asset, Liability, and Equity account balances from cycle to cycle because the business doesn't start each cycle by getting rid of old assets and buying new assets, paying off and then taking on new debt, or paying out all claims to owners and then collecting the money again.

Tackling the Big Decision: Cash-basis or Accrual Accounting

Before starting to record transactions, you must decide whether to use cash-basis or accrual accounting. The crucial difference between these two processes is in how you record your cash transactions.

Waiting for funds with cash-basis accounting

With *cash-basis accounting,* you record all transactions in the books when cash actually changes hands, meaning when cash payment is received by the company from customers or paid out by the company for purchases or other services. Cash receipt or payment can be in the form of cash, check, credit card, electronic transfer, or other means used to pay for an item.

Cash-basis accounting can't be used if a store sells products on store credit and bills the customer at a later date. There is no provision to record and track money due from customers at some time in the future in the cash-basis accounting method. That's also true for purchases. With the cash-basis accounting method, the owner only records the purchase of supplies or goods that will later be sold when he actually pays cash. If he buys goods on credit to be paid later, he doesn't record the transaction until the cash is actually paid out.

Depending on the size of your business, you may want to start out with cash-basis accounting. Many small businesses run by a sole proprietor or a small group of partners use cash-basis accounting because it's easy. But as the business grows, the business owners find it necessary to switch to accrual accounting in order to more accurately track revenues and expenses.

Cash-basis accounting does a good job of tracking cash flow, but it does a poor job of matching revenues earned with money laid out for expenses. This deficiency is a problem particularly when, as it often happens, a company buys products in one month and sells those products in the next month. For example, you buy products in June with the intent to sell, and pay $1,000 cash. You don't sell the products until July, and that's when you receive cash for the sales. When you close the books at the end of June, you have to show the $1,000 expense with no revenue to offset it, meaning you have a loss that month. When you sell the products for $1,500 in July, you have a $1,500 profit. So, your monthly report for June shows a $1,000 loss, and your monthly report for July shows a $1,500 profit, when in actuality you had revenues of $500 over the two months.

For the most part, this book concentrates on the accrual accounting method. If you choose to use cash-basis accounting, don't panic: You'll still find most of the bookkeeping information here useful, but you don't need to maintain some of the accounts, such as Accounts Receivable and Accounts Payable, because you aren't recording transactions until cash actually changes hands. If you're using a cash-basis accounting system and sell things on credit, though, you'd better have a way to track what people owe you.

Recording right away with accrual accounting

With *accrual accounting*, you record all transactions in the books when they occur, even if no cash changes hands. For example, if you sell on store credit, you record the transaction immediately and enter it into an Accounts

Receivable account until you receive payment. If you buy goods on credit, you immediately enter the transaction into an Accounts Payable account until you pay out cash.

Like cash-basis accounting, accrual accounting has its drawbacks. It does a good job of matching revenues and expenses, but it does a poor job of tracking cash. Because you record revenue when the transaction occurs and not when you collect the cash, your income statement can look great even if you don't have cash in the bank. For example, suppose you're running a contracting company and completing jobs on a daily basis. You can record the revenue upon completion of the job even if you haven't yet collected the cash. If your customers are slow to pay, you may end up with lots of revenue but little cash.

Many companies that use the accrual accounting method also monitor cash flow on a weekly basis to be sure they have enough cash on hand to operate the business. If your business is seasonal, such as a landscaping business with little to do during the winter months, you can establish short-term lines of credit through your bank to maintain cash flow through the lean times.

Seeing Double with Double-Entry Bookkeeping

All businesses, whether they use the cash-basis accounting method or the accrual accounting method, use *double-entry bookkeeping* to keep their books. A practice that helps minimize errors and increase the chance that your books balance, double-entry bookkeeping gets its name because you enter all transactions twice.

When it comes to double-entry bookkeeping, the key formula for the balance sheet (Assets = Liabilities + Equity) plays a major role.

In order to adjust the balance of accounts in the bookkeeping world, you use a combination of *debits* and *credits*. You may think of a debit as a subtraction because you've found that debits usually mean a decrease in your bank balance. On the other hand, you've probably been excited to find unexpected credits in your bank or credit card that mean more money has been added to the account in your favor. Now, forget all that you ever learned about debits or credits. In the world of bookkeeping, their meanings aren't so simple.

The only definite thing when it comes to debits and credits in the bookkeeping world is that a debit is on the left side of a transaction and a credit is on the right side of a transaction. Everything beyond that can get very muddled. Don't worry if you're finding this concept very difficult to grasp. You get plenty of practice using these concepts throughout this book.

Before getting into all the technical mumbo jumbo of double-entry bookkeeping, here's an example of the practice in action. Suppose you purchase a new desk that costs $1,500 for your office. This transaction actually has two parts: You spend an asset — cash — to buy another asset — furniture. So, you must adjust two accounts in your company's books: the Cash account and the Furniture account. Here's what the transaction looks like in a bookkeeping entry:

Account	Debit	Credit
Furniture	$1,500	
Cash		$1,500

To purchase a new desk for the office.

In this transaction, you record the accounts impacted by the transaction. The debit increases the value of the Furniture account, and the credit decreases the value of the Cash account. For this transaction, both accounts impacted are asset accounts, so, looking at how the balance sheet is affected, you can see that the only changes are to the asset side of the balance sheet equation:

Assets = Liabilities + Equity

Furniture increase = Cash decreases = No change to total assets

In this case, the books stay in balance because the exact dollar amount that increases the value of your Furniture account decreases the value of your Cash account. At the bottom of any journal entry, you should include a brief explanation that explains the purpose for the entry. The first example indicates this entry was "To purchase a new desk for the office."

To show you how you record a transaction if it impacts both sides of the balance sheet equation, here's an example that shows how to record the purchase of inventory. Suppose you purchase $5,000 worth of widgets on credit. (Haven't you always wondered what widgets were? You won't find the answer here. They're just commonly used in accounting examples to represent something that's purchased.) These new widgets add value to your Inventory Asset account and also add value to your Accounts Payable account. (Remember, the Accounts Payable account is a Liability account where you track bills that need to be paid at some point in the future.) Here's how the bookkeeping transaction for your widget purchase looks:

Account	Debit	Credit
Inventory	$5,000	
Accounts Payable		$5,000

To purchase widgets for sale to customers.

Here's how this transaction affects the balance sheet equation:

Assets = Liabilities + Equity

Inventory increases = Accounts Payable increases = No change

In this case, the books stay in balance because both sides of the equation increase by $5,000.

You can see from the two example transactions how double-entry bookkeeping helps to keep your books in balance — as long as you make sure each entry into the books is balanced. Balancing your entries may look simple here, but sometimes bookkeeping entries can get very complex when more than two accounts are impacted by the transaction. Don't worry, you don't have to understand it totally now. You'll see how to enter transactions throughout the book. Again, this is just a quick overview to introduce the subject.

Differentiating Debits and Credits

Because bookkeeping's debits and credits are different from the ones you're used to encountering, you're probably wondering how you're supposed to know whether a debit or credit will increase or decrease an account. Believe it or not, identifying the difference will become second nature as you start making regular bookkeeping entries. But to make things easier, Table 1-1 is a chart that's commonly used by all bookkeepers and accountants.

Copy Table 1-1 and post it at your desk when you start keeping your own books. It will help you keep your debits and credits straight!

Table 1-1	How Credits and Debits Impact Your Accounts	
Account Type	*Debits*	*Credits*
Assets	Increase	Decrease
Liabilities	Decrease	Increase
Income	Decrease	Increase
Expenses	Increase	Decrease

Chapter 2

Charting the Accounts

Can you imagine the mess your checkbook would be if you didn't record each check you wrote? You've probably forgotten to record a check or two on occasion, but you certainly learn your lesson when you realize that an important payment bounces as a result. Yikes!

Keeping the books of a business can be a lot more difficult than maintaining a personal checkbook. Each business transaction must be carefully recorded to make sure it goes into the right account. This careful bookkeeping gives you an effective tool for figuring out how well the business is doing financially.

As a bookkeeper, you need a road map to help you determine where to record all those transactions. This road map is called the Chart of Accounts. This chapter tells you how to set up the Chart of Accounts, which includes many different accounts. It also reviews the types of transactions you enter into each type of account in order to track the key parts of any business: assets, liabilities, equity, revenue, and expenses.

Getting to Know the Chart of Accounts

The *Chart of Accounts* is the road map that a business creates to organize its financial transactions. After all, you can't record a transaction until you know where to put it! Essentially, this chart is a list of all the accounts a business has, organized in a specific order; each account has a description that includes the type of account and the types of transactions that should be entered into that account. Every business creates its own Chart of Accounts based on how the business is operated, so you're unlikely to find two businesses with the exact same Charts of Accounts.

However, some basic organizational and structural characteristics are common to all Charts of Accounts. The organization and structure are designed around two key financial reports: the *balance sheet,* which shows what your business owns and what it owes, and the *income statement,* which shows how much money your business took in from sales and how much money it spent to generate those sales. (You can find out more about balance sheets in Book II Chapter 4 and income statements in Book II Chapter 5.)

The Chart of Accounts starts with the balance sheet accounts, which include the following:

- ✔ **Current Assets:** Includes all accounts that track things the company owns and expects to use in the next 12 months, such as cash, accounts receivable (money collected from customers), and inventory

- ✔ **Long-term Assets:** Includes all accounts that track things the company owns that have a lifespan of more than 12 months, such as buildings, furniture, and equipment

- ✔ **Current Liabilities:** Includes all accounts that track debts the company must pay over the next 12 months, such as accounts payable (bills from vendors, contractors, and consultants), interest payable, and credit cards payable

- ✔ **Long-term Liabilities:** Includes all accounts that track debts the company must pay over a period of time longer than the next 12 months, such as mortgages payable and bonds payable

- ✔ **Equity:** Includes all accounts that track the owners of the company and their claims against the company's assets, which include any money invested in the company, any money taken out of the company, and any earnings that have been reinvested in the company

The rest of the chart is filled with income statement accounts, which include

- ✔ **Revenue:** Includes all accounts that track sales of goods and services as well as revenue generated for the company by other means

- ✔ **Cost of Goods Sold:** Includes all accounts that track the direct costs involved in selling the company's goods or services

- ✔ **Expenses:** Includes all accounts that track expenses related to running the business that aren't directly tied to the sale of individual products or services

When developing the Chart of Accounts, you start by listing all the Asset accounts, the Liability accounts, the Equity accounts, the Revenue accounts, and finally, the Expense accounts. All these accounts come from two places: the balance sheet and the income statement.

This chapter reviews the key account types found in most businesses, but this list isn't cast in stone. You should develop an account list that makes the most sense for how you operate your business and the financial information you want to track. As you explore the accounts that make up the Chart of Accounts, you'll see how the structure may differ for different businesses.

The Chart of Accounts is a money management tool that helps you track your business transactions, so set it up in a way that provides you with the financial information you need to make smart business decisions. You'll probably tweak the accounts in your chart annually and, if necessary, you may add accounts during the year if you find something for which you want more detailed tracking. You can add accounts during the year, but it's best not to delete accounts until the end of a 12-month reporting period. Book IV Chapter 6 discusses adding and deleting accounts from your books.

Starting with the Balance Sheet Accounts

The first part of the Chart of Accounts is made up of balance sheet accounts, which break down into the following three categories:

- ✔ **Asset:** These accounts are used to track what the business owns. Assets include cash on hand, furniture, buildings, vehicles, and so on.

- ✔ **Liability:** These accounts track what the business owes, or, more specifically, claims that lenders have against the business's assets. For example, mortgages on buildings and lines of credit are two common types of liabilities.

- ✔ **Equity:** These accounts track what the owners put into the business and the claims owners have against assets. For example, stockholders are company owners that have claims against the business's assets.

The balance sheet accounts, and the financial report they make up, are so-called because they have to *balance* out. The value of the assets must be equal to the claims made against those assets. (Remember, these claims are liabilities made by lenders and equity made by owners.)

Book II Chapter 4 discusses the balance sheet in greater detail, including how it's prepared and used. This section, however, examines the basic components of the balance sheet, as reflected in the Chart of Accounts.

Tackling assets

First on the chart are always the accounts that track what the company owns — its assets: current assets and long-term assets.

Current assets

Current assets are the key assets that your business uses up during a 12-month period and will likely not be there the next year. The accounts that reflect current assets on the Chart of Accounts are as follows:

- ✔ **Cash in Checking:** Any company's primary account is the checking account used for operating activities. This is the account used to deposit revenues and pay expenses. Some companies have more than one operating account in this category; for example, a company with many divisions may have an operating account for each division.

- ✔ **Cash in Savings:** This account is used for surplus cash. Any cash for which there is no immediate plan is deposited in an interest-earning savings account so that it can at least earn interest while the company decides what to do with it.

- ✔ **Cash on Hand:** This account is used to track any cash kept at retail stores or in the office. In retail stores, cash must be kept in registers in order to provide change to customers. In the office, petty cash is often kept around for immediate cash needs that pop up from time to time. This account helps you keep track of the cash held outside a financial institution.

- ✔ **Accounts Receivable:** If you offer your products or services to customers on store credit (meaning *your* store credit system), then you need this account to track the customers who buy on your dime.

  Accounts Receivable isn't used to track purchases made on other types of credit cards because your business gets paid directly by banks, not customers, when other credit cards are used. Head to Book III Chapter 2 to read more about this scenario and the corresponding type of account.

- ✔ **Inventory:** This account tracks the products on hand to sell to your customers. The value of the assets in this account varies depending on how you decide to track the flow of inventory in and out of the business. Book III Chapter 1 discusses inventory valuation and tracking in greater detail.

- ✔ **Prepaid Insurance:** This account tracks insurance you pay in advance that's credited as it's used up each month. For example, if you own a building and prepay one year in advance, each month you reduce the amount that you prepaid by 1/12 as the prepayment is used up.

Depending upon the type of business you're setting up, you may have other current asset accounts that you decide to track. For example, if you're starting a service business in consulting, you're likely to have a Consulting account for tracking cash collected for those services. If you run a business in which you barter assets (such as trading your services for paper goods), you may add a Barter account for business-to-business barter.

Long-term assets

Long-term assets are assets that you anticipate your business will use for more than 12 months. This section lists some of the most common long-term assets, starting with the key accounts related to buildings and factories owned by the company:

- ✓ **Land:** This account tracks the land owned by the company. The value of the land is based on the cost of purchasing it. Land value is tracked separately from the value of any buildings standing on that land because land isn't depreciated in value, but buildings must be depreciated. *Depreciation* is an accounting method that shows an asset is being used up. Book IV Chapter 1 talks more about depreciation.

- ✓ **Buildings:** This account tracks the value of any buildings a business owns. As with land, the value of the building is based on the cost of purchasing it. The key difference between buildings and land is that the building's value is depreciated, as discussed in the previous bullet.

- ✓ **Accumulated Depreciation – Buildings:** This account tracks the cumulative amount a building is depreciated over its useful lifespan. Book IV Chapter 1 talks more about how to calculate depreciation.

- ✓ **Leasehold Improvements:** This account tracks the value of improvements to buildings or other facilities that a business leases rather than purchases. Frequently when a business leases a property, it must pay for any improvements necessary in order to use that property the way it's needed. For example, if a business leases a store in a strip mall, it's likely that the space leased is an empty shell or filled with shelving and other items that may not match the particular needs of the business. As with buildings, leasehold improvements are depreciated as the value of the asset ages.

- ✓ **Accumulated Depreciation – Leasehold Improvements:** This account tracks the cumulative amount depreciated for leasehold improvements.

The following are the types of accounts for smaller long-term assets, such as vehicles and furniture:

- **Vehicles:** This account tracks any cars, trucks, or other vehicles owned by the business. The initial value of any vehicle is listed in this account based on the total cost paid to put the vehicle in service. Sometimes this value is more than the purchase price if additions were needed to make the vehicle usable for the particular type of business. For example, if a business provides transportation for the handicapped and must add additional equipment to a vehicle in order to serve the needs of its customers, that additional equipment is added to the value of the vehicle. Vehicles also depreciate through their useful lifespan.

- **Accumulated Depreciation – Vehicles:** This account tracks the depreciation of all vehicles owned by the company.

- **Furniture and Fixtures:** This account tracks any furniture or fixtures purchased for use in the business. The account includes the value of all chairs, desks, store fixtures, and shelving needed to operate the business. The value of the furniture and fixtures in this account is based on the cost of purchasing these items. These items are depreciated during their useful lifespan.

- **Accumulated Depreciation – Furniture and Fixtures:** This account tracks the accumulated depreciation of all furniture and fixtures.

- **Equipment:** This account tracks equipment that was purchased for use for more than one year, such as computers, copiers, tools, and cash registers. The value of the equipment is based on the cost to purchase these items. Equipment is also depreciated to show that over time it gets used up and must be replaced.

- **Accumulated Depreciation – Equipment:** This account tracks the accumulated depreciation of all the equipment.

The following accounts track the long-term assets that you can't touch but that still represent things of value owned by the company, such as organization costs, patents, and copyrights. These are called *intangible assets,* and the accounts that track them include

- **Organization Costs:** This account tracks initial start-up expenses to get the business off the ground. Many such expenses can't be written off in the first year. For example, special licenses and legal fees must be written off over a number of years using a method similar to depreciation, called *amortization,* which is also tracked. Book IV Chapter 1 discusses amortization in greater detail.

- **Amortization – Organization Costs:** This account tracks the accumulated amortization of organization costs during the period in which they're being written-off.

- ✔ **Patents:** This account tracks the costs associated with *patents,* grants made by governments that guarantee to the inventor of a product or service the exclusive right to make, use, and sell that product or service over a set period of time. Like organization costs, patent costs are amortized. The value of this asset is based on the expenses the company incurs to get the right to patent the product.

- ✔ **Amortization – Patents:** This account tracks the accumulated amortization of a business's patents.

- ✔ **Copyrights:** This account tracks the costs incurred to establish copyrights, the legal rights given to an author, playwright, publisher, or any other distributor of a publication or production for a unique work of literature, music, drama, or art. This legal right expires after a set number of years, so its value is amortized as the copyright gets used up.

- ✔ **Goodwill:** This account is only needed if a company buys another company for more than the actual value of its tangible assets. Goodwill reflects the intangible value of this purchase for things like company reputation, store locations, customer base, and other items that increase the value of the business bought.

If you hold a lot of assets that aren't of great value, you can also set up an "Other Assets" account to track them. Any asset you track in the Other Assets account that you later want to track individually can be shifted to its own account. Book IV Chapter 6 discusses adjusting the Chart of Accounts.

Laying out your liabilities

After you cover assets, the next stop on the bookkeeping highway is the accounts that track what your business owes to others. These "others" can include vendors from which you buy products or supplies, financial institutions from which you borrow money, and anyone else who lends money to your business. Like assets, liabilities are lumped into two types: current liabilities and long-term liabilities.

Current liabilities

Current liabilities are debts due in the next 12 months. Some of the most common types of current liabilities accounts that appear on the Chart of Accounts are

- ✔ **Accounts Payable:** Tracks money the company owes to vendors, contractors, suppliers, and consultants that must be paid in less than a year. Most of these liabilities must be paid 30 to 90 days from billing.

✔ **Sales Tax Collected:** You may not think of sales tax as a liability, but because the business collects the tax from the customer and doesn't pay it immediately to the government entity, the taxes collected become a liability tracked in this account. A business usually collects sales tax throughout the month and then pays it to the local, state, or federal government on a monthly basis. Book V Chapter 4 discusses paying sales taxes in greater detail.

✔ **Accrued Payroll Taxes:** This account tracks payroll taxes collected from employees to pay state, local, or federal income taxes as well as Social Security and Medicare taxes. Companies don't have to pay these taxes to the government entities immediately, so depending on the size of the payroll, companies may pay payroll taxes on a monthly or quarterly basis. Book III Chapter 3 discusses how to handle payroll taxes.

✔ **Credit Cards Payable:** This account tracks all credit-card accounts to which the business is liable. Most companies use credit cards as short-term debt and pay them off completely at the end of each month, but some smaller companies carry credit-card balances over a longer period of time. Because credit cards often have a much higher interest rate than most lines of credits, most companies transfer any credit-card debt they can't pay entirely at the end of a month to a line of credit at a bank. When it comes to your Chart of Accounts, you can set up one Credit Card Payable account, but you may want to set up a separate account for each card your company holds to improve tracking credit-card usage.

How you set up your current liabilities and how many individual accounts you establish depends on how detailed you want to track each type of liability. For example, you can set up separate current liability accounts for major vendors if you find that approach provides you with a better money management tool. For example, suppose that a small hardware retail store buys most of the tools it sells from Snap-on. To keep better control of its spending with Snap-on, the bookkeeper sets up a specific account called Accounts Payable – Snap-on, which is used only for tracking invoices and payments to that vendor. In this example, all other invoices and payments to other vendors and suppliers are tracked in the general Accounts Payable account.

Long-term liabilities

Long-term liabilities are debts due in more than 12 months. The number of long-term liability accounts you maintain on your Chart of Accounts depends on your debt structure. The two most common types are

✔ **Loans Payable:** This account tracks any long-term loans, such as a mortgage on your business building. Most businesses have separate loans payable accounts for each of their long-term loans. For example, you could have Loans Payable – Mortgage Bank for your building and Loans Payable – Car Bank for your vehicle loan.

✔ **Notes Payable:** Some businesses borrow money from other businesses using *notes,* a method of borrowing that doesn't require the company to put up an asset, such as a mortgage on a building or a car loan, as collateral. This account tracks any notes due.

In addition to any separate long-term debt you may want to track in its own account, you may also want to set up an account called Other Liabilities that you can use to track types of debt that are so insignificant to the business that you don't think they need their own accounts.

Eyeing the equity

Every business is owned by somebody. *Equity accounts* track owners' contributions to the business as well as their share of ownership. For a corporation, ownership is tracked by the sale of individual shares of stock because each stockholder owns a portion of the business. In smaller companies that are owned by one person or a group of people, equity is tracked using Capital and Drawing accounts. Here are the basic equity accounts that appear in the Chart of Accounts:

✔ **Common Stock:** This account reflects the value of outstanding shares of stock sold to investors. A company calculates this value by multiplying the number of shares issued by the value of each share of stock. Only corporations need to establish this account.

✔ **Retained Earnings:** This account tracks the profits or losses accumulated since a business was opened. At the end of each year, the profit or loss calculated on the income statement is used to adjust the value of this account. For example, if a company made a $100,000 profit in the past year, the Retained Earnings account would be increased by that amount; if the company lost $100,000, then that amount would be subtracted from this account.

✔ **Capital:** This account is only necessary for small, unincorporated businesses. The Capital account reflects the amount of initial money the business owner contributed to the company as well as owner contributions made after the initial start-up. The value of this account is based on cash contributions and other assets contributed by the business owner, such as equipment, vehicles, or buildings. If a small company has several different partners, then each partner gets his or her own Capital account to track his or her contributions.

✔ **Drawing:** This account is only necessary for businesses that aren't incorporated. It tracks any money that a business owner takes out of the business. If the business has several partners, each partner gets his or her own Drawing account to track what he or she takes out of the business.

Tracking the Income Statement Accounts

The income statement is made up of two types of accounts:

- **Revenue:** These accounts track all money coming into the business, including sales, interest earned on savings, and any other methods used to generate income.

- **Expenses:** These accounts track all money that a business spends in order to keep itself afloat.

The bottom line of the income statement shows whether your business made a profit or a loss for a specified period of time. Book II Chapter 5 discusses the income statement in detail. This section examines the various accounts that make up the income statement portion of the Chart of Accounts.

Recording the money you make

First up in the income statement portion of the Chart of Accounts are accounts that track revenue coming into the business. If you choose to offer discounts or accept returns, that activity also falls within the revenue grouping. The most common income accounts are

- **Sales of Goods or Services:** This account, which appears at the top of every income statement, tracks all the money that the company earns selling its products, services, or both.

- **Sales Discounts:** Because most businesses offer discounts to encourage sales, this account tracks any reductions to the full price of merchandise.

- **Sales Returns:** This account tracks transactions related to returns, when a customer returns a product because he or she is unhappy with it for some reason.

When you examine an income statement from a company other than the one you own or are working for, you usually see the following accounts summarized as one line item called Revenue or Net Revenue. Because not all income is generated by sales of products or services, other income accounts that may appear on a Chart of Accounts include

- **Other Income:** If a company takes in income from a source other than its primary business activity, that income is recorded in this account. For example, a company that encourages recycling and earns income from the items recycled records that income in this account.

✔ **Interest Income:** This account tracks any income earned by collecting interest on a company's savings accounts. If the company loans money to employees or to another company and earns interest on that money, that interest is recorded in this account as well.

✔ **Sale of Fixed Assets:** Any time a company sells a fixed asset, such as a car or furniture, any revenue from the sale is recorded in this account. A company should only record revenue remaining after subtracting the accumulated depreciation from the original cost of the asset.

Tracking the Cost of Sales

Before you can sell a product, you must spend some money to either buy or make that product. The type of account used to track the money spent is called a Cost of Goods Sold account. The most common are

✔ **Purchases:** Tracks the purchases of all items you plan to sell.

✔ **Purchase Discount:** Tracks the discounts you may receive from vendors if you pay for your purchase quickly. For example, a company may give you a 2 percent discount on your purchase if you pay the bill in 10 days rather than wait until the end of the 30-day payment allotment.

✔ **Purchase Returns:** If you're unhappy with a product you've bought, record the value of any returns in this account.

✔ **Freight Charges:** Charges related to shipping items you purchase for later sale. You may or may not want to keep track of this detail.

✔ **Other Sales Costs:** This is a catchall account for anything that doesn't fit into one of the other Cost of Goods Sold accounts.

Acknowledging the money you spend

Expense accounts take the cake for the longest list of individual accounts. Any money you spend on the business that can't be tied directly to the sale of an individual product falls under the expense account category. For example, advertising a storewide sale isn't directly tied to the sale of any one product, so the costs associated with advertising fall under this category.

The Chart of Accounts mirrors your business operations, so it's up to you to decide how much detail you want to keep in your expense accounts. Most businesses have expenses that are unique to their operations, so your list will probably be longer than the one presented here. However, you also may find that you don't need some of these accounts.

On your Chart of Accounts, the expense accounts don't have to appear in any specific order, so they are listed here alphabetically. Here are the most common expense accounts:

- ✓ **Advertising:** Tracks expenses involved in promoting a business or its products. Money spent on newspaper, television, magazine, and radio advertising is recorded here as well as any money spent to print flyers and mailings to customers. For community events such as cancer walks or crafts fairs, associated costs are tracked in this account as well.

- ✓ **Bank Service Charges:** This account tracks any charges made by a bank to service a company's bank accounts.

- ✓ **Dues and Subscriptions:** This account tracks expenses related to business club membership or subscriptions to magazines.

- ✓ **Equipment Rental:** This account tracks expenses related to renting equipment for a short-term project. For example, a business that needs to rent a truck to pick up some new fixtures for its store records that truck rental in this account.

- ✓ **Insurance:** Tracks any money paid to buy insurance. Many businesses break this down into several accounts, such as Insurance – Employees Group, which tracks any expenses paid for employee insurance, or Insurance – Officers' Life, which tracks money spent to buy insurance to protect the life of a key owner or officer of the company. Companies often insure their key owners and executives because an unexpected death, especially for a small company, may mean facing many unexpected expenses in order to keep the company's doors open. In such a case, insurance proceeds can be used to cover those expenses.

- ✓ **Legal and Accounting:** This account tracks any money that's paid for legal or accounting advice.

- ✓ **Miscellaneous Expenses:** This is a catchall account for expenses that don't fit into one of a company's established accounts. If certain miscellaneous expenses occur frequently, a company may choose to add an account to the Chart of Accounts and move related expenses into that new account by subtracting all related transactions from the Miscellaneous Expenses account and adding them to the new account. With this shuffle, it's important to carefully balance out the adjusting transaction to avoid any errors or double counting.

- ✓ **Office Expense:** This account tracks any items purchased in order to run an office. For example, office supplies such as paper and pens or business cards fit in this account. As with miscellaneous expenses, a company may choose to track some office expense items in their own accounts. For example, if you find your office is using a lot of copy paper and you want to track that separately, you set up a Copy Paper expense account. Just be sure you really need the detail because the number of accounts can get unwieldy.

✔ **Payroll Taxes:** This account tracks any taxes paid related to employee payroll, such as the employer's share of Social Security and Medicare, unemployment compensation, and workers' compensation.

✔ **Postage:** Tracks money spent on stamps and shipping. If a company does a large amount of shipping through vendors such as UPS or Federal Express, it may want to track that spending in separate accounts for each vendor. This option is particularly helpful for small companies that sell over the Internet or through catalog sales.

✔ **Rent Expense:** Tracks rental costs for a business's office or retail space.

✔ **Salaries and Wages:** This account tracks any money paid to employees as salary or wages.

✔ **Supplies:** This account tracks any business supplies that don't fit into the category of office supplies. For example, supplies needed for the operation of retail stores are tracked using this account.

✔ **Travel and Entertainment:** This account tracks money spent for business purposes on travel or entertainment. Some business separate these expenses into several accounts, such as Travel and Entertainment – Meals, Travel and Entertainment – Travel, and Travel and Entertainment – Entertainment, to keep a close watch.

✔ **Telephone:** This account tracks all business expenses related to the telephone and telephone calls.

✔ **Utilities:** Tracks money paid for utilities (electricity, gas, and water).

✔ **Vehicles:** Tracks expenses related to the operation of company vehicles.

Setting Up Your Chart of Accounts

You can use the lists of accounts provided in this chapter to get started setting up your business's own Chart of Accounts. There's really no secret — just make a list of the accounts that apply to your business.

Don't panic if you can't think of every type of account you may need for your business. It's very easy to add to the Chart of Accounts at any time. Just add the account to the list and distribute the revised list to any employees that use it. (Even employees not involved in bookkeeping need a copy of your Chart of Accounts if they code invoices or other transactions and indicate to which account those transactions should be recorded.)

The Chart of Accounts usually includes at least three columns:

- ✔ **Account:** Lists the account names
- ✔ **Type:** Lists the type of account: asset, liability, equity, income, cost of goods sold, or expense
- ✔ **Description:** Contains a description of the type of transaction that should be recorded in the account

Many companies also assign numbers to the accounts, to be used for coding charges. If your company is using a computerized system, the computer automatically assigns the account number. Otherwise, you need to plan out your own numbering system. The most common number system is as follows:

- ✔ Asset accounts: 1,000 to 1,999
- ✔ Liability accounts: 2,000 to 2,999
- ✔ Equity accounts: 3,000 to 3,999
- ✔ Sales and Cost of Goods Sold accounts: 4,000 to 4,999
- ✔ Expense accounts: 5,000 to 6,999

This numbering system matches the one used by computerized accounting systems, making it easy at some future time to automate the books using a computerized accounting system. A number of different Charts of Accounts have been developed. When you get your computerized system, whichever accounting software you use, all you need to do is review the chart options for the type of business you run included with that software, delete any accounts you don't want, and add any new accounts that fit your business plan.

If you're setting up your Chart of Accounts manually, be sure to leave a lot of room between accounts to add new accounts. For example, number your Cash in Checking account 1,000 and your Accounts Receivable account 1,100. That leaves you plenty of room to add other accounts to track cash.

Figure 2-1 is a Chart of Accounts from QuickBooks 2014. Asset accounts are first, followed by liability, equity, income, and expense accounts.

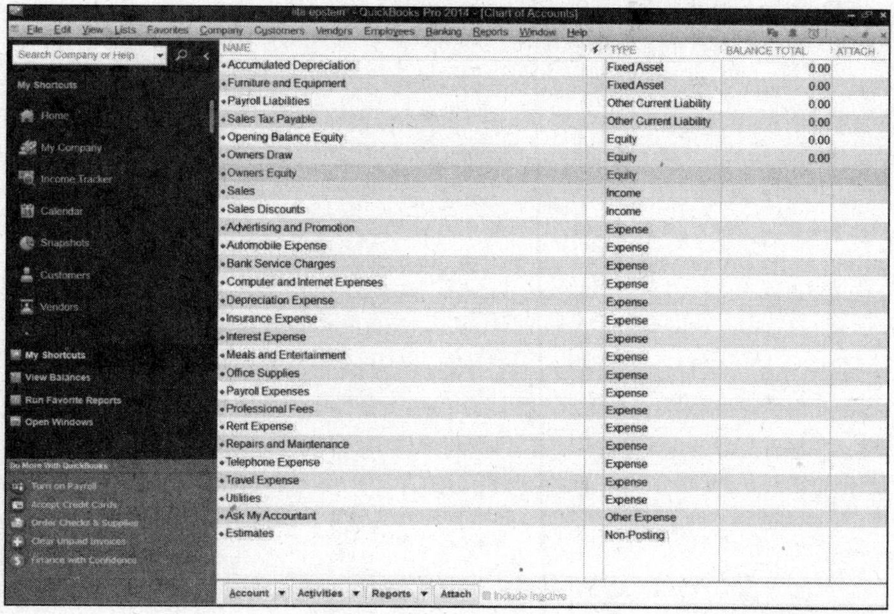

Figure 2-1:
The top portion of a sample Chart of Accounts.

© John Wiley & Sons, Inc.

Chapter 3

The General Ledger

As a bookkeeper, you may be dreaming of having one source that you can turn to when you need to review all entries that impact your business's accounts. (Okay, so maybe that's not exactly what you're dreaming about.) The General Ledger is your dream come true. It's where you find a summary of transactions and a record of the accounts that those transactions impact.

In this chapter, you discover the purpose of the General Ledger. It tells you how to not only develop entries for the Ledger but also enter (or post) them. In addition, it explains how you can change already posted information or correct entries in the Ledger and how this entire process is streamlined when you use a computerized accounting system.

The Eyes and Ears of a Business

Of course, the book known as the General Ledger isn't alive, so it can't actually see or speak. But wouldn't it be nice if it could just tell you all its secrets about what happens with your money? That would certainly make it a lot easier to track down any bookkeeping problems or errors.

Instead, the General Ledger serves as the figurative eyes and ears of bookkeepers and accountants who want to know what financial transactions have taken place historically in a business. By reading the General Ledger — not exactly interesting reading, unless you just love numbers — you can see, account by account, every transaction that has taken place in the business.

(And to uncover more details about those transactions, you can turn to your business's journals, where transactions are kept on a daily basis. See Chapter 5 for the lowdown on journals.)

The General Ledger is the granddaddy of your business. You can find all the transactions that ever occurred in the history of the business in the General Ledger account. It's the one place you need to go to find transactions that impact Cash, Inventory, Accounts Receivable, Accounts Payable, and any other account included in your business's Chart of Accounts. (See Book I Chapter 2 for more on setting up the Chart of Accounts and the kinds of transactions you can find in each.)

Developing Entries for the Ledger

Because your business's transactions are first entered into journals, you develop many of the entries for the General Ledger based on information pulled from the appropriate journal. For example, cash receipts and the accounts that are impacted by those receipts are listed in the Cash Receipts journal. Cash disbursements and the accounts impacted by those disbursements are listed in the Cash Disbursements journal. The same is true for transactions found in the Sales journal, Purchases journal, General journal, and any other special journals you may be using in your business.

At the end of each month, you summarize each journal by adding up the columns and then use that summary to develop an entry for the General Ledger. That takes a lot less time than entering every transaction in the General Ledger.

Book I Chapter 4 introduces you to the process of entering transactions and summarizing journals. Near the end of that chapter, this entry for the General Ledger appears:

Account	Debit	Credit
Cash	$2,900	
Accounts Receivable		$500
Sales		$900
Capital		$1,500

Note that the Debits and Credits are in balance — $2,900 each. Remember all entries to the General Ledger must be balanced entries. That's the cardinal rule of double-entry bookkeeping. (For more details about double-entry bookkeeping, check out Book I Chapter 1.)

In this entry, the Cash account is increased by $2,900 to show that cash was received. The Accounts Receivable account is decreased by $500 to show customers paid their bills, and the money is no longer due. The Sales account is increased by $900, because additional revenue was collected. The Capital account is increased by $1,500 because the owner put more cash into the business.

Figures 3-1 through 3-4 summarize the remaining journal pages prepared in Book I Chapter 4, resulting in the following entries for the General Ledger:

Figure 3-1 — Summarized Cash Disbursements Journal
Figure 3-2 — Summarized Sales Journal
Figure 3-3 — Summarized Purchases Journal
Figure 3-4 — Summarized General Journal

Figure 3-1 shows a summary of the Cash Disbursements journal for a business.

Figure 3-1:
Summarizing cash transactions so they can be posted to the General Ledger.

Cheesecake Shop
Cash Disbursements Journal
March 2014

Date	Account Debited	Check #	PR	General Debit	Account Payable Debit	Salaries Debit	Cash Credit
3/1	Rent	1065		$800			$800
3/3	Accounts Payable - Henry's	1066			$500		$500
3/3	Accounts Payable - Helen's	1067			$250		$250
3/4	Salaries	1068				$350	$350
3/10	Credit Card Payable - AmBank	1069		$150			$150
	March General Ledger Summary				$750	$350	$2,050

© John Wiley & Sons, Inc.

The following General Ledger entry is based on the transactions that appear in Figure 3-1:

Account	*Debit*	*Credit*
Rent	$800	
Accounts Payable	$750	
Salaries	$350	
Credit Card Payable	$150	
Cash		$2,050

This General Ledger summary balances out at $2,050 each for the debits and credits. The Cash account is decreased to show the cash outlay, the Rent and Salaries expense accounts are increased to show the additional expenses, and the Accounts Payable and Credit Card Payable accounts are decreased to show that bills were paid and are no longer due.

Figure 3-2 shows the Sales journal for a sample business.

Figure 3-2:
Summari-
zing sales
transactions
so they can
be posted to
the General
Ledger.

Cheesecake Shop
Sales Journal
March 2014

Date	Customer Account Debited	PR	Invoice Number	Accounts Receivable Debit	Sales Credit
3/1	S. Smith		243	$200	$200
3/1	Charlie's Garage		244	$300	$300
3/3	P. Perry		245	$100	$100
3/5	J. Jones		246	$200	$200
	March General Ledger Summary			$800	$800

© John Wiley & Sons, Inc.

The following General Ledger entry is based on the transactions that appear in Figure 3-2:

Account	Debit	Credit
Accounts Receivable	$800	
Sales		$800

Note that this entry is balanced. The Accounts Receivable account is increased to show that customers owe the business money because they bought items on store credit. The Sales account is increased to show that even though no cash changed hands, the business in Figure 3-2 took in revenue. Cash will be collected when the customers pay their bills.

Figure 3-3 shows the business's Purchases journal for one month. The following General Ledger entry is based on the transactions that appear in Figure 3-3:

Account	Debit	Credit
Purchases	$925	
Accounts Payable		$925

Book I

Keeping the
Books

Like the entry for the Sales account, this entry is balanced. The Accounts Payable account is increased to show that money is due to vendors, and the Purchases expense account is also increased to show that more supplies were purchased.

Figure 3-4 shows the General journal for a sample business. The following General Ledger entry is based on the transactions that appear in Figure 3-4:

Account	Debit	Credit
Sales Return	$60	
Accounts Payable	$200	
Vehicles	$10,000	
Accounts Receivable		$60
Purchase Return		$200
Capital		$10,000

Checking for balance — Debits and Credits both total to $10,260.

In this entry, the Sales Return and Purchase Return accounts are increased to show additional returns. The Accounts Payable and Accounts Receivable accounts are both decreased to show that money is no longer owed. The Vehicles account is increased to show new company assets, and the Capital account, which is where the owner's deposits into the business are tracked, is increased accordingly.

Figure 3-3:
Summari-
zing goods
to be sold
transactions
so they can
be posted to
the General
Ledger.

				Purchases	Accounts Payable
			Invoice		
Date	Vendor Account Credited	PR	Number	Debit	Credit
3/1	Supplies from Henry's		1575	$750	$750
3/3	Packaging Boxes from Barry's		1235	$100	$100
3/5	Paper Goods from Helen's		1745	$75	$75
	March General Ledger Summary			$925	$925

Cheesecake Shop
Purchases Journal
March 2014

© John Wiley & Sons, Inc.

Cheesecake Shop General Journal March 2014					
Date Account	PR	General Debit	General Credit	Accounts Payable Debit	Accounts Receivable Credit
3/3 Sales Return		$60			
S. Smith					$60
Credit Memo 124					
3/5 Henry's Bakery Supplies				$200	
Purchase Return			$200		
Debit Memo 346					
3/5 Vehicles		$10,000			
Owner Capital			$10,000		
Transfer of Owner's Vehicle to Business					
March General Ledger Summary				$200	$60

Figure 3-4:
Summarizing miscellaneous transactions so they can be posted to the General Ledger.

Posting Entries to the Ledger

After you summarize your journals and develop all the entries you need for the General Ledger (see the previous section), you post your entries into the General Ledger accounts.

When posting to the General Ledger, include transaction dollar amounts as well as references to where material was originally entered into the books so you can track a transaction back if a question arises later. For example, you may wonder what a number means, your boss or the owner may wonder why certain money was spent, or an auditor (an outside accountant who checks your work for accuracy) could raise a question.

Whatever the reason someone is questioning an entry in the General Ledger, you definitely want to be able to find the point of original entry for every transaction in every account. Use the reference information that guides you to where the original detail about the transaction is located in the journals to answer any question that arises.

For this particular business, three of the accounts — Cash, Accounts Receivable, and Accounts Payable — are carried over month to month, so each has an opening balance. Just to keep things simple, this example starts each account with a $2,000 balance. One of the accounts, Sales, is closed at the end of each accounting period, so it starts with a zero balance.

Most businesses close their books at the end of each month and do financial reports. Others close them at the end of a quarter or end of a year. (Book V Chapter 6 talks more about which accounts are closed at the end of each accounting period and which accounts remain open, as well as why that is the case.) For the purposes of this example, it's assumed that this business closes its books monthly. And the figures that follow only give examples for the first five days of the month to keep things simple.

As you review the figures for the various accounts in this example, take notice that the balance of some accounts increases when a debit is recorded and decreases when a credit is recorded. Others increase when a credit is recorded and decrease when a debit is recorded. That's the mystery of debits, credits, and double-entry accounting. (For more, flip to Book I Chapter 1.)

The Cash account (see Figure 3-5) increases with debits and decreases with credits. Ideally, the Cash account always ends with a debit balance, which means there's still money in the account. A credit balance in the cash account indicates that the business is overdrawn, and you know what that means — checks are returned for nonpayment.

Book I

Keeping the Books

Figure 3-5:
Cash
account in
the General
Ledger.

		Cheesecake Shop			
		Cash			
		March 2014			
Date	Description	Ref. #	Debit	Credit	Balance
	Opening Balance				$2,000
3/31	From Cash Receipts Journal	Journal P2	$2,900		
3/31	From Cash Disbursements Journal	Journal P3		$2,050	
	March Closing Balance				$2,850

© John Wiley & Sons, Inc.

The Accounts Receivable account (see Figure 3-6) increases with debits and decreases with credits. Ideally, this account also has a debit balance that indicates the amount still due from customer purchases. If no money is due from customers, the account balance is zero. A zero balance isn't necessarily a bad thing if all customers have paid their bills. However, a zero balance may be a sign that your sales have slumped, which could be bad news.

The Accounts Payable account (see Figure 3-7) increases with credits and decreases with debits. Usually, this account has a credit balance because money is still due to vendors, contractors, and others. A zero balance here equals no outstanding bills.

		Cheesecake Shop Accounts Receivable March 2014			
Date	Description	Ref. #	Debit	Credit	Balance
	Opening Balance				$2,000
3/31	From Cash Receipts Journal	Journal P2		$500	
3/31	From Sales Journal	Journal P3	$800		
3/31	Credit Memo 124 (General Journal)	Journal P3		$60	
	March Closing Balance				$2,240

© John Wiley & Sons, Inc.

		Cheesecake Shop Accounts Payable March 2014			
Date	Description	Ref. #	Debit	Credit	Balance
	Opening Balance				$2,000
3/31	From Accounts Payable	Journal P2	$750		
3/31	From Purchases Journal	Journal P3		$925	
3/31	Debit Memo 346 (General Journal)	Journal P5	$200		
	March Closing Balance				$1,975

© John Wiley & Sons, Inc.

These three accounts — Cash, Accounts Receivable, and Accounts Payable — are part of the balance sheet, covered in Book II Chapter 4. Asset accounts on the balance sheet usually carry debit balances because they reflect assets (in this case, cash) owned by the business. Cash and Accounts Receivable are asset accounts. Liability and Equity accounts usually carry credit balances because Liability accounts show claims made by creditors (in other words, money owed by the company to financial institutions, vendors, or others), and Equity accounts show claims made by owners (in other words, how much money the owners have put into the business). Accounts Payable is a liability account.

Here's how these accounts impact the balance of the company:

Assets	= Liabilities + Equity
Cash (debit balance)	= Accounts Payable (credit balance)
Accounts Receivable (usually debit balance)	

The Sales account (see Figure 3-8) isn't a balance sheet account. Instead, it's used in developing the income statement, which shows whether or not a company made money in the period being examined. (For the lowdown on income statements, see Book II Chapter 5.) Credits and debits are pretty straightforward when it comes to the Sales account: Credits increase the account, and debits decrease it. The Sales account usually carries a credit balance, which is a good thing because it means the company had income.

What's that you say? The Sales account should carry a credit balance? That may sound strange, so let me explain the relationship between the Sales account and the balance sheet. The Sales account is one of the accounts that feeds the bottom line of the income statement, which shows whether your business made a profit or suffered a loss. A profit means that you earned more through sales than you paid out in costs or expenses. Expense and cost accounts usually carry a debit balance.

The income statement's bottom line figure shows whether or not the company made a profit. If Sales account credits exceed expense and cost account debits, then the company made a profit. That profit would be in the form of a credit, which then gets added to the Equity account called Retained Earnings, which tracks how much of your company's profits were reinvested into the company to grow it. If the company lost money, and the bottom line of the income statement showed that cost and expenses exceeded sales, then the number would be a debit. That debit would be subtracted from the balance in Retained Earnings to show the reduction to profits reinvested in the company.

Figure 3-8: Sales account in the General Ledger.

Cheesecake Shop
Sales
March 2014

Date	Description	Ref. #	Debit	Credit	Balance
	Opening Balance				$0
3/31	From Cash Receipts Journal	Journal P2		$900	
3/31	From Sales Journal	Journal P3		$800	
	March Closing Balance				$1,700

If your company earns a profit at the end of the accounting period, the Retained Earnings account increases thanks to a credit from the Sales account. If you lose money, your Retained Earnings account decreases.

Because the Retained Earnings account is an Equity account and Equity accounts usually carry credit balances, Retained Earnings usually carries a credit balance as well.

After you post all the Ledger entries, you need to record details about where you posted the transactions on the journal pages (see Book I Chapter 4 for more on journals).

Adjusting for Ledger Errors

Your entries in the General Ledger aren't cast in stone. If necessary, you can always change or correct an entry with what's called an *adjusting entry*. Four of the most common reasons for General Ledger adjustments are

- **Depreciation:** A business shows the aging of its assets through depreciation. Each year, a portion of the original cost of an asset is written off as an expense, and that change is noted as an adjusting entry. Determining how much should be written off is a complicated process that Book IV Chapter 1 explains in greater detail.

- **Prepaid expenses:** Expenses that are paid up front, such as a year's worth of insurance, are allocated by the month using an adjusting entry. This type of adjusting entry is usually done as part of the closing process at the end of an accounting period. Book IV Chapter 6 shows you how to develop entries related to prepaid expenses.

- **Adding an account:** Accounts can be added by way of adjusting entries at any time during the year. If the new account is being created to track transactions separately that once appeared in another account, you must move all transactions already in the books to the new account. You do this transfer with an adjusting entry to reflect the change.

- **Deleting an account:** Accounts should only be deleted at the end of an accounting period. The next section shows you the type of entries you need to make in the General Ledger.

Book IV Chapter 6 talks more about adjusting entries and how you can use them.

Using Computerized Transactions to Post and Adjust in the General Ledger

If you keep your books using a computerized accounting system, posting to the General Ledger is actually done behind the scenes by your accounting software. You can view your transactions right on the screen. This section shows you how using two simple steps in QuickBooks Pro 2014, without ever having to make a General Ledger entry. Other computerized accounting programs let you view transactions on the screen too. QuickBooks is used for examples throughout the book because it's the most popular system:

1. **In My Shortcuts, scroll down to "Accnt" to pull up the Chart of Accounts (see Figure 3-9).**

2. **Click on the account for which you want more detail. In Figure 3-10, I look into Accounts Payable and see the transactions when bills were recorded or paid.**

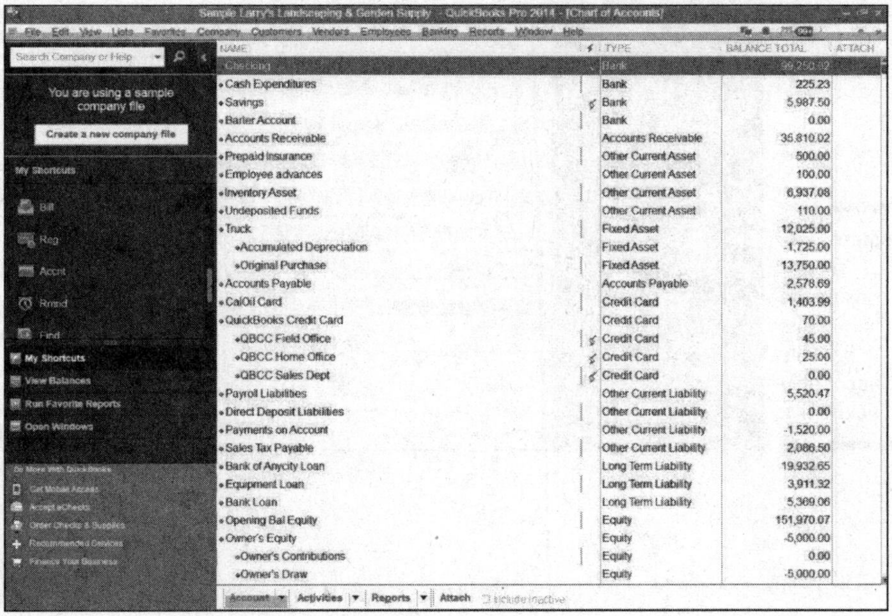

Figure 3-9: A Chart of Accounts as it appears in QuickBooks.

If you need to make an adjustment to a payment that appears in your computerized system, highlight the transaction, click Edit Transaction in the line below the account name, and make the necessary changes.

As you navigate the General Ledger created by your computerized bookkeeping system, you can see how easy it would be for someone to make changes that alter your financial transactions and possibly cause serious harm to your business. For example, someone could reduce or alter your bills to customers or change the amount due to a vendor. Be sure that you can trust whoever has access to your computerized system and that you have set up secure password access. Also, establish a series of checks and balances for managing your business's cash and accounts. Book I Chapter 5 covers safety and security measures in greater detail.

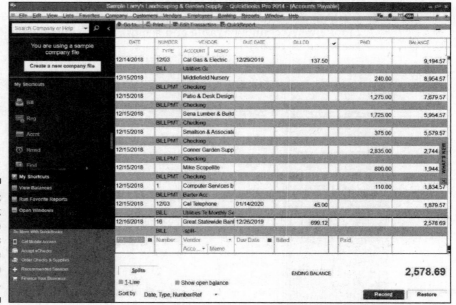

Figure 3-10: A peek inside the Accounts Payable account in QuickBooks.

Chapter 4

Keeping Journals

When it comes to doing your books, you must start somewhere. You could take a shortcut and just list every transaction in the affected accounts, but after recording hundreds and maybe thousands of transactions in just one month, imagine what a nightmare you'd face if your books didn't balance and you had to find the error. It would be like looking for a needle in a haystack — a haystack of numbers!

Because you enter every transaction in two places — that is, as a debit in one account and a credit in another account — in a double-entry bookkeeping system, you need to have a place where you can easily match those debits and credits. (For more on the double-entry system, flip back to Book I Chapter 1.)

Long ago, bookkeepers developed a system of *journals* to give businesses a starting point for each transaction. This chapter introduces you to the process of journalizing your transactions; it tells you how to set up and use journals, how to post the transactions to accounts impacted, and how to simplify this entire process by using a computerized bookkeeping program.

Establishing a Transaction's Point of Entry

In most companies that don't use computerized bookkeeping programs, a transaction's original point of entry into the bookkeeping system is through a system of journals.

Each transaction goes in the appropriate journal in chronological order. The entry should include information about the date of the transaction, the accounts to which the transaction was posted, and the source material used for developing the transaction.

If, at some point in the future, you need to track how a credit or debit ended up in a particular account, you can find the necessary detail in the journal where you first posted the transaction. (Before it's posted to various accounts in the bookkeeping system, each transaction gets a reference number to help you backtrack to the original entry point.) For example, suppose a customer calls you and wants to know why his account has a $500 charge. To find the answer, you go to the posting in the customer's account, track the charge back to its original point of entry in the Sales journal, use that information to locate the source for the charge, make a copy of the source (most likely a sales invoice or receipt), and mail the evidence to the customer.

If you've filed everything properly, you should have no trouble finding the original source material and settling any issue that arises regarding any transaction. For more on what papers you need to keep and how to file them, see Book I Chapter 5.

It's perfectly acceptable to keep one general journal for all your transactions, but one big journal can be very hard to manage because you'll likely have thousands of entries in that journal by the end of the year. Instead, most businesses employ a system of journals that includes a Cash Receipts journal for incoming cash and a Cash Disbursements journal for outgoing cash. Not all transactions involve cash, however, so the two most common noncash journals are the Sales journal and the Purchases journal. The sections that follow show you how to set up and use each of these journals.

When Cash Changes Hands

Most businesses deal with cash transactions every day, and as a business owner, you definitely want to know where every penny is going. The best way to get a quick daily summary of cash transactions is by reviewing the entries in your Cash Receipts journal and Cash Disbursements journal.

Keeping track of incoming cash

The Cash Receipts journal is the first place you record cash received by your business. The majority of cash received each day comes from daily sales;

other possible sources of cash include deposits of capital from the company's owner, customer bill payments, new loan proceeds, and interest from savings accounts.

Each entry in the Cash Receipts journal must not only indicate how the cash was received but also designate the account into which the cash will be deposited. Remember, in double-entry bookkeeping, every transaction is entered twice — once as a debit and once as a credit. For example, cash taken in for sales is credited to the Sales account and debited to the Cash account. In this case, both accounts increase in value. (For more about debits and credits, flip back to Book I Chapter 1.)

In the Cash Receipts journal, the Cash account is always the debit because it's where you initially deposit your money. The credits vary depending upon the source of the funds. Figure 4-1 shows you what a series of transactions look like when they're entered into a Cash Receipts journal.

Figure 4-1: The first point of entry for incoming cash is the Cash Receipts journal.

Cheesecake Shop
Cash Receipts Journal
March 2014

Prepared by:_____ Date _____

Approved by: _____ Date_____

Date	Account Credited	PR	General Credit	Accounts Receivable Credit	Sales Credit	Cash Debit
3/1	Sales				$300	$300
3/2	Sales				$250	$250
3/3	Ck. 121 from S. Smith			$200		$200
3/3	Sales				$150	$150
3/4	Owner Capital		$1,500			$1,500
3/5	Ck 125 from J. Jones			$100		$100
3/5	Ck 567 from P. Perry			$200		$200
3/5	Sales				$200	$200

© John Wiley & Sons, Inc.

You record most of your incoming cash daily because it's cash received by the cashier, called *cash register sales* or simply *sales* in the journal. When you record checks received from customers, you list the customer's check number and name as well as the amount. In Figure 4-1, the only other cash received is a cash deposit from H.G. (the owner) to cover a cash shortfall.

The Cash Receipts journal in Figure 4-1 has seven columns of information:

- ✔ **Date:** The date of the transaction.
- ✔ **Account Credited:** The name of the account credited.

✓ **PR (post reference):** Where the transaction will be posted at the end of the month. This information is filled in at the end of the month when you do the posting to the General Ledger accounts. If the entry to be posted to the accounts is summarized and totaled at the bottom of the page, you can just put a check mark next to the entry in the PR column. For transactions listed in the General Credit or General Debit column, you should indicate an account number for the account into which the transaction is posted.

✓ **General Credit:** Transactions that don't have their own columns; these transactions are entered individually into the accounts impacted.

For example, according to Figure 4-1, H.G. deposited $1,500 of his own money into the Capital account on March 4th in order to pay bills. The credit shown there will be posted to the Capital account at the end of the month because the Capital account tracks all information about assets H.G. pays into the business.

✓ **Accounts Receivable Credit:** Any transactions that are posted to the Accounts Receivable account (which tracks information about customers who buy products on store credit).

✓ **Sales Credit:** Credits for the Sales account.

✓ **Cash Debit:** Anything that will be added to the Cash account.

You can set up your Cash Receipts journal with more columns if you have accounts with frequent cash receipts. The big advantage to having individual columns for active accounts is that, when you total the columns at the end of the month, the total for the active accounts is the only thing you have to add to the General Ledger accounts, which is a lot less work then entering every Sales transaction individually in the General Ledger account. This approach saves a lot of time posting to accounts that involve multiple transactions every month. Individual transactions listed in the General Credits column each need to be entered into the affected accounts separately, which takes a lot more time that just entering a column total.

As you can see in Figure 4-1, the top-right corner of the journal page has a place for the person who prepared the journal to sign and date and for someone who approves the entries to sign and date as well. If your business deals with cash, it's always a good idea to have a number of checks and balances to ensure that cash is properly handled and recorded. For more safety measures, see Book I Chapter 5.

Following outgoing cash

Cash going out of the business to pay bills, salaries, rents, and other necessities has its own journal, the Cash Disbursements journal. This journal is the point of original entry for all business cash paid out to others.

No business person likes to see money go out the door, but imagine what creditors, vendors, and others would think if they didn't get the money they were due. Put yourself in their shoes: Would you be able to buy needed supplies if other companies didn't pay what they owed you? Not a chance.

You need to track your outgoing cash just as carefully as you track incoming cash (see the preceding section). Each entry in the Cash Disbursements journal must not only indicate how much cash was paid out but also designate which account will be decreased in value because of the cash disbursal. For example, cash disbursed to pay bills is credited to the Cash account (which goes down in value) and is debited to the account from which the bill or loan is paid, such as Accounts Payable. The debit decreases the amount still owed in the Accounts Payable account.

In the Cash Disbursements journal, the Cash account is always the credit, and the debits vary depending upon the outstanding debts to be paid. Figure 4-2 shows you what a series of transactions look like when they're entered in a Cash Disbursements journal.

Figure 4-2:
The first point of entry for outgoing cash is the Cash Disbursements journal.

	Cheesecake Shop Cash Disbursements Journal March 2014						
Date	Account Debited	Check #	PR	General Debit	Account Payable Debit	Salaries Debit	Cash Credit
3/1	Rent	1065		$800			$800
3/3	Accounts Payable - Henry's	1066			$500		$500
3/3	Accounts Payable - Helen's	1067			$250		$250
3/4	Salaries	1068				$350	$350
3/10	Credit Card Payable - AmBank	1069		$150			$150

© *John Wiley & Sons, Inc.*

The Cash Disbursements journal in Figure 4-2 has eight columns of information:

✓ **Date:** The date of the transaction.

✓ **Account Debited:** The name of the account debited as well as any detail about the reason for the debit.

✓ **Check #:** The number of the check used to pay the debt.

✓ **PR (post reference):** Where the transaction will be posted at the end of the month. This information is filled in at the end of the month when you do the posting to the General Ledger accounts. If the entry to be posted to the accounts is summarized and totaled at the bottom of the page, you can just put a check mark next to the entry in the PR column. For transactions listed in the General Credit or General Debit columns, you should indicate an account number for the account into which the transaction is posted.

- ✔ **General Debit:** Any transactions that don't have their own columns; these transactions are entered individually into the accounts they impact.

  For example, according to Figure 4-2, rent was paid on March 1st and will be indicated by a debit in the Rent Expense.

- ✔ **Accounts Payable Debit:** Any transactions that are posted to the Accounts Payable account (which tracks bills due).

- ✔ **Salaries Debit:** Debits to the Salaries expense account, which increase the amount of salaries expenses paid in a particular month.

- ✔ **Cash Credit:** Anything that's deducted from the Cash account.

You can set up your Cash Disbursements journal with more columns if you have accounts with frequent cash disbursals. For example, in Figure 4-2, the bookkeeper for this fictional company added one column each for Accounts Payable and Salaries because cash for both accounts is disbursed multiple times during the month. Rather than having to list each disbursement in the Accounts Payable and Salaries accounts, she can just total each journal column at the end of the month and add totals to the appropriate accounts. This approach sure saves a lot of time when you're working with your most active accounts.

Managing Sales Like a Pro

Not all sales involve the collection of cash; many stores allow customers to buy products on store credit using a store credit card. (Not a bank-issued credit card — in that case, the bank, not the store or company making the sale, is the one who has to worry about collecting from the customer.)

Instead, store credit comes into play when a customer is allowed to take a store's products without paying immediately because he has an account that's billed monthly. This can be done by using a credit card issued by the store or some other method the company uses to track credit purchases by customers, such as having the customer sign a sales receipt indicating that the amount should be charged to the customer's account.

Sales made on store credit don't involve cash until the customer pays his bill. (In contrast, with credit-card sales, the store gets a cash payment from the card-issuing bank before the customer even pays the credit-card bill.) If your

Book I.

Keeping the Books

company sells on store credit, the total value of the products bought on any particular day becomes an item for the Accounts Receivable account, which tracks all money due from customers. Book III Chapter 2 talks more about managing accounts receivable.

Before allowing customers to buy on credit, your company should require customers to apply for credit in advance so that you can check their credit references.

When something's sold on store credit, usually the cashier drafts an invoice for the customer to sign when picking up the product. The invoice lists the items purchased and the total amount due. After getting the customer's signature, the invoice is tracked in both the Accounts Payable account and the customer's individual account.

Transactions for sales made by store credit first enter your books in the Sales journal. Each entry in the Sales journal must indicate the customer's name, the invoice number, and the amount charged.

In the Sales journal, the Accounts Receivable account is debited, which increases in value. The bookkeeper must also remember to make an entry to the customer's account records because the customer has not yet paid for the item and will have to be billed for it. The transaction also increases the value of the Sales account, which is credited.

Figure 4-3 shows a few days' worth of transactions related to store credit.

Figure 4-3:
The first point of entry for sales made on store credit is the Sales journal.

	Cheesecake Shop Sales Journal March 2014				
Date	Customer Account Debited	PR	Invoice Number	Accounts Receivable Debit	Sales Credit
3/1	S. Smith		243	$200	$200
3/1	Charlie's Garage		244	$300	$300
3/3	P. Perry		245	$100	$100
3/3	J. Jones		246	$200	$200

© John Wiley & Sons, Inc.

The Sales journal in Figure 4-3 has six columns of information:

✔ **Date:** The date of the transaction.

✔ **Customer Account Debited:** The name of the customer whose account should be debited.

✔ **PR (post reference):** Where the transaction will be posted at the end of the month. This information is filled in at the end of the month when you do the posting to the General Ledger accounts. If the entry to be posted to the accounts is summarized and totaled at the bottom of the page, you can just put a check mark next to the entry in the PR column. For transactions listed in the General Credit or General Debit columns, you should indicate an account number for the account into which the transaction is posted.

✔ **Invoice Number:** The invoice number for the purchase.

✔ **Accounts Receivable Debit:** Increases to the Accounts Receivable account.

✔ **Sales Credit:** Increases to the Sales account.

At the end of the month, the bookkeeper can just total the Accounts Receivable and Sales columns shown in Figure 4-3 and post the totals to those General Ledger accounts. She doesn't need to post all the details because she can always refer back to the Sales journal. However, each invoice noted in the Sales journal must be carefully recorded in each customer's account. Otherwise, the bookkeeper doesn't know who and how much to bill.

Keeping Track of Purchases

Purchases of products to be sold to customers at a later date are a key type of noncash transaction. All businesses must have something to sell, whether they manufacture it themselves or buy a finished product from some other company. Businesses usually make these purchases on credit from the company that makes the product. In this case, the business becomes the customer of another business.

Transactions for purchases bought on credit first enter your books in the Purchases journal. Each entry in the Purchases journal must indicate the vendor from whom the purchase was made, the vendor's invoice number, and the amount charged.

In the Purchases journal, the Accounts Payable account is credited, and the Purchases account is debited, meaning both accounts increase in value. The Accounts Payable account increases because the company now owes more money to creditors, and the Purchases account increases because the amount spent on goods to be sold goes up.

Figure 4-4 shows some store purchase transactions as they appear in the company's Purchases journal.

Figure 4-4:
The first point of entry for purchases bought on credit is the Purchases journal.

Date	Vendor Account Credited	PR	Invoice Number	Purchases Debit	Accounts Payable Credit
	Cheesecake Shop Purchases Journal March 2014				
3/1	Supplies from Henry's		1575	$750	$750
3/3	Packaging Boxes from Barry's		1235	$100	$100
3/5	Paper Goods from Helen's		1745	$75	$75

© *John Wiley & Sons, Inc.*

The Purchases journal in Figure 4-4 has six columns of information:

- ✔ **Date:** The date of the transaction.

- ✔ **Vendor Account Credited:** The name of the vendor from whom the purchases were made.

- ✔ **PR (post reference):** Where information about the transaction will be posted at the end of the month. This information is filled in at the end of the month when you do the posting to the General Ledger accounts. If the entry to be posted to the accounts is summarized and totaled at the bottom of the page, you can just put a check mark next to the entry in the PR column. For transactions listed in the General Credit or General Debit columns, you should indicate an account number for the account into which the transaction is posted.

- ✔ **Invoice Number:** The invoice number for the purchase assigned by the vendor.

- ✔ **Purchases Debit:** Additions to the Purchases account.

- ✔ **Accounts Payable Credit:** Increases to the Accounts Payable account.

At the end of the month, the bookkeeper can just total the Purchases and Accounts Payable columns and post the totals to the corresponding General Ledger accounts. She can refer back to the Purchases journal for details if necessary. However, each invoice should be carefully recorded in each vendor's accounts so that there's a running total of outstanding bills for each vendor. Otherwise, the bookkeeper doesn't know who and how much is owed.

Dealing with Transactions that Don't Fit

Not all your transactions fit in one of the four main journals (Cash Receipts, Cash Disbursements, Sales, and Purchases). If you need to establish other special journals as the original points of entry for transactions, go ahead. The sky's the limit!

If you keep your books the old-fashioned way — on paper — be aware that paper is vulnerable to being mistakenly lost or destroyed. In this case, you may want to consider keeping the number of journals you maintain to a minimum.

For transactions that don't fit in the "big four" journals but don't necessarily warrant the creation of their own journals, you should consider keeping a General Journal for miscellaneous transactions. Using columnar paper similar to what's used for the other four journals, create the following columns:

- **Date:** The date of the transaction.

- **Account:** The account impacted by the transaction. More detail is needed here because the General Ledger impacts so many different accounts with so many different types of transactions. For example, you will find only sales transactions in the Sales journal and Purchase transactions in the Purchase journal, but you could find any type of transaction in the General journal affecting many less active accounts.

- **PR (post reference):** Where information about the transaction will be posted at the end of the month. This information is filled in at the end of the month when you do the posting to the General Ledger accounts. If the entry to be posted to the accounts is summarized and totaled at the bottom of the page, you can just put a check mark next to the entry in the PR column. For transactions listed in the General Credit or General Debit columns, you should indicate an account number for the account into which the transaction is posted.

- **General Debit:** Contains most debits.

- **General Credit:** Contains most credits.

If you have certain accounts for which you expect a lot of activity, you can start a column for those accounts, too. Figure 4-5 adds columns for Accounts Payable and Accounts Receivable. The big advantage of having a separate column for an account is that you'll be able to total that column at the end of the month and just put the total in the General Ledger. You won't have to enter each transaction separately.

Many businesses also add columns for Accounts Receivable and Accounts Payable because those accounts are commonly impacted by noncash transactions.

All the transactions in this General journal are noncash transactions. Cash transactions should go into one of the two cash journals: Cash Receipts (see the section "Keeping track of incoming cash") and Cash Disbursements (see the section "Following outgoing cash").

In a General journal, transactions need to be entered on multiple lines because each transaction impacts at least two accounts (and sometimes more than two). For example, in the General journal shown in Figure 4-5, the first transaction listed is the return of a cheesecake by S. Smith. This return of products sold must be posted to the customer's account as a credit as well as to the Accounts Receivable account. Also, the Sales Return account, where the business tracks all products returned by the customer, has to be debited.

March 5 — Return a portion of purchase from Henry's Bakery Supplies, $200, Debit memo 346. When a business returns a product purchased, it is tracked in the Purchase Return account, which is credited. A debit must also be made to the Accounts Payable account, as well as vendor's account, since less money is now owed. Cash does not change hands with this transaction.

March 5 — H.G. transferred car to business, $10,000. This transaction is posted to the Vehicle asset account and the Capital account in Owner's Equity. Rather than deposit cash into the business, H.G. made his personal vehicle a business asset.

Figure 4-5: The point of entry for miscellaneous transactions is the General journal.

Cheesecake Shop
General Journal
March 2014

Date	Account	PR	General Debit	General Credit	Accounts Payable Debit	Accounts Receivable Credit
3/3	Sales Return		$60			
	S. Smith					$60
	Credit Memo 124					
3/5	Henry's Bakery Supplies				$200	
	Purchase Return			$200		
	Debit Memo 346					
3/5	Vehicles		$10,000			
	Owner Capital			$10,000		
	Transfer of Owner's Vehicle to Business					

In addition to the five columns already mentioned, the General journal in Figure 4-5 has the following two columns:

- **Accounts Payable Debit:** Decreases to the Accounts Payable account.

- The bookkeeper working with this journal anticipated that many of the company's transactions would impact Accounts Payable. She created this column so that she can subtotal it and make just one entry to the Accounts Payable account in the General Ledger.

- **Accounts Receivable Credit:** Decreases to the Accounts Receivable account.

At the end of the month, the bookkeeper can just total this journal's Accounts Payable and Accounts Receivable columns and post those totals to the corresponding General Ledger accounts. All transaction details remain in the General journal. However, because the miscellaneous transactions impact General Ledger accounts, the transactions need to be posted to each affected account separately (see the next section).

Posting Journal Information to Accounts

When you close your books at the end of the month, you summarize all the journals — that is, you total the columns and post the information to update all the accounts involved.

Posting journal pages is a four-step process:

1. **Number each journal page at the top if it isn't already numbered.**

2. **Total any column that's not titled General Debit or General Credit.** Any transactions recorded in the General Debit or General Credit columns need to be recorded individually in the General Ledger.

3. **Post the entries to the General Ledger account.** Each transaction in the General Credit or General Debit column must be posted separately. You just need to post totals to the General Ledger for the other columns in which transactions for more active accounts were entered in the General journal. List the date and journal page number as well as the amount of the debit or credit, so you can quickly find the entry for the original transaction if you need more details.

The General Ledger account only shows debit or credit (whichever is appropriate to the transaction). Only the journals have both sides of a transaction. (Book I Chapter 3 shows you how to work with General Ledger accounts.)

4. **In the PR column of the journal, record information about where the entry is posted.** If the entry to be posted to the accounts is summarized and totaled at the bottom of the page, you can just put a check mark next to the entry in the PR column. For transactions listed in the General Credit or General Debit columns, you should indicate an account number for the account into which the transaction is posted. This process helps you confirm that you've posted all entries in the General Ledger.

Posting to the General Ledger is done at the end of an accounting period as part of the process of closing the accounts. Book IV Chapter 4 covers the closing process in detail.

Figure 4-6 shows a summarized journal page, specifically the Cash Receipts journal. You can see that entries that are listed in the Sales Credit and Cash Debit columns on the Cash Receipts journal are just checked in the PR column. Only one entry was placed in the General Credit column, and that entry has an account number in the PR column. Although not all the transactions for the month are listed, which would of course be a much longer list, you will see how to summarize the journal at the end of the month.

	Cheesecake Shop Cash Receipts Journal March 2014					
Date	Account Credited	PR	General Credit	Accounts Receivable Credit	Sales Credit	Cash Debit
3/1	Sales	x			$300	$300
3/2	Sales	x			$250	$250
3/3	Ck. 121 from S. Smith	x		$200		$200
3/3	Sales	x			$150	$150
3/4	Owner Capital	3300	$1,500			$1,500
3/5	Ck 125 from J. Jones	x		$100		$100
3/5	Ck 567 from P. Perry	x		$200		$200
3/5	Sales	x			$200	$200
	March Summary		$1,500	$500	$900	$2,900

Figure 4-6: Summary of Cash Receipts journal entries after the first five days.

© John Wiley & Sons, Inc.

As you can see in Figure 4-6, after summarizing the Cash Receipts journal, there are only four General Ledger accounts (General Credit, Accounts Receivable Credit, Sales Credit, and Cash Debit) and three customer accounts

(S. Smith, J. Jones, and P. Perry) into which you need to post entries. Even better, the entries balance: $2,900 in debits and $2,900 in credits! (The customer accounts total $500, which is good news because it's the same amount credited to Accounts Receivable. The Accounts Receivable account is decreased by $500 because payments were received, as is the amount due from the individual customer accounts.)

Simplifying Your Journaling with Computerized Accounting

The process of posting first to the journals and then to the General Ledger and individual customer or vendor accounts can be a very time-consuming job. Luckily, most businesses today use computerized accounting software, so the same information doesn't need to be entered so many times. The computer does the work for you.

If you're working with a computerized accounting software package (see Book I Chapter 6), you only have to enter a transaction once. All the detail that normally needs to be entered into one of the journal pages, one of the General Ledger accounts, and customer, vendor and other accounts is posted automatically. Voilà!

The method by which you initially enter your transaction varies depending on the type of transaction. To show you what's involved in making entries into a computerized accounting system, the following figures show one entry each from the Cash Receipts journal (see Figure 4-7 for a customer payment), the Cash Disbursements journal (see Figure 4-8 for a list of bills to be paid), and the Sales journal (see Figure 4-9 for an invoice). (The screenshots are all from QuickBooks, a popular computerized bookkeeping system.)

As you can see in Figure 4-7, to enter the customer payment, all you need to do is type the customer's name in the box labeled Received From. All outstanding invoices then appear. You can put a check mark next to the invoices to be paid, indicate the payment method (in this case, a check), enter the check number, and click Save & Close.

When you use a software package to track your cash receipts, the following accounts are automatically updated:

✔ The Cash account is debited the appropriate amount.

✔ The Accounts Receivable account is credited the appropriate amount.

✔ The corresponding customer account is credited the appropriate amount.

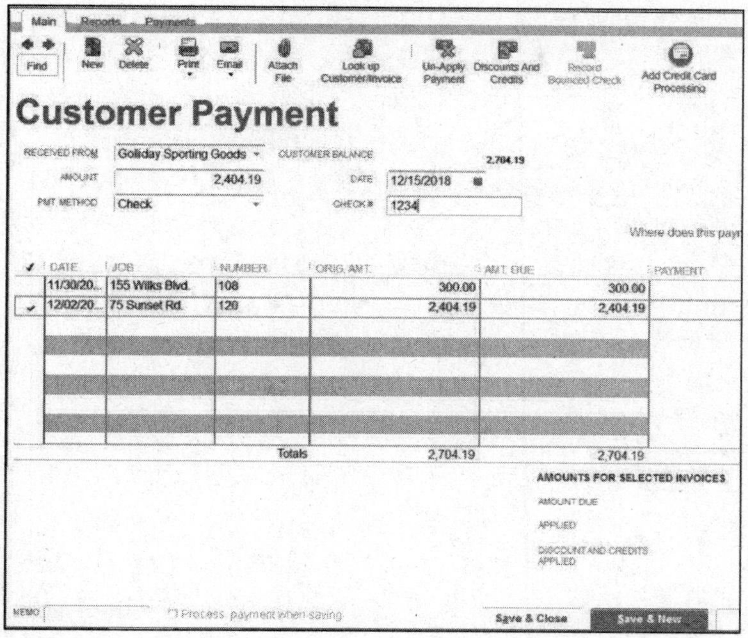

Figure 4-7:
Customer
Payment
entry form.

That's much simpler than adding the transaction to the Cash Receipts journal, closing out the journal at the end of the month, adding the transactions to the accounts impacted by the cash receipts, and then (finally!) closing out the books.

Cash disbursements are even easier than cash receipts when you've got a computerized system on your side. For example when paying bills (see Figure 4-8), all you need to do is go to the bill-paying screen for QuickBooks. In this example, all the bills due are listed, so all you need to do is select the bills you want to pay, and the system automatically sets the payments in motion.

The bill-paying perks of this system include the following:

✔ Checks can be automatically printed by the software package.

✔ Each of the vendor accounts is updated to show that payment is made.

✔ The Accounts Payable account is debited the appropriate amount for your transaction, which decreases the amount due to vendors.

✔ The Cash account is credited the appropriate amount for your transaction, which decreases the amount of cash available (because it's designated for use to pay corresponding bills).

SELECT BILLS TO BE PAID

Show bills   ◉ Due on or before   12/25/2018   ▦
          ◉ Show all bills

Filter By
Sort By Due Date

	DATE DUE	VENDOR	REF. NO.	DISC. DATE	AMT. DUE	DISC. USED	CREDITS USED	AMT. T
☐	09/01/2019	Conner Garde...			127.20	0.00	0.00	
☐	12/25/2019	Townley Insura...			427.62	0.00	0.00	
☐	12/26/2019	Great Statewid...	16		699.12	0.00	0.00	
☐	12/27/2019	Nolan Hardwar...			610.00	0.00	0.00	
☐	12/29/2019	Cal Gas & Ele...	12/03		137.50	0.00	0.00	
☐	01/12/2020	Robert Carr M...			196.25	0.00	0.00	
☐	01/14/2020	Cal Telephone	12/03		45.00	0.00	0.00	
				Totals	2,242.69	0.00	0.00	

Select All Bills

DISCOUNT & CREDIT INFORMATION FOR HIGHLIGHTED BILL
Vendor   Terms   Number of Credits
Bill Ref. No.   Sugg. Discount   0.00   Total Credits Available

Go to Bill   Set Discount   Set Credits

PAYMENT
Date   Method   Account
12/15/2018 ▦   Check   ◉ To be printed   Checking
                                   ◉ Assign check number   **Ending Balance**

Figure 4-8:
List of bills
to be paid.

When you make the necessary entries into your computerized accounting system for the information that would normally be found in a Sales journal (for example, when a customer pays for your product on credit), you can automatically create an invoice for the purchase. Figure 4-9 shows what that invoice looks like when generated by a computerized accounting system. Adding the customer name in the box marked "Customer" automatically fills in all the necessary customer information. The date appears automatically, and the system assigns a customer invoice number. You add the quantity and select the type of product bought in the "Item Code" section, and the rest of the invoice is calculated automatically. When the invoice is final, you can print it and send it off to the customer.

Once the customer name is chosen, the system automatically fills in the billing information. If sales taxes are indicated in the customer's information, then those figures are automatically calculated as well. In Figure 4-9, you can see the sales tax percentage of 8.25%. All the bookkeeper needs to do is add shipping information, the P.O. number, and the items ordered. The invoice is then automatically calculated.

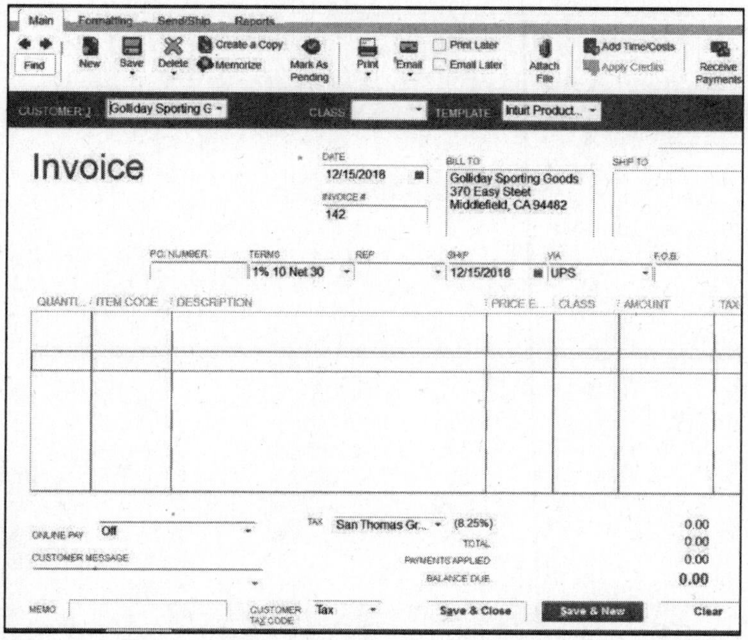

Figure 4-9:
Customer
Invoice
entry form.

Filling out the invoice in the accounting system also updates the affected accounts:

- ✔ The Accounts Receivable account is debited the appropriate amount, which increases the amount due from customers by that amount.

- ✔ The Sales account is credited the appropriate amount, which increases the revenue received by that amount.

- ✔ The invoice is added to the customer's outstanding bills so that when the customer makes a payment, the outstanding invoice appears on the payment screen.

Chapter 5

Controlling Your Records

- -

In This Chapter

▶ Protecting your business's cash

▶ Maintaining proper paperwork

▶ Divvying up responsibilities

▶ Insuring your cash handlers

- -

*E*very business takes in cash in some form. Whether in the form of dollar bills, checks, credit cards, or electronic payment, it's all eventually deposited as cash into the business's accounts. Before you take in that first penny, controlling that cash and making sure none of it walks out the door improperly should be your first concern as a businessperson.

Finding the right level of cash control while at the same time allowing your employees the flexibility to sell your products or services and provide ongoing customer service can be a monumental task. If you don't have enough controls, you risk theft or embezzlement. Yet if you have too many controls, employees may miss sales or anger customers.

This chapter explains the basic protections you need to put in place to be sure all cash coming into or going out of your business is clearly documented and controlled. It also reviews the type of paperwork you need to document the use of cash and other business assets. Finally, it covers how to organize your staff to properly control the flow of your assets and insure yourself against possible misappropriation of those assets.

Putting Controls on Your Business's Cash

Think about how careful you are with your personal cash. You find various ways to protect how you carry it around, you dole it out carefully to your family members, and you may even hide cash in a safe place in the house just in case you need it for unexpected purposes.

If you're that protective of your cash when you're the only one who handles it, consider the vulnerability of business cash. After all, unless you're a one-person shop, you aren't the only one handling the cash for your business. You have some employees encountering incoming cash at cash registers and others opening the mail and finding checks for orders to purchase products or pay bills and checks from other sources. And don't forget that employees may need petty cash to pay for mail sent COD (Collect on Delivery) or to pay for other unexpected, low-cost needs.

If you were around to watch every transaction in which cash enters your business, you wouldn't have time to do the things you need to do to grow your business. If your business is small enough, you can maintain control of cash going out by signing all checks, but as soon as the business grows, you may not have time for that either.

You can drive yourself crazy with worry about all this cash flow, but the truth is that just putting in place the proper controls for your cash can help protect your business's family jewels. Cash flows through your business in four key ways:

- ✔ Deposits and payments into and out of your checking accounts
- ✔ Deposits and payments into and out of your savings accounts
- ✔ Petty cash funds in critical locations where fast cash may be needed
- ✔ Transactions made in your cash registers

The following sections cover some key controls for each of these cash flow points.

Checking accounts

Almost every dime that comes into your business flows through your business's checking account (at least that's what *should* happen). Whether it's cash collected at your cash registers, payments received in the mail, cash used to fill the cash registers, petty cash accounts, payments sent out to pay business obligations, or any other cash need, this cash enters and exits your checking account. That's why your checking account is your main tool for protecting your cash flow.

Choosing the right bank

Finding the right bank to help you set up your checking account and the controls that limit access to that account is crucial. When evaluating your banking options, ask yourself the following questions:

✔ Does this bank have a branch that's conveniently located to my business?

✔ Does this bank operate at times when I need it most?

✔ Does this bank offer secure ways to deposit cash even when the bank is closed?

Most banks have secure drop boxes for cash so you can deposit receipts as quickly as possible at the end of the business day rather than secure the cash overnight yourself.

Visit local bank branches yourself, and check out the type of business services each bank offers. Pay particular attention to

✔ The type of personal attention you receive.

✔ What type of charges may be tacked on for this personal attention.

✔ How questions are handled.

Some banks require business account holders to call a centralized line for assistance rather than depend on local branches. Some banks are even adding charges today if you use a teller rather than an ATM (automatic teller machine). Other banks charge for every transaction, whether it's a deposit, withdrawal, or a check. Many have charges that differ for business accounts, and most have charges on printing checks. If you're planning to accept credit cards, compare the services offered for that as well.

Deciding on types of checks

After you choose your bank, you need to consider what type of checks you want to use in your business. For example, you need different checks depending upon whether you handwrite each check or print checks from your computerized accounting system.

If you plan to write your checks, you'll most likely use a business voucher check in a three-ring binder; this type of check consists of a voucher on the left and a check on the right (see Figure 5-1). This arrangement provides the best control for manual checks because each check and voucher are numbered. When a check is written, the voucher should be filled out with details about the date, the check's recipient, and the purpose of the check. The voucher also has a space to keep a running total of your balance in the account.

If you plan to print checks from your computerized accounting system, you'll need to order checks that match that system's programming. Each computer software program has a unique template for printing checks. Figure 5-2 shows a common layout for business voucher checks printed by your computerized accounting system. You can see there are actually three sections in a blank computerized check: the check in the middle with two relatively blank sections on either side.

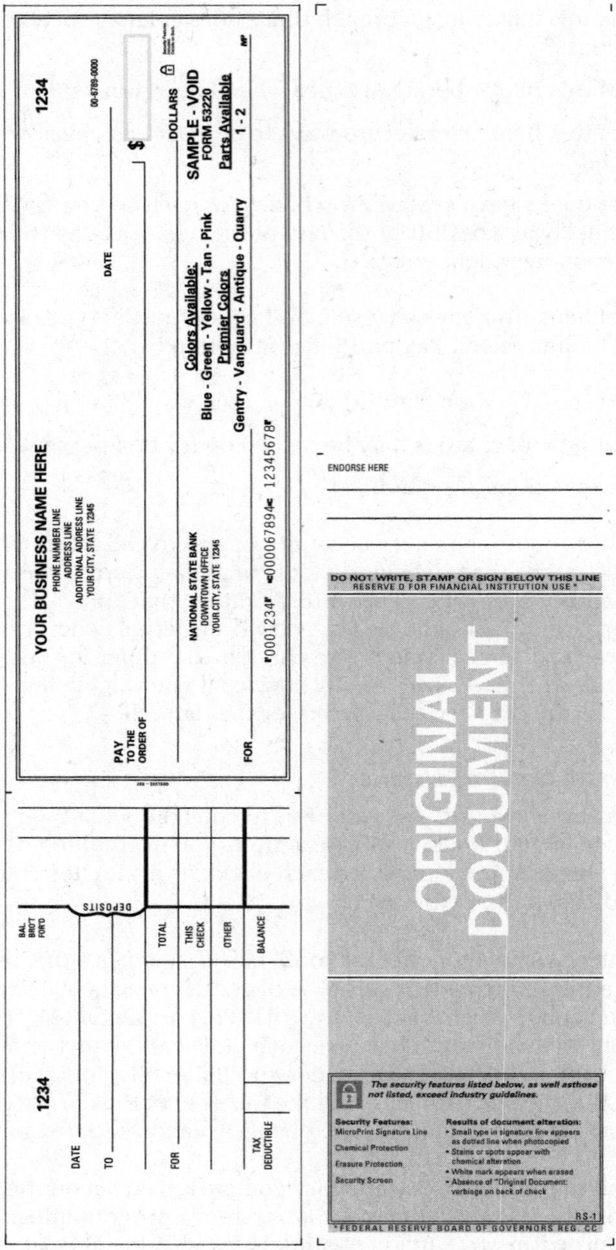

Figure 5-1:
A business voucher check is used by many businesses that manually write out their checks.

Check samples courtesy of Deluxe.com

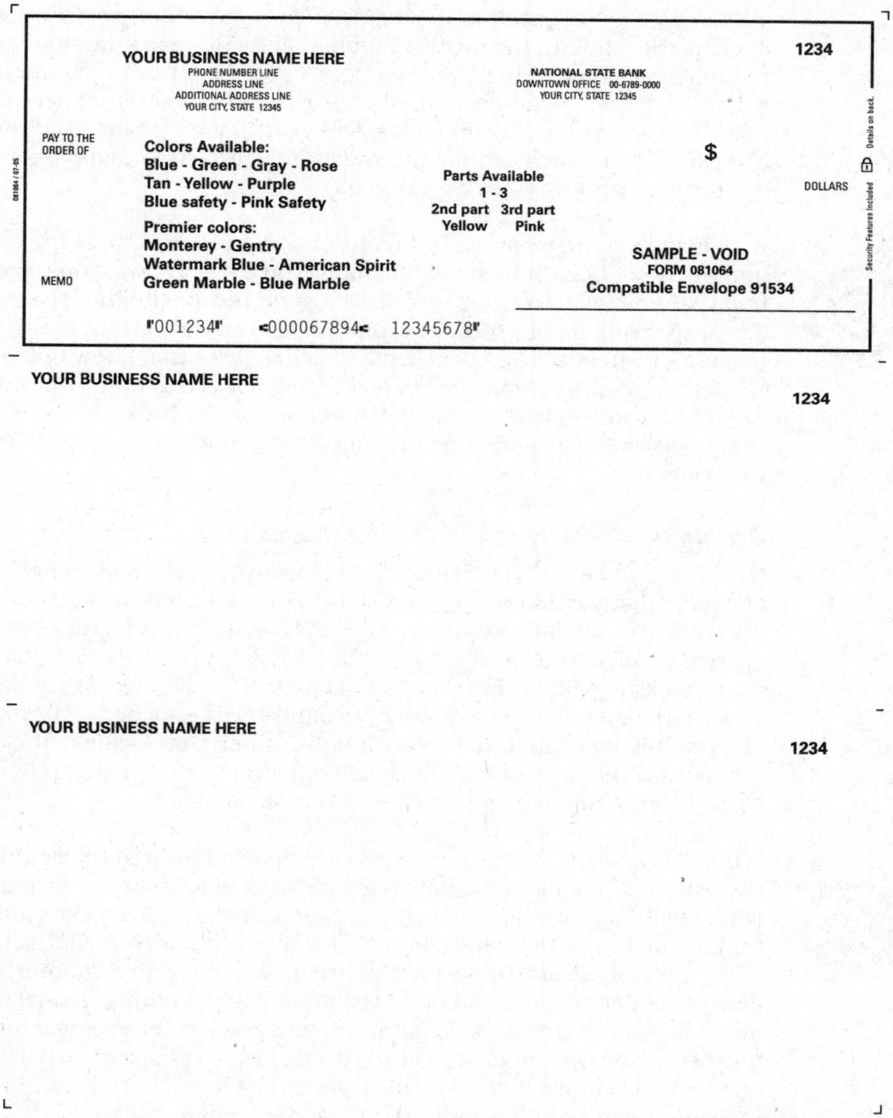

YOUR BUSINESS NAME HERE
PHONE NUMBER LINE
ADDRESS LINE
ADDITIONAL ADDRESS LINE
YOUR CITY, STATE 12345

1234

NATIONAL STATE BANK
DOWNTOWN OFFICE 00-6789-0000
YOUR CITY, STATE 12345

PAY TO THE
ORDER OF

Colors Available:
Blue - Green - Gray - Rose
Tan - Yellow - Purple
Blue safety - Pink Safety

Premier colors:
Monterey - Gentry
Watermark Blue - American Spirit
Green Marble - Blue Marble

Parts Available
1 - 3
2nd part   3rd part
Yellow   Pink

$

DOLLARS

SAMPLE - VOID
FORM 081064
Compatible Envelope 91534

MEMO

081064 / 07-05

Security Features Included

Details on back.

⌐"001234⌐"   ⌐000067894⌐   12345678⌐"

YOUR BUSINESS NAME HERE

1234

YOUR BUSINESS NAME HERE

1234

Figure 5-2:
Computer-
printed
checks
usually
pre-print the
business's
name. This
check is
compatible
with
QuickBooks.

Check samples courtesy of Deluxe.com

For one of the blank sections, you set up your computer accounting system to print out the detail you'd expect to find on a manual voucher — the date, name of the recipient, and purpose of the check. You keep this stub as a control for check use. In the other blank section, you print the information that the recipient needs. For example, if it's a check to pay an outstanding invoice, you include all information the vendor needs to properly credit that invoice, such as the amount, the invoice number, and your account number. If it's a payroll check, one of the blank sections should contain all the required payroll information including amount of gross check, amount of net check, taxes taken out, totals for current check, and year-to-date totals. Send the check and portion that includes detail needed by your vendor, employee, or other recipient to whoever you intend to pay.

Initially, when the business is small, you can keep control of the outflow of money by signing each check. But as the business grows, you'll probably find that you need to delegate check-signing responsibilities to someone else, especially if your business requires you to travel frequently. Many small business owners set up check-signing procedures that allow one or two of their staff people to sign checks up to a designated amount, such as $5,000. Any checks above that designated amount require the owner's or the signature of an employee and a second designated person, such as an officer of the company.

Arranging deposits to the checking account

Of course, you aren't just withdrawing from your business's checking account (that would be a big problem). You also need to deposit money into that account, and you want to be sure your deposit slips contain all the needed detail as well as documentation to back up the deposit information. Most banks provide printed deposit slips with all the necessary detail to be sure the money is deposited in the appropriate account. They also usually provide you with a "for deposit only" stamp that includes the account number for the back of the checks. (If you don't get that stamp from the bank, be sure to have one made as soon as possible.)

Whoever opens your business mail should be instructed to use that "for deposit only" stamp immediately on the back of any check received in the mail. Stamping "for deposit only" on the back of a check makes it a lot harder for anyone to use that check for other than its intended business purposes. (The "Dividing staff responsibilities" section, later in this chapter, talks more about controls for incoming cash.) If you get both personal and business checks sent to the same address, you need to set up some instructions for the person opening the mail regarding how to differentiate the types of checks and how each type of check should be handled to best protect your incoming cash, whether for business or personal purposes.

To secure incoming cash even more carefully, some businesses set up lock box services with a bank. Customers or others sending checks to the business mail checks to a post office box number that goes directly to the bank, and a bank employee opens and deposits the checks right into the business's account.

You may think that making bank deposits is as easy as 1-2-3, but when it comes to business deposits and multiple checks, things get a bit more complicated. To properly make deposits to your business's checking account, follow these steps:

1. **Record on the deposit slip the numbers of all checks being deposited as well as the total cash being deposited.**

2. **Make photocopies of all checks being deposited so that you have a record in case something gets lost or misplaced at the bank.**

3. **After you make the deposit, attach the copies of all the checks to the deposit receipt and add any detail regarding the source of the deposited cash; file everything in your daily bank folder.**

   (The section "Keeping the Right Paperwork," later in this chapter, talks more about filing.)

Savings accounts

Some businesses find they have more cash than they need to meet their immediate plans. Rather than keep that extra cash in a non-interest bearing account, many businesses open a savings account to store the extra cash stash.

If you're a small business owner with few employees, you'll probably be the one to control the flow of money into and out of your savings account. As you grow and find that you need to delegate the responsibility for the business's savings, be sure to think carefully about who gets access and how you will document the flow of funds into and out of the savings account.

Petty cash accounts

Every business needs unexpected cash on almost a weekly basis. Whether it's money to pay the postman when he brings a letter or package COD, money to buy a few emergency stamps to get the mail out, or money for some office supplies needed before the next delivery, businesses need to keep some cash on hand, called *petty cash,* for unexpected expenses.

You certainly don't want to have a lot of cash sitting around in the office, but you should keep $50 to $100 in a petty cash box. If you find that you're faced with cash expenses more or less often than you initially expected, you can adjust the amount kept in petty cash accordingly.

No matter how much you keep in petty cash, be sure you set up a good control system that requires anyone who uses the cash to write a voucher that specifies how much was used and why. If possible, you should also ask that a cash receipt from the store or post office, for example, be attached to the voucher in order to justify the cash withdrawal. In most cases, a staff person buys something for the business and then gets reimbursed for that expense. If the expense is small enough, you can reimburse it by using the petty cash fund. If the expense is more than a few dollars, you'd likely ask the person to fill out an expense account form and get reimbursed by check. Petty cash usually is used for minor expenses of $5 to $10 or less.

The best control for petty cash is to pick one person in the office to manage the use of petty cash. Before giving that person more cash, he or she should be able to prove the absence of cash used and why it was used.

Cash registers

Have you ever gone into a business and tried to pay with a large bill only to find out the cashier can't make change? It's frustrating, but it happens in many businesses, especially when they don't carefully monitor the money in their cash registers. Most businesses empty cash registers each night and put any cash not being deposited in the bank that night into a safe. Some businesses today aren't even using traditional cash registers. They use portable devices to take orders and then a cash drawer to manage cash receipts and disbursements. Even if your business is using something other than a traditional cash register, the basics of cash handling remain the same.

Many businesses instruct their cashiers to periodically deposit their cash in a company safe throughout the day and get a paper voucher to show the cash deposited. These daytime deposits minimize the cash held in the cash draw in case the store is the victim of a robbery.

All these types of controls are necessary parts of modern business operations, but they can have consequences that make customers angry. Most customers will just walk out the door and not come back if they can't buy what they want using the bills they have on hand.

At the beginning of the day, cashiers usually start out with a set amount of cash in the register or cash drawer. As they collect money and give out change, the register records the transactions. At the end of the day, the cashier must count out the amount of change left in the register or cash drawer, run a copy of all transactions that passed through that register, and total the cash collected. Then the cashier must prove that the amount of cash remaining in that register or cash drawer totals the amount of cash at the beginning of the day plus the amount of cash collected during the day. After the cashier balances the register or cash drawer, the staff person in charge of cash deposits (usually the store manager or someone on the accounting or bookkeeping staff) takes all cash out except the amount that will be needed for the next day and deposits it in the bank.

In addition to having the proper amount of cash on hand necessary to give customers the change they need, you also must make sure that your cashiers are giving the right amount of change and actually recording all sales on their cash registers or other portable devices. Keeping an eye on cashier activities is good business practice, but it's also a way to protect cash theft by your employees. There are three ways cashiers can pocket some extra cash:

- ✔ **They don't record the sale and instead pocket the cash.** The best deterrent to this type of theft is supervision. You can decrease the likelihood of theft through unrecorded sales by printing up sales tickets that the cashier must use to enter a sale and open the cash drawer. If cash register transactions don't match sales receipts, then the cashier must show a voided transaction for the missing ticket or explain why the cash drawer was opened without a ticket.

- ✔ **They don't provide a sales receipt and instead pocket the cash.** In this scenario the cashier neglects to give a sales receipt to one customer in line. The cashier gives the next customer the unused sales receipt but doesn't actually record the second transaction in the cash register or other mobile device. Instead, he or she just pockets the cash. In the company's books, the second sale never took place. The customer whose sale wasn't recorded has a valid receipt though it may not match exactly what he bought, so he likely won't notice any problem unless he wants to return something later. Your best defense against this type of deception is to post a sign reminding all customers that they should get a receipt for all purchases and that the receipt is required to get a refund or exchange. Providing numbered sales receipts that include a duplicate copy can also help prevent this problem; cashiers need to produce the duplicates at the end of the day when proving the amount of cash flow that passed through their registers.

In addition to protection from theft by cashiers, the printed sales receipt system can be used to carefully monitor and prevent shoplifters from getting money for merchandise they never bought. For example, suppose a shoplifter took a blouse out of a store, as well as some blank sales receipts. The next day the shoplifter comes back with the blouse and one of the stolen sales receipts filled out as though the blouse had actually been purchased the day before. You can spot the fraud because that sales receipt is part of a numbered batch of sales receipts that you've already identified as missing or stolen. You can quickly identify that the customer never paid for the merchandise and call the police.

✔ **They record a false credit voucher and keep the cash for themselves.** In this case the cashier wrote up a credit voucher for a nonexistent customer and then pocketed the cash themselves. Most stores control this problem by using a numbered credit voucher system, so each credit can be carefully monitored with some detail that proves it's based on a previous customer purchase, such as a sales receipt. Also, stores usually require that a manager reviews the reason for the credit voucher, whether a return or exchange, and approves the transaction before cash or credit is given. When the bookkeeper records the sales return in the books, the number for the credit voucher is recorded with the transaction so that she can easily find the detail about that credit voucher if a question is raised later about the transaction.

Even if cashiers don't deliberately pocket cash, they can do so inadvertently by giving the wrong change. If you run a retail outlet, training and supervising your cashiers is a critical task that you must either handle yourself or hand over to a trusted employee.

Keeping the Right Paperwork

When it comes to handling cash, whether you're talking about the cash register, deposits into your checking accounts, or petty cash withdrawals, you can see that a lot of paper changes hands. In order to properly control the movement of cash into and out of your business, careful documentation is key. And don't forget about organization; you need to be able to find that documentation if questions about cash flow arise later.

Monitoring cash flow isn't the only reason you need to keep loads of paperwork. In order to do your taxes and write off business expenses, you have to have receipts for expenses. You also need details about the money you paid to employees and taxes collected for your employees in order to file the proper reports with government entities. (Book III Chapter 4 covers dealing with the government relating to employee matters, and Book V Chapter 5 discusses paying taxes.) Setting up a good filing system and knowing what to keep and for how long to keep it is very important for any small businessperson.

Some businesses are switching to electronic filing. They scan images of all paperwork and save it on their computers and backup devices. Even if your company has switched to an electronic filing system, the basics of what needs to be kept are the same. Rather than file cabinets, you use external drives and create file folders on those drives. Electronic filing systems can make it easier to find needed paperwork because of their search capabilities. This chapter focuses on a traditional filing system. If your company uses electronic filing, ask your accounting department for a short review on how to make the best use of your company's system.

Creating a filing system

To get started setting up your filing system, you need some supplies, specifically

- ✔ **Filing cabinets:** This one's pretty self-explanatory — it's hard to have a filing system with nothing to keep the files in.

- ✔ **File folders:** Use these to set up separate files for each of your vendors, employees, and customers who buy on store credit, as well as files for backup information on each of your transactions. Many bookkeepers file transaction information by the date the transaction was added to their journal. If the transaction relates to a customer, vendor, or employee, they add a duplicate copy of the transaction to the individual files as well.

  Even if you have a computerized accounting system, you need to file paperwork related to the transactions you enter into your computer system. You should still maintain employee, vendor, and customer files in hard copy just in case something goes wrong, like if your computer system crashes and you need the originals to restore the data. Of course, you should avoid that type of crisis at all costs and back up your computerized accounting system's data regularly. Daily backups are best; one week is the longest you should ever go without a backup.

- ✔ **Three-ring binders:** These binders are great for things like your Chart of Accounts (see Book I Chapter 2), your General Ledger (Book I Chapter 3), and your system of journals (Book I Chapter 4) because you'll be adding to these documents regularly, and the binders make it easy to add additional pages. Be sure to number the pages as you add them to the binder, so you can quickly spot a missing page. How many binders you need depends on how many financial transactions you have each accounting period. You can keep everything in one binder, or you may want to set up a binder for the Chart of Accounts and General Ledger and then a separate binder for each of your active journals. It's your decision based on what makes your job easier.

- ✔ **Expandable files:** These are the best way to keep track of current vendor activity and any bills that may be due. Make sure you have

  - **An alphabetical file:** Use this file to track all your outstanding purchase orders by vendor. After you fill the order, you can file all details about that order in the vendor's individual file in case questions about the order arise later.

  - **A 12-month file:** Use this file to keep track of bills that you need to pay. Simply place the bill in the slot for the month that it's due. Many companies also use a 30-day expandable file. At the beginning of the month, the bills are placed in the 30-day expandable file based on the dates that they need to be paid. This approach provides a quick and organized visual reminder for bills that are due.

If you're using a computerized accounting system, you likely don't need the expandable files because your accounting system can remind you when bills are due (as long as you added the information to the system when the bill arrived).

✔ **Blank computer disks or other storage media:** Use these to back up your computerized system on a weekly or, better yet, daily basis. Keep the backup disks in a fire safe or some place that won't be affected if the business is destroyed by a fire. (A fire safe is a must for any business; it's the best way to keep critical financial data safe.)

Figuring out what to keep and for how long

As you can probably imagine, the pile of paperwork you need to hold on to can get very large very quickly. As they see their files getting thicker and thicker, most business people wonder what they can toss, what they really need to keep, and how long they need to keep it.

Generally, you should keep most transaction-related paperwork for as long as the tax man can come and audit your books. For most types of audits, that's three years after you file your return. But if you failed to file taxes or filed taxes fraudulently (though of course you wouldn't do that), you may be questioned by the IRS at any time because there's no statute of limitations in these cases.

The tax man isn't the only reason to keep records around longer than one year. You may need proof-of-purchase information for your insurance company if an asset is lost, stolen, or destroyed by fire or other accident. Also, you need to hang on to information regarding any business loan until it's paid off, just in case the bank questions how much you paid. After the loan's paid off, be sure to keep proof of payment indefinitely in case a question about the loan ever arises. Information about real estate and other asset holdings also should be kept around for as long as you hold the asset and for at least three years after the asset is sold. And it's necessary to keep information about employees for at least three years after the employee leaves. (If any legal action arises regarding that employee's job tenure after the employee leaves, the statute of limitations for legal action is at most three years.)

Keep the current year's files easily accessible in a designated filing area and keep the most recent past year's files in accessible filing cabinets if you have room. Box up records when they hit the two-year-old mark, and put them in storage. Be sure to date your boxed records with information about what they are, when they were put into storage, and when it's okay to destroy them. So many people forget that detail about when it's safe to destroy the boxes, so they just pile up until total desperation sets in and there's no more room. Then someone must take the time to sort through the boxes and figure out what needs to be kept and what can be destroyed, and that's not a fun job. Note that destroying financial records (or any sensitive records) means shredding them yourself or hiring a shredding service — not tossing them in the trash or recycling bin.

Generally, keep information about all transactions around for about three years. After that, make a list of things you want to hold on to longer for other reasons, such as asset holdings and loan information. Check with your lawyer and accountant to get their recommendations on what to keep and for how long.

Protecting Your Business Against Internal Fraud

Many business people start their operations by carefully hiring people they can trust, thinking "We're family — they'll never steal from me." Unfortunately, those who have learned the truth are the ones who put too much trust in just one employee.

Too often a business owner finds out too late that even the most loyal employee may steal from the company if the opportunity arises and the temptation becomes too great — or if the employee finds himself caught up in a serious personal financial dilemma and needs fast cash. After introducing you to the various ways people can steal from a company, this section talks about steps you can take to prevent it.

Facing the reality of financial fraud

The four basic types of financial fraud are as follows:

- **Embezzlement,** also called *larceny,* which is the illegal use of funds by a person who controls those funds. For example, a bookkeeper may use company money for his own personal needs. Many times, embezzlement stories don't make it into the paper because business people are so embarrassed that they choose to keep the affair quiet instead. They usually settle privately with the embezzler rather than face public scrutiny.

✔ **Internal theft,** which is the stealing of company assets by employees, such as taking office supplies or products the company sells without paying for them. Internal theft is often the culprit behind inventory shrinkage.

✔ **Payoffs and kickbacks,** which are situations in which employees accept cash or other benefits in exchange for access to the company's business, often creating a scenario where the company that the employee works for pays more for the goods or products than necessary. That extra money finds its way into the pocket of the employee who helped facilitate the access. For example, say Company A wants to sell its products to Company B. An employee in Company B helps Company A get in the door. Company A prices its product a bit higher and gives the employee of Company B that extra profit in the form of a kickback for helping it out. A payoff is paid before the sale is made, essentially saying "please." A kickback is paid after the sale is made, essentially saying "thank you." In reality, payoffs and kickbacks are a form of bribery, but few companies report or litigate this problem (although sometimes employees are fired when deals are uncovered).

✔ **Skimming,** which occurs when employees take money from receipts and don't record the revenue on the books.

Although any of these financial crimes can happen in a small business, the one that hits small businesses the hardest is embezzlement. Embezzlement happens most frequently in small businesses when one person has access or control over most of the company's financial activities. For example, a bookkeeper may write checks, make deposits, and balance the monthly bank statement — talk about having your fingers in a very big cookie jar.

Caught with fingers in the cookie jar

Alice is a bookkeeper who's been with Company A for a long time. She got promoted to office manager after she was with the company for 20 years. She's like a family member to the business owner, who trusts her implicitly. Because he's so busy with other aspects of running the business, he gives her control of the daily grind of cash flow. The beloved office manager handles or supervises all incoming and outgoing cash, proves out the bank statements, handles payroll, signs all the checks, and files the business's tax returns.

All that control gives her the opportunity, credibility, and access to embezzle a lot of money. At first, the trust was well founded, and Alice handled her new responsibilities very well. But after about three years in the role as office manager, her son was struck with a severe illness, and the medical bills continued to mount.

Alice decides to pay herself more money. She adds her husband or other family members to the payroll and documents the checks for them as consulting expenses. She draws large cash checks to buy nonexistent office supplies and equipment, and then, worst of all, she files the company's tax returns and pockets the money that should go to paying the taxes due. The business owner doesn't find out about the problem until the IRS comes calling, and by then, the office manager is retired and moved away.

Sound far-fetched? Well, it's not. You may not hear this exact scenario, but you're likely to see stories in your local newspaper about similar embezzlement schemes.

Employee embezzlement and theft cost companies more than customer theft

According to the National White Collar Crime Center, internal theft by employees is the largest single component of white-collar crime. You don't hear much about it, though, because many businesses choose to keep it quiet. The reality is that employee theft and embezzlement in the United States are estimated to cost employers over $240 billion per year (when the theft of intellectual property is included) or over $500 million per day. Total cost to businesses is ten times more than the amount lost through all other crimes against businesses combined. Banks, for example, report 95 percent of their theft losses from employee misdeeds as opposed to 5 percent of theft losses from bank robberies and customer theft. Four key situations in the workplace provide opportunities for theft and embezzlement: poor internal controls, too much control given to certain individuals, lax management, and failure to adequately prescreen employees.

Dividing staff responsibilities

Your primary protection against financial crime is properly separating staff responsibilities when the flow of business cash is involved. Basically, you should never have one person handle more than one of the following tasks:

- **Bookkeeping:** Involves reviewing and entering all transactions into the company's books. The bookkeeper makes sure that transactions are accurate, valid, appropriate, and have the proper authorization. For example, if a transaction requires paying a vendor, the bookkeeper makes sure the charges are accurate and that someone with proper authority has approved the payment. The bookkeeper can review documentation of cash receipts and the overnight deposits taken to the bank, but he or she shouldn't be the person who actually makes the deposit.

Also, if the bookkeeper is responsible for handling payments from external parties, such as customers or vendors, he or she shouldn't be the one to enter those transactions in the books.

✓ **Authorization:** Involves being the manager or managers delegated to authorize expenditures for their departments. You may decide that transactions over a certain amount must have two or more authorizations before checks can be sent to pay a bill. Authorization levels should be clearly spelled out and followed by all, even the owner or president of the company. (Remember, as owner, you set the tone for how the rest of the office operates; if you take shortcuts, you set a bad example and undermine the system you put in place.)

✓ **Money-handling:** Involves direct contact with incoming cash or revenue, whether check, credit card, or store credit transactions, as well as outgoing cash flow. The person who handles money directly, such as a cashier, shouldn't be the one who prepares and makes bank deposits. Likewise, the person writing checks to pay company bills shouldn't be authorized to sign those checks; to be safe, one person should prepare the checks based on authorized documentation, and a second person should sign those checks after reviewing the authorized documentation.

When setting up your cash-handling systems, try to think like an embezzler to figure out ways someone could take advantage of a system.

✓ **Financial report preparation and analysis:** Involves the actual preparation of the financial reports and any analysis of those reports. Financial reports should be prepared by someone who's not involved in the day-to-day entering of transactions in the books. For most small businesses, the bookkeeper turns over the raw reports from the computerized accounting system to an outside accountant who reviews the materials and prepares the financial reports. In addition, he or she does a financial analysis of the business activity results for the previous accounting period.

Of course, if you're just starting up a small business, you don't have enough staff to separate all these duties. Until you do have that capability, be sure to stay heavily involved in the inflow and outflow of cash in your business.

✓ **Open your business's bank statements every month, and keep a close watch on the transactions.** Someone else can be given the responsibility to prove out the statement, but you should still keep an eye on the transactions listed.

✓ **Periodically look at your business check voucher system to be sure there aren't missing checks.** A bookkeeper who knows you periodically check the books is less likely to find an opportunity for theft or embezzlement. If you find that a check or page of checks is missing, act quickly to find out if the checks were used legitimately. If you can't find the answer, call your bank and put a stop on the missing check numbers.

> ✔ **Periodically observe cash handling by your cashiers and managers to be sure they're following the rules you've established.** It's known as *management by walking around* — the more often you're out there, the less likely you are to be a victim of employee theft and fraud.

Balancing control costs

As a small businessperson, you'll always be trying to balance the cost of protecting your cash and assets with the cost of adequately separating those duties. It can be a big mistake to put in too many controls that end up costing you money. For example, you may put in inventory controls that require salespeople to contact one particular person who has the key to your product warehouse. This kind of control may prevent employee theft, but it also may result in lost sales because salespeople can't find the key-holder when they're dealing with an interested customer. In the end, the customer gets mad, and you lose the sale.

When you put controls in place, talk to your staff both before and after instituting the controls to see how they're working and to check for any unforeseen problems. Be willing and able to adjust your controls to balance the business needs of selling your products, managing the cash flow, and keeping your eye on making a profit.

Generally, as you make rules for your internal controls, be sure that the cost of protecting an asset is no more than the asset you're trying to protect. For example, don't go overboard to protect office supplies by forcing your staff to sit around waiting for hours to access needed supplies while you and a manager are at a meeting away from the office.

Ask yourself these four questions as you design your internal controls:

> ✔ What exactly do I want to prevent or detect — errors, sloppiness, theft, fraud, or embezzlement?
>
> ✔ Do I face the problem frequently?
>
> ✔ What do I estimate the loss to be?
>
> ✔ What will it cost me to implement the change in procedures to prevent or detect the problem?

You can't answer these questions all by yourself, so consult with your managers and the staff that will be impacted by the changes. Get their answers to these questions, and listen to their feedback.

When you finish putting together the new internal control rule, be sure to document why you decided to implement the rule and the information you collected in developing it. After it's been in place for a while, test your assumptions. Be sure you're in fact detecting the errors, theft, fraud, or embezzlement that you hoped and expected to detect. Check the costs of keeping the rule in place by looking at cash outlay, employee time and morale, and the impact on customer service. If you find any problems with your internal controls, take the time to fix them and change the rule, again documenting the process. With detailed documentation, if two or three years down the road someone questions why he or she is doing something, you'll have the answers and be able to determine if the problem is still a valid one and if the rule is still necessary or needs to be changed.

Insuring Your Cash through Employee Bonding

If you have employees who handle a lot of cash, insuring your business against theft is an absolute must. This insurance, called *fidelity bonds,* helps you protect yourself against theft and reduce your risk of loss. Employee bonding is a common part of an overall business insurance package.

If you carry a fidelity bond on your cash handlers, you're covered for losses sustained by any employee who's bonded. You also have coverage if an employee's act causes losses to a client of your business. For example, if you're a financial consultant and your bookkeeper embezzles a client's cash, you're protected for the loss.

Fidelity bonds are a type of insurance that you can buy through the company that handles your business insurance policies. The cost varies greatly depending on the type of business you operate and the amount of cash or other assets that are handled by the employees you want to bond. If an employee steals from you or one of your customers, the insurance covers the loss.

Employers bond employees who handle cash, as well as employees who may be in a position to steal something other than cash. For example, a janitorial service bonds its workers in case a worker steals something from one of its customers. If a customer reports something missing, the insurance company that bonded the employee covers the loss. Without a bond, an employer must pay back the customer for any loss.

Chapter 6

Computer Options for Bookkeeping

In This Chapter

▶ Finding the right accounting software for your business

▶ Getting your computerized books up and running

Some small business owners who have been around a while still do things the old-fashioned way — they keep their books in paper journals and ledgers. However, in this age of technology and instant information, the majority of today's businesses computerize their books.

Not only is computerized bookkeeping easier, it minimizes the chance of errors because most of the work done to a computerized system's ledgers and journals (see Book I Chapters 3 and 4, respectively) involves inputting data on forms that can be understood even by someone without training in accounting or bookkeeping. The person entering the information doesn't need to know whether something is a debit or credit (see Book I Chapter 1 for an explanation of the difference) because the computerized system takes care of everything.

Mobile accounting is also becoming popular, with major accounting software packages now available as online tools that can be accessed from any mobile device. Companies with multiple locations, if they purchase an online accounting software package for multiple users, can allow employees to log on from anywhere and access a central accounting system.

This chapter explores the three top accounting software packages for small businesses, discusses the basics of setting up your own computerized books, talks about how you can customize a program for your business, and gives you some pointers on converting your manual bookkeeping system into a computerized one.

Surveying Your Software Options

More than 50 different types of accounting software programs are on the market, and all are designed to computerize your bookkeeping. The more sophisticated ones target specific industry needs, such as food services or utilities, and can cost thousands of dollars. To check out those options, visit `http://findaccountingsoftware.com`, where you can browse for accounting software that's grouped by industry.

Luckily, as a small businessperson, you probably don't need all the bells and whistles offered by the top-of-the-line programs. Instead, the three software programs reviewed in this chapter can meet the needs of most small business people. Using one of the three systems recommended in this chapter, you can get started with an initial investment of as little as $40. It may not be fancy, but basic computerized accounting software can do a fine job of helping you keep your books. And you can always upgrade to a more expensive program, if needed, as your business grows.

The three programs that meet any small business's basic bookkeeping needs are Bookkeeper, QuickBooks, and Sage 50 (formerly known as Peachtree Accounting). The most affordable of the three is Bookkeeper, which has been priced as low as $31 at various Internet sites. QuickBooks and Sage 50 both offer simple systems. QuickBooks Online Simple Start and Sage 50 First Step can get you started for under $100. But if you can afford it, consider stepping up at least to QuickBooks Pro or Sage 50 Pro. The costs vary depending on the number of people you want to have access to the software, but you would need to expect to pay at least $200 more.

Accounting software packages are updated almost every year. That's because tax laws and laws involving many other aspects of operating a business change so often. In addition, computer software companies are always improving their products to make computerized accounting programs more user-friendly, so be sure that you always buy the most current version of an accounting software package.

No matter what computerized system you choose, always be sure that you set up a daily backup plan to save your data in another location. This may be an external hard drive or an online backup system. That way if your computer crashes you won't lose all your accounting data.

Bookkeeper

Bookkeeper 2015 (`www.avanquest.com/USA/software/bookkeeper-2015-502578`) is a cost-effective choice for bookkeeping software if you're just starting up and don't have sophisticated bookkeeping or accounting needs. You can prepare invoices, pay bills, write checks, manage inventory, track receivables, bill customers, and prepare payroll. But as of this writing there is no online version offered, and it only receives minor updates periodically.

The program includes accounting templates for things like sales orders, quotes, receipts, and other basic needs. More than 125 reports and charts are included that you can customize to your accounting needs.

You can purchase add-ons for processing payroll and credit-card processing. However, the add-on features don't work as well as features that are included in an original software package, such as the ones included as part of QuickBooks.

Bookkeeping 2015 does not offer the ability to scale up, which means as your business grows, you need to find another package for your business needs. So consider this program only if you plan to keep your business small with just basic accounting needs.

Sage 50 Pro

Sage 50 (`http://na.sage.com/us/sage-50-accounting/pro`) is an excellent software package for your bookkeeping and accounting needs, but it's definitely not recommended if you're a novice. You need to be familiar with accounting jargon just to use the Sage 50 system, and its interface isn't as user-friendly as the ones for Bookkeeper and QuickBooks.

To use Sage 50, you definitely need to know your way around the General Ledger and be comfortable with accounting terms such as Account Reconciliation, Accounts Payable, and Cash Receipts journal. Although Sage 50 offers training options inside the program, it lacks the sophistication of the excellent learning center now offered by QuickBooks. So if you're a beginner, which is probably the case because you bought this book, starting with this software is not recommended.

Sage 50 offers inventory-management tools that are the best in its class. New versions of the software even automatically generate purchase orders when inventory reaches a user-specified level. You can also export Sage 50 customer, vendor, and employee databases into Microsoft Word and use the data with Word's mail-merge feature to send emails or letters.

Sage 50 Pro costs around $350 a year, but you may be able to find it cheaper by searching the Internet. Payroll processing is an extra $250 for up to 50 employees. If you want to be able to integrate your shipping with UPS, have more than one user, control users by screen-level security, have advanced inventory or job costing capabilities, or have an audit trail of your work, you need to start with Sage 50 Premium, which starts at around $449 for up to five users. Enterprise and cloud solutions are also available for Sage 50 Premium at an additional cost if you want to have mobile access.

Sage 50 offers a utility that makes it easy to use to convert data from Intuit's QuickBooks. You can also import files from Quicken, the popular financial/ money-management software package. There's no conversion tool for Microsoft Excel data, but you can import and export Excel files into the program without problems. Check out Jane Kelly's *Sage 50 Accounts for Dummies* (Wiley, 2012) to get a better feel for this program, its capabilities, and how to use it.

QuickBooks Pro

QuickBooks (`http://quickbooks.intuit.com/pro/`) offers the best of both worlds: an easy user interface (for the novice) and extensive bookkeeping and accounting features (for the experienced bookkeeper or accountant). That's why QuickBooks is used to demonstrate various bookkeeping functions throughout this book. More small business owners today use QuickBooks than any other small business accounting software package. It is the number one software on the Top Ten Reviews site as well (`http://accounting-software-review.toptenreviews.com/small-business/`). Note that you can check out reviews about other top ten accounting programs at this website.

QuickBooks offers the novice an extensive learning center, which walks you through every type of key transaction with an interactive program that not only shows you how to do the function but also explains the basics of bookkeeping. You don't have to use the tutorial, but the option pops up when you do a task for the first time, so the choice is always yours. You also can go back to the learning center to review at any time. For additional information on this software, check out *QuickBooks 2015 For Dummies* (Wiley, 2014) by Stephen L. Nelson.

Most people have a love/hate relationship with Intuit support (Intuit's the company that makes QuickBooks). Many have had good support experiences not only with QuickBooks but also with its other popular software packages, such as TurboTax and Quicken. Others have complained loudly about support problems.

Add-ons and fees

All the accounting programs recommended in this section offer add-ons and features you're likely to need:

✔ **Tax updates:** If you have employees and want up-to-date tax information and forms to do your payroll using your accounting software, you need to buy an update each year.

✔ **Online credit-card processing and electronic bill paying:** Having the capabilities to perform these tasks means additional fees. In fact, QuickBooks advertises its add-ons

in these areas throughout its system; you can see the advertisements pop up on a number of screens.

✔ **Point-of-sale software:** This add-on helps you integrate your sales at the cash register with your accounting software.

Before signing on for one of the add-ons be sure you understand what the fees will be. Usually, you're advised of the additional costs whenever you try to do anything that incurs extra fees.

QuickBooks Online Simple Start may be able to meet most of your bookkeeping and accounting needs. At the time of this writing, the pricing ranges from $7.99 a month to $23.97 a month, depending on the features you want. It gives you mobile access from your PC, Mac, iPad/iPhone device, or Android phone or tablet. If you want to integrate your bookkeeping with a point-of-sale package, which integrates cash register sales, you need to get QuickBooks Pro, which starts at around $199. You also need to upgrade to QuickBooks Pro if you want to do inventory management, generate purchase orders from estimates or sales orders, do job costing and estimates, automatically create a budget, or integrate your data for use with Microsoft Word and Excel programs. Payroll services also can be added for an additional cost, depending on the size of your payroll.

QuickBooks is the most versatile software if you plan to use other software packages along with it. It can share data with more than 325 popular business software applications. Sales, customer, and financial data can be shared easily too, so you don't have to enter that information twice. To find out if QuickBooks can share data with the business software applications you're currently using or plan to use, access their online chat feature at www.quickbooks.inuit.com and then click the Chat button. Operators are standing by.

Setting Up Your Computerized Books

After you pick your software, the hard work is done because actually setting up the package will probably take you less time than researching your options and picking which one to get. All three packages discussed here have good start-up tutorials to help you set up the books. QuickBooks even has an interactive interview that asks questions about all aspects of how you want to run your business and then sets up what you'll need based on your answers.

Bookkeeper, Sage 50, and QuickBooks all produce a number of sample Charts of Accounts (see Book I Chapter 2) that automatically appear after you choose the type of business you plan to run and upon which industry that business falls. All three programs ask you to enter a company name, address, and tax identification number to get started. Then they generate a Chart of Accounts for the business type selected. Start with one of the charts offered by the software, like the one in Figure 6-1, and then tweak it to your business's needs.

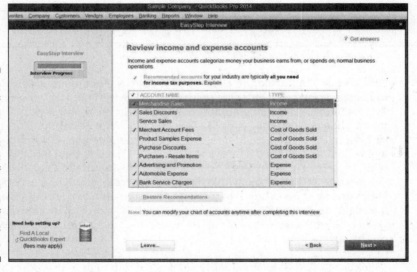

Figure 6-1:
As part of the initial interview, QuickBooks generates a Chart of Accounts based on the type of business you have.

If you're operating as a sole proprietor or your business is based on a partnership and you don't have a federal tax ID for the business, you can use your Social Security number. You then select an accounting period (see Figure 6-2). If the calendar year is your accounting period, you don't have to change anything. But if you operate your business based on another period of 12 months, such as September 1 to August 31, you must enter that information.

If you don't change your accounting period to match how you plan to develop your financial statements, then you have to delete the business from the system and start over.

Fiscal year

Many retail businesses don't close their books at the end of December because the holiday season is not a good time to be closing out for the year. With gift cards and other new ways to give gifts, purchases after the holiday can be very active. So, many retail businesses operate on a fiscal year of February 1 to January 31, so they can close the books well after the holiday season ends.

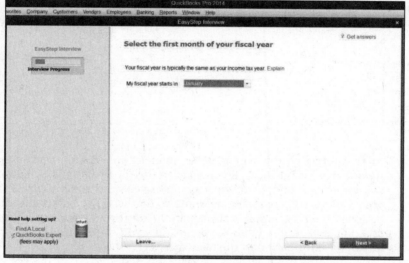

Figure 6-2: QuickBooks asks about calendar year or fiscal. For fiscal, you choose the month that you start your business operations.

After you set up your business, you can customize the software so that it matches your business's needs.

Customizing software to match your operations

With the basics set up (see the preceding section), you can customize the software to fit your business's operations. For example, you're able to pick the type of invoices and other business forms you want to use.

This is also the time to input information about your bank accounts and other key financial data (see Figure 6-3). Your main business bank account is the one that should be used for the first account listed in your software program, Cash in Checking.

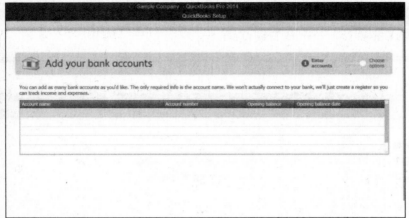

Figure 6-3:
QuickBooks collects information about your bank accounts as part of the initial interview.

After entering your bank and other financial information, you enter data unique to your business. If you want to use the program's budgeting features, you enter your budget information before entering other data. Then you add your vendor and customer accounts so that when you start entering transactions, the information is already in the system. If you don't have any outstanding bills or customer payments due, you can wait and enter vendor and customer information as the need arises.

If you have payments to be made or money to be collected from customers, be sure to input that information so your system is ready when it comes time to pay the bills or input a customer payment. Also, you don't want to forget to pay a bill or collect from a customer!

You may be able to import data about your customers, vendors, and employees from software packages you're currently using to track that information, such as Microsoft Excel or Access. Full instructions for importing data come with the software program you choose.

Don't panic about entering everything into your computerized system right away. All programs make it very easy to add customers, vendors, and employees at any time.

Other information collected includes the type of accounting method you'll be using — either cash-basis or accrual accounting. (Book I Chapter 1 talks about both.) You also need to enter information about whether or not you collect sales taxes from your customers and, if you do, the sales tax rates. Also, you can pick a format for your invoices, set up payroll data, and make arrangements for how you want to pay bills.

Converting your manual bookkeeping to a computerized system

If you're converting a manual bookkeeping system to a computerized system, your conversion will take a bit more time than just starting fresh because you need to be sure your new system starts with information that matches your current books. The process for entering your initial data varies depending on the software you've chosen, so it's beyond the scope of this book to go into detail about that process here. To ensure that you properly convert your bookkeeping system, use the information that comes with your software; read through the manual, review the startup suggestions made as you set up the system, and pick the methods that best match your style of operating.

The best time to convert is at the end of an accounting period. That way, you won't have to do a lot of extra work adding transactions that already occurred during a period. For example, if you decide to computerize your accounting system on March 15, you'd have to add all the transactions that occurred between March 1 and March 15 into your new system. It's just easier to wait until April 1 to get started even if you buy the software on March 15. While you can convert to a computerized accounting system at the end of a month, your best time to do it is at the end of a calendar or fiscal year. Otherwise, you have to input data for all the months of the year that have passed.

Whenever you decide to start your computerized bookkeeping, use the data from your trial balance that you used to close the books at the end of your most recent accounting period. (Book IV Chapter 5 explains how to prepare a trial balance.) In the computerized system, enter the balances for each of the accounts in your trial balance. Asset, liability, and equity accounts should have carry-over balances, but income and expense accounts should have zero balances.

Of course, if you're starting a new business, you won't have a previous trial balance. Then you just enter any balances you might have in your cash accounts, any assets your business may own as it starts up, and any liabilities that your business may already owe relating to startup expenses.

You also add any contributions from owners that were made to get the business started in the Equity accounts.

After you enter all the appropriate data, run a series of financial reports, such as an income statement and balance sheet, to be sure the data is entered and formatted the way you like it. It's a lot easier to change formatting when the system isn't chock-full of data.

You need to be sure that you've entered the right numbers, so verify that the new accounting system's financial reports match what you created manually. If the numbers are different, now's the time to figure out why. Otherwise the reports you do at the end of the accounting period will be wrong. If the numbers don't match, don't assume the only place an error could be is in the data entered. You may find that the error is in the reports you developed manually. Of course, check your entries first, but if the income statement and balance sheet still don't look right, double-check your trial balances as well.

Chapter 7

Financial Statements and Accounting Standards

*T*his chapter presents a brief introduction to the three primary business financial statements: the *income statement*, the *balance sheet*, and the *statement of cash flows*. In this chapter, you get more interesting tidbits about these three *financials*, as they're sometimes called. Then, in Book II Chapters 4–6, you really get the goods. Remember when you were learning to ride a bicycle? This chapter is like getting on the bike and learning to keep your balance. In this chapter, you put on your training wheels and start riding. Then, when you're ready, the really meaty upcoming chapters just mentioned explain all 21 gears of the financial statements bicycle, and then some.

This chapter explains that *net income* — which is the bottom-line profit of a business reported in its income statement — does not produce cash flow of the same amount. Profit-making activities cause many changes in the financial condition of a business, not just in the cash account. Many people assume that making a profit increases a business's cash balance by the same amount, and that's the end of it. Making profit leaves many footprints on the financial condition of a business, which you learn in this chapter.

This chapter also briefly discusses financial accounting and reporting standards. Businesses should comply with established accounting standards that govern the recording of revenue, income, expenses, and losses; put values on assets and liabilities; and present and disclose information in financial reports. The basic idea is that all businesses should follow uniform methods for measuring and reporting profit performance, and reporting financial condition and cash flows. Consistency in accounting from business to business is the goal. This chapter explains who makes the rules and discusses important recent developments: the internationalization of accounting standards and the increasing divide between financial reporting by public and private companies.

Reviewing the Basic Content of Financial Statements

This chapter focuses on the basic *information components* of each financial statement reported by a business. This first step doesn't address the grouping of these information packets within each financial statement. The first step is to just get a good idea of the information content reported in financial statements. The second step is to become familiar with more details about the "architecture," rules of classification, and other features of financial statements, which is covered in Book II Chapters 4–6.

Realizing that form follows function in financial statements

You need realistic business examples to understand the three primary financial statements. The information content of a business's financial statements depends on whether the business sells products or services. For example, the financial statements of a movie theater chain are different from those of a bank, which are different from those of an airline, which are different from an automobile manufacturer. This section uses two examples that fit a wide variety of businesses.

The first example is a business that sells *products*. The second example is for a business that sells *services*. Note that the two financial statements differ to some degree — not entirely, but in some important respects. The point is that the form of its financial statements follows the function of the business and how it makes profit — whether the business sells products or services to bring in the needed revenue to cover expenses and to provide enough profit after expenses.

Here are the particulars about the product business example:

- ✔ It sells products to other businesses (not on the retail level).
- ✔ It sells on credit, and its customers take a month or so before they pay.
- ✔ It holds a fairly large stock of products awaiting sale (its *inventory*).

✔ It owns a wide variety of long-term operating assets that have useful lives from 3 to 30 years or longer (building, machines, tools, computers, office furniture, and so on).

✔ It has been in business for many years and has made a consistent profit.

✔ It borrows money for part of the total capital it needs.

✔ It's organized as a corporation and pays federal and state income taxes on its annual taxable income.

✔ It has never been in bankruptcy and is not facing any immediate financial difficulties.

The product company's annual income statement for the year just ended, its balance sheet at the end of the year, and its statement of cash flows for the year are presented in following the sections.

For comparison, financial statements are also presented for a service company. This company doesn't sell products, and it makes no sales on credit; cash is collected at the time of making sales. These are the two main differences compared with the product company.

Dollar amounts in financial statements are typically rounded off, either by not presenting the last three digits (when rounded off to the nearest thousand) or by not presenting the last six digits (when rounded to the nearest million by large companies). This section strikes a compromise on this issue — it shows the last three digits for each item as 000, which means that the amount has been rounded off but still shows all digits. Many smaller businesses report their financial statement dollar amounts out to the last dollar, or even the last penny, for that matter. Keep in mind that too many digits in a dollar amount are hard to comprehend.

The financial statement examples for the product and service businesses are stepping-stone illustrations that are concerned mainly with the basic information components in each statement. Full-blown, classified financial statements are presented in Book II Chapters 4–6. (You are no doubt anxious to get to those chapters — remember, patience is a virtue.) The financial statements in this chapter do not include all the information you see in actual financial statements. Also, descriptive labels are used for each item rather than the terse and technical titles you see in actual financial statements. And most subtotals that you see in actual financial statements have been stripped out because they are not necessary at this point. So, with all these caveats in mind, let's get going.

Financial statements are rather stiff and formal. No slang or street language is allowed, and you'll never see a swear word in one. Financial statements would get a G in the movies rating system. Seldom do you see any graphics or artwork in a financial statement itself, although you do see a fair amount of photos and graphics on other pages in the financial reports of public companies. And there's virtually no humor in financial reports. Sorry.

Income statements

The *income statement* is the all-important financial statement that summarizes the profit-making activities of a business over a period of time. Figure 7-1 shows the basic information content of the external income statement for our product company example. *External* means that the financial statement is released outside the business to those entitled to receive it — primarily its shareowners and lenders. Internal financial statements stay within the business and are used mainly by its managers; they are not circulated outside the business because they contain competitive and confidential information.

Company's Name
Income Statement
For Most Recent Year

Sales revenue		$10,400,000
Cost of goods sold expense		$6,240,000
Gross margin		$4,160,000
Selling, general, and administrative expenses	$3,235,000	
Interest expense	$125,000	
Income tax expense	$280,000	
Total other expenses		$3,640,000
Net income		$520,000

Figure 7-1: Income statement for a business that sells products.

Income statement for a product company

Figure 7-1 presents the major ingredients of the income statement for a product company. As you might expect, it starts with sales revenue on the top line. Then the cost of the products (goods) sold is deducted from sales revenue to report *gross margin* (also called gross profit), which is a preliminary, or "first" line, measure of profit before other expenses are taken into account. Next other types of expenses are listed, and their total is deducted from gross margin to reach the final bottom line, called *net income*. Virtually all income statements disclose at least these four expenses. (A business can report more types of expenses in its external income statement, and many do.)

Cost of goods sold expense and selling, general, and administrative expenses take the biggest bites out of sales revenue. The other two expenses (interest and income tax) are relatively small as a percent of annual sales revenue but important enough in their own right to be reported separately. And though you may not need this reminder, bottom-line profit (net income) is the amount of sales revenue in excess of its total expenses. If either sales revenue or any of the expense amounts are wrong, then profit is wrong.

Income statement for a service company

Figure 7-2 presents the income statement for a company that sells services (instead of products). Same dollar size as the product company. Notice that annual sales revenue is $10,400,000 for both companies. And total expenses are the same at $9,880,000. (For the product company its $6,240,000 cost of goods sold expense plus its $3,640,000 of other expenses is $9,880,000.) Therefore, net income for both companies is $520,000.

Company's Name
Income Statement
For Most Recent Year

Sales revenue		$10,400,000
Operating expenses	$6,240,000	
Selling, general, and administrative expenses	$3,235,000	
Interest expense	$125,000	
Income tax expense	$280,000	
Total expenses		$9,880,000
Net income		$520,000

Figure 7-2: Income statement for a business that sells services.

The service business does not sell a product; therefore, it does not have the cost of goods sold expense, and accordingly does not report a gross margin line in its income statement. In place of cost of goods sold, it has other types of expenses. In Figure 7-2, operating expenses are $6,240,000 in place of cost of goods sold expense. Service companies differ on how they report their operating expenses. For example, United Airlines breaks out the cost of aircraft fuel, and landing fees. The largest expense of the insurance company State Farm is payments on claims. The movie chain AMC reports film exhibition costs separate from its other operating expenses.

Income statement pointers

Most product and service businesses break out one or more expenses instead of disclosing just one very broad category for all selling, general, and administrative expenses. For example, a business could disclose expenses for advertising and sales promotion, depreciation, salaries and wages, research and development, and delivery and shipping — though reporting these expenses varies quite a bit from business to business. Businesses do not disclose the compensation of top management in their external financial reports, although this information can be found in the proxy statements of public companies that are filed with the Securities and Exchange Commission. Details disclosed about operating expenses in externally reported financial reports vary from business to business. Financial reporting standards are rather permissive on this point.

Inside most businesses an income statement is called a *P&L (profit and loss) report*. These internal profit performance reports to the managers of a business include a good deal more detailed information about expenses and about sales revenue also. Reporting just four expenses to managers (as shown in Figures 7-1 and 7-2) would not do.

Sales revenue is from the sales of products or services to customers. You also see the term *income*, which generally refers to amounts earned by a business from sources other than sales; for example, a real estate rental business receives rental income from its tenants. (In the two examples for a product and a service company, the businesses have only sales revenue.)

Net income, being the bottom line of the income statement after deducting all expenses from sales revenue (and income, if any), is called, not surprisingly, the *bottom line*. It is also called *net earnings*. A few companies call it *profit* or *net profit*, but such terminology is not common.

The income statement gets the most attention from business managers, lenders, and investors (not that they ignore the other two financial statements). The much-abbreviated versions of income statements that you see in the financial press, such as in *The Wall Street Journal,* report the top line (sales revenue and income) and the bottom line (net income) and not much more. Refer to Book II Chapter 5 for more information on income statements.

Balance sheets

A more accurate name for a balance sheet is *statement of financial condition,* or *statement of financial position*. But the term *balance sheet* has caught on, and most people use this term. Keep in mind that the "balance" is not important, but rather the information reported in this financial statement. In brief, a balance sheet summarizes on the one hand the assets of the business and on the other hand the sources of the assets. The sources have claims, or entitlements against the assets of the business. Looking at assets is only half the picture. The other half consists of the liabilities and owner equity claims on the assets. Cash is listed first and other assets are listed in the order of their nearness to cash. Liabilities are listed in order of their due dates (the earliest first, and so on). Liabilities are listed ahead of owners' equity.

Balance sheet for a product company

Figure 7-3 shows the building blocks (basic information components) of a typical balance sheet for a business that sells products on credit. One reason the balance sheet is called by this name is that its two sides balance, or are equal in total amounts. In the example, the $5.2 million total of assets equals the $5.2 million total of liabilities and owners' equity. The balance or equality of total assets on the one side of the scale and the sum of liabilities plus owners' equity on the other side of the scale is expressed in the *accounting equation,* discussed back in Book I Chapter 1. ***Note:*** The balance sheet example shown in Figure 7-3 concentrates on the essential elements in this financial statement. In a financial report, the balance sheet includes additional features and frills, explained in Book II Chapter 4.

Company's Name
Balance Sheet
At End of Most Recent Year

Assets

Cash	$1,000,000
Receivables from sales made on credit	$800,000
Inventory of unsold products, at cost	$1,560,000
Long-term operating assets, at cost less cumulative amount charged off to depreciation expense	$1,840,000
Total assets	$5,200,000

Liabilities and Owners' Equity

Non-interest bearing liabilities from purchases on credit and for unpaid expenses	$650,000
Interest-bearing debt	$2,080,000
Owners' equity capital invested in business plus profit earned and retained in business	$2,470,000
Total liabilities and owners' equity	$5,200,000

Figure 7-3:
Balance sheet for a company that sells products on credit.

Let's take a quick walk through the balance sheet (Figure 7-3). For a company that sells products on credit, assets are reported in the following order: First is cash; then receivables; then cost of products held for sale; and finally the long-term operating assets of the business. Moving to the other side of the balance sheet, the liabilities section starts with the trade liabilities (from buying on credit) and liabilities for unpaid expenses. Following these operating liabilities is the interest-bearing debt of the business. Owners' equity sources are then reported below liabilities. Each of these information packets is called an *account* — so a balance sheet has a composite of asset accounts, liability accounts, and owners' equity accounts.

Balance sheet for a service company

Figure 7-4 presents the typical balance sheet components for a business that sells services (instead of products). Recall that the service company example does not sell on credit; it collects cash at the point of sale. Notice right away that this service business example does not have two sizable assets that the product company has — receivables from credit sales and inventory of products held for sale. Therefore, the total assets of our service company example are considerably smaller. The product company has $5,200,000 total assets (Figure 7-3), whereas the service company has only $2,840,000 total assets (Figure 7-4).

Company's Name
Balance Sheet
At End of Most Recent Year

Assets

Cash	$1,000,000
Long-term operating assets, at cost less cumulative amount charged off to depreciation expense	$1,840,000
Total assets	$2,840,000

Liabilities and Owners' Equity

Non-interest bearing liabilities from purchases on credit and for unpaid expenses	$650,000
Interest-bearing debt	$1,000,000
Owners' equity capital invested in business plus profit earned and retained in business	$1,190,000
Total liabilities and owners' equity	$2,840,000

Figure 7-4: Balance sheet for a service company.

The smaller amount of total assets of the service business means that the other side of its balance sheet is correspondingly smaller as well. In plain terms, this means that the service company does not need to borrow as much money or raise as much capital from its equity owners compared with the product business. Notice, for example, that the interest-bearing debt of the service company is $1.0 million (Figure 7-4) compared with over

$2.0 million for the product company (Figure 7-3). Likewise, the total amount of owners' equity for the service business is much smaller than the product company.

Balance sheet pointers

Businesses need a variety of assets. You have *cash,* of course, which every business needs. When selling on credit, a business records a *receivable* that is collected later (typically 30 days or longer). Businesses that sell products carry an *inventory* of products awaiting sale to customers. Businesses need long-term resources that have the generic name *property, plant, and equipment*; this group includes buildings, vehicles, tools, machines, and other resources needed in their operations. All these, and more, go under the collective name "assets."

As you might suspect, the particular assets reported in the balance sheet depend on which assets the business owns. Just four basic types of assets are included in Figure 7-3. These are the hardcore assets that a business selling products on credit would have. It's possible that such a business could lease (or rent) virtually all of its long-term operating assets instead of owning them, in which case the business would report no such assets. In this example, the business owns these so-called *fixed assets.* They are *fixed* because they are held for use in the operations of the business and are not for sale, and their usefulness lasts several years or longer.

So, where does a business get the money to buy its assets? Most businesses borrow money on the basis of interest-bearing notes or other credit instruments for part of the total capital they need for their assets. Also, businesses buy many things on credit and at the balance sheet date, owe money to their suppliers, which will be paid in the future. These operating liabilities are never grouped with interest-bearing debt in the balance sheet. The accountant would be tied to the stake for doing such a thing. Note that liabilities are not intermingled among assets — this is a definite no-no in financial reporting. You cannot subtract certain liabilities from certain assets and only report the net balance. You would be given 20 lashes for doing so.

Could a business's total liabilities be greater than its total assets? Well, not likely — unless the business has been losing money hand over fist. In the vast majority of cases, a business has more total assets than total liabilities. Why? For two reasons:

- Its owners have invested money in the business.

- The business has earned profit over the years, and some (or all) of the profit has been retained in the business. Making profit increases assets; if not all the profit is distributed to owners, the company's assets rise by the amount of profit retained.

In the product company example (refer to Figure 7-3), owners' equity is about $2.5 million, or $2.47 million to be more exact. Sometimes this amount is referred to as *net worth*, because it equals total assets minus total liabilities. However, net worth can be misleading because it implies that the business is worth the amount recorded in its owners' equity accounts. The market value of a business, when it needs to be known, depends on many factors. The amount of owners' equity reported in a balance sheet, which is called its *book value,* is not irrelevant in setting a market value on the business — but it is usually not the dominant factor. The amount of owners' equity in a balance sheet is based on the history of capital invested in the business by its owners and the history of its profit performance and distributions from profit.

A balance sheet could be whipped up anytime you want, say at the end of every day. In fact, some businesses (such as banks and other financial institutions) need daily balance sheets, but most businesses do not prepare balance sheets that often. Typically, preparing a balance sheet at the end of each month is adequate for general management purpose — although a manager may need to take a look at the business's balance sheet in the middle of the month. In external financial reports (those released outside the business to its lenders and investors), a balance sheet is required at the close of business on the last day of the income statement period. If its annual or quarterly income statement ends, say, September 30; then the business reports its balance sheet at the close of business on September 30.

The profit *for the most recent period* is found in the income statement; periodic profit is not reported in the balance sheet. The profit reported in the income statement is before any distributions from profit to owners. The cumulative amount of profit over the years that has not been distributed to its owners is reported in the owners' equity section of the company's balance sheet.

By the way, notice that the balance sheet in Figure 7-3 is presented in a top and bottom format, instead of a left and right side format. Either the vertical or horizontal mode of display is acceptable. You see both the portrait and the landscape layouts in financial reports. For a whole lot more on the balance sheet, head for Book II Chapter 4.

Statement of cash flows

To survive and thrive, business managers confront three financial imperatives:

- ✔ Make an adequate profit
- ✔ Keep financial condition out of trouble and in good shape
- ✔ Control cash flows

The income statement reports whether the business made a profit. The balance sheet reports the financial condition of the business. The third imperative is reported on in the *statement of cash flows,* which presents a summary of the business's sources and uses of cash during the income statement period.

Smart business managers hardly get the word *net income* (or profit) out of their mouths before mentioning *cash flow.* Successful business managers tell you that they have to manage both profit *and* cash flow; you can't do one and ignore the other. Business managers have to deal with a two-headed dragon in this respect. Ignoring cash flow can pull the rug out from under a successful profit formula.

In the statement of cash flows, the cash activity of the business during the period is grouped into three basic types of transactions: *profit-making* transactions, *investing* transactions, and *financing* transactions. Figure 7-5 presents just the net cash effects of each of these three types of transactions for the product company example. These are the basic information components of the statement. The net increase or decrease in cash from the three types of cash activities during the period is added to or subtracted from the beginning cash balance to get the cash balance at the end of the year.

Company's Name
Statement of Cash Flows
For Most Recent Year

Cash effect during period from *operating activities* (collecting cash from sales and paying cash for expenses)	$400,000
Cash effect during period from making investments in long-term operating assets	($450,000)
Cash effect during period from transactions with lenders and owners	$200,000
Cash increase during period	$150,000
Cash balance at start of period	$850,000
Cash balance at end of period	$1,000,000

Figure 7-5: Statement of cash flows.

In the product company example, the business earned $520,000 profit (net income) during the year (see Figure 7-1). The result of its profit-making activities was to increase its cash $400,000, which you see in the first part of the statement of cash flows (see Figure 7-5). This still leaves $120,000 of profit to explain, which the next section covers. The actual cash inflows from revenues and outflows for expenses run on a different timetable than when the sales revenue and expenses are recorded for determining profit.

The second part of the statement of cash flows sums up the long-term investments made by the business during the year, such as constructing a new production plant or replacing machinery and equipment. If the business sold any of its long-term assets, it reports the cash inflows from these divestments in this section of the statement of cash flows. The cash flows of other investment activities (if any) are reported in this part of the statement as well. As you can see in part of the statement of cash flows (see Figure 7-5), the business invested $450,000 in new long-term operating assets (trucks, equipment, tools, and computers).

The third part of the statement sums up the dealings between the business and its sources of capital during the period — borrowing money from lenders and raising new capital from its owners. Cash outflows to pay debt are reported in this section, as well as cash distributions from profit paid to the owners of the business. The third part of the statement reports that the result of these transactions was to increase cash $200,000 (see Figure 7-5). By the way, in this product company example, the business did not make cash distributions from profit to its owners. It probably could have, but it didn't — which is an important point discuss in the upcoming section "Why no cash distribution from profit?".

As you see in Figure 7-5, the net result of the three types of cash activities was a $150,000 increase during the year. The increase is added to the cash balance at the start of the year to get the cash balance at the end of the year, which is $1.0 million. **Note:** The $150,000 cash increase during the year (in this example) is never referred to as a cash flow *bottom line,* or any such thing. The term *bottom line* is strictly reserved for the last line of the income statement, which reports net income — the final profit after all expenses are deducted.

It would be nice if statements of cash flows were relatively straightforward and easy to understand, but they're not. The statements of cash flows of most businesses are frustratingly difficult to read. Not to scare you off, but actual cash flow statements have much more detail than the brief introduction to this financial statement in Figure 7-5.

A statement of cash flows for the service company example would look virtually the same as for the product company example, except that the cash effect for each type of cash activity would be different amounts. Two factors can cause the cash flow from profit-making (operating) activities of a product company to swing widely from its bottom-line profit: changes in receivables, and changes in inventory. A service company does not have these two assets, so its cash flow from profit holds on a steadier course with profit.

REMEMBER

Imagine you have a highlighter pen in your hand, and the three basic financial statements of a business are in front of you. What are the most important numbers to mark? Financial statements do *not* have any numbers highlighted; they do not come with headlines like newspapers. You have to find your own headlines. *Bottom-line profit* (net income) in the income statement is one number you would mark for sure. Another key number is *cash flow from operating activities* in the statement of cash flows. For much more info, Book II Chapter 6 is devoted to cash flows.

A note about the statement of changes in shareowners' equity

Many financial reports of businesses include a *fourth* financial statement — or at least it's called a "statement." It's really a summary of the changes in the constitutive elements of owners' equity (stockholders' equity of a corporation). The corporation is one basic type of legal structure that businesses use. Book II Chapter 3 explains the alternative legal structures available for conducting business operations.

When a business has a complex owner's equity structure, a separate summary of changes in the several different components of owners' equity during the period is useful for the owners, the board of directors, and the top-level managers. On the other hand, in some cases the only changes in owners' equity during the period were earning profit and distributing part of the cash flow from profit to owners. In this situation there is not much need for a summary of changes in owners' equity. The financial statements reader can easily find profit in the income statement and cash distributions from profit (if any) in the statement of cash flows. See the section "Why no cash distribution from profit?" later in this chapter for the product company example.

Contrasting Profit and Cash Flow from Profit

Look again at the income statement in Figure 7-1. The product company in our example earned $520,000 net income for the year. However, its statement of cash flows for the same year in Figure 7-5 reports that its profit-making, or operating, activities increased cash only $400,000 during the year. This gap between profit and cash flow from operating activities is not unusual. So, what happened to the other $120,000 of profit? Where is it? Is there some accounting sleight of hand going on? Did the business really earn $520,000 net income if cash increased only $400,000? Those are good questions. This section tries to answer them without hitting you over the head with a lot of technical details at this point.

Here's one scenario that explains the $120,000 difference between profit (net income) and cash flow from profit (operating activities):

✔ Suppose the business collected $50,000 less cash from customers during the year than the total sales revenue reported in its income statement. (Remember that the business sells on credit, and its customers take time before actually paying the business.) Therefore, there's a cash inflow lag between booking sales and collecting cash from customers. As a result, the business's cash inflow from customers was $50,000 less than the sales revenue amount used to calculate profit for the year. This would be reflected on the balance sheet as an increase in accounts receivable

✔ Also suppose that during the year the business made cash payments connected with its expenses that were $70,000 higher than the total amount of expenses reported in the income statement. For example, a business that sells products buys or makes the products, and then holds the products in inventory for some time before it sells the items to customers. Cash is paid out before the cost of goods sold expense is recorded. This is one example of a difference between cash flow connected with an expense and the amount recorded in the income statement for the expense.

In this scenario, the two factors cause cash flow from profit-making (operating) activities to be $120,000 less than the net income earned for the year. Cash collections from customers were $50,000 less than sales revenue, and cash payments for expenses were $70,000 more than the amount of expenses recorded to the year. Book II Chapter 6 explores the several factors that cause cash flow and bottom-line profit to diverge.

At this point the key idea to hold in mind is that the sales revenue reported in the income statement does not equal cash collections from customers during the year, and expenses do not equal cash payments during the year. Cash collections from sales minus cash payments for expenses gives cash flow from a company's profit-making activities; sales revenue minus expenses gives the net income earned for the year. Cash flow almost always is different from net income. Sorry. That's just how the cookie crumbles.

Gleaning Key Information from Financial Statements

The whole point of reporting financial statements is to provide important information to people who have a financial interest in the business — mainly its outside investors and lenders. From that information, investors and lenders are able to answer key questions about the financial performance and condition of the business. This section discusses a few of these key questions.

How's profit performance?

Investors use two important measures to judge a company's annual profit performance. Here, the example uses the data from Figures 7-1 and 7-3 for the product company. Of course you can do the same ratio calculations for the service business example. For convenience the dollar amounts here are expressed in thousands:

- ✔ **Return on sales** = profit as a percent of annual sales revenue:

    $520 bottom-line annual profit (net income) ÷ $10,400 annual sales revenue = 5.0%

- ✔ **Return on equity** = profit as a percent of owners' equity:

    $520 bottom-line annual profit (net income) ÷ $2,470 owners' equity = 21.1%

Profit looks pretty thin compared with annual sales revenue. The company earns only 5 percent return on sales. In other words, 95 cents out of every sales dollar goes for expenses, and the company keeps only 5 cents for profit. (Many businesses earn 10 percent or higher return on sales.) However, when profit is compared with owners' equity, things look a lot better. The business earns more than 21 percent profit on its owners' equity. It's doubtful that you have many investments earning 21 percent per year.

Return on sales varies among different types of business, of course. If this example were a grocery store chain, 5 percent is not bad. When looking at these numbers, you need to know what's standard in your industry to know if it's good or bad.

Is there enough cash?

Cash is the lubricant of business activity. Realistically, a business can't operate with a zero cash balance. It can't wait to open the morning mail to see how much cash it will have for the day's needs (although some businesses try to operate on a shoestring cash balance). A business should keep enough cash on hand to keep things running smoothly even when there are interruptions in the normal inflows of cash. A business has to meet its payroll on time, for example. Keeping an adequate balance in the checking account serves as a buffer against unforeseen disruptions in normal cash inflows.

At the end of the year, the product company in our example has $1 million cash on hand (refer to Figure 7-3). This cash balance is available for general business purposes. (If there are restrictions on how it can use its cash balance, the business is obligated to disclose the restrictions.) Is $1 million enough? Interestingly, businesses do not have to comment on their cash balance.

The business has $650,000 in operating liabilities that will come due for payment over the next month or so (refer to Figure 7-3). So, it has enough cash to pay these liabilities. But it doesn't have enough cash on hand to pay its operating liabilities and its $2.08 million interest-bearing debt (refer to Figure 7-2 again). Lenders don't expect a business to keep a cash balance more than the amount of debt; this condition would defeat the very purpose of lending money to the business, which is to have the business put the money to good use and be able to pay interest on the debt.

Lenders are more interested in the ability of the business to control its cash flows, so that when the time comes to pay off loans it will be able to do so. They know that the other, non-cash assets of the business will be converted into cash flow. Receivables will be collected, and products held in inventory will be sold and the sales will generate cash flow. So, you shouldn't focus just on cash; you should throw the net wider and look at the other assets as well.

Taking this broader approach, the business has $1 million cash, $800,000 receivables, and $1.56 million inventory, which adds up to $3.36 million of cash and cash potential. Relative to its $2.73 million total liabilities ($650,000 operating liabilities plus $2.08 million debt), the business looks in pretty good shape. On the other hand, if it turns out that the business is not able to collect its receivables and is not able to sell its products, it would end up in deep doo-doo.

One other way to look at a business's cash balance is to express its cash balance in terms of how many days of sales the amount represents. In the example, the business has an ending cash balance equal to 35 days of sales, calculated as follows:

$10,400,000 annual sales revenue ÷ 365 days = $28,493 sales per day

$1,000,000 cash balance ÷ $28,493 sales per day = 35 days

The business's cash balance equals a little more than one month of sales activity, which most lenders and investors would consider adequate.

Can you trust financial statement numbers?

Whether the financial statements are correct or not depends on the answers to two basic questions:

- ✔ Does the business have a reliable accounting system in place and employ competent accountants?
- ✔ Have its managers manipulated the business's accounting methods or deliberately falsified the numbers?

It would be awesome if the answer to the first question was always yes, and the answer to the second question was always no. But you know better, don't you?

There are a lot of crooks and dishonest persons in the business world who think nothing of manipulating the accounting numbers and cooking the books. Also, organized crime is involved in many businesses. And, sad to say, many businesses don't put much effort into keeping their accounting systems up to speed, and they skimp on hiring competent accountants. In short, there is a risk that the financial statements of a business could be incorrect and seriously misleading.

To increase the credibility of their financial statements, many businesses hire independent CPA auditors to examine their accounting systems and records and to express opinions on whether the financial statements conform to established standards. In fact, some business lenders insist on an annual audit by an independent CPA firm as a condition of making the loan. The outside, non-management investors in a privately owned business could vote to have annual CPA audits of the financial statements. Public companies have no choice; under federal securities laws, a public company is required to have annual audits by an independent CPA firm.

Two points: CPA audits are not cheap, yet these audits are not always effective in rooting out financial reporting fraud by managers. Unfortunately, there have been many cases of CPA auditors not detecting serious financial fraud that had been going on for years right under their auditing noses. Cleverly concealed fraud is very difficult to uncover unless you stumble over it by accident. CPAs are supposed to apply *professional skepticism* in doing their audits, but this doesn't always lead to discovery of fraud.

Why no cash distribution from profit?

In this product company example, the business did not distribute any of its profit for the year to its owners. Distributions from profit by a business corporation are called *dividends*. (The total amount distributed is divided up among the stockholders, hence the term "dividends.") Cash distributions from profit to owners are included in the third section of the statement of cash flows (refer to Figure 7-5). But, in the example, the business did not make any cash distributions from profit — even though it earned $520,000 net income (refer to Figure 7-1). Why not?

The business realized $400,000 cash flow from its profit-making (operating) activities (refer to Figure 7-3). In most cases, this would be the upper limit on how much cash a business would distribute from profit to its owners. So you might very well ask whether the business should have distributed, say, at least half of its cash flow from profit, or $200,000, to its owners. If you owned 20 percent of the ownership shares of the business, you would have received 20 percent, or $40,000, of the distribution. But you got no cash return on your investment in the business. Your shares should be worth more because the profit for the year increased the company's owners' equity. But you did not see any of this increase in your wallet.

Deciding whether to make cash distributions from profit to shareowners is in the hands of the directors of a business corporation. Its shareowners elect the directors, and in theory the directors act in the best interests of the shareowners. So, evidently the directors thought the business had better use for the $400,000 cash flow from profit than distributing some of it to shareowners. Generally the main reason for not making cash distributions from profit is to finance the growth of the business — to use all the cash flow from profit for expanding the assets needed by the business at the higher sales level. Ideally, the directors of the business would explain their decision not to distribute any money from profit to the shareowners. But, generally, no such comments are made in financial reports.

Is making profit ethical?

Many people have the view that making profit is unethical; they think profit is a form of theft — from employees who are not paid enough, from customers who are charged too much, from finding loopholes in the tax laws, and so on. (Profit critics usually don't say anything about the ethical aspects of a loss; they don't address the question of who should absorb the effects of a loss.) Profit critics are sometimes proved right because some businesses make profit by using illegal or unethical means, such as false advertising, selling unsafe products, paying employees lower wages than they are legally entitled to, deliberately under-funding retirement plans for employees, and other immoral tactics. Of course in making profit, a business should comply with all applicable laws, conduct itself in an ethical manner, and play fair with everyone it deals with. Most businesses strive to behave according to high ethical standards, although under pressure they cut corners and take the low road in certain areas. Keep in mind that businesses provide jobs, pay several kinds of taxes, and are essential cogs in the economic system. Even though they are not perfect angels, where would we be without them?

Keeping in Step with Accounting and Financial Reporting Standards

The unimpeded flow of capital is critical in a free market economic system and in the international flow of capital between countries. Investors and lenders put their capital to work where they think they can get the best returns on their investments consistent with the risks they're willing to take. To make these decisions, they need the accounting information provided in financial statements of businesses.

Imagine the confusion that would result if every business were permitted to invent its own accounting methods for measuring profit and for putting values on assets and liabilities. What if every business adopted its own individual accounting terminology and followed its own style for presenting financial statements? Such a state of affairs would be a Tower of Babel.

Recognizing U.S. standards

The authoritative standards and rules that govern financial accounting and reporting by businesses in the United States are called *generally accepted accounting principles (GAAP)*. When you read the financial statements of a business, you're entitled to assume that the business has fully complied with GAAP in reporting its cash flows, profit-making activities, and financial condition — *unless* the business makes very clear that it has prepared its financial statements using some other basis of accounting or has deviated from GAAP in one or more significant respects.

If GAAP is not the basis for preparing its financial statements, a business should make very clear which other basis of accounting is being used and avoid using titles for its financial statements that are associated with GAAP. For example, if a business uses a simple cash receipts and cash disbursements basis of accounting — which falls way short of GAAP — it should not use the terms *income statement* and *balance sheet*. These terms are part and parcel of GAAP, and their use as titles for financial statements implies that the business is using GAAP.

You're lucky that there's no room here for a lengthy historical discourse on the development of accounting and financial reporting standards in the United States. The general consensus (backed by law) is that businesses should use consistent accounting methods and terminology. General Motors and Microsoft should use the same accounting methods; so should Wells Fargo and Apple. Of course, businesses in different industries have different types of transactions, but the same types of transactions should be accounted for in the same way. That is the goal.

There are upwards of 10,000 public companies in the United States and easily more than a million private-owned businesses. Now, should all these businesses use the same accounting methods, terminology, and presentation styles for their financial statements? The ideal answer is that all businesses *should* use the same rulebook of GAAP. However, the rulebook permits alternative accounting methods for some transactions. Furthermore, accountants have to interpret the rules as they apply GAAP in actual situations. The devil is in the details.

In the United States, GAAP constitute the gold standard for preparing financial statements of business entities. The presumption is that any deviations from GAAP would cause misleading financial statements. If a business honestly thinks it should deviate from GAAP — in order to better reflect the economic reality of its transactions or situation — it should make very clear that it has not complied with GAAP in one or more respects. If deviations from GAAP are not disclosed, the business may have legal exposure to those who relied on the information in its financial report and suffered a loss attributable to the misleading nature of the information.

Unfortunately, the mechanisms and processes of issuing and enforcing financial reporting and accounting standards are in a state of flux. The biggest changes in the works have to do with the push to internationalize the standards, and the movements toward setting different standards for private companies and for small and medium sized business entities.

Financial accounting and reporting by government and not-for-profit entities

In the grand scheme of things, the world of financial accounting and reporting can be divided into two hemispheres: for-profit business entities and not-for-profit entities. A large body of authoritative rules and standards called *generally accepted accounting principles (GAAP)* have been hammered out over the years to govern accounting methods and financial reporting of business entities in the United States. Accounting and financial reporting standards have also evolved and been established for government and not-for-profit entities. This book centers on business accounting methods and financial reporting. Financial reporting by government and not-for-profit entities is a broad and diverse territory, and a full treatment of it is well beyond the scope of this book.

People generally don't demand financial reports from government and not-for-profit organizations. Federal, state, and local government entities issue financial reports that are in the public domain, although few taxpayers are interested

in reading them. When you donate money to a charity, school, or church, you don't always get financial reports in return. On the other hand, many private, not-for-profit organizations issue financial reports to their members — credit unions, homeowners' associations, country clubs, mutual insurance companies (owned by their policy holders), pension plans, labor unions, healthcare providers, and so on. The members or participants may have an equity interest or ownership share in the organization and, thus, they need financial reports to apprise them of their financial status with the entity.

Government and other not-for profit entities should comply with the established accounting and financial reporting standards that apply to their type of entity. *Caution:* Many not-for-profit entities use accounting methods different than business GAAP — in some cases very different — and the terminology in their financial reports is somewhat different than in the financial reports of business entities.

Getting to know the U.S. standard setters

Okay, so everyone reading a financial report is entitled to assume that GAAP have been followed (unless the business clearly discloses that it is using another basis of accounting). The basic idea behind the development of GAAP is to measure profit and to value assets and liabilities *consistently* from business to business — to establish broad-scale uniformity in accounting methods for all businesses. The idea is to make sure that all accountants are singing the same tune from the same hymnal. The authoritative bodies write the tunes that accountants have to sing.

Who are these authoritative bodies? In the United States, the highest-ranking authority in the private (non-government) sector for making pronouncements on GAAP — and for keeping these accounting standards up-to-date — is the

Financial Accounting Standards Board (FASB). Also, the federal Securities and Exchange Commission (SEC) has broad powers over accounting and financial reporting standards for companies whose securities (stocks and bonds) are publicly traded. Actually, the SEC outranks the FASB because it derives its authority from federal securities laws that govern the public issuance and trading in securities. The SEC has on occasion overridden the FASB, but not very often.

GAAP also include minimum requirements for *disclosure,* which refers to how information is classified and presented in financial statements and to the types of information that have to be included with the financial statements, mainly in the form of footnotes. The SEC makes the disclosure rules for public companies. Disclosure rules for private companies are controlled by GAAP. Book II Chapter 7 explains the disclosures that are required in addition to the three primary financial statements of a business (the income statement, balance sheet, and statement of cash flows).

Internationalization of accounting standards (maybe, maybe not)

Although it's a bit of an overstatement, today the investment of capital knows no borders. U.S. capital is invested in European and other countries, and capital from other countries is invested in U.S. businesses. In short, the flow of capital has become international. U.S. GAAP does not bind accounting and financial reporting standards in other countries, and in fact there are significant differences that cause problems in comparing the financial statements of U.S. companies with those in Europe and other countries.

Outside the United States, the main authoritative accounting standards setter is the International Accounting Standards Board (IASB), which is based in London. The IASB was founded in 2001. Over 7,000 public companies have their securities listed on the several stock exchanges in the European Union (EU) countries. In many regards, the IASB operates in a manner similar to the Financial Accounting Standards Board (FASB) in the United States, and the two have very similar missions. The IASB has already issued many standards, which are called International Financial Reporting Standards.

For some time, the FASB and IASB have been working together toward developing global standards that all businesses would follow, regardless of which country a business is domiciled. Of course political issues and national pride come into play. The term *harmonization* is favored, which sidesteps difficult issues regarding the future roles of the FASB and IASB in the issuance of international accounting standards. However, the SEC recently put out a study that could delay if not kill the efforts toward one set of universal financial reporting and accounting standards. Also, the two rule-making bodies have had fundamental disagreements on certain accounting issues. It seems doubtful that a full-fledged universal set of standards will be agreed upon. But stay tuned; it's hard to predict the final outcome.

Divorcing public and private companies

Traditionally, GAAP and financial reporting standards were viewed as equally applicable to public companies (generally large corporations) and private companies (generally smaller). Today, however, we are witnessing a growing distinction between accounting and financial reporting standards for public versus private companies. Although most accountants don't like to admit it, there's always been a de facto divergence in actual financial reporting practices by private companies compared with the more rigorously enforced standards for public companies. For example, a surprising number of private companies still do not include a statement of cash flows in their financial reports, even though this has been a GAAP requirement since 1975.

Although it's hard to prove one way or the other, my view is that the financial reports of private businesses generally measure up to GAAP standards in all significant respects. At the same time, however, there's little doubt that the financial reports of some private companies fall short. As a matter of fact, in the invitation to comment on the proposal to establish an advisory committee for private company accounting standards, the FASB said "compliance with GAAP standards for many for-profit private companies is a choice rather than a requirement because private companies can often control who receives their financial information." Recently a *Private Company Council (PCC)* was established separate from the FASB, but subject to oversight by the FASB. This arrangement is in the early stages at this point, but the PCC will probably become more autonomous from the FASB over time.

Private companies do not have many of the accounting problems of large, public companies. For example, many public companies deal in complex derivative instruments, issue stock options to managers, provide highly developed defined-benefit retirement and health benefit plans for their employees, enter into complicated inter-company investment and joint venture operations, have complex organizational structures, and so on. Most private companies do not have to deal with these issues.

The AICPA, the national association of CPAs, has started a project to develop an *Other Comprehensive Basis of Accounting* for privately held small and medium sized entities. Oh boy! What a confusing time for accounting standards. The upshot seems to be that we are drifting towards separate accounting standards for larger public companies versus smaller private companies. Just how different the two sets of standards will be is open to speculation.

Following the rules and bending the rules

An oft-repeated story concerns three persons interviewing for an important accounting position. They are asked one key question: "What's 2 plus 2?" The first candidate answers, "It's 4," and is told, "Don't call us, we'll call you." The second candidate answers, "Well, most of the time the answer is 4, but sometimes it's 3 and sometimes it's 5." The third candidate answers: "What do you want the answer to be?" Guess who gets the job. This story exaggerates, of course, but it does have an element of truth.

The point is that interpreting GAAP is not cut-and-dried. Many accounting standards leave a lot of wiggle room for interpretation. *Guidelines* would be a better word to describe many accounting rules. Deciding how to account for certain transactions and situations requires seasoned judgment and careful analysis of the rules. Furthermore, many estimates have to be made. (See the sidebar "Depending on estimates and assumptions.") Deciding on accounting methods requires, above all else, *good faith*.

A business may resort to "creative" accounting to make profit for the period look better, or to make its year-to-year profit less erratic than it really is (which is called *income smoothing*). Like lawyers who know where to find loopholes, accountants can come up with inventive interpretations that stay within the boundaries of GAAP. These creative accounting techniques are also called *massaging the numbers*. Massaging the numbers can get out of hand and become accounting fraud, also called *cooking the books*. Massaging the numbers has some basis in honest differences for interpreting the facts. Cooking the books goes way beyond interpreting facts; this fraud consists of *inventing* facts and good old-fashioned chicanery. Book II Chapter 8 talks more about accounting fraud.

Depending on estimates and assumptions

The importance of estimates and assumptions in financial statement accounting is illustrated in a footnote you see in many annual financial reports such as the following:

"The preparation of financial statements in conformity with generally accepted accounting principles requires management to make estimates and assumptions that affect reported amounts. Examples of the more significant estimates include: accruals and reserves for warranty and product liability losses, post-employment benefits, environmental costs, income taxes, and plant closing costs."

Accounting estimates should be based on the best available information, of course, but most estimates are subjective and arbitrary to some extent. The accountant can choose either pessimistic or optimistic estimates, and thereby record either conservative profit numbers or more aggressive profit numbers. One key prediction made in preparing financial statements is called the *going-concern assumption.* The accountant assumes that the business is not facing imminent shutdown of its operations and the forced liquidations of its assets, and that it will continue as usual for the foreseeable future. This rather important pillar of accounting has received renewed attention in the aftermath of the recession of 2008. If a business is in the middle of bankruptcy proceedings, the accountant changes focus to the liquidation values of its assets.

Book II
Accounting and Financial Reports

	Assets	=	Liabilities		Owners' Equity	
			Operating Liabilities	+ Debt	Invested Captial	+ Retained Earnings
Revenue	$10,000			n/a	n/a	$10,000
Expenses	($8,100)		$400	n/a	n/a	($8,500)
Profit	$1,900		$400			$1,500

In this book . . .

- Look at the three most important documents: the balance sheet, the income statement, and the statement of cash flows
- Learn the correct way to report profit
- Understand business structures, from sole proprietorships to different types of corporation
- Learn how to read a balance sheet to find assets, liabilities, and equity
- Determine a company's expenses and analyze profits and losses
- Examine the statement of cash flow
- Keep up to date on accounting and financial reporting standards
- Take a close look at the cost of goods sold and depreciation expenses

Chapter 1

Financial Report Basics

*F*inancial reports give a snapshot of a company's value at the end of a particular period, as well as a view of the company's operations and whether it made a profit. The business world couldn't function without financial reports. Yes, fewer scandals would be exposed because companies wouldn't be tempted to paint false but pretty financial pictures, but you'd still need a way to gauge a firm's financial health.

At this point in time, nothing's available that can possibly replace financial reports. Nothing can be substituted that'd give investors, financial institutions, and government agencies the information they need to make decisions about a company. And without financial reports, the folks who work for a company wouldn't know how to make it more efficient and profitable because they wouldn't have a summary of its financial activities during previous business periods. These financial summaries help companies look at their successes and failures and make plans for future improvements.

The first part of this chapter introduces you to the many facets of financial reports and shows you how internal and external players use them to evaluate a company's financial health.

The second part of the chapter tackles annual reports in particular. No doubt the financial statements are the meat of any annual report, but lots of trimmings make up an annual report, and you need to be able to read and understand them. Although companies must follow set rules for how they format the key financial statements, how they present the rest of the report is left to their creativity.

Some companies spend millions of dollars putting on a glossy show with color pictures throughout the report. Others put out a plain-vanilla, black-and-white version without pictures. Still, the major components of an annual report are standard, although the order in which companies present them may vary.

Figuring Out Financial Reporting

Financial reporting gives readers a summary of what happens in a company based purely on the numbers. The numbers that tell the tale include the following:

- **Assets:** The cash, marketable securities, buildings, land, tools, equipment, vehicles, copyrights, patents, and any other items needed to run a business that a company holds.
- **Liabilities:** Money a company owes to outsiders, such as loans, bonds, and unpaid bills.
- **Equity:** Money invested in the company.
- **Sales:** Products or services that customers purchase.
- **Costs and expenses:** Money spent to operate a business, such as expenditures for production, compensation for employees, operation of buildings and factories, or supplies to run the offices.
- **Profit or loss:** The amount of money a company earns or loses.
- **Cash flow:** The amount of money that flows into and out of a business during the time period being reported.

Without financial reporting, you'd have no idea where a company stands financially. Sure, you'd know how much money the business has in its bank accounts, but you wouldn't know how much is still due to come in from customers, how much inventory is being held in the warehouse and on the shelf, how much the firm owes, or even how much the firm owns. As an investor, if you don't know these details, you can't possibly make an objective decision about whether the company is making money and whether investing in the company's future is worthwhile.

Preparing the reports

A company's accounting department is the key source of its financial reports. This department is responsible for monitoring the numbers and putting together the reports. The numbers are the products of a process called *double-entry bookkeeping* or *double-entry accounting,* which requires a company to record resources and the assets it uses to get those resources (refer to Book I Chapter 1 for more on double-entry accounting). For example, if you buy a chair, you must spend another asset, such as cash. An entry in the double-entry accounting system shows both sides of that transaction — the cash account is reduced by the chair's price, and the furniture account value is increased by the chair's price.

This crucial method of accounting gives companies the ability to record and track business activity in a standardized way. Accounting methods are constantly updated to reflect the business environment as financial transactions become more complex.

Seeing why financial reporting counts (and who's counting)

Many people count on the information companies present in financial reports. Here are some key groups of readers and why they need accurate information:

- ✔ **Executives and managers:** They need information to know how well the company is doing financially and to find out about problem areas so they can make changes to improve the company's performance.

- ✔ **Employees:** They need to know how well they're meeting or exceeding their goals and where they need to improve. For example, if a salesperson has to make $50,000 in sales during the month, she needs a financial report at the end of the month to gauge how well she did in meeting that goal. If she believes that she met her goal but the financial report doesn't show that she did, she must provide details to defend her production levels. Most salespeople are paid according to their sales production. Without financial reports, they'd have no idea what their compensation is based on.

  Employees also make career and retirement investment decisions based on the company's financial reports. If the reports are misleading or false, employees may lose most, if not all, of their 401(k) retirement savings, and their long-term financial futures may be at risk.

- ✔ **Creditors:** They need to understand a company's financial results to determine whether to risk lending more money to the company and to find out whether the firm is meeting the minimum requirements of any loan programs that are already in place.

  If a firm's financial reports are false or misleading, creditors may loan money at an interest rate that doesn't truly reflect the risks they're taking. And by trusting the misleading information, they may miss out on a better opportunity.

Book II

Accounting and Financial Reports

✔ **Investors:** They need information to judge whether a company is a good investment. If investors think that a company is on a growth path because of the financial information it reports, but those reports turn out to be false, investors can pay, big time. They may buy stock at inflated prices and risk the loss of capital as the truth comes out, or they may miss out on better investing opportunities.

✔ **Government agencies:** These agencies need to be sure that companies comply with regulations set at the state and federal levels. They also need to be certain that companies accurately inform the public about their financial position.

✔ **Analysts:** They need information to develop analytical reviews for clients who are considering the company for investments or additional loan funds.

✔ **Financial reporters:** They need to provide accurate coverage of a company's operations to the general public, which helps make investors aware of the critical financial issues facing the company and any changes the company makes in its operations.

✔ **Competitors:** Every company's bigwigs read their competitors' financial reports. If these reports are based on false numbers, the financial playing field gets distorted. A well-run company could make a bad decision to keep up with the false numbers of a competitor and end up reducing its own profitability.

Companies don't produce financial reports only for public consumption. Many financial reports are prepared for internal use only. These internal reports help managers accomplish these tasks:

✔ Find out which of the business's operations are producing a profit and which are operating at a loss

✔ Determine which departments or divisions need to receive additional resources to encourage growth

✔ Identify unsuccessful departments or divisions and make needed changes to turn around the troubled section or kill the project

✔ Determine staffing and inventory levels needed to respond to customer demand

✔ Review customer accounts to identify slow-paying or nonpaying customers, to devise collection methods and develop guidelines for when a customer should be cut off from future orders

✔ Prepare production schedules and review production levels

This list identifies just a few of the many uses companies have for their internal financial reports. The actual list is endless and is limited only by the imagination of the executives and managers who want to find ways to use the numbers to make business decisions.

Checking Out Types of Reporting

Not every company needs to prepare financial statements, but any company seeking to raise cash through stock sales or by borrowing funds certainly does. How public these statements must be depends on the business's structure.

Most businesses are *private companies,* which share these statements only with a small group of stakeholders: managers, investors, suppliers, vendors, and the financial institutions that they do business with. As long as a company doesn't sell shares of stock to the general public, it doesn't have to make its financial statements public. Book II Chapter 3 talks more about the reporting rules for private companies.

Public companies, which sell stock on the open market, must file a series of reports with the Securities and Exchange Commission (SEC) each year if they have at least 500 investors or at least $10 million in assets. Smaller companies that have incorporated and sold stock must report to the state in which they incorporated, but they aren't required to file with the SEC. You can find more details about the SEC's reporting requirements for public companies in Book II Chapter 3.

Even if a firm doesn't need to make its financial reports public, if it wants to raise cash outside a very small circle of friends, it has to prepare financial statements and have a certified public accountant (CPA) *audit* them, or certify that the financial statements meet the requirements of the generally accepted accounting principles (or GAAP, which you can find out more about in the section "Keeping the number crunchers in line," later in this chapter). Few banks consider loaning large sums of money to businesses without audited financial statements. Investors who aren't involved in the daily management of a business also usually require audited financial statements.

Keeping everyone informed

One big change in a company's operations after it decides to publicly sell stock is that it must report publicly on both a quarterly and annual basis to its stockholders. Companies send these reports directly to their stockholders, to analysts, and to the major financial institutions that help fund their operations through loans or bonds. The reports often include glossy pictures and pleasingly designed graphics at the beginning, keeping the less eye-pleasing financial reports that meet the SEC's requirements in the back.

Book II

Accounting and Financial Reports

Quarterly reports

Companies must release *quarterly reports* within 45 days of the quarter's end. Companies with holdings over $75 million must file more quickly. In addition to the three key financial statements — the *balance sheet,* the *income statement,* and the *statement of cash flows* (check out the upcoming section "Getting to the meat of the matter" for details on these documents) — the company must state whether a CPA has audited or reviewed (a much less intensive look at the data) the numbers. A report reviewed rather than audited by a CPA holds less weight.

Annual reports

Most small companies must file their *annual reports* within 90 days of the end of their fiscal year. Companies with over $700 million in assets must file their reports within 60 days; for $75 to 700 million, the deadline is 75 days. The annual report includes the information presented in the quarterly reports and much more, including a full business description, details about the management team and its compensation, and details about any filings done during the year.

Most major companies put a lot of money into producing glossy reports filled with information and pictures designed to make a good impression on the public. The marketing or public relations department, not the financial or accounting department, writes much of the summary information. Too often, annual reports are puff pieces that carefully hide any negative information in the *notes to the financial statements,* which is the section that offers additional details about the numbers provided in those statements. Read between the lines — especially the tiny print at the back of the report — to get some critical information about the accounting methods used, any pending lawsuits, or other information that may negatively impact results in the future.

Following the rules: Government requirements

Reports for the government are more extensive than the glossy reports sent to shareholders (see the preceding section). Companies must file many types of forms with the SEC, but this chapter focuses on three of them:

✔ **The 10-K:** This form is the annual report that provides a comprehensive overview of a company's business and financial activities.

Firms must file this report within 90 days of the end of the fiscal year (companies with more than $75 million in assets must file within 75 days; those with more than $700 million, in 60 days). In addition to the information included in the glossy annual reports sent to shareholders (see the preceding section), investors can find more detailed information about company history, organizational structure, equity holdings, subsidiaries, employee stock purchase and savings plans, incorporation, legal proceedings, controls and procedures, executive compensation, accounting fees and services, and changes or disagreements with accountants about financial disclosures.

✔ **The 10-Q:** This form is the quarterly report that describes key financial information about the prior three months. Most companies must file this report within 45 days of the end of the quarter (firms with more than $75 million in assets must file within 40 days). In addition to the information sent directly to shareholders, this form includes details about the company's market risk, controls and procedures, legal proceedings, and defaults on payments.

✔ **The 8-K:** This form is a periodic report that accounts for any major events that may impact a company's financial position. Examples of major events include the acquisition of another company, the sale of a company or division, bankruptcy, the resignation of directors, or a change in the fiscal year. When a major event occurs, the company must file a report with the SEC within four days of the event.

Book II

Accounting and Financial Reports

You can access reports filed with the SEC online at Edgar, which is run by the SEC. To use Edgar, go to www.sec.gov/edgar.shtml.

Going global

Many companies these days operate across national borders. For years, each country had its own set of rules for preparing financial reports to meet government regulations. Global companies had to keep separate sets of books and report results under different sets of rules in each country in which they operated.

Today most countries have agreed to accept the International Financial Reporting Standards developed by the London-based International Accounting Standards Board (IASB). Beginning in 2002, the United States agreed to look at ways to converge the IFRS and the U.S. GAAP. The U.S. allows companies based outside its borders to file required reports using either U.S. GAAP or IFRS, but U.S.-based companies must still use GAAP to file their reports. The process of converging U.S. standards with international standards is still a work in process.

Staying within the walls of the company: Internal reporting

Not all of an accounting department's financial reporting is done for public consumption. In fact, companies usually produce many more internal reports than external ones to keep management informed. Firms can design their internal reports in whatever way makes sense to their operations.

Each department head usually receives a report from the top managers showing the department's expenses and revenue and whether it's meeting its budget. If the department's numbers vary significantly from the amount that was budgeted, the report indicates red flags. The department head usually needs to investigate the differences and report what the department is doing to correct any problems. Even if the difference is increased revenue (which can be good news), the manager needs to know why the difference exists, because an error in the data input could have occurred.

Reports on inventory are critical, not only for managing the products on hand, but also for knowing when to order new inventory.

Tracking cash is vital to the day-to-day operations of any company. The frequency of a company's cash reporting depends on the volatility of its cash status — the more volatile the cash, the more likely the company needs frequent reporting to be sure that it has cash on hand to pay its bills. Some large firms actually provide cash reporting to their managers daily. Book II Chapter 6 talks more about cash flows.

Finding the roots of financial reporting

Accounting practices can be traced back to the Renaissance, but financial reporting wasn't recognized as a necessity until centuries later.

✔ **1494:** Italian monk Luca Pacioli became known as the "father of accounting" for his book *Everything about Arithmetic, Geometry and Proportions,* which includes a section on double-entry accounting. Pacioli warned his readers that an accountant shouldn't go to sleep at night until his debits equal his credits.

✔ **1600–1800:** Besides the East India Company, and early public company that formed in 1600 in England, for-profit corporations started to appear in substantial numbers in Europe as early as the 18th century. In 1800, only about 330 corporations operated in the United States.

✔ **1800s:** As public ownership of stock increased, regulators realized that some standardized distribution of information to investors was a priority. The New York

Stock Exchange was the first to jump into the fray, and in 1853, it began requiring companies listed on the exchange to provide statements of shares outstanding and capital resources.

✔ **1929:** Before the stock market crash, equity investing became a passion. People borrowed money to get into the market, paying higher and higher prices for stock. Sound familiar? Not too different from what occurred just before the 2000 crash of technology and Internet stocks.

✔ **1933–1934:** Congress created the SEC and gave it authority to develop financial accounting and reporting standards and rules to deter companies from distributing misleading information.

✔ **1973:** The Financial Accounting Standards Board (FASB) was created to establish standards for financial accounting and reporting. The SEC recognized the generally accepted accounting principles (GAAP) as the official reporting standards for federal securities laws.

✔ **1984:** The FASB formed the Emerging Issues Task Force, which keeps an eye on changes in business operations and sets standards before new practices become entrenched.

✔ **2002:** The FASB began work with the International Accounting Standards Board (IASB) to converge international financial reporting systems.

Book II

Accounting and Financial Reports

Introducing the Annual Report

The annual report gives more details about a company's business and financial activities than any other report. This document is primarily for shareholders, although any member of the general public can request a copy. Glossy pictures and graphics fill the front of the report, highlighting what the company wants you to know. After that, you find the full details about the company's business and financial operations; most companies include the full 10-K that they file with the SEC.

Breaking down the parts

The annual report is broken into the following parts, which are covered in detail in the next section:

✔ **Highlights:** These are a narrative summary of the previous year's activities and general information about the company, its history, its products, and its business lines.

✔ **Letter from the president or chief executive officer (CEO):** This letter is directed to the shareholders and discusses the company's key successes or explains any major failures.

- ✔ **Auditors' report:** This report tells you whether the numbers are accurate or whether you need to have any concerns about the future operation of the business.

- ✔ **Management's discussion and analysis:** In this part, you find management's discussion of the financial results and other factors that impact the company's operations.

- ✔ **Financial statements:** The key financial statements are the balance sheet, income statement, and statement of cash flows. In the financial statements, you find the actual financial results for the year. For details about this part of the report, check out the following section, "Getting to the meat of the matter."

- ✔ **Notes to the financial statements:** In the notes, you find details about how the numbers were derived.

- ✔ **Other information:** In this part, you find information about the company's key executives and managers, officers, board members, and locations, along with new facilities that have opened in the past year.

Getting to the meat of the matter

No doubt, the most critical part of the annual report for anyone who wants to know how well a company did financially is the financial statements section, which includes the balance sheet, the income statement, and the statement of cash flows. Book II Chapters 4–6 cover these three statements in detail, but this section provides a quick summary.

The balance sheet

The *balance sheet* gives a snapshot of the company's financial condition. On a balance sheet, you find assets, liabilities, and equity. The balance sheet got its name because the total assets must equal the total liabilities plus the total equities so that the value of the company is in balance. Here's the equation:

Assets = Liabilities + Equities

Assets appear on the left side of a balance sheet, and liabilities and equities are on the right side. Assets are broken down into *current assets* (holdings that the company will use in the next 12 months, such as cash and savings) and *long-term assets* (holdings that the company will use longer than a 12-month period, such as buildings, land, and equipment).

Liabilities are broken down into *current liabilities* (payments on bills or debts that are due in the next 12 months) and *long-term liabilities* (payments on debt that are due after the next 12 months).

The equities portion of the balance sheet can be called *owner's equity* (when an individual or partners closely hold a company) or *shareholders' equity* (when shares of stock have been sold to raise cash). Book II Chapter 4 talks more about what information goes into a balance sheet.

The income statement

The *income statement,* also known as the *profit and loss statement (P&L),* gets the most attention from investors. This statement shows a summary of the financial activities of one quarter or an entire year. Many companies prepare P&Ls on a monthly basis for internal use. Investors always focus on the exciting parts of the statement: revenue, net income, and earnings per share of stock.

In the income statement, you also find out how much the company is spending to produce or purchase the products or services it sells, how much the company costs to operate, how much it pays in interest, and how much it pays in income tax. To find out more about the information you can find on an income statement, go to Book II Chapter 5.

The statement of cash flows

The *statement of cash flows* is relatively new to the financial reporting game. The SEC didn't require companies to file it with the other financial reports until 1988. Basically, the statement of cash flows is similar to the income statement, in that it reports a company's performance over time. But instead of focusing on profit or loss, it focuses on how cash flows through the business. This statement has three sections: cash from operations, cash from investing, and cash from financing. Book II Chapter 6 talks more about the statement of cash flows.

Book II

Accounting and Financial Reports

Keeping the number crunchers in line

Every public company's internal accounting team and external audit team must answer to government entities. The primary government entity responsible for overseeing corporate reporting is the SEC. Its staff reviews reports filed with the SEC. If SEC employees have any questions or want additional information, they notify the company after reviewing the reports.

Financial statements filed with the SEC and for public consumption must adhere to the *generally accepted accounting principles* (GAAP). To meet the demands of these rules, financial reporting must be relevant, reliable, consistent, and presented in a way that allows the report reader to compare the results to prior years, as well as to other companies' financial results.

With GAAP in place, you may wonder why so many accounting scandals have hit the front pages of newspapers around the country for the past few years.

Filing statements according to GAAP has become a game for many companies. Unfortunately, investors and regulators find that companies don't always engage in transactions for the economic benefit of the shareholders, but sometimes do so to make their reports look better and to meet the quarterly expectations of Wall Street. Many times, companies look financially stronger than they actually are. For example, as scandals have come to light, companies have been found to overstate income, equity, and cash flows while understating debt.

Digging Deeper into the Annual Report

When you see a fat, glossy annual report from a company, you can be certain that you'll find a lot of fluff in it and probably a lot of spin about all the good things the company accomplished. No matter how fancy or plain the annual report is, as a careful reader, you need to focus on four key parts, listed in order:

- **Auditors' report:** A statement by the auditors regarding the findings of their audit of the company's books

- **Financial statements:** The balance sheet, income statement, and statement of cash flows

- **Notes to the financial statements:** Additional information on the data in the financial statements

- **Management's discussion and analysis:** Management's perspective regarding the company's results

This section explains why these four parts of an annual report are so critical. It also defines the other parts of an annual report and their purposes.

Most people think of numbers when they hear the words *annual report,* but any savvy investor can find a lot more useful information in the report than just numbers. Some parts of the report are fluff pieces written for public consumption, but others can give you great insight into the company's prospects, as well as suggest some areas of management concern. You just need to be a detective: Read between the lines, and read the fine print.

Debunking the letter to shareholders

What would an annual report be if not an opportunity for the head honchos to tout their company's fabulousness? Near the front of most annual reports, you find a letter to the shareholders from the chief executive officer (CEO) and the chairman of the board; other key executives may have signed their names, too.

Don't put too much stock in this letter, no matter how appealing it looks and how exciting its message is. Few CEOs actually write the letter to shareholders; the company's public relations department usually carefully designs the letter to highlight the positive aspects of the company's year. Negative results, when mentioned at all, are typically hidden in the middle of a paragraph somewhere in the middle of the letter.

In these letters, you usually find information about the key business activities for the year, such as a general statement about the company's financial condition, performance summaries of key divisions or subsidiaries that were the shining stars, and the company's major prospects.

Don't let these letters fool you. They *will* focus on the positive news and try to minimize the bad news. Do read the company's optimistic view, but don't depend on this letter to make a decision about whether to invest in the company. You can find more definitive information in other parts of the report to help you make investment decisions.

Book II

Accounting and Financial Reports

Translating the language of letters to shareholders

Maintaining a long and proud tradition, letters to shareholders present companies in the best possible light using a positive spin to hide whatever trouble may lie under the surface. A careless reader may feel reassured by the everything's-hunky-dory tone, but a few often-used niceties may tip off careful readers that things aren't necessarily what they seem.

- A company frequently uses *challenging* when it's facing significant difficulties selling its product or service.

- *Restructuring* means something isn't working. Find out what that something is and how much the company is spending to fix the problem.

- Sometimes letters to shareholders gloss over mistakes by using phrases like "corrective actions are being taken." Look for details about both the cause and the plan for corrective actions in the notes to the financial statements or the management's discussion and analysis.

- If you come across the term *difficulties*, look for details on those difficulties highlighted in the management's discussion and analysis or notes to the financial statements.

The best place to find full details on these issues is in the notes to the financial statements or the management's discussion and analysis. For more on these sections, go to "Getting the skinny from management" and "Reading the notes," later in this chapter.

Making sense of the corporate message

After the letter to shareholders, but before the juicy information, you usually find more rah-rah text in the form of a summary of the company's key achievements throughout the year. Like the president's letter, these pages present more of the type of message the corporation wants to portray, which may or may not give you the true picture. Few companies include much information about negative results in this section. Often chock-full of glossy, colorful images, this section is pure public relations fluff that focuses on the year's top performance highlights.

Although you may enjoy the pictures, don't count on the info printed around them to help you make any decisions about the company. Even if a company doesn't use pretty color pictures, this section usually includes bold graphics and lots of headlines that focus on the successes. Don't expect to find any warning signs in this image-setting section.

Although this section is basically advertising, it may give you a good overview of what the company does and the key parts of its operations. The firm generally presents its key divisions or units, highlights the top products within these divisions, and gives a brief summary of the financial results of the top divisions. In addition, you usually find some discussion of market share and position in the market of the company's key products or services.

Meeting the people in charge

Want to find out who's running the place? After the corporate message, one or two pages list the members of the board of directors and sometimes a brief bio of each member. You also find a listing of top executives or managers and their responsibilities. If you want to complain to someone at the top, this is where you can find out where to send your letters!

But seriously, reviewing the backgrounds of the company's leaders can help you get an idea of the experience these leaders bring to the company. If they don't impress you, it may be a good sign that you should walk away from the investment.

Finding basic shareholder information

At the end of the key financial statements, you usually find a *statement of shareholders' equity,* which is a summary of changes to shareholders' equity over the past three years. The key parts of this statement for current-year results are in the equity section of the balance sheet (one of the key financial statements discussed in greater detail in Book II Chapter 4).

This information is good to know because you can get an overview of changes to shareholders' equity over the past three years, but you don't need this information to analyze a company's prospects. When this text talks about how to analyze results by using information about shareholders' equity, it uses numbers you can find on the balance sheet.

Getting the skinny from management

The management's discussion and analysis (MD&A) section is one of the most important sections of an annual report. The MD&A may not be the most fun section to look at, but in it you find the key discussions about what went smoothly over the year and what went wrong.

Read the MD&A section carefully. It has a lot of the meat-and-potatoes information that gives you details about how the company's doing.

The Securities and Exchange Commission (SEC) monitors the MD&A section closely to make sure that companies present all critical information about current operations, capital, and liquidity. Management must also include forward-looking statements about known market and economic trends that may impact the company's liquidity and material events, as well as uncertainties that may cause reported information to not necessarily reflect future operating results or future financial conditions. For example, if a company manufactures its products in a country that's facing political upheaval or labor strife, those conditions may impact the company's ability to continue manufacturing its products at the same low cost. The company must report this information, indicating how this situation may impact its future earning potential.

The SEC pays special attention to a number of key factors that the MD&A is supposed to cover:

✔ **Revenue recognition:** In a retail store, recognizing revenue can be a relatively straightforward process: A customer buys a product off the shelves, and the revenue is *recognized* — that is, recorded in the company's books. But matters aren't that cut-and-dried in many complex corporate deals. For example, in the computer and hardware industries, revenue recognition can be complex because purchase contracts frequently include multiple parts, such as software, hardware, services, and training. When a company actually recognizes the revenue for each of these parts can vary, depending on the terms of a contract.

Book II

Accounting and Financial Reports

When reading financial reports for a particular industry, reviewing how management describes its revenue-recognition process compared to similar companies in the same industry is important.

✔ **Restructuring charges:** When a company restructures a portion of itself — which can include shutting down factories, disbanding a major division, or enacting other major changes related to how the company operates — management discusses the impact this had on the company (or may have in the future). This portion of the report explains costs for employee severance, facility shutdowns, and other expenses related to restructuring.

✔ **Impairments to assets:** The SEC expects companies to report any losses to assets in a timely manner. If an asset is damaged or destroyed, or for any reason loses value, companies must report that loss to shareholders. Look for information about the loss of value to assets in the MD&A. Also look for information about the depreciation or amortization of these assets.

✔ **Pension plans:** Accounting for pension plans includes many assumptions, such as the amount of interest or other gains the company expects to make on the assets it holds in its pension plans and the expenses the company anticipates paying out when employees retire. If the company has a pension plan for its employees, you'll find a discussion about how the company finances this plan and whether it expects to have difficulty meeting its plan's requirements.

✔ **Environmental and product liabilities:** All companies face some liability for products that fail to operate as expected or products that may cause damage to an individual or property. In some industries — such as oil, gas, and chemicals — an error can cause considerable environmental damage. You've probably heard stories about a chemical spill destroying a local stream or drinking water supply, or an oil spill wiping out an area's entire ecological system. In the MD&A section, the company must acknowledge the liabilities it faces and the way it prepares financially for the possibility of taking a loss after paying the liability. The company must estimate its potential losses and disclose the amount of money it has set aside or the insurance it has to protect against such losses.

✔ **Stock-based compensation:** To attract and keep top executives, many companies offer *stock incentives* (such as shares of stock as bonuses) as part of an employee compensation package. This part of the annual report must mention details of any stock-based compensation. Many recent scandals have included disclosures of unusually lavish stock-based compensation programs for top executives. Keep a watchful eye (or ear) out for discussion of bonuses or other employee compensation that involves giving employees shares of stock or selling employees' shares of stock below the market value.

✔ **Allowance for doubtful accounts:** Any company that offers credit to customers will encounter some nonpayers in the group. Management must discuss what it allows for loss on accounts that aren't paid and whether this allowance increased or decreased from the previous year. An increase in the allowance for doubtful accounts may indicate a problem with collections or be a sign of significant problems in the industry as a whole.

The discussion in this section of the annual report can get technical. If you don't understand what you read, you can always make a call to the investor relations department to ask for clarification. Whenever you're considering a major investment in a company's stock, be certain that you understand the key points in the MD&A. Any time you find the information beyond your comprehension, don't hesitate to research further and ask a lot of questions before investing in the stock.

In the MD&A, managers focus on three key areas: company operations, capital resources, and liquidity.

Company operations

Management commentary on this topic focuses on the income the company's operations generate and the expenses related to them. To get an idea of how well the company may perform in the future, look for the following:

✔ Discussion about whether sales increased or decreased

✔ Details on how well the company's various product lines performed

✔ Explanations of economic or market conditions that may have impacted the company's performance

The MD&A section also discusses these areas:

✔ **Distribution systems:** How products are distributed.

✔ **Product improvements:** Changes to products that improve their performance or appearance.

✔ **Manufacturing capacity:** The number of manufacturing plants and their production capability. The MD&A also mentions the percentage of the company's manufacturing capacity that it's using. For example, if the firm uses only 50 percent of its manufacturing capacity, it may have a lot of extra resources that are idle. If the company is using 100 percent of its manufacturing capacity, it may have maxed out its resources and may need to expand.

✔ **Research and development projects:** The research or development the business is doing to develop new products or improve current products.

The manager also comments on key profit results and how they may differ from the previous year's projections.

Management as a whole?

Also look for cost information related to product manufacturing or purchase. Cost-control problems may mean that future results won't be as good as the current year, especially if management mentions that the cost of raw materials isn't stable.

Look for statements about interest expenses, major competition, inflation, or other factors that may impact the success of future operations.

Capital resources

A company's *capital resources* are its assets and its ability to fund its operations for the long term. In addition to a statement that the company is in a strong financial position, you'll find discussions on these topics:

- Acquisitions or major expansion plans
- Any major capital expenses carried out over the past year or planned in future years
- Company debt
- Plans the company may have for taking on new debt
- Other key points about the company's cash flow

Liquidity

A company's *liquidity* is its cash position and its ability to pay its bills on a short-term or day-to-day basis.

Getting guarantees from management

Management has been required to include a section called "Corporate Responsibility for Financial Reports" or "Management's Responsibility for Financial Reports" since the financial reporting scandals of the late 1990s and early 2000s. When the Sarbanes-Oxley Act of 2002 passed Congress, this guarantee became more critical.

Today the chief executive officer (CEO) and chief financial officer (CFO) must prepare a statement to accompany the audit report to certify that, "based on such officer's knowledge, the financial statements, and other financial information included in the report, fairly present in all material respects the financial condition and results of operations of the issuer as of, and for, the periods presented in the report," according to Section 302 of the Act.

Executives were asked to provide these letters in the past, but this new requirement must include a certified statement, signed and notarized for public view, indicating that management takes full responsibility and can be held legally accountable for what's in the financial reports.

Executives can now be held personally responsible for their actions and may face up to a five-year prison term, fines, and other disciplinary action. They may also face civil and criminal litigation, and the SEC may bar them from serving as a corporate officer or director.

CEOs and CFOs have responded to this new requirement by looking for ways to shield their money and property from shareholder lawsuits and federal prosecution. The key question not yet answered is whether we will actually see this enforced and whether it will protect investors and the public from the corporate scandals we have seen in the past.

Bringing the auditors' answers to light

Any publicly traded company must provide financial reports that outside auditors have examined. You usually find the *auditors' report* (a letter from the auditors to the company's board of directors and shareholders) either before the financial information or immediately following it.

Before you read the financial statements or the notes to the financial statements, be sure that you've read the auditors' report. You read the auditors' report first to find out whether the auditor raised any red flags about the company's financial results. But you don't find the answers to these questions in the auditors' report. To find the details, you need to read the MD&A, the financial statements, and the notes to the financial statements. But if you haven't read the auditors' report first, you may overlook some critical details.

To lend credibility to management's assurances, companies call in independent auditors from an outside accounting firm to audit their internal controls and financial statements. Auditors don't check every transaction, so their reports don't give you 100 percent assurance that the financial statements don't include misstatements about the company's assets and liabilities. Auditors don't endorse the company's financial position or give indications about whether the company is a good investment.

Most standard auditors' reports include these three paragraphs:

- ✔ **Introductory paragraph:** Here you find information about the time period the audit covers and who's responsible for the financial statements. In most cases, this paragraph states that management is responsible for the financial statements and that the auditors only express an opinion about the financial statements based on their audit. Essentially, this is a "protect your fanny" paragraph in which the auditors attempt to limit their responsibility for possible inaccuracies.

- ✔ **Scope paragraph:** In this paragraph, the auditors describe how they carried out the audit, including a statement that they used *generally accepted audit standards*. These standards require that auditors plan and prepare their audit to be reasonably sure that the financial statements are free of material misstatements. A *material misstatement* is an error that significantly impacts the company's financial position, such as reporting revenue before it's actually earned.

- ✔ **Opinion paragraph:** Here the auditors state their opinion of the financial statements. If the auditors don't find any problems with the statements, they simply say that these statements are prepared "in conformity with generally accepted accounting principles" (or GAAP). For more on GAAP, see Book II Chapter 3.

When an auditors' report follows the outline described here, it's called a *standard auditors' report*. And because no qualifiers (or red flags) limit the auditors' opinions, it's also an *unqualified audit report*.

If the auditors find a problem, the report is a *nonstandard auditors' report*. In a nonstandard report, auditors must explain their opinions in a *qualified audit report* — in other words, they qualify their opinions and note problem areas. A nonstandard auditors' report and a standard auditors' report have the same structure; the only difference is that the nonstandard report includes information about the problems the auditors found.

When you see a nonstandard auditors' report, be sure that you find a discussion of the problems in the MD&A and in the notes to the financial statements. Also, when reading the MD&A, be certain that you understand how management is handling the problems the auditors noted and how these problems may impact the company's long-term financial prospects before you invest your hard-earned dollars. (Call the investor relations department to ask for clarification, if you need to.) If you've already invested, look carefully at the issues to be sure you want to continue holding your stock in the company.

A nonstandard auditors' report may include paragraphs that discuss problems the auditors found, such as the following:

✔ **Work performed by a different auditor:** In many cases, this isn't a major problem. Maybe a different auditor handled the audit in previous years or audited a subsidiary of a newly acquired company.

But whenever a company changes auditors, you need to know why it made the change, and you need to research the issue. You probably won't find the reason for the change in the annual report, so you may have to research the change in news reports or analysts' reports. Because changing auditors can negatively impact a firm's stock price, companies are usually very careful about doing so. Wall Street typically gets concerned whenever a change of auditors occurs because it can be a sign of a major accounting problem that hasn't surfaced yet.

✔ **Accounting policy changes:** If a company decides to change its accounting policies or how it applies an accounting method, the auditors must note the change in a nonstandard auditors' report. These changes may not indicate a problem, and if the auditors agree that the company had a good reason for making the change, you most likely have no reason for concern. For example, if the company changed how it reported an asset because the SEC required that change, then it's a good reason for making the change.

If the auditors disagree with the company's decision to change accounting methods, they question the change and provide a *qualified opinion* (discussed later in this section) in the nonstandard auditors' report. If their report indicates a change in accounting policy, be sure to look in the notes portion of the annual report for the full explanation of the change and how it may impact the financial statements. When companies change an accounting policy or method, the change impacts your ability to compare the previous year's results to the results for the current year.

✔ **Material uncertainties:** If the auditors find an area of uncertainty, it's impossible for management or the auditors to determine the potential financial consequences of an event. Uncertainties may include debt-agreement violations, damages the company must pay if it loses a pending lawsuit, or the loss of a major customer or market share. If the auditors believe that these material uncertainties may impact future earnings, they include a paragraph about the uncertainty and give a qualified opinion.

If a loss is probable and the auditors can estimate it, the financial statements usually reflect this loss, and the auditors give an unqualified opinion. So in reality, the impact of a known loss can be a greater problem than a possible loss with unknown consequences. The company and the auditors have a responsibility to make you aware of the uncertainty so that you can factor it into any decisions you make about your potential dealings with or investment in the company.

Book II

Accounting and Financial Reports

✔ **Going-concern problems:** If the auditors have substantial doubt that the company has the ability to stay in business, they indicate that the company has a *going-concern problem*. Problems that can lead to this type of paragraph in the auditors' report include ongoing losses, capital deficiencies, or a significant contract dispute. If you see a statement by the auditors that the company has a going-concern problem, it's a major red flag and a good indication that you don't want to invest in this company.

✔ **Specific disclosures:** Sometimes auditors indicate concerns about a specific financial matter but still give the company a nonqualified opinion.

Many times the auditor believes that these are matters the public needs to know about but aren't signs of a serious problem. For example, if the company is doing business with another company that has officers involved in both firms, the auditor may note this issue in a special paragraph. The notes to the financial statements explain any specific disclosure in greater detail.

✔ **Qualified opinions:** Any time the auditors issue a nonstandard report, they also issue a qualified opinion in the final paragraph of the report. A qualified opinion isn't always cause for alarm, but it does mean that you need to do additional research to make sure you understand the qualification. Sometimes a qualified opinion simply indicates that the auditors didn't have sufficient information available at the time of the audit to determine whether the issue raised will have a significant financial impact on the company. Look in the notes to the financial statements or the MD&A for any explanation of the matter that caused the auditors to issue a qualified opinion.

Summarizing the Financial Data

Knowing that most people won't spend the time to read all the way through the annual report, many companies summarize their numbers in various ways. The two most common ways to summarize are to highlight the financial data presented in the financial statements and to summarize some key information in the notes to the financial statements. But beware: Most summaries highlight the good news and skip over the bad.

Finding the highlights

The highlights to the financial data summarize the financial results for the year being reported. Typically, this summary is called the *financial highlights,* but companies can be creative because this section isn't a required part of the report. And because the highlights aren't required, they're not always presented according to GAAP rules, so don't count on their accuracy. You usually find the financial highlights at the front of the annual report, after the letter from the CEO and chairman of the board. Some companies include them inside the annual report's back cover.

You frequently find financial highlights at the front of the annual report, designed in a graphically pleasing way. Most companies show either a 10-year or 11-year summary that doesn't include much detail but allows you to see the firm's growth trends. Although this type of summary can be a good historical overview, don't count on it. Instead, do your own research of the company's financial history to be sure that you're aware of both the good and the bad news. Remember that even outstanding companies have some bad years that they want to gloss over.

Reading the notes

The notes to the financial statements is the section where you find any warts on a company's financial record. The notes are a required part of the annual report, and they give you the details behind the numbers presented in the financial statements. Companies like to hide their problems in the notes; in fact, most companies even print this part of the annual report in smaller type.

Most of the details in the notes discuss the impact that the following business aspects may have on the company's future financial health:

- ✔ Accounting methods used
- ✔ Changes to accounting methods
- ✔ Key financial commitments that can impact current and future operations
- ✔ Lease obligations
- ✔ Pension and retirement benefits

If any red flags pop up in a company's annual report, this part is where you can find the financial details and explanations. The auditors' report probably highlights any potential problems and red flags that you want to search for in the notes. You may also find problems mentioned in the MD&A section, but the notes section probably covers the full explanations for these problems in greater detail.

Don't get turned off by the visually unpleasing presentation. The notes to the financial statements is one of the most critical parts of the annual report.

Chapter 2

Reporting Profit

This chapter lifts up the hood and explains how the profit engine runs. Making a profit is, of course, the main financial goal of a business. (Nonprofit organizations and government entities don't aim to make profit, but they should at least break even and avoid a deficit.) Measuring profit is a challenge. Determining the correct amounts for revenue and expenses to record is no walk in the park.

Managers have the demanding tasks of making sales and controlling expenses, and accountants have the tough job of measuring revenue and expenses and preparing financial reports that summarize the profit-making activities. Also, accountants are called on to help business managers analyze profit for decision-making, which is covered in Book V Chapter 1. And accountants prepare profit budgets for managers, covered in Book V Chapter 2.

This chapter explains how profit activities are reported in a business's financial reports to its owners and lenders. Revenue and expenses change the financial condition of the business, a fact often overlooked when reading a profit report. Business managers, creditors, and owners should understand the vital connections between revenue and expenses and their corresponding assets and liabilities.

Introducing Income Statements

At the risk of oversimplification, businesses make profit in three basic ways:

✔ Selling *products* (with allied services) and controlling the cost of the products sold and other operating costs

✔ Selling *services* and controlling the cost of providing the services and other operating costs

✔ *Investing* in assets that generate investment income and market value gains and controlling operating costs

Obviously, this list isn't exhaustive, but it captures a large swath of business activity. This chapter concentrates on reporting the first and second ways of making profit: selling products and selling services. *Products* range from automobiles to computers to food to clothes to jewelry. *Services* range from transportation to entertainment to consulting. The customers of a business may be the final consumers in the economic chain, or a business may sell to other businesses.

Looking at a product business

Figure 2-1 presents a typical profit report for a *product-oriented* business; this report, called the *income statement,* would be sent to its outside owners and lenders. The report could just as easily be called the *net income statement* because the bottom-line profit term preferred by accountants is *net income,* but the word *net* is dropped off the title and it's most often called the income statement. Alternative titles for the external profit report include *earnings statement, operating statement, statement of operating results,* and *statement of earnings.* (***Note:*** Profit reports distributed to managers inside a business are usually called *P&L* [profit and loss] statements, but this moniker is not used in external financial reporting.)

The heading of an income statement identifies the business (which in this example is incorporated — thus the term "Inc." following the name), the financial statement title ("Income Statement"), and the time period summarized by the statement ("Year Ended December 31, 2015"). The legal organization structures of businesses are covered in Book II Chapter 3.

You may be tempted to start reading an income statement at the bottom line. But this financial report is designed for you to read from the top line (sales revenue) and proceed down to the last — the bottom line (net income). Each step down the ladder in an income statement involves the deduction of an expense. In Figure 2-1, four expenses are deducted from the sales revenue amount, and four profit lines are given: gross margin; operating earnings; earnings before income tax; and, finally, net income.

Typical Product Business, Inc.
Income Statement
For Year Ended December 31, 2013

Sales Revenue	$26,000,000
Cost of Goods Sold Expense	14,300,000
Gross Margin	$11,700,000
Selling, General and Administrative Expenses	8,700,000
Operating Earnings	$3,000,000
Interest Expense	400,000
Earnings Before Income Tax	$2,600,000
Income Tax Expense	910,000
Net Income	$1,690,000

Figure 2-1:
Typical income statement for a business that sells products.

Book II

Accounting and Financial Reports

Looking at a service business

For comparison, Figure 2-2 presents a typical income statement for a *service-oriented* business. I keep the sales revenue and operating earnings the same for both businesses, so you can compare the two. If a business sells services and does not sell products, it does not have a cost of goods sold expense; therefore, the company does not show a gross margin line. Notice in Figure 2-2 that the first profit line is *operating earnings*, which is profit before interest and income tax. The business in Figure 2-2 discloses three broad types of expenses. In passing you might notice that the interest expense for the service business is lower than for the product business (see Figure 2-1). Therefore, it has higher earnings before income tax and higher net income.

You find many variations in the reporting of expenses. A business — whether a product or service company — has fairly wide latitude regarding the number of expense lines to disclose in its external income statement. Accounting standards do not dictate that particular expenses must be disclosed. Public companies must disclose certain expenses in their publicly available fillings with the federal Securities and Exchange Commission (SEC). Filing reports to the SEC is one thing; in their reports to shareholders, most businesses are relatively stingy regarding how many expenses are revealed in their income statements.

Typical Service Business, Inc.
Income Statement
For Year Ended December 31, 2013

Sales Revenue	$26,000,000
Marketing and Selling Expenses	4,325,000
Operating and Administrative Expenses	8,700,000
Employee Compensation Expenses	9,975,000
Operating Earnings	$3,000,000
Interest Expense	200,000
Earnings Before Income Tax	$2,800,000
Income Tax Expense	980,000
Net Income	$1,820,000

Figure 2-2:
Typical
income
statement
for a service
business.

Taking care of some housekeeping details

There are a few things about income statements that accountants assume everyone knows but, in fact, are not obvious to many people. (Accountants do this a lot: They assume that the people using financial statements know a good deal about the customs and conventions of financial reporting, so they don't make things as clear as they could.) For an accountant, the following facts are second nature:

- **Minus signs are missing.** Expenses are deductions from sales revenue, but hardly ever do you see minus signs in front of expense amounts to indicate that they are deductions. Forget about minus signs in income statements, and in other financial statements as well. Sometimes parentheses are put around a deduction to signal that it's a negative number, but that's the most you can expect to see.

- **Your eye is drawn to the bottom line.** Putting a double underline under the final (bottom-line) profit number for emphasis is common practice but not universal. Instead, net income may be shown in bold type. You generally don't see anything as garish as a fat arrow pointing to the profit number or a big smiley encircling the profit number — but again, tastes vary.

- **Profit isn't usually called** *profit.* As you see in Figures 2-1 and 2-2, bottom-line profit is called *net income.* Businesses use other terms as well, such as *net earnings* or just *earnings.* (Can't accountants agree on anything?) In this book, the terms *net income* and *profit* are used interchangeably.

✔ **You don't get details about sales revenue.** The sales revenue amount in an income statement is the combined total of all sales during the year; you can't tell how many different sales were made, how many different customers the company sold products or services to, or how the sales were distributed over the 12 months of the year. (Public companies are required to release quarterly income statements during the year, and they include a special summary of quarter-by-quarter results in their annual financial reports; private businesses may or may not release quarterly sales data.) Sales revenue does not include sales and excise taxes that the business collects from its customers and remits to the government.

Note: In addition to sales revenue from selling products and/or services, a business may have income from other sources. For instance, a business may have earnings from investments in marketable securities. In its income statement, investment income goes on a separate line and is not commingled with sales revenue. (The businesses featured in Figures 2-1 and 2-2 do not have investment income.)

✔ **Gross margin matters.** The *cost of goods sold* expense is the cost of products sold to customers, the sales revenue of which is reported on the *sales revenue* line. The idea is to match up the sales revenue of goods sold with the cost of goods sold and show the *gross margin* (also called *gross profit),* which is the profit before other expenses are deducted. The other expenses could in total be more than gross margin, in which case the business would have a net loss for the period. (A bottom-line loss usually has parentheses around it to emphasize that it's a negative number.)

Note: Companies that sell services rather than products (such as airlines, movie theaters, and CPA firms) do not have a cost of goods sold expense line in their income statements, as mentioned earlier. Nevertheless some service companies report a cost of sales expense, and these businesses may also report corresponding gross margin line of sorts. This is one more example of the variation in financial reporting from business to business.

✔ **Operating costs are lumped together.** The broad category *selling, general, and administrative expenses* (refer to Figure 2-1) consists of a wide variety of costs of operating the business and making sales. Some examples are:

- Labor costs (employee wages and salaries, plus retirement benefits, health insurance, and payroll taxes paid by the business)

- Insurance premiums

- Property taxes on buildings and land

- Cost of gas and electric utilities

Book II

Accounting and Financial Reports

- Travel and entertainment costs

- Telephone and Internet charges

- Depreciation of operating assets that are used more than one year (including buildings, land improvements, cars and trucks, computers, office furniture, tools and machinery, and shelving)

- Advertising and sales promotion expenditures

- Legal and audit costs

As with sales revenue, you don't get much detail about operating expenses in a typical income statement.

Your job: Asking questions!

The worst thing you can do when presented with an income statement is to be a passive reader. You should be inquisitive. An income statement is not fulfilling its purpose unless you grab it by its numbers and start asking questions.

For example, you should be curious regarding the size of the business. Another question to ask is: How does profit compare with sales revenue for the year? Profit (net income) equals what's left over from sales revenue after you deduct all expenses. The business featured in Figure 2-1 squeezed $1.69 million profit from its $26 million sales revenue for the year, which equals 6.5 percent. (The service business did a little better; see Figure 2-2.) This ratio of profit to sales revenue means expenses absorbed 93.5 percent of sales revenue. Although it may seem rather thin, a 6.5 percent profit margin on sales is quite acceptable for many businesses. (Some businesses consistently make a bottom-line profit of 10 to 20 percent of sales, and others are satisfied with a 1 or 2 percent profit on sales revenue.) Profit ratios on sales vary widely from industry to industry.

Accounting standards are relatively silent regarding which expenses have to be disclosed on the face of an income statement or elsewhere in a financial report. For example, the amount a business spends on advertising does not have to be disclosed. (In contrast, the rules for filing financial reports with the SEC require disclosure of certain expenses, such as repairs and maintenance expenses. Keep in mind that the SEC rules apply only to public businesses.) Established in May 2012, Private Company Council (PCC) may decide to lay down some rules regarding expense disclosure by private businesses. Although this particular issue doesn't appear to be currently on the PPC's agenda, it is well within the purview of the Council's mandate. In the product business example shown in Figure 2-1, expenses such as labor costs and advertising expenditures are buried in the all-inclusive *selling, general,*

and administrative expenses line. (If the business manufactures the products it sells instead of buying them from another business, a good part of its annual labor cost is included in its *cost of goods sold* expense.) Some companies disclose specific expenses such as advertising and marketing costs, research and development costs, and other significant expenses. In short, income statement expense disclosure practices vary considerably from business to business.

Another set of questions you should ask in reading an income statement concern the *profit performance* of the business. Refer again to the product company's profit performance report (refer to Figure 2-1). Profit-wise, how did the business do? Underneath this question is the implicit question: relative to what? Generally speaking, three sorts of benchmarks are used for evaluating profit performance:

Book II

Accounting and Financial Reports

✔ Broad, industry-wide performance averages

✔ Immediate competitors' performances

✔ The business's own performance in recent years

Finding Profit

Your job is asking pertinent questions. Okay, so here's an important question: What happened to the product company's financial condition as the result of earning $1.69 million net income for the year (refer to Figure 2-1)? The financial condition of a business consists of its assets on the one side and its liabilities and owners' equity on the other side. (The financial condition of a business at a point in time is reported in its *balance sheet,* discussed in detail in Book I Chapter 3.)

To phrase the question a little differently: How did the company's assets, liabilities, and owners' equity change during the year as the result of its revenue and expense transactions that yielded $1.69 million profit? Revenue and expenses are not ephemeral things, like smoke blowing in the wind. These two components of profit cause real changes in assets and liabilities. Figure 2-3 summarizes the effects of recording revenue on the one hand, and expenses on the opposite hand. A business may also record a *gain*, which has the same effect as revenue (that is, an increase in an asset or a decrease in a liability). And a business may record a *loss* in addition to its normal operating expenses. A loss has the same effect as an expense (that is, a decrease in an asset or an increase in a liability).

	Assets	=	Liabilities		Owners' Equity	
			Operating Liabilities +	Debt	Invested Captial +	Retained Earnings
Revenue	+		−	n/a	n/a	+
Expenses	−		+	n/a	n/a	−

Figure 2-3: Financial effects of revenue and expenses.

Figure 2-3 expands the accounting equation (Assets = Liabilities + Owners' Equity) by separating two distinct kinds of liabilities and two distinct sources of owners' equity. Certain liabilities emanate naturally out of the normal operating activities of the business, from buying things on credit and delaying payment for expenses. These are called *operating liabilities*. *Debt* is from borrowing money. Interest is paid on debt; interest is not paid on operating liabilities. Debt can run for many months or years; operating liabilities are generally payable in 30 to 120 days.

Owners' equity comes from two sources. The first source is capital invested in the business by its shareowners at the start of the business, and from time to time thereafter if the business needs more capital from its owners. The second source is profit earned by the business that is not distributed, or paid out to its owners. The retention of profit increases the owners' equity of the business. The second source of owners' equity is called *retained earnings*.

So, the owners' equity of a business increases for two quite different reasons: The owners invest money in the business, and the business makes a profit. Naturally, a business keeps two types of accounts for owners' equity: one for invested capital and one for retained earnings. In most situations not all of annual profit is distributed to owners but is retained in the business. Unfortunately, the retained earnings account sounds like an asset in the minds of many people. It is not! It is a source-of-assets account, not an asset account. It's on the right-hand side of the accounting equation; assets are on the left side.

One important lesson of Figure 2-3 is that debt and owners' equity-invested capital are *not* involved in recording revenue and expenses. Notice that revenue is recorded by increasing an asset or decreasing a liability. Revenue increases retained earnings (before expenses are considered). Some businesses receive cash from their customers before delivering the product or service, such as newspapers, insurance companies, airlines, and so on. When the money is first received it's recorded in an operating liability account. Later, when the product or service is delivered to the customer, the appropriate amount is recorded as a decrease in the liability.

Expenses are the opposite of revenue, as Figure 2-3 shows. In recording an expense an asset is decreased or an operating liability is increased. Expenses also decrease retained earnings of course. Figure 2-4 shows an example where the business recorded $10,000 revenue (or $10,000,000 rounded off if you prefer). We assume that the business does not collect money in advance from its customers, so all the revenue for the period was recorded by increases in assets. If the business had no expenses its retained earnings would have increased $10,000 during the period (see the increase in this owners' equity account Figure 2-4). But, of course, the business did have expenses.

Book II

Accounting and Financial Reports

Figure 2-4: Financial effects of making profit through end of year.

	Assets	=	Liabilities		Owners' Equity	
			Operating Liabilities	+ Debt	Invested Captial	+ Retained Earnings
Revenue	$10,000			n/a	n/a	$10,000
Expenses	($8,100)		$400	n/a	n/a	($8,500)
Profit	$1,900		$400			$1,500

The business recorded $8,500 in expenses during the period, so notice that retained earnings decreases this amount. The $8,500 in expenses had the impact of decreasing assets $8,100 and increasing operating liabilities $400. Don't overlook the fact that expenses impact both assets and operating liabilities.

The bottom line, as the saying goes in the business world, is that the business earned $1,500 profit. Check out the profit line in Figure 2-4. Retained earnings increased $1,500. What's the makeup of this profit? Assets increased $1,900 (good) and operating liabilities increased $400 (bad), for a net positive effect of $1,500, the amount of profit for the period. Whew! Even this simple example takes several steps to understand. But that's the nature of profit. You can't get around the fact that assets and operating liabilities change in the process of making profit. The next section explores in more detail which particular assets and operating liabilities are involved in recording revenue and expenses. Gains and losses are discussed later in the chapter in the section "Reporting Extraordinary Gains and Losses".

The product business in the Figure 2-1 example earned $1.69 million profit for the year. Therefore, its retained earnings increased this amount because the bottom-line amount of net income for the period is recorded in this owners' equity account. You know this for sure, but what you can't tell from the income statement is how the assets and operating liabilities of the business were affected by its sale and expense activities during the period.

The financial gyrations in assets and operating liabilities from profit-making activities is especially important for business managers to understand and pay attention to because they have to manage and control the changes. It would be dangerous to simply assume that making a profit has only beneficial effects on assets and liabilities. One of the main purposes of the statement of cash flows, discussed in Book I Chapter 4, is to summarize the financial changes caused by the profit activities of the business during the year.

To summarize, the product company's $1.69 million net income resulted in some combination of changes in its assets and operating liabilities, such that its owners' equity (specifically, retained earnings) increased $1.69 million. One such scenario is given in Figure 2-5, which reflects the company's profit-making activities through the end of the year. By year end most of the operating liabilities that were initially recorded for expenses have been paid, which is reflected in the $24,010,000 decrease in assets. Still, operating liabilities did increase $300,000 during the year. Cash has not yet been used to pay these liabilities. The upcoming section "Summing Up the Diverse Financial Effects of Making Profit" discusses these changes in more detail.

		Assets	=	Liabilities			Owners' Equity		
				Operating Liabilities	+	Debt	Invested Captial	+	Retained Earnings
Figure 2-5: Financial changes from profit-making activities through end of year.	Revenue	$26,000,000							$26,000,000
	Expenses	($24,010,000)		$300,000					($24,310,000)
	Profit	$1,990,000		$300,000		n/a	n/a		$1,690,000

Getting Particular about Assets and Operating Liabilities

The sales and expense activities of a business involve inflows and outflows of cash, as I'm sure you know. What you may not know, however, is that the profit-making process of a business that sells products on credit also involves four other basic assets and three basic types of operating liabilities. Each of the following sections explains one of these assets and operating liabilities. This gives you a better understanding of what's involved in making profit and how profit-making activities change the financial make up of a business.

Making sales on credit → Accounts receivable asset

Many businesses allow their customers to buy their products or services on credit. They use an asset account called *accounts receivable* to record the total amount owed to the business by its customers who have made purchases "on the cuff" and haven't paid yet. In most cases, a business doesn't collect all its receivables by the end of the year, especially for credit sales that occur in the last weeks of the year. It records the sales revenue and the cost of goods sold expense for these sales as soon as a sale is completed and products are delivered to the customers. This is one feature of the *accrual basis of accounting,* which records revenue when sales are made and records expenses when these costs are incurred.

When sales are made on credit, the accounts receivable asset account is increased; later, when cash is received from the customer, cash is increased and the accounts receivable account is decreased. Collecting the cash is the follow-up transaction trailing along after the sale is recorded. So, there is a two-step process: Make the sale, and Collect cash from the customer. Through the end of the year the amount of cash collections may be less than the total recorded sales revenue, in which case the accounts receivable asset account increases from the start to the end of the period. The amount of the asset increase had not been collected in cash by the end of the year. Cash flow is lower by the amount of the asset increase.

The balance of accounts receivable at the end of the year is the amount of sales revenue that has not yet been converted to cash. Accounts receivable represents cash waiting in the wings to be collected in the near future (assuming that all customers pay their accounts owed to the business on time). Until the money is actually received, the business is without the cash inflow. Cash flow is explained in more depth in Book I Chapter 4.

Selling products → Inventory asset

The *cost of goods sold* is one of the primary expenses of businesses that sell products. (In Figure 2-1, notice that this expense is equal to more than half the sales revenue for the year.) This expense is just what its name implies: the cost that a business pays for the products it sells to customers. A business makes profit by setting its sales prices high enough to cover the costs of products sold, the costs of operating the business, interest on borrowed money, and income taxes (assuming that the business pays income tax), with something left over for profit.

Book II

Accounting and Financial Reports

When the business acquires a product, the cost of the product goes into an *inventory asset* account (and, of course, the cost is either deducted from the cash account or added to a liability account, depending on whether the business pays with cash or buys on credit). When a customer buys that product, the business transfers the cost of the product from the inventory asset account to the *cost of goods sold* expense account because the product is no longer in the business's inventory; the product has been delivered to the customer.

The first layer in the income statement of a product company is deducting the cost of goods sold expense from the sales revenue for the goods sold. Almost all businesses that sell products report the cost of goods sold as a separate expense in their income statements, as you see in Figure 2-1. Most report this expense as shown in Figure 2-1 so that gross margin is reported. But some product companies simply report cost of goods sold as one expense among many and do not call attention to gross margin. For example, Ford Motor and General Mills (think Cheerios) do not report gross margin.

A business that sells products needs to have a stock of those products on hand to sell to its customers. This stockpile of goods on the shelves (or in storage space in the backroom) waiting to be sold is called *inventory*. When you drive by an auto dealer and see all the cars, SUVs, and pickup trucks waiting to be sold, remember that these products are inventory. The cost of unsold products (goods held in inventory) is not yet an expense; only after the products are actually sold does the cost get listed as an expense. In this way, the cost of goods sold expense is correctly matched against the sales revenue from the goods sold. Correctly matching expenses against sales revenue is the essence of accounting for profit.

So, the cost of goods sold expense involves two steps: the products to be sold are purchased or manufactured; later, the products are sold at which time the expense is recorded. A business may acquire more products than it sells during the year. In this case the inventory asset account increases by the cost of the unsold products. The cost of goods sold expense would have an albatross around its neck, as it were — the increase in inventory of products not yet sold by the end of the period.

Prepaying operating costs → Prepaid expense asset

Prepaid expenses are the opposite of unpaid expenses. For example, a business buys fire insurance and general liability insurance (in case a customer who slips on a wet floor or is insulted by a careless salesperson sues the business). Insurance premiums must be paid ahead of time, before coverage starts. The premium cost is allocated to expense in the actual periods benefited. At the end of the year, the business may be only halfway through the insurance coverage period, so it charges off only half the premium cost as an expense. (For a six-month policy, you charge one-sixth of the premium cost to each of the six months covered.) So at the time the premium is paid, the entire amount is recorded in the prepaid expenses asset account, and for each month of coverage, the appropriate fraction of the cost is transferred to the insurance expense account.

Another example of something initially put in the prepaid expenses asset account is when a business pays cash to stock up on office supplies that it may not use for several months. The cost is recorded in the prepaid expenses asset account at the time of purchase; when the supplies are used, the appropriate amount is subtracted from the prepaid expenses asset account and recorded in the office supplies expense account.

Using the prepaid expenses asset account is not so much for the purpose of reporting all the assets of a business, because the balance in the account compared with other assets and total assets is typically small. Rather, using this account is an example of allocating costs to expenses in the period benefited by the costs, which isn't always the same period in which the business pays those costs. The prepayment of these expenses lays the groundwork for continuing operations seamlessly into the next year.

So, for some expenses there is a two-step process: the expenses paid for in advance and the cost of the advance payment is allocated to expense over time. As with inventory, a business may prepay more than is recorded as expense during the period, in which case the prepaid expenses asset account increases.

Fixed assets → Depreciation expense

Long-term operating assets that are not held for sale in the ordinary course of business are called generically *fixed assets*; these include buildings, machinery, office equipment, vehicles, computers and data-processing equipment, shelving and cabinets, and so on. *Depreciation* refers to spreading out the cost of a fixed asset over the years of its useful life to a business, instead of charging the entire cost to expense in the year of purchase. That way, each year of use bears a share of the total cost. For example, autos and light trucks are typically depreciated over five years; the idea is to charge a fraction of the total cost to depreciation expense during each of the five years. (The actual fraction each year depends on which method of depreciation is used, a topic covered in Book I Chapter 5.)

Of course, depreciation applies only to fixed assets that you buy, not those you rent or lease. If you lease or rent fixed assets, which is quite common, the rent you pay each month is charged to *rent expense*. Depreciation is a real expense but not a cash outlay expense in the year it is recorded. The cash outlay occurs when the fixed asset is acquired.

Take a look back at the product company example in Figure 2-1. From the information supplied in its income statement, we don't know how much depreciation expense the business recorded in 2015. However, the footnotes to its financial statements reveal this amount. In 2015, the business recorded $775,000 depreciation expense. Basically, this expense decreases the book value (the recorded value) of its depreciable assets. Book I Chapter 3 goes into more detail regarding how depreciation expense is recorded.

Unpaid expenses → Accounts payable, accrued expenses payable, and income tax payable

A typical business pays many expenses *after* the period in which the expenses are recorded. Following are some common examples:

- ✔ A business hires a law firm that does a lot of legal work during the year, but the company doesn't pay the bill until the following year.

- ✔ A business matches retirement contributions made by its employees but doesn't pay its share until the following year.

- ✔ A business has unpaid bills for telephone service, gas, electricity, and water that it used during the year.

Accountants use three different types of liability accounts to record a business's unpaid expenses:

- ✔ **Accounts payable:** This account is used for items that the business buys on credit and for which it receives an invoice (a bill). For example, your business receives an invoice from its lawyers for legal work done. As soon as you receive the invoice, you record in the accounts payable liability account the amount that you owe. Later, when you pay the invoice, you subtract that amount from the accounts payable account, and your cash goes down by the same amount.

- ✔ **Accrued expenses payable:** A business has to make estimates for several unpaid costs at the end of the year because it hasn't received invoices or other types of bills for them. Examples of accrued expenses include the following:

- Unused vacation and sick days that employees carry over to the following year, which the business has to pay for in the coming year

- Unpaid bonuses to salespeople

- The cost of future repairs and part replacements on products that customers have bought and haven't yet returned for repair

- The daily accumulation of interest on borrowed money that won't be paid until the end of the loan period

Without invoices to reference, you have to examine your business operations carefully to determine which liabilities of this sort to record.

✔ **Income tax payable:** This account is used for income taxes that a business still owes to the IRS at the end of the year. The income tax expense for the year is the total amount based on the taxable income for the entire year. Your business may not pay 100 percent of its income tax expense during the year; it may owe a small fraction to the IRS at year's end. You record the unpaid amount in the income tax payable account.

Note: A business may be organized legally as a *pass-through tax entity* for income tax purposes, which means that it doesn't pay income tax itself but instead passes its taxable income on to its owners. Book VII Chapter 1 explains these types of business entities. The example offered here is for a business that is an ordinary corporation that pays income tax.

Book II

Accounting and Financial Reports

Summing Up the Diverse Financial Effects of Making Profit

Business managers should understand not only how to make profit, but also the full range of financial effects of making profit. Profit does not simply mean an increase in cash. Sales revenue and expenses affect several assets other than cash and operating liabilities. It's hard to overemphasize the importance of understanding this fact.

The *profit-making activities* of a business include more than just recording revenue and expenses. Additional transactions are needed, which take place before or after revenue and expenses occur. These before-and-after transactions include the following:

✔ Collecting cash from customers for credit sales made to them, which takes place after recording the sales revenue

✔ Purchasing (or manufacturing) products that are put in inventory and held there until the products are sold sometime later, at which time the cost of products sold is charged to expense in order to match up with the revenue from the sale

✔ Paying certain costs in advance of when they are charged to expense

✔ Paying for products bought on credit and for other items that are not charged to expense until sometime after the purchase

✔ Paying for expenses that have been recorded sometime earlier

✔ Making payments to the government for income tax expense that has already been recorded

To sum up, the profit-making activities of a business include both making sales and incurring expenses as well as the various transactions that take place before and after the occurrence of revenue and expenses. Only revenue and expenses are reported in the income statement; however, the other transactions change assets and liabilities, and they definitely affect cash flow. Book II Chapter 6 explains how the changes in assets and liabilities caused by the allied transactions affect cash flow.

Figure 2-6 is a summary of the changes in assets and operating liabilities through the end of the year caused by the product company's profit-making activities. Keep in mind that these changes include the sales and expense transactions and the preparatory and follow-through transactions. This sort of summary can be prepared for business managers, but is not presented in external financial reports.

Figure 2-6: Changes in assets and operating liabilities from profit-making activities through end of year for product company (in thousands of dollars).

Assets		Operating Liabilities		Retained Earnings
Cash	$1,515	Payables for purchases on credit	$125	
Receivables from credit sales	$450	Accrual of unpaid expenses	$150	
Inventory of unsold products	$725	Income tax payable	$25	
Prepaid expenses	$75			
Depreciable assets	($775)			
Total assets	$1,990 −	Total operating liabilities	$300 =	$1,690 Profit

Notice the differences in Figure 2-6 compared with the earlier accounting equation-based figures. The columns for debt and owners' equity-invested capital are not included because these two are not affected by the profit-making activities of the business. In other words, making profit affects only assets, operating liabilities, and retained earnings. The bottom line in Figure 2-6 shows that the $1,990,000 total increase in assets minus the $300,000 total increase in operating liabilities equals the $1,690,000 profit for the year.

With the summary in Figure 2-6, you can find profit. The summary reveals what profit consists of, or the substance of profit based on the profit-making activities of the business. The $1,515,000 increase in cash is the largest component of profit for the year, and the other changes in assets and operating liabilities fill out the rest of the picture. The business is $1,690,000 better off from earning that much profit. This better-offness is distributed over five assets and three liabilities. You can't look only to cash. You have to look at the other changes as well.

Reporting Extraordinary Gains and Losses

The income statement examples shown in Figures 2-1 and 2-2 are sanitized versions when compared with actual income statements in external financial reports. Suppose you took the trouble to read 100 income statements. You'd be surprised at the wide range of things you'd find in these statements.

Many businesses report *unusual, extraordinary gains and losses* in addition to their usual revenue, income, and expenses. Remember that recording a gain increases an asset or decreases a liability. And, recording a loss decreases an asset or increases a liability. When a business has recorded an extraordinary gain or loss during the period, its income statement is divided into two sections:

✔ The first section presents the *ordinary, continuing sales, income, and expense operations* of the business for the year.

✔ The second section presents any *unusual, extraordinary, and nonrecurring gains and losses* that the business recorded in the year.

The road to profit is anything but smooth and straight. Every business experiences an occasional *discontinuity* — a serious disruption that comes out of the blue, doesn't happen regularly or often, and can dramatically affect its bottom-line profit. In other words, a discontinuity is something that disturbs the basic continuity of its operations or the regular flow of profit-making activities.

Here are some examples of discontinuities or out of left field types of impacts:

- ✓ **Downsizing and restructuring the business:** Layoffs require severance pay or trigger early retirement costs; major segments of the business may be disposed of, causing large losses.

- ✓ **Abandoning product lines:** When you decide to discontinue selling a line of products, you lose at least some of the money that you paid for obtaining or manufacturing the products, either because you sell the products for less than you paid or because you just dump the products you can't sell.

- ✓ **Settling lawsuits and other legal actions:** Damages and fines that you pay — as well as awards that you *receive* in a favorable ruling — are obviously nonrecurring extraordinary losses or gains (unless you're in the habit of being taken to court every year).

- ✓ **Writing down (also called *writing off*) damaged and impaired assets:** If products become damaged and unsellable, or fixed assets need to be replaced unexpectedly, you need to remove these items from the assets accounts. Even when certain assets are in good physical condition, if they lose their ability to generate future sales or other benefits to the business, accounting rules say that the assets have to be taken off the books or at least written down to lower book values.

- ✓ **Changing accounting methods:** A business may decide to use a different method for recording revenue and expenses than it did in the past, in some cases because the accounting rules (set by the authoritative accounting governing bodies) have changed. Often, the new method requires a business to record a one-time cumulative effect caused by the switch in accounting method. These special items can be huge.

- ✓ **Correcting errors from previous financial reports:** If you or your accountant discovers that a past financial report had an accounting error, you make a catch-up correction entry, which means that you record a loss or gain that had nothing to do with your performance this year.

According to financial reporting standards, a business must make these one-time losses and gains very visible in its income statement. So in addition to the main part of the income statement that reports normal profit activities, a business with unusual, extraordinary losses or gains must add a second layer to the income statement to disclose these out-of-the-ordinary happenings.

If a business has no unusual gains or losses in the year, its income statement ends with one bottom line, usually called *net income* (which is the situation shown in Figures 2-1 and 2-2). When an income statement includes a second layer, that line becomes *net income from continuing operations before unusual gains and losses.* Below this line, each significant, nonrecurring gain or loss appears.

Say that a business suffered a relatively minor loss from quitting a product line and a very large loss from a major lawsuit whose final verdict went against the business. The second layer of the business's income statement would look something like the following (in thousands of dollars):

Net income from continuing operations	$267,000
Discontinued operations, net of income taxes	($20,000)
Earnings before effect of legal verdict	$247,000
Loss due to legal verdict, net of income taxes	($456,000)
Net earnings (loss)	($209,000)

The gains and losses reported in the second layer of an external income statement are generally complex and may be quite difficult to follow. So where does that leave you? In assessing the implications of extraordinary gains and losses, use the following questions as guidelines:

- ✔ Were the annual profits reported in prior years overstated?

- ✔ Why wasn't the loss or gain recorded on a more piecemeal and gradual year-by-year basis instead of as a one-time charge?

- ✔ Was the loss or gain really a surprising and sudden event that could not have been anticipated?

- ✔ Will such a loss or gain occur again in the future?

Every company that stays in business for more than a couple of years experiences a discontinuity of one sort or another. But beware of a business that takes advantage of discontinuities in the following ways:

- ✔ **Discontinuities become continuities:** This business makes an extraordinary loss or gain a regular feature on its income statement. Every year or so, the business loses a major lawsuit, abandons product lines, or restructures itself. It reports "nonrecurring" gains or losses from the same source on a recurring basis.

- ✔ **A discontinuity is used as an opportunity to record all sorts of write-downs and losses:** When recording an unusual loss (such as settling a lawsuit), the business opts to record other losses at the same time, and everything but the kitchen sink (and sometimes that, too) gets written off. This so-called *big-bath* strategy says that you may as well take a big bath now in order to avoid taking little showers in the future.

A business may just have bad (or good) luck regarding extraordinary events that its managers could not have predicted. If a business is facing a major, unavoidable expense this year, cleaning out all its expenses in the same year so it can start off fresh next year can be a clever, legitimate accounting tactic. But where do you draw the line between these accounting manipulations and fraud? Stay alert to these potential problems.

Correcting Common Misconceptions About Profit

Many people (perhaps the majority) think that the amount of the bottom-line profit increases cash by the same amount. This is not true, as shown in Figure 2-6 and as explained in Book I Chapter 4. In almost all situations, the assets and operating liabilities used in recording profit had changes during the period that inflate or deflate cash flow from profit. This is not an easy lesson to learn. Sure, it would be simpler if profit equals cash flow, but it doesn't. Sorry, but that's the way it is.

Another broad misconception about profit is that the numbers reported in the income statement are precise and accurate and can be relied on down to the last dollar. Call this the *exactitude* misconception. Virtually every dollar amount you see in an income statement probably would have been different if a different accountant had been in charge. Business transactions can get very complex and require forecasts and estimates. Different accountants would arrive at different interpretations of the "facts" and, therefore, record different amounts of revenue and expenses. Hopefully the accountant keeps consistent over time, so that year-to-year comparisons are valid.

Another serious misconception is that if profit is good, the financial condition of the business is good. At the time of writing, the profit of Apple Computer is very good. But you shouldn't automatically assume that its financial condition is equally good. Still, if you look in Apple's balance sheet, you'll find that its financial condition is very good indeed. (It has more cash and marketable investments on hand than the economies of many countries.) The point is that its bottom line doesn't tell you anything about the financial condition of the business. You find this in the balance sheet.

Closing Comments

The income statement occupies center stage; the bright spotlight is on this financial statement because it reports profit or loss for the period. But remember that a business reports three primary financial statements — the other two being the balance sheet and the statement of cash flows, discussed in the next two chapters. The three statements are like a three-ring circus. The income statement may draw the most attention, but you have to watch what's going on in all three places. As important as profit is to the financial success of a business, the income statement is not an island unto itself.

Also, keep in mind that financial statements are supplemented with footnotes and contain other commentary from the business's executives. If the financial statements have been audited, the CPA firm includes a short report stating whether the financial statements have been prepared in conformity with the appropriate accounting standards.

An income statement you read and rely on — as a business manager, investor, or lender — may not be true and accurate. In most cases, businesses prepare their financial statements in good faith, and their profit accounting is honest. They may bend the rules a little, but basically their accounting methods are within the boundaries of GAAP even though the business puts a favorable spin on its profit number.

But some businesses resort to accounting fraud and deliberately distort their profit numbers. In this case, an income statement reports false and misleading sales revenue and/or expenses in order to make the bottom-line profit appear to be better than the facts would support. If the fraud is discovered at a later time, the business puts out revised financial statements. Basically, the business in this situation rewrites its profit history.

By the way, look at Figure 2-6 again. This summary provides a road map of sorts for understanding accounting fraud. The fraudster knows that he has to cover up and conceal his accounting fraud. Suppose the fraudster wants to make reported profit higher. But how? The fraudster has to overstate revenue or understate expenses. *And*, he has to overstate one of the assets or understate one of the operating liabilities you see in Figure 2-6. The crook cannot simply jack up revenue or downsize an expense. To keep things in order the fraudster has to balance the error in the income statement with an error in an asset or operating liability. If revenue is overstated, for example, most likely the ending balance of receivables is overstated the same amount.

It would be nice if financial reporting fraud didn't happen very often, but the number of high-profile accounting fraud cases in the past several years has been truly alarming. The CPA auditors of these companies did not catch the accounting fraud, even though this is one purpose of an audit. Investors who relied on the fraudulent income statements ended up suffering large losses.

Book II

Accounting and Financial Reports

There were different auditing standards in place at that time. Back then, most auditors probably would not have considered detecting fraud to be one of the "purposes" of their audit. Those high-isibility cases, however, have resulted in new auditing standards — namely, SAS 99, adopted in 2002, which requires the auditors to consider the "fraud triangle" and to have brainstorming sessions with management to consider how their financial statements may be subject to material misstatements due to fraud.

When you read a financial report, keep in mind the risk that the financial statements may be "stage managed" to some extent — to make year-to-year reported profit look a little smoother and less erratic, and to make the financial condition of the business appear a little better. Regretfully, financial statements don't always tell it as it is. Rather, the chief executive and chief accountant of the business fiddle with the financial statements to some extent.

Chapter 3

Exploring Business Structures

*A*ll businesses need to prepare key financial statements, but some businesses can prepare less formal statements than others. The way a business is legally organized greatly impacts the way it reports its financials to the public and the depth of that reporting.

For a small business, financial reporting is needed only to monitor the success or failure of operations. But as the business grows, and as more outsiders — such as investors and creditors — become involved, financial reporting becomes more formalized until the company reaches the point at which audited financial statements are required.

Each business structure also follows a different set of rules about what financial information the business must file with state, local, and federal agencies. This first part of this chapter reviews the basics of how each type of business structure is organized, how taxation differs, which forms the business must file, and what types of financial reports are required.

Not every company wants to be under public scrutiny. Although some firms operate in the public arena by selling shares to the general public on the open market, others prefer to keep ownership within a closed circle of friends or investors. When company owners contemplate whether to keep their business private or to take it public, they're making a decision that can permanently change the company's direction.

The second part of this chapter explains the differences between public and private companies, the advantages and disadvantages of each, and how the decision about whether to go public or stay private impacts a company's financial reporting requirements. It also describes the process involved when company owners decide to take their business public.

Flying Solo: Sole Proprietorships

The simplest business structure is the *sole proprietorship* — the IRS's automatic classification for any business that an individual starts. Most new businesses with only one owner start out as sole proprietorships, and many never grow into anything larger. Others start adding partners and staff and may realize that incorporating is a wise decision for legal purposes. (Check out "Seeking Protection with Limited Liability Companies" and "Shielding Your Assets: S and C Corporations," later in the chapter, to find out more about incorporating.)

To start a business as a sole proprietor, you don't have to do anything official, like file government papers or register with the IRS. In fact, unless you formally *incorporate* — that is, follow a process that makes the business a separate legal entity — the IRS considers the business to be a sole proprietorship. (Incorporation and the process of forming corporations are discussed in the upcoming section "Shielding Your Assets: S and C Corporations.")

The fact that the business isn't a separate legal entity is the biggest risk of a sole proprietorship. All debts or claims against the business are filed against the sole proprietor's personal property. If a sole proprietor is sued, insurance is the only form of protection against losing everything.

Keeping taxes personal

Sole proprietorships aren't taxable entities, and sole proprietors don't have to fill out separate tax forms for their businesses. The only financial reporting sole proprietors must do is add a few forms about their business entity to their personal tax returns.

Most sole proprietors add Schedule C — a "Profit or Loss from Business" form — to their personal tax returns, but some may qualify to use an even simpler form, called Schedule C-EZ, "Net Profit from Business." In addition, a sole proprietor must pay both the employer and employee sides of Social Security and Medicare taxes using Schedule SE, "Self-Employment Tax." These taxes total 15.3 percent of *net business income,* or the business income after all business expenses have been subtracted.

Sole proprietors in specialized businesses may have different IRS forms to fill out. Farmers use Schedule F, "Profit or Loss from Farming." People who own rental real estate but don't operate a real estate business use Schedule E, "Supplemental Income and Loss." Schedule E profits are not subject to SE tax.

Reviewing requirements for reporting

Financial reporting requirements don't exist for sole proprietors unless they seek funding from outside sources, such as a bank loan or a loan from the U.S. Small Business Administration. When a business seeks outside funding, the funding source likely provides guidelines for how the business should present financial information.

When sole proprietors apply for a business loan, they fill out a form that shows their assets and liabilities. In addition, they're usually required to provide a basic profit and loss statement. Depending on the size of the loan, they may even have to submit a formal business plan stating their goals, objectives, and implementation plans.

Even though financial reports aren't required for a sole proprietorship that isn't seeking outside funding, it makes good business sense to complete periodic profit and loss statements to keep tabs on how well the business is doing and to find any problems before they become too huge to fix. These reports don't have to adhere to formal generally accepted accounting principles, but honesty is the best policy. You're fooling only yourself if you decide to make your financial condition look better on paper than it really is.

Joining Forces: Partnerships

The IRS automatically considers any business started by more than one person a *partnership*. Each person in the partnership is equally liable for the activities of the business, but because more than one person is involved, a partnership is a slightly more complicated company type than a sole proprietorship. Partners have to sort out the following legal issues:

- How they divide profits
- How they can sell the business
- What happens if one partner becomes sick or dies
- How they dissolve the partnership if one of the partners wants out

Because of the number of options, a partnership is the most flexible business structure for a business that involves more than one person. But to avoid future problems that can destroy an otherwise successful business, partners should decide on all these issues before opening their business's doors.

Partnering up on taxes

Partnerships aren't taxable entities, but partners do have to file a "U.S. Return of Partnership Income" using IRS Form 1065. This form, which shows income, deductions, and other tax-related business data, is for information purposes only. It lists each partner's share of taxable income, called a Schedule K-1, "Partner's Share of Income, Credits, Deductions, Etc." Each individual partner must report that income on his or her personal tax return.

Meeting reporting requirements

Unless a partnership seeks outside funding, its financial reports don't have to be presented in any special way because the reports don't have to satisfy anyone but the partners. Partnerships do need reports to monitor the success or failure of business operations, but they don't have to be completed to meet GAAP standards (see Book I Chapter 7 for more on accounting standards). Usually, when more than one person is involved, the partners decide among themselves what type of financial reporting is required and who's responsible for preparing those reports.

If the partnership seeks funding from a bank or investors, more formal reporting may be needed, such as audited financial statements and business plans.

Seeking Protection with Limited Liability Companies

A partnership or sole proprietorship can limit its liability by using an entity called a *limited liability company,* or LLC. First established in the United States about 30 years ago, LLCs didn't become popular until the mid-1990s, when most states approved them.

This business form actually falls somewhere between a corporation and a partnership or sole proprietorship in terms of protection by the law. Because

LLCs are state entities, any legal protections offered to the owners of an LLC are dependent on the laws of the state where it's established. In most states, LLC owners get the same legal protection from lawsuits as the federal law provides to corporations, but unlike the federal laws, these protections haven't been tested fully in the state courts.

Reporting requirements for LLCs aren't as strict as they are for a corporation, but many partnerships do decide to have their books audited to satisfy all the partners that the financial information is being kept accurately and within internal control procedures determined by the partners.

Taking stock of taxes

LLCs let sole proprietorships and partnerships have their cake and eat it, too: They get the same legal protection from liability as a corporation but don't have to pay corporate taxes or file all the forms required of a corporation. In fact, the IRS treats LLCs as partnerships or sole proprietorships unless they ask to be taxed as corporations by using Form 8832, "Entity Classification Election."

Reviewing reporting requirements

The issues of business formation and business reporting are essentially the same for a partnership and a sole proprietorship, whether or not the entity files as an LLC. To shield themselves from liability, many large legal and accounting firms file as LLCs rather than take the more formal route of incorporating. When LLCs seek outside funding, either by selling shares of ownership or by seeking loans, the IRS requires their financial reporting to be more formal. Some partnerships form as LLPs, or Limited Liability Partnerships. In an LLP, one partner is *not* responsible for the other partner's actions. In some countries, an LLP must have at least one general partner with unlimited liability.

Shielding Your Assets:
S and C Corporations

Company owners seeking the greatest level of protection may choose to incorporate their businesses. The courts have clearly determined that corporations are separate legal entities, and their owners are protected from claims filed against the corporation's activities (provided the corporation follows all the rules and regulations to insure the corporate veil cannot be pierced.). An owner (shareholder) in a corporation can't get sued or face collections because of actions the corporation takes.

The veil of protection makes a powerful case in favor of incorporating. However, the obligations that come with incorporating are tremendous, and a corporation needs significant resources to pay for the required legal and accounting services. Many businesses don't incorporate and choose instead to stay unincorporated or to organize as an LLC to avoid these additional costs.

Before incorporating, a business must first form a board of directors, even if that means including spouses and children on the board. (Imagine what those family board meetings are like!)

Boards can be made up of both corporation owners and nonowners. Any board member who isn't an owner can be paid for his service on the board.

Before incorporating, a company must also divvy up ownership in the form of stock. Most small businesses don't trade their stock on an open exchange. Instead, they sell it privately among friends and investors.

Corporations are separate tax entities, so they must file tax returns and pay taxes or find ways to avoid them by using deductions. Two types of corporate structures exist:

- ✔ **S corporations:** These corporations have fewer than 100 shareholders and function like partnerships but give owners additional legal protection.

- ✔ **C corporations:** These corporations are separate legal entities formed for the purpose of operating a business. They're actually treated in the courts as individual entities, just like people. Incorporation allows owners to limit their liability from the corporation's actions. Owners must split their ownership by using shares of stock, which is a requirement specified as part of corporate law. As an investor, you're most likely to be a shareholder in a C corporation.

Paying taxes the corporate way

If a company organizes as an S corporation, it can avoid corporate taxation but still keep its legal protection. S corporations are essentially treated as partnerships for tax purposes, with profits and losses passed through to the shareholders, who then report the income or loss on their personal tax returns.

The biggest disadvantage of the S corporation is the way profits and losses are distributed. Although a partnership has a lot of flexibility in divvying up profits and losses among the partners, S corporations must divide them based on the amount of stock each shareholder owns. This structure can be a big problem if one of the owners has primarily given cash and bought stock while another owner is primarily responsible for day-to-day business operations. Because the owner responsible for operations didn't purchase stock, he isn't eligible for the profits unless he receives stock ownership as part of his contract with the company.

Only relatively small businesses can avoid taxation as a corporation. After a corporation has more than 100 shareholders, it loses its status as an S corporation. In addition, only U.S. residents can hold S corporation stock. Nonresident aliens (that is, citizens of another country) and nonhuman entities (such as other corporations or partnerships) don't qualify as owners. However, some tax-exempt organizations — including pension plans, profit-sharing plans, and stock bonus plans — *can* be shareholders in an S corporation.

Book II

Accounting and Financial Reports

One big disadvantage of the C corporation is that its profits are taxed twice — once through the corporate entity and once as dividends paid to its owners. C corporation owners can get profits only through dividends, but they can pay themselves a salary.

Unlike S corporations, partnerships, and sole proprietorships, which pass any profits and losses to their owners, who then report them on their personal income tax forms, C corporations must file their own tax forms and pay taxes on any profits.

Paying the high price of incorporation

C corporations must pay the following tax rates:

Taxable Income	C Corporation Tax Rate
$0–$50,000	15%
$50,001–$75,000	25%
$75,001–$100,000	34%
$100,001–$335,000	39%
$335,001–$10,000,000	34%
$10,000,001–$15,000,000	35%
$15,000,001–$18,333,333	38%
Over $18,333,333	35%

Although you may think that C corporation tax rates look higher than individual tax rates, in reality, many corporations avoid taxes completely by taking advantage of loopholes and deductions in the tax code. Most major corporations have an entire tax department whose sole responsibility is to find ways to avoid taxation.

Getting familiar with reporting requirements

A company must meet several requirements to keep its corporate veil of protection in place. For example, corporations must hold board meetings, and the minutes from those meetings detail the actions the company must take to prove it's operating as a corporation. The actions that must be shown in the minutes include:

- ✔ Establishment of banking associations and any changes to those arrangements

- ✔ Loans from either shareholders or third parties

- ✔ The sale or redemption of stock shares

- ✔ The payment of dividends

- ✔ Authorization of salaries or bonuses for officers and key executives (Yep, those multimillion-dollar bonuses you've been hearing about as major corporate scandals must be voted on in board meetings. The actual list of salaries doesn't have to be in the minutes but can be included as an attachment.)

- ✔ Any purchases, sales, or leases of corporate assets

- ✔ The purchase of another company

- ✔ Any merger with another company

- ✔ Changes to the Articles of Incorporation or bylaws

- ✔ Election of corporate officers and directors

These corporate minutes are official records of the company, and the IRS, state taxing authorities, and courts can review them. If a company and its owners are sued and the company wants to invoke the veil of corporate protection, it must have these board minutes in place to prove that it operated as a corporation.

If a C corporation's ownership is kept among family and friends, it can be flexible about its reporting requirements. However, many C corporations have outside investors and creditors who require formal financial reporting that meets GAAP standards (for more on this topic, see Book I Chapter 7). Also, most C corporations must have their financial reports audited.

Investigating Private Companies

Private companies don't sell stock to the general public, so they don't have to report to the government (except for filing their tax returns, of course) or answer to the public. No matter how big or small these companies are, they can operate behind closed doors.

A private company gives owners the freedom to make choices for the firm without having to worry about outside investors' opinions. Of course, to maintain that freedom, the company must be able to raise the funds necessary for the business to grow — through either profits, debt funding, or investments from family and friends.

Checking out the benefits

Private companies maintain absolute control over business operations. With absolute control, owners don't have to worry about what the public thinks of its operations, nor do they have to worry about the quarterly race to meet

---

Keeping it in the family

Mars, one of the world's largest private companies, makes some of your favorite candies — 3 Musketeers, M&M's, and Snickers. Mars has never gone public, which means it has never sold its shares of stock to the general public. The company is still owned and operated by the family that founded it.

Frank and Ethel Mars, who made candy in the kitchen of their Tacoma, Washington, home, started Mars in 1911. Their first worldwide success was the Milky Way bar, which became known as the Mars bar in Europe in the 1920s.

Today Mars is a $30 billion business with operations in more than 56 countries and sales of its products in over 100 countries. Mars isn't just making candy anymore, either. It also manufactures Whiskas and Pedigree pet food, Uncle Ben's rice products, vending systems,

electronics for automated payment systems, and information technology related to its manufacturing operations. The family is still in control of all these businesses and makes the decisions about which businesses to add to its portfolio.

One of Mars's five key principles that shape its business is "Freedom." The company's statement about the importance of freedom clearly describes why the family decided to stay private:

Mars is one of the world's largest privately owned corporations. This private ownership is a deliberate choice. Many other companies began as Mars did, but as they grew larger and required new sources of funds, they sold stocks or incurred restrictive debt to fuel their business. To extend their growth, they exchanged a portion of their freedom. We believe growth and prosperity can be achieved another way.

the numbers to satisfy Wall Street's profit watch. The company's owners are the only ones who worry about profit levels and whether the company is meeting its goals, which they can do in the privacy of a boardroom. Further advantages of private ownership include

- ✔ **Confidentiality:** Private companies can keep their records under wraps, unlike public companies, which must file quarterly financial statements with the Securities and Exchange Commission (SEC) and various state agencies. Competitors can take advantage of the information that public companies disclose, whereas private companies can leave their competitors guessing and even hide a short-term problem.

  Owners of private companies also like the secrecy they can keep about their personal net worth. Although public companies must disclose the number of shares their officers, directors, and major shareholders hold, private companies have no obligation to release these ownership details.

- ✔ **Flexibility:** In private companies, family members can easily decide how much to pay one another, whether to allow private loans to one another, and whether to award lucrative fringe benefits or other financial incentives, all without having to worry about shareholder scrutiny. Public companies must answer to their shareholders for any bonuses or other incentives they give to top executives. Private-company owners can take out whatever money they want without worrying about the best interests of outside investors, such as shareholders. Any disagreements the owners have about how they disburse their assets remain behind closed doors.

- ✔ **Greater financial freedom:** Private companies can carefully select how to raise money for the business and with whom to make financial arrangements. After public companies offer their stock in the public markets, they have no control over who buys their shares and becomes a future owner.

If a private company receives funding from experienced investors, it doesn't face the same scrutiny that a public company does. Publicly disclosed financial statements are required only when stock is sold to the general public, not when shares are traded privately among a small group of investors.

Defining disadvantages

The biggest disadvantage a private company faces is its limited ability to raise large sums of cash. Because a private company doesn't sell stock or offer bonds to the general public, it spends a lot more time than a public company does finding investors or creditors who are willing to risk their funds. And many investors don't want to invest in a company that's controlled by a small group of people and that lacks the oversight of public scrutiny.

If a private company needs cash, it must perform one or more of the following tasks:

✔ Arrange for a loan with a financial institution

✔ Sell additional shares of stock to existing owners

✔ Ask for help from an *angel,* a private investor willing to help a small business get started with some upfront cash

✔ Get funds from a *venture capitalist,* someone who invests in startup businesses, providing the necessary cash in exchange for some portion of ownership

These options for raising money may present a problem for a private company because of the following:

✔ A company's borrowing capability is limited and based on how much capital the owners have invested in the company. A financial institution requires that a certain portion of the capital needed to operate the business — sometimes as much as 50 percent — come from the owners. Just as when you want to borrow money to buy a home, the bank requires you to put up some cash before it loans you the rest. The same is true for companies that want a business loan.

✔ Persuading outside investors to put up a significant amount of cash if the owners want to maintain control of the business is no easy feat. Often major outside investors seek a greater role in company operations by acquiring a significant share of the ownership and asking for several seats on the board of directors.

✔ Finding the right investment partner can be difficult. When private-company owners seek outside investors, they must ensure that the potential investors have the same vision and goals for the business that they do.

Book II

Accounting and Financial Reports

Another major disadvantage that a private company faces is that the owners' net worth is likely tied almost completely to the value of the company. If a business fails, the owners may lose everything and may even be left with a huge debt. If owners take their company public, however, they can sell some of their stock and diversify their portfolios, thereby reducing their portfolios' risk.

Figuring out reporting

Reporting requirements for a private company vary based on its agreements with stakeholders. Outside investors in a private company usually establish reporting requirements as part of the agreement to invest funds in the business. A private company circulates its reports among its closed group of stakeholders — executives, managers, creditors, and investors — and doesn't have to share them with the public.

Private or Publix?

Publix Super Markets is a private company owned by more than 112,000 shareholders. You can think of it as a semipublic company. However, until Publix actually decides to sell stock on a public exchange — if it ever does — it's classified as a private company. Publix makes its stock available during designated public offerings that are open only to its employees and nonemployee members of its board of directors. It also offers employees a stock ownership plan, which has more than 122,000 participants. So even though Publix stock isn't sold on a stock exchange, Publix must file public financial reports with the SEC.

A private company must file financial reports with the SEC when it has more than 500 common shareholders and $10 million in assets, as set by the Securities and Exchange Act of 1934. Congress passed this act so that private companies that reach the size of public companies and acquire a certain mass of outside ownership have the same reporting obligations as public companies. (See the nearby sidebar "Private or Publix?" for an example of this type of company.)

When a private company's stock ownership and assets exceed the limits set by the Securities and Exchange Act of 1934, the company must file a Form 10, which includes a description of the business and its officers, similar to an initial public offering (also known as an IPO, which is the first public sale of a company's stock). After the company files Form 10, the SEC requires it to file quarterly and annual reports.

In some cases, private companies buy back stock from their current shareholders to keep the number of individuals who own stock under the 500 limit. But generally, when a company deals with the financial expenses of publicly reporting its earnings and can no longer keep its veil of secrecy, the pressure builds to go public and gain greater access to the funds needed to grow even larger.

Understanding Public Companies

A company that offers shares of stock on the open market is a *public company*. Public company owners don't make decisions based solely on their preferences — they must always consider the opinions of the business's outside investors.

Before a company goes public, it must meet certain criteria. Generally, investment bankers (who are actually responsible for selling the stock) require that a private company generate at least $10 million to $20 million in annual sales, with profits of about $1 million.

(Exceptions to this rule exist, however, and some smaller companies do go public.) Before going public, company owners must ask themselves the following questions:

- Can my firm maintain a high growth rate to attract investors?
- Does enough public awareness of my company and its products or services exist to make a successful public offering?
- Is my business operating in a hot industry that will help attract investors?
- Can my company perform as well as, and preferably better than, its competition?
- Can my firm afford the ongoing cost of financial auditing requirements (which can be as high as $2 million a year for a small company)?

If company owners are confident in their answers to these questions, they may want to take their business public. But they need to keep in mind the advantages and disadvantages of going public, which is a long, expensive process that takes months and sometimes even years.

Companies don't take themselves public alone — they hire investment bankers to steer the process to completion. Investment bankers usually get multimillion-dollar fees or commissions for taking a company public. The upcoming section "Entering a Whole New World: How a Company Goes from Private to Public" talks more about this.

Book II

Accounting and Financial Reports

Going public, losing jobs

Public company founders who don't keep their investors happy can find themselves out on the street and no longer involved in the company they started. Steve Jobs and Steve Wozniak, who started Apple Computer, found out the hard way that selling stock on the public market can ultimately take the company away from the founders.

Jobs and Wozniak became multimillionaires after Apple Computer went public, but shareholders ousted them from their leadership roles in a management shake-up in 1984. Wozniak decided to leave Apple soon after the shake-up. Apple's new CEO announced that he couldn't find a role for Jobs in the company's operations in 1985.

Interestingly, Jobs ended up as the head of Apple again in 1998, when the shareholders turned to him to rescue the company from failure. He engineered a legendary comeback for Apple before his death in 2011.

Examining the perks

If a company goes public, its primary benefit is that it gains access to additional capital (more cash), which can be critical if it's a high-growth business that needs money to take advantage of its growth potential. A secondary benefit is that company owners can become millionaires, or even billionaires, overnight if the initial public offering (IPO) is successful. The largest one to date was the IPO of Alibaba, the "Chinese Amazon," which raised a whopping $25 billion in September of 2014.

Being a public company has a number of other benefits:

- **New corporate cash:** At some point, a growing company usually maxes out its ability to borrow funds, and it must find people willing to invest in the business. Selling stock to the general public can be a great way for a company to raise cash without being obligated to pay interest on the money.

- **Owner diversification:** People who start a new business typically put a good chunk of their assets into starting the business and then reinvest most of the profits in the business in order to grow the company. Frequently, founders have a large share of their assets tied up in the company. Selling shares publicly allows owners to take out some of their investment and diversify their holdings in other investments, which reduces the risks to their personal portfolios.

- **Increased liquidity:** *Liquidity* is a company's ability to quickly turn an asset into cash (if it isn't already cash). People who own shares in a closely held private company may have a lot of assets but little chance to actually turn those assets into cash. Selling privately owned shares of stock is very difficult. Going public gives the stock a set market value and creates more potential buyers for the stock.

- **Company value:** Company owners benefit by knowing their firm's worth for a number of reasons. If one of the key owners dies, state and federal inheritance tax appraisers must set the company's value for estate tax purposes. Many times, these values are set too high for private companies, which can cause all kinds of problems for other owners and family members. Going public sets an absolute value for the shares held by all company shareholders and prevents problems with valuation. Also, businesses that want to offer shares of stock to their employees as incentives find that recruiting with this incentive is much easier when the stock is sold on the open market.

Looking at the negative side

Regardless of the many advantages of being a public company, a great many disadvantages also exist:

- ✔ **Costs:** Paying the costs of providing audited financial statements that meet the requirements of the SEC or state agencies can be very expensive — sometimes as high as $2 million annually. Investor relations can also add significant costs in employee time, printing, and mailing expenses.

- ✔ **Control:** As stock sells on the open market, more shareholders enter the picture, giving each one the right to vote on key company decisions. The original owners and closed circle of investors no longer have absolute control of the company.

- ✔ **Disclosure:** A private company can hide difficulties it may be having, but a public company must report its problems, exposing any weaknesses to competitors, who can access detailed information about the company's operations by getting copies of the required financial reports. In addition, the net worth of a public company's owners is widely known because they must disclose their stock holdings as part of these reports.

Book II

Accounting and Financial Reports

- ✔ **Cash control:** In a private company, owners can decide their own salary and benefits, as well as the salary and benefits of any family member or friend involved in running the business. In a public company, the board of directors must approve and report any major cash withdrawals, whether for salary or loans, to shareholders.

- ✔ **Lack of liquidity:** When a company goes public, a constant flow of buyers for the stock isn't guaranteed. For a stock to be liquid, a shareholder must be able to convert that stock to cash. Small companies that don't have wide distribution of their stock can be hard to sell on the open market. The market price may even be lower than the actual value of the firm's assets because of a lack of competition for shares of the stock. When not enough competition exists, shareholders have a hard time selling the stock and converting it to cash, making the investment nonliquid.

A failed IPO or a failure to live up to shareholders' expectations can change what may have been a good business for the founders into a bankrupt entity. Although founders may be willing to ride out the losses for a while, shareholders rarely are. Many IPOs that raised millions before the Internet stock crash in 2000 are now defunct companies.

Filing and more filing: Government and shareholder reports

Public companies must file an unending stream of reports with the SEC. They must file financial reports quarterly as well as annually. They also must file reports after specific events, such as bankruptcy or the sale of a company division.

Quarterly reports

Each quarter, public companies must file financial statements on Form 10Q, in addition to information about the company's market risk, controls and procedures, legal proceedings, and defaults on payments.

Yearly report

Each year, public companies must file an annual report with audited financial statements and information about

- ✔ **Company history:** How the company was started, who started it, and how it grew to its current level of operations
- ✔ **Organizational structure:** How the company is organized, who the key executives are, and who reports to whom
- ✔ **Equity holdings:** A list of the major shareholders and a summary of all outstanding stock
- ✔ **Subsidiaries:** Other businesses that the company owns wholly or partially
- ✔ **Employee stock purchase and savings plans:** Plans that allow employees to own stock by purchasing it or participating in a savings plan
- ✔ **Incorporation:** Information about where the company is incorporated
- ✔ **Legal proceedings:** Information about any ongoing legal matters that may be material to the company
- ✔ **Changes or disagreements with accountants:** Information about financial disclosures, controls and procedures, executive compensation, and accounting fees and services

In addition to the regular reports, public companies must file an 8-K, a form for reporting any major events that can impact the company's financial position. A major event may be the acquisition of another company, the sale of a company or division, bankruptcy, the resignation of directors, or a change in the fiscal year. A public company must report any event that falls under this requirement on the 8-K to the SEC within four days of the event's occurrence.

The rules of the Sarbanes-Oxley Act

All the scandals about public companies that emerged in the early 2000s have made this entire reporting process riskier and more costly for company owners. In 2002, Congress passed a bill called the Sarbanes-Oxley Act to try to correct some of the problems in financial reporting. This bill passed as details emerged about how corporate officials from companies like Enron, MCI, and Tyco hid information from the SEC.

New SEC rules issued after the Sarbanes-Oxley Act passed require CEOs and CFOs to certify financial and other information contained in their quarterly and annual reports. They must certify that

- ✔ They've established, maintained, and regularly evaluated effective disclosure controls and procedures.

- ✔ They've made disclosures to the auditors and audit committee of the board of directors about internal controls.

- ✔ They've included information in the quarterly and annual reports about their evaluation of the controls in place, as well as about any significant changes in their internal controls or any other factors that could significantly affect controls after the initial evaluation.

If a CEO or CFO certifies this information and that information later proves to be false, he or she can end up facing criminal charges. Since the passage of the Sarbanes-Oxley Act, companies have delayed releasing financial reports if the CEO or CFO has any questions rather than risk charges. You'll probably hear more about delays in reporting as CEOs and CFOs become more reluctant to sign off on financial reports that may have questionable information. Shareholders often panic when they hear about a delay, and stock prices drop.

The Sarbanes-Oxley Act has added significant costs to the entire process of completing financial reports, affecting the following components:

- ✔ **Documentation:** Companies must document and develop policies and procedures relating to their internal controls over financial reporting. Although an outside accounting firm can assist with the documentation process, managers must be actively involved in the process of assessing internal controls — they can't delegate this responsibility to an external firm.

- ✔ **Audit fees:** Independent audit firms now look a lot more closely at financial statements and internal controls in place over financial reporting, and the SEC's Public Company Accounting Oversight Board (PCAOB) now regulates the accounting profession. The PCAOB inspects accounting firms to be sure they're in compliance with the Sarbanes-Oxley Act and SEC rules.

- ✔ **Legal fees:** Because companies need lawyers to help them comply with the new provisions of the Sarbanes-Oxley Act, their legal expenses are increasing.

- ✔ **Information technology:** Complying with the Sarbanes-Oxley Act requires both hardware and software upgrades to meet the internal control requirements and the speedier reporting requirements.

Book II

Accounting and Financial Reports

Bearing the burden and expense of Sarbanes-Oxley

Many major corporations already had the internal controls in place and produced the documentation that the Sarbanes-Oxley Act required. Smaller companies were hit harder with these new requirements. The SEC's only concession for smaller companies was *when* they must be in compliance with the new rules on internal controls: All small businesses had to be in compliance by November 2004.

The rules imposed by Sarbanes-Oxley were such a significant burden on small companies that some of them decided to buy out shareholders and make the companies private again, or merge with larger companies, or even liquidate.

When a private company thinks about going public, it must consider whether the process is worth the costs. With the new Sarbanes-Oxley rules in place, a small company pays close to $3 million in legal, accounting, and other costs of being public. Before Sarbanes-Oxley, these costs totaled closer to $2 million. Large corporations budget more than $7 million to cover the costs of being a public company nowadays.

✔ **Boards of directors:** Most companies must restructure their board of directors and audit committees to meet the Sarbanes-Oxley Act's requirements, ensuring that independent board members control key audit decisions. The structure and operation of nominating and compensation committees must eliminate even the appearance of conflicts of interest. Companies must make provisions to give shareholders direct input in corporate governance decisions. Businesses also must provide additional education to board members to be sure they understand their responsibilities to shareholders.

Entering a Whole New World: How a Company Goes from Private to Public

So the owners of a company have finally decided to sell the company's stock publicly. Now what? This section describes the role of an investment banker in helping a company sell its stock and explains the process of making a public offering.

Teaming up with an investment banker

The first step after a company decides to go public is to choose who will handle the sales and which market to sell the stock on. Few firms have the capacity to approach the public stock markets on their own. Instead, they hire an investment banker to help them through the complicated process of going public. A well-known investment banker can lend credibility to a little-known small company, which makes selling the stock easier.

Investment bankers help a company in the following ways:

- **They prepare the required SEC documents and register the new stock offering with the SEC.** These documents must include information about the company (its products, services, and markets) and its officers and directors. Additionally, they must include information about the risks the firm faces, how the business plans to use the money raised, any outstanding legal problems, holdings of company insiders, and, of course, audited financial statements.

- **They price the stock so it's attractive to potential investors.** If the stock is priced too high, the offering could fall flat on its face, with few shares sold. If the stock is priced too low, the company could miss out on potential cash that investors, who buy IPO shares, can get as a windfall from quickly turning around and selling the stock at a profit.

- **They negotiate the price at which the stock is offered to the general public and the guarantees they give to the company owners for selling the stock.** An investment banker can give an *underwriting guarantee,* which guarantees the amount of money that will be raised. In this scenario, the banker buys the stock from the company and then resells it to the public. Usually, an investment banker puts together a syndicate of investment bankers who help find buyers for the stock.

  Another method that's sometimes used is called a *best efforts agreement.* In this scenario, the investment banker tries to sell the stock but doesn't guarantee the number of shares that will sell.

- **They decide which stock exchange to list the stock on.** The New York Stock Exchange (NYSE) has the highest level of requirements. If a company wants to list on this exchange, it must have a pretax income of at least $10 million over the last three years and 2,200 or more shareholders. The NASDAQ has lower requirements. Companies can also sell stock over the counter, which means the stock isn't listed on any exchange, so selling the stock both as an IPO and after the IPO is much harder.

Book II

Accounting and Financial Reports

Making a public offering

After the company and the investment banker agree to work together and set the terms for the public offering, as well as the commission structure (how the investment banker gets paid), the banker prepares the registration statement to be filed with the SEC.

After the registration is filed, the SEC imposes a "cooling-off period" to give itself time to investigate the offering and to make sure the documents disclose all necessary information. The length of the cooling-off period depends on how complete the documents are and whether the SEC asks for additional information. During the cooling-off period, the underwriter produces the *red herring,* which is an initial prospectus that includes the information in the SEC registration without the stock price or effective date.

After the underwriter completes the red herring, the company and the investment bankers do *road shows* — presentations held around the country to introduce the business to major institutional investors and start building interest in the pending IPO. A company can't transact sales until the SEC approves the registration information, but it can start generating excitement and getting feedback about the IPO at these meetings.

When the SEC finishes its investigation and approves the offering, the company can set an *effective date,* or the date of the stock offering. The company and investment bankers then sit down and establish a final stock price. Although they discuss the stock price in initial conversations, they can't set the final price until they know the actual effective date. Market conditions can change significantly from the time the company first talks with investment bankers and the date when the stock is finally offered publicly. Sometimes the company and investment banker decide to withdraw or delay an IPO if a market crisis creates a bad climate for introducing a new stock or if the road shows don't identify enough interested major investors.

After the stock price is set, the stock is sold to the public. The company gets the proceeds minus any commissions it pays to the investment bankers.

Chapter 4

The Balance Sheet: Assets, Liabilities, and Equity

*P*icture a tightrope walker carefully making her way across a tightrope. Now imagine that she's carrying plates of equal weight on both sides of a wobbling rod. What would happen if one of those plates were heavier than the other? You don't have to understand squat about physics to know that it wouldn't be a pretty sight.

Just as a tightrope walker must be in balance, so must a company's financial position. If the assets aren't equal to the claims against those assets, then that company's financial position isn't in balance, and everything topples over. This chapter introduces you to the balance sheet, which gives the financial report reader a snapshot of a company's financial position.

Understanding the Balance Equation

A company keeps track of its financial balance on a *balance sheet,* a summary of the company's financial standing at a particular point in time. To understand balance sheets, you first have to understand the following terms, which typically appear on a balance sheet:

✔ **Assets:** Anything the company owns, from cash, to inventory, to the paper it prints the reports on

✔ **Liabilities:** Debts the company owes

✔ **Equity:** Claims made by the company's owners, such as shares of stock

The assets a company owns are equal to the claims against that company, by either debtors (liability) or owners (equity). The claims side must equal the assets side for the balance sheet to stay in balance. The parts always balance according to this formula:

> Assets = Liabilities + Equity

As a company and its assets grow, its liabilities and equities grow in similar proportion. For example, whenever a company buys a major asset, such as a building, it has to either use another asset to pay for the building or use a combination of assets and liabilities (such as bonds or a mortgage) or equity (owner's money or outstanding shares of stock).

Introducing the Balance Sheet

Trying to read a balance sheet without having a grasp of its parts is a little like trying to translate a language you've never spoken — you may recognize the letters, but the words don't mean much. Unlike a foreign language, however, a balance sheet is pretty easy to get a fix on as soon as you figure out a few basics.

Digging into dates

The first parts to notice when looking at the financial statements are the dates indicated at the top of the statements. You need to know what date or period of time the financial statements cover. This information is particularly critical when you start comparing results among companies. You don't want to compare the 2015 results of one firm with the 2014 results of another. Economic conditions certainly vary, and the comparison doesn't give you an accurate view of how well the companies competed in similar economic conditions.

On a balance sheet, the date at the top is written after "As of," meaning that the balance sheet reports a company's financial status on that particular day. A balance sheet differs from other kinds of financial statements, such as the income statement or statement of cash flows, which show information for a period of time such as a year, a quarter, or a month. Book II Chapter 5 covers income statements, and statements of cash flows are discussed in Book II Chapter 6.

If a company's balance sheet states "As of December 31, 2015," the company is most likely operating on the calendar year. Not all firms end their business year at the end of the calendar year, however. Many companies operate on a fiscal year instead, which means they pick a 12-month period that more accurately reflects their business cycles. For example, most retail companies end their fiscal year on January 31. The best time of year for major retail sales is during the holiday season and post-holiday season, so stores close the books after those periods end.

To show you how economic conditions can make comparing the balance sheets of two companies difficult during two different fiscal years, consider an example surrounding the terrorist attacks on September 11, 2001.

If one company's fiscal year runs from September 1 to August 31 and another's runs from January 1 to December 31, the results may be very different. The company that reports from September 1, 2000, to August 31, 2001, wasn't impacted by that devastating event on its 2000/2001 financial reports. Its holiday season sales from October 2000 to December 2000 are likely much different from those of the company that reports from January 1, 2001, to December 31, 2001, because those results include sales after September 11, when the economy slowed considerably. However, the first company's balance sheet for September 1, 2001, to August 31, 2002, shows the full impact of the attacks on its financial position.

When a year is more than a year

Things can get confusing if a company picks a certain point in time instead of an actual date for its fiscal year. For example, a company can decide to end its fiscal year on the last Friday of a particular month, which means its fiscal year is sometimes 52 weeks and sometimes 53 weeks. If a firm chooses a point in time instead of a year-end or month-end date, you usually find an explanation in the notes to the financial statements about how it handles its 52- and 53-week years, which can get convoluted.

For example, Darden Restaurants explained its 52- and 53-week years when it released its 2009 annual report like this:

"We operate on a 52/53 week fiscal year, which ends on the last Sunday in May. Fiscal 2009 consisted of 53 weeks of operation. Fiscal 2008 and 2007 each consisted of 52 weeks of operation."

Looking at this paragraph, you can see the complications of a fiscal year ending on a set period in time instead of one that ends on the last day of a month. The quarter with the extra week is 17 weeks. Comparing a 16-week quarter with a 17-week quarter can be misleading because an extra week of sales certainly looks better.

Nailing down the numbers

As you start reading the financial reports of large corporations, you see that they don't use large numbers to show billion-dollar results (1,000,000,000) or carry off an amount to the last possible cent, such as 1,123,456,789.99. Imagine how difficult reading such detailed financial statements would be!

At the top of a balance sheet or any other financial report, you see a statement indicating that the numbers are in millions, thousands, or however the company decides to round the numbers. For example, if a billion-dollar company indicates that numbers are in millions, you see 1 billion represented as 1,000 and 35 million as 35. The 1,123,456,789.99 figure would appear as 1,123.

Rounding off numbers makes a report easier on the eye, but be sure you know how companies are rounding their numbers before you start comparing financial statements among them. This issue is particularly crucial when you compare a large company with a smaller one. The large company may round to millions, whereas the smaller company may round to thousands.

Figuring out format

Balance sheets come in three different styles: the account format, the report format, and the financial position format. The following figures show a sample of each format using simple numbers to give you an idea of what you can expect to see. Of course, real balance sheets have much larger and more complex numbers.

Account format

The *account format* is a horizontal presentation of the numbers, as Figure 4-1 shows.

A balanced sheet shows total assets equal to total liabilities/equity.

Current assets	$300	Current liabilities	$200
Long-term assets	$150	Long-term liabilities	$100
Other assets	$ 50	Total liabilities	$300
		Shareholders' equity	$200
Total assets	$500	Total liabilities/equity	$500

Figure 4-1: The account format.

Report format

The *report format* is a vertical presentation of the numbers. You can check it out in Figure 4-2.

Current assets	$300
Long-term assets	$150
Other assets	$ 50
Total assets	$500
Current liabilities	$200
Long-term liabilities	$100
Total liabilities	$300
Shareholders' equity	$200
Total liabilities/equity	$500

Figure 4-2: The report format.

© John Wiley & Son

Book II

Accounting and Financial Reports

Financial position format

American companies rarely use the *financial position format,* although it is common internationally, especially in Europe. The key difference between this format and the other two is that it has two lines that don't appear on the account and report formats:

- ✔ **Working capital:** This line indicates the current assets the company has available to pay bills. You find the working capital by subtracting the current assets from the current liabilities.

- ✔ **Net assets:** This line shows what's left for the company's owners after all liabilities have been subtracted from total assets.

Figure 4-3 shows you what the financial position format looks like. (Keep in mind that *noncurrent assets* are long-term assets as well as assets that aren't current but also aren't long term, such as stock ownership in another company.)

As investing becomes more globalized, you may start comparing U.S. companies with foreign companies. Or perhaps you are considering buying stock directly in European or other foreign companies. You need to become more familiar with the financial position format if you want to read reports from foreign companies.

Current assets	$300
Less: current liabilities	$200
Working capital	$100
Plus: noncurrent assets	$200
Total assets less	
current liabilities	$300
Less: long-term liabilities	$100
Net assets	$200

Figure 4-3: The financial position format.

© John Wiley & Son

Ogling Assets

Anything a company owns is considered an asset. *Assets* can include something as basic as cash or as massive as a factory. A company must have assets to operate the business. The asset side of a balance sheet gives you a summary of what the company owns.

Current assets

Anything a company owns that it can convert to cash in less than a year is a current asset. Without these funds, the company wouldn't be able to pay its bills and would have to close its doors. Cash, of course, is an important component of this part of the balance sheet, but a company uses other assets during the year to pay the bills.

Cash

For companies, cash is basically the same as what you carry around in your pocket or keep in your checking and savings accounts. Keeping track of the money is a lot more complex for companies, however, because they usually keep it in many different locations. Every multimillion-dollar corporation has numerous locations, and every location needs cash.

Even in a *centralized accounting system,* in which all bills are paid in the same place and all money is collected and put in the bank at the same time, a company keeps cash in more than one location. Keeping most of the money in the bank and having a little cash on hand for incidental expenses doesn't work for most companies.

For example, retail outlets and banks need to keep cash in every cash register or under the control of every teller to be able to transact business with their customers. Yet a company must have a way of tracking its cash and knowing exactly how much it has at the end of every day (and sometimes several times a day, for high-volume businesses). The cash drawer must be counted out, and the person counting out the draw must show that the amount of cash matches up with the total that the day's transactions indicate should be there.

If a company has a number of locations, each location likely needs a bank to deposit receipts and get cash as needed. So a large corporation has a maze of bank accounts, cash registers, petty cash, and other places where cash is kept daily. At the end of every day, each company location calculates the cash total and reports it to the centralized accounting area.

The amount of cash that you see on the balance sheet is the amount of cash found at all company locations on the particular day for which the balance sheet was created.

Managing cash is one of the hardest jobs because cash can so easily disappear if proper internal controls aren't in place. Internal controls for monitoring cash are usually among the strictest in any company. If this subject interests you, you can find out more about it in any basic accounting book, such as *Accounting For Dummies,* 5th Edition, by John A. Tracy (John Wiley & Sons, 2013).

Book II

Accounting and Financial Reports

Accounts receivable

Any company that allows its customers to buy on credit has an accounts receivable line on its balance sheet. *Accounts receivable* is a collection of individual customer accounts listing money that customers owe the company for products or services they've already received.

A company must carefully monitor not only whether a customer pays, but also how quickly she pays. If a customer makes her payments later and later, the company must determine whether to allow her to get additional credit or to block further purchases. Although the sales may look good, a nonpaying customer hurts a company because she's taking out — and failing to pay for — inventory that another customer could've bought. Too many nonpaying or late-paying customers can severely hurt a company's cash-flow position, which means the firm may not have the cash it needs to pay the bills.

Comparing a company's accounts receivable line over a number of years gives you a good idea of how well the company is doing collecting late-paying customers' accounts. Although you may see a company report positive sales numbers and a major increase in sales, if the accounts-receivable number is also rising rapidly, the business may be having trouble collecting the money on those accounts.

Marketable securities

Marketable securities are a type of liquid asset, meaning they can easily be converted to cash. They include holdings such as stocks, bonds, and other securities that are bought and sold daily.

Securities that a company buys primarily as a place to hold on to assets until the company decides how to use the money for its operations or growth are considered *trading securities.* Marketable securities held as current assets fit in this category. A company must report these assets at their fair value based on the market value of the stock or bond on the day the company prepares its financial report.

A firm must report any *unrealized losses or gains* — changes in the value of a holding that it hasn't sold — on marketable securities on its balance sheet to show the impact of those losses or gains on the company's earnings. The amount you find on the balance sheet is the *net marketable value*, the book value of the securities adjusted for any gains or losses that haven't been realized.

The balance sheet is the show for general consumption, but the notes to the financial statements are where you find the small print that most people don't read. You'll find lots of juicy details in the notes that you don't want to miss.

Inventory

Any products a company holds ready for sale are considered *inventory.* The inventory on the balance sheet is valued at the cost to the company, not at the price the company hopes to sell the product for. Companies can pick from among five different methods to track inventory, and the method they choose can significantly impact the bottom line. Following are the different inventory tracking systems:

- ✓ **First in, first out (FIFO):** This system assumes that the oldest goods are sold first, and it's used when a company is concerned about spoilage or obsolescence. Food stores use FIFO because items that sit on the shelves too long spoil. Computer firms use it because their products quickly become outdated, and they need to sell the older products first. Assuming that older goods cost less than newer goods, FIFO makes the bottom line look better because the lowest cost is assigned to the goods sold, increasing the net profit from sales.

- ✓ **Last in, first out (LIFO):** This system assumes that the newest inventory is sold first. Companies with products that don't spoil or become obsolete can use this system. The bottom line can be significantly affected if the cost of goods to be sold is continually rising. The most expensive goods that come in last are assumed to be the first sold. LIFO increases the cost of goods figured, which, in turn, lowers the net income from sales and decreases a company's tax liability because its profits are lower after the higher costs are subtracted. Hardware stores that sell hammers, nails, screws, and other items that have been the same for years and won't spoil are good candidates for LIFO.

✔ **Average costing:** This system reflects the cost of inventory most accurately and gives a company a good view of its inventory's cost trends. As the company receives each new shipment of inventory, it calculates an average cost for each product by adding in the new inventory. If the firm frequently faces inventory prices that go up and down, average costing can help level out the peaks and valleys of inventory costs throughout the year. Because the price of gasoline rises and falls almost every day, gas stations usually use this type of system.

✔ **Specific identification:** This system tracks the actual cost of each individual piece of inventory. Companies that sell big-ticket items or items with differing accessories or upgrades (such as cars) commonly use this system. For example, each car that comes onto the lot has a different set of features, so the price of each car differs.

✔ **Lower of cost or market (LCM):** This system sets the value of inventory based on which is lower — the actual cost of the products on hand or the current market value. Companies that sell products with market values that fluctuate significantly use this system. For instance, a brokerage house that sells marketable securities may use this system.

Book II

Accounting and Financial Reports

You usually find some information on the type of inventory system a company uses in the notes to the financial statements. Any significant detail about inventory costs appears in the notes section or in the management's discussion and analysis section.

After a company chooses a type of inventory system, it must use that system for the rest of its corporate life unless it files special explanations with its tax returns to explain the reasons for changing systems. Because the way companies track inventory costs can have a significant impact on the net income and the amount of taxes due, the IRS closely monitors any changes in inventory tracking methods.

Long-term assets

Assets that a company plans to hold for more than one year belong in the long-term assets section of the balance sheet. Long-term assets include land and buildings; capitalized leases; leasehold improvements; machinery and equipment; furniture and fixtures; tools, dies, and molds; intangible assets; and others. This section of the balance sheet shows you the assets that a company has to build its products and sell its goods.

Land and buildings

Companies list any buildings they own on the balance sheet's *land and buildings* line. Companies must depreciate (show that the asset is gradually being used up by deducting a portion of its value) the value of their buildings each year, but the land portion of ownership isn't depreciated.

Many people believe that depreciating the value of a building actually results in undervaluing a company's assets. The IRS allows 39 years for depreciation of a building; after that time, the building is considered valueless. That fact may be true in many cases, such as with factories that need to be updated to current-day production methods, but a well-maintained office building usually lasts longer. A company that has owned a building for 20 or more years may, in fact, show the value of that building depreciated below its market value.

Real estate over the past 20 years has appreciated (gone up in value) greatly in most areas of the country. So, a building's value may actually increase because of market appreciation. You can't figure out this appreciation by looking at the financial reports, though. You have to find research reports written by analysts or the financial press to determine the true value of these assets.

Sometimes you see an indication that a company holds *hidden assets* — they're hidden from your view when you read the financial reports because you have no idea what the true marketable value of the buildings and land may be. For example, an office building that a company purchased for $390,000 and held for 20 years may have a marketable value of $1 million if it were sold today but has been depreciated to $190,000 over the past 20 years.

Capitalized leases

Whenever a company takes possession of or constructs a building by using a lease agreement that contains an option to purchase that property at some point in the future, you see a line item on the balance sheet called *capitalized leases*. It means that, at some point in the future, the company may likely own the property and then can add the property's value to its total assets owned. You can usually find a full explanation of the lease agreement in the notes to the financial statements.

Leasehold improvements

Companies track improvements to property they lease and don't own in the *leasehold improvements account* on the balance sheet. These items are depreciated because the improvements will likely lose value as they age.

Machinery and equipment

Companies track and summarize all machinery and equipment used in their facilities or by their employees in the *machinery and equipment accounts* on the balance sheet. These assets depreciate just like buildings, but for shorter periods of time, depending on the company's estimate of their useful life.

Furniture and fixtures

Some companies have a line item for *furniture and fixtures,* whereas others group these items in machinery and equipment or other assets. You're more likely to find furniture and fixture line items on the balance sheet of major retail chains that hold significant furniture and fixture assets in their retail outlets than on the balance sheet for manufacturing companies that don't have retail outlets.

Tools, dies, and molds

You find *tools, dies, and molds* on the balance sheet of manufacturing companies, but not on the balance sheet of businesses that don't manufacture their own products. Tools, dies, and molds that are unique and are developed specifically by or for a company can have significant value. This value is amortized, which is similar to the depreciation of other tangible assets.

Intangible assets

Any assets that aren't physical — such as patents, copyrights, trademarks, and goodwill — are considered *intangible assets.* Patents, copyrights, and trademarks are actually registered with the government, and a company holds exclusive rights to these items. If another company wants to use something that's patented, copyrighted, or trademarked, it must pay a fee to use that asset.

Patents give companies the right to dominate the market for a particular product. For example, pharmaceutical companies can be the sole source for a drug that's still under patent. Copyrights also give companies exclusive rights for sale. Copyrighted books can be printed only by the publisher or individual who owns that copyright, or by someone who has bought the rights from the copyright owner.

Goodwill is a different type of asset, reflecting the value of a company's locations, customer base, or consumer loyalty, for example. Firms essentially purchase goodwill when they buy another company for a price that's higher than the value of the company's tangible assets or market value. The premium that's paid for the company is kept in an account called *Goodwill* that's shown on the balance sheet.

Other assets

Other assets is a catchall line item for items that don't fit into one of the balance sheet's other asset categories. The items shown in this category vary by company; some firms group both tangible and intangible assets here.

Book II

Accounting and Financial Reports

Other companies may put unconsolidated subsidiaries or affiliates in this category. Whenever a company owns less than a controlling share of another company (less than 50 percent) but more than 20 percent, it must list the ownership as an *unconsolidated subsidiary* (a subsidiary that's partially but not fully owned) or an *affiliate* (a company that's associated with the corporation but not fully owned).

Ownership of less than 20 percent of another company's stock is tracked as a marketable security (see the section "Marketable securities," earlier in this chapter). Long before a firm reaches even the 20 percent mark, you usually find discussion of its buying habits in the financial press or in analysts' reports. Talk of a possible merger or acquisition often begins when a company reaches the 20 percent mark.

You usually don't find more than a line item that totals all unconsolidated subsidiaries or affiliates. Sometimes the notes to the financial statements or the management's discussion and analysis sections mention more detail, but you often can't tell by reading the financial reports and looking at this category what other businesses the company owns. You have to read the financial press or analyst reports to find out the details.

Accumulated depreciation

On a balance sheet, you may see numerous line items that start with accumulated depreciation. These line items appear under the type of asset whose value is being depreciated or shown as a total at the bottom of long-term assets. *Accumulated depreciation* is the total amount depreciated against tangible assets over the life span of the assets shown on the balance sheet.

Although some companies show accumulated depreciation under each of the long-term assets, it's becoming common for companies to total accumulated depreciation at the bottom of the balance sheet's long-term assets section. This method of reporting makes it harder for you to determine the actual age of the assets because depreciation isn't indicated by each type of asset. You have no idea which assets have depreciated the most — in other words, which ones are the oldest.

The age of machinery and factories can be a significant factor in trying to determine a company's future cost and growth prospects. A firm with mostly aging plants needs to spend more money on repair or replacement than a company that has mostly new facilities. Look for discussion of this in the management's discussion and analysis or the notes to the financial statements. If you don't find this information there, you have to dig deeper by reading analyst reports or reports in the financial press. For example, the toy companies Mattel and Hasbro both show their property, plant, and equipment on one line in the balance sheet, but you find a complete breakdown in the notes to the financial statements.

Looking at Liabilities

Companies must spend money to conduct their day-to-day operations. Whenever a company makes a commitment to spend money on credit, be it short-term credit using a credit card or long-term credit using a mortgage, that commitment becomes a debt or liability.

Current liabilities

Current liabilities are any obligations that a company must pay during the next 12 months. These include short-term borrowings, the current portion of long-term debt, accounts payable, and accrued liabilities. If a company can't pay these bills, it may go into bankruptcy or out of business.

Short-term borrowings

Short-term borrowings are usually lines of credit a company takes to manage cash flow. A company borrowing this way isn't much different from you using a credit card or personal loan to pay bills until your next paycheck. As you know, these types of loans usually carry the highest interest-rate charges, so if a firm can't repay them quickly, it converts the debt to something longer term with lower interest rates.

This type of liability should be a relatively low number on the balance sheet, compared with other liabilities. A number that isn't low may be a sign of trouble, indicating that the company is having difficulty securing long-term debt or meeting its cash obligations.

Current portion of long-term debt

This line item of the balance sheet shows payments due on long-term debt during the current fiscal year. The long-term liabilities section reflects any portion of the debt that a company owes beyond the current 12 months.

Accounts payable

Companies list money they owe to others for products, services, supplies, and other short-term needs (invoices due in less than 12 months) in *accounts payable*. They record payments due to vendors, suppliers, contractors, and other companies they do business with.

Accrued liabilities

Liabilities that a company has accrued but hasn't yet paid at the time it prepares the balance sheet are totaled in *accrued liabilities.* For example, companies include income taxes, royalties, advertising, payroll, management incentives, and employee taxes they haven't yet paid in this line item. Sometimes a firm breaks out items individually, like income taxes payable, without using a catchall line item called accrued liabilities. When you look in the notes, you see more details about the types of financial obligations included and the total of each type of liability.

Long-term liabilities

Any money a business must pay out for more than 12 months in the future is considered a long-term liability. Long-term liabilities don't throw a company into bankruptcy, but if they become too large, the company may have trouble paying its bills in the future.

Many companies keep the long-term liabilities section short and sweet, and group almost everything under one lump sum, such as long-term debt. *Long-term debt* includes mortgages on buildings, loans on machinery or equipment, or bonds the company needs to repay at some point in the future. Other companies break out the type of debt, showing mortgages payable, loans payable, and bonds payable.

For example, both Hasbro and Mattel take the short-and-sweet route, giving the financial report reader little detail on the balance sheet. Instead, a reader must dig through the notes and management's discussion and analysis to find more details about the liabilities.

You can find more details about what a company actually groups in the other liability category in the notes to the financial statements. (Guess you're getting used to that phrase!)

Navigating the Equity Maze

The final piece of the balancing equation is equity. All companies are owned by somebody, and the claims that owners have against the assets the company owns are called *equity.* In a small company, the equity owners are individuals or partners. In a corporation, the equity owners are shareholders.

Stock

Stock represents a portion of ownership in a company. Each share of stock has a certain value, based on the price placed on the stock when it's originally sold to investors. The current market value of the stock doesn't affect this price; any increase in the stock's value after its initial offering to the public isn't reflected here. The market gains or losses are actually taken by the shareholders, not the company, when the stock is bought and sold on the market.

Some companies issue two types of stock:

✔ **Common stock:** These shareholders own a portion of the company and have a vote on issues. If the board decides to pay *dividends* (a certain portion per share it pays to common shareholders from profits), common shareholders get their portion of those dividends as long as the preferred shareholders have been paid in full.

✔ **Preferred stock:** These shareholders own stock that's actually somewhere in between common stock and a *bond* (a long-term liability to be paid back over a number of years). Although they don't get back the principal they pay for the stock, as a bondholder does, these shareholders have first dibs on any dividends.

Preferred shareholders are guaranteed a certain dividend each year. If a company doesn't pay dividends for some reason, it accrues these dividends for future years and pays them when it has enough money. A company must pay preferred shareholders their accrued dividends before it pays any money to common shareholders. The disadvantage for preferred shareholders is that they have no voting rights in the company.

You may also find Treasury stock in the equity section of the balance sheet. This is stock that the company has bought back from shareholders. Many companies did that between 2008 and 2013, so look for that on balance sheets. When a company buys back stock, it means fewer shares on the market. With fewer shares available for purchase on the open market, stock prices tend to rise.

If a firm goes bankrupt, the bondholders hold first claim on any money remaining after the company pays the employees and *secured debtors* (debtors who've loaned money based on specific assets, such as a mortgage on a building). The preferred shareholders are next in line; the common shareholders are at the bottom of the heap and are frequently left with valueless stock.

Retained earnings

Each year, companies make a choice to either pay out their net profit to their shareholders or retain all or some of the profit for reinvesting in the company. Any profit a company doesn't pay to shareholders over the years accumulates in an account called *retained earnings*.

Capital

You don't find this line item on a corporation's financial statement, but you'll likely find it on the balance sheet of a small company that isn't publicly owned. *Capital* is the money that the company's founders initially invested.

If you don't see this line item on the balance sheet of a small, privately owned company, the owners likely didn't invest their own capital to get started, or they already took out their initial capital when the company began to earn money.

Drawing

Drawing is another line item you don't see on a corporation's financial statement. Only unincorporated businesses have a drawing account. This line item tracks money that the owners take out from the yearly profits of a business. After a company is incorporated, owners can take money as salary or dividends, but not on a drawing account.

Chapter 5

The Income Statement

*E*very businessperson needs to know how well the business has done over the past month, quarter, or year. Without that information, he has no idea where his business has come from and where it may go next. Even a small business that has no obligation to report to the public is sure to do income statements on at least a quarterly or (more likely) monthly basis to find out whether the business made a profit or took a loss.

The income statement you see in public financial statements is likely very different from the one you see if you work for the company. The primary difference is the detail in certain line items.

This chapter reviews the detail that goes into an income statement, but don't be surprised if some of the detail never shows up in the financial reports you get as a company outsider. Much of the detail is considered confidential and doesn't go to people outside the company. This detailed information is included so you know what's behind the numbers you do see. If you're a company insider, this additional information can help you understand the internal reports you receive.

Introducing the Income Statement

The *income statement* is where you find out whether a company made a profit or took a loss. You also find information about the company's revenues, its sales levels, the costs it incurred to make those sales, and the expenses it paid to operate the business. These are the key parts of the statement:

- ✔ **Sales or revenues:** How much money the business took in from its sales to customers.

- ✔ **Cost of goods sold:** What it cost the company to produce or purchase the goods it sold.

- ✔ **Expenses:** How much the company spent on advertising, administration, rent, salaries, and everything else that's involved in operating a business to support the sales process.

- ✔ **Net income or loss:** The bottom line that tells you whether the company made a profit or operated at a loss.

The income statement is one of the three reports the Securities and Exchange Commission (SEC) and the Financial Accounting Standards Board (FASB) require. In fact, the FASB specifies that the income statement provide a report of comprehensive income, which means the report must reflect any changes to a company's equity during a given period of time that are caused by transactions, events, or other circumstances involving transactions with non-owner sources. In simpler terms, this statement must reflect any changes in equity that aren't raised by investments from owners or distributed to owners.

When looking at an income statement, you can expect to find a report of either

- ✔ **Excess of revenues over expenses:** This report means the company earned a profit.

- ✔ **Excess of expenses over revenues:** This report means the company faced a loss.

Because the income statement shows profits and losses, some people like to call it the profit and loss statement (or P&L), but that isn't actually one of its official names. In addition to "statement of income," the income statement has a number of official names that you may find in a financial report:

- ✔ Statement of operations
- ✔ Statement of earnings
- ✔ Statement of operating results

Digging into dates

Income statements reflect an *operating period,* which means that they show results for a specific length of time. At the top of an income statement, you see the phrase "Years Ended" or "Fiscal Years Ended" and the month the period ended for an annual financial statement. You may also see "Quarters Ended" or "Months Ended" for reports based on shorter periods of time. Companies are required to show at least three periods of data on their income statements, so if you're looking at a statement for 2014, you'll also find columns for 2013 and 2012.

Many people believe you need to analyze at least five years' worth of data if you're thinking about investing in a company. You can easily get hold of this data by ordering a two-year-old annual report along with the current one. You can also find most annual and quarterly reports online at a company's web-site or by visiting the SEC's Edgar website (`www.sec.gov/edgar.shtml`), which posts all financial reports filed with the SEC. Because each report must have three years' worth of data, a 2014 report shows data for 2013 and 2012, too. And a 2011 report shows 2010 and 2009 data also. So you actually have six years' worth of data with these reports.

Book II

Accounting and Financial Reports

Figuring out format

Not all income statements look alike. Basically, companies can choose to use one of two formats for the income statement: the single-step or the multistep.

Both formats give you the same bottom-line information. The key difference between them is whether they summarize that information to make analyzing it easier. The single-step format is easier to produce, but the multistep format gives you a number of subtotals throughout the statement that make analyzing a company's results easier. Most public corporations use the multistep format, but many smaller companies that don't have to report to the general public use the single-step format.

Single-step format

The *single-step format* groups all data into two categories: revenue and expenses. Revenue includes income from sales, interest income, and gains from sales of equipment. It also includes income that a company raises from its regular operations or from one-time transactions, such as from the sale of a building. Expenses include all the costs that are involved in bringing in the revenue.

The single-step format (see Figure 5-1) gets its name because you perform only one step to figure out a company's net income — you subtract the expenses from the revenue.

Revenues	
Sales	$1,000
Interest income	200
Total Revenue	**$1,200**
Expenses	
Cost of goods sold	$ 500
Depreciation	50
Advertising	50
Salaries and wages	100
Insurance	50
Research and development	100
Supplies	50
Interest expense	50
Income taxes	50
Total Expenses	**$1,000**
Net Income	**$ 200**

Figure 5-1:
The single-step format.

© John Wiley & Son

Multistep format

The *multistep format* divides the income statement into several sections and gives the reader some critical subtotals that make analyzing the data much easier and quicker. Even though the single-step and multistep income statements include the same revenue and expense information, they group the information differently. The key difference is that the multistep format has the following four profit lines:

- ✔ **Gross profit:** This line reflects the profit generated from sales minus the cost of the goods sold.

- ✔ **Income from operations:** This line reflects the operating income the company earned after subtracting all its operating expenses.

- ✔ **Income before taxes:** This line reflects all income earned — which can include gains on equipment sales, interest revenue, and other revenue not generated by sales — before subtracting taxes or interest expenses.

- ✔ **Net income (or Net loss):** This line reflects the bottom line — whether the company made a profit.

Many companies add even more profit lines, like earnings before interest, taxes, depreciation, and amortization, known as EBITDA for short (see the section "EBITDA," later in this chapter).

Some companies that have discontinued operations include that information in the line item for continuing operations. But it's better for the financial report reader if that information is on a separate line; otherwise, the reader doesn't know what the actual profit or loss is from continuing operations. I delve a bit deeper into these various profit lines in "Sorting Out the Profit and Loss Types," later in this chapter.

Figure 5-2 shows the multistep format, using the same items as in the single-step format example (refer to Figure 5-1).

Book II

Accounting and Financial Reports

Revenues	
Sales	$1000
Cost of goods sold	$ 500
Gross Profits	**$ 500**
Operating Expenses	
Advertising	50
Salaries and wages	100
Insurance	50
Research and development	100
Supplies	50
Operating Income	**$ 150**
Other Income	
Interest income	200
Other Expenses	
Interest expense	50
Depreciation	50
Income before Taxes	**$ 250**
Income taxes	50
Net Income	**$ 200**

Figure 5-2: The multistep format.

© John Wiley & Son

Delving into the Tricky Business of Revenues

You may think that figuring out when to count something as revenue is a relatively simple procedure. Well, forget that. Revenue acknowledgment is one of the most complex issues on the income statement. In fact, you may have noticed that, with the recent corporation scandals, the most common reason companies have gotten into trouble has to do with the issue of misstated revenues.

This section defines revenue and explains the three line items that make up the revenue portion of the income statement: sales, cost of goods sold, and gross profit.

Defining revenue

When a company recognizes something as revenue, it doesn't always mean that cash changed hands, nor does it always mean that a product was even delivered. Accrual accounting leaves room for deciding when a company actually records revenue. A company recognizes revenue when it earns it and recognizes expenses when it incurs them, without regard to whether cash changes hands. You can find out more about accounting basics in Book I Chapter 1.

Because accrual accounting doesn't require that a company actually have the cash in hand to count something as revenue, senior managers can play games to make the bottom line look the way they want it to look by either counting or not counting income. Sometimes they acknowledge more income than they should to improve the financial reports; other times they reduce income to reduce the tax bite.

When a company wants to count something as revenue, several factors can make that decision rather muddy, leaving questions about whether a particular sale should be counted:

✔ **If the seller and buyer haven't agreed on the final price for the merchandise and service, the seller can't count the revenue collected.**

For example, when a company is in the middle of negotiating a contract for a sale of a major item such as a car or appliance, it can't include that sale as revenue until the final price has been set and a contract obligating the buyer is in place.

✔ **If the buyer doesn't pay for the merchandise until the company resells it to a retail outlet (which may be the case for a company that works with a distributor) or to the customer, the company can't count the revenue until the sale to the customer is final.**

For example, publishers frequently allow bookstores to return unsold books within a certain amount of time. If there's a good chance that some portion of the product may be returned unsold, companies must take this into account when reporting revenues. For instance, a publisher uses historical data to estimate what percentage of books will be returned and adjusts sales downward to reflect those likely returns.

✔ **If the buyer and seller are related, revenue isn't acknowledged in the same way.**

No, not kissing cousins. This is when the buyer is the parent company or subsidiary of the seller. In that case, companies must handle the transaction as an internal transfer of assets.

✔ **If the buyer isn't obligated to pay for the merchandise because it's stolen or physically destroyed before it's delivered or sold, the company can't acknowledge the revenue until the merchandise is actually sold.**

For example, a toy company works with a distributor or other middleman to get its toys into retail stores. If the middleman doesn't have to pay for those toys until they're delivered or sold to retailers, the manufacturer can't count the toys it shipped to the middleman as revenue until the middleman completes the sale.

✔ **If the seller is obligated to provide significant services to the buyer or aid in reselling the product, the seller can't count the sale of that product as revenue until the sale is actually completed with the final customer.**

For example, many manufacturers of technical products offer installation or follow-up services for a new product as part of the sales promotion. If those services are a significant part of the final sale, the manufacturer can't count that sale as revenue until the installation or service has been completed with the customer. Items shipped for sale to local retailers under these conditions aren't considered sold, so they can't be counted as revenue.

Adjusting sales

Not all products sell for their list price. Companies frequently use discounts, returns, or allowances to reduce the prices of products or services. Whenever a firm sells a product at a discount, it needs to keep track of those discounts, as well as its returns and allowances. It's the only way the company can truly analyze how much money it's making on the sale of its products and how accurately it's pricing the products to sell in the marketplace.

If a company must offer too many discounts, it's usually a sign of a weak or very competitive market. If a company has a lot of returns, it may be a sign of a quality-control problem or a sign that the product isn't living up to customers' expectations. The sales adjustments discussed here help a company track and analyze its sales and recognize any negative trends.

As a financial report reader, you don't see the specifics about discounts in the income statement, but you may find some mention of significant discounting in the notes to the financial statements. Here are the most common types of adjustments companies make to their sales:

- **Volume discounts:** To get more items in the marketplace, manufacturers offer major retailers *volume discounts,* which means these retailers agree to buy a large number of a manufacturer's product so they can save a certain percentage of money off the price. One of the reasons you get such good prices at discount sellers like Walmart and Target is that they buy products from the manufacturer at greatly discounted prices. Because they purchase for thousands of stores, they can buy a large number of goods at one time. Volume discounts reduce the revenue of the company that gives them.

- **Returns:** *Returns* are arrangements between the buyer and seller that allow the buyer to return goods for a number of reasons. Surely you've returned goods that you didn't like, that didn't fit, or that possibly didn't even work. Returns are subtracted from a company's revenue.

- **Allowances:** Gift cards and other accounts that a customer pays for up front are actually liabilities on the balance sheet for a store, because the customer hasn't yet selected the merchandise and the sale isn't complete. Revenues are collected up front, but at some point in the future, merchandise will be taken off the shelves and the company won't receive additional cash.

Most companies don't show you the details of their discounts, returns, and allowances, but they do track them and adjust their revenue accordingly. When you see a *net sales* or *net revenue* figure (the company's sales minus any adjustments) at the top of an income statement, the company has already adjusted the figure for these items.

Internally, managers see the details of these adjustments in the sales area of the income statement so that they can track trends for discounts, returns, and allowances. Tracking such trends is an important aspect of the managerial process. If a manager notices that any of these line items show a dramatic increase, she needs to investigate the reason for the increase. For example, an increase in discounts may mean that the company has to consistently offer its products for less money, which then may mean that the market is softening and fewer customers are buying fewer products. A dramatic increase in returns may mean that the products the business is selling have a defect that needs to be corrected.

Considering cost of goods sold

Like the *Sales* line item, the *Cost of goods sold* (what it costs to manufacture or purchase the goods being sold) line item has many different pieces that make up its calculation on the income sheet. You don't see the details for this line item unless you're a company manager. Few firms report the details of their cost of goods sold to the general public.

Items that make up the cost of goods sold vary depending on whether a company manufactures the goods in-house or purchases them. If the company manufactures them in-house, you track the costs all the way from the point of raw materials and include the labor involved in building the product. If the company purchases its goods, it tracks the purchases of the goods as they're made.

In fact, a manufacturing firm tracks several levels of inventory, including

- ✔ **Raw materials:** The materials used for manufacturing

- ✔ **Work-in-process inventory:** Products in the process of being constructed

- ✔ **Finished-goods inventory:** Products ready for sale

Sometimes tracking begins from the time the raw materials are purchased, with adjustments based on discounts, returns, or allowances given. Companies also add to the income statement's cost of goods sold section freight charges and any other costs involved directly in acquiring goods to be sold.

When a company finally sells the product, it becomes a *Cost of goods sold* line item. Managing costs during the production phase is critical for all manufacturing companies. Managers in this type of business receive regular reports that include the cost details. Trends that show dramatically increasing costs certainly must be investigated as quickly as possible because the company must consider a price change to maintain its profit margin.

Even if a company is only a service company, it likely has costs for the services it provides. In this case, the line item may be called *Cost of services sold* instead of *Cost of goods sold*. You may even see a line item called *Cost of goods or services sold* if a company gets revenue from the sale of both goods and services.

Gauging gross profit

The *Gross profit* line item in the income statement's revenue section is simply a calculation of net revenue or net sales minus the cost of goods sold. Basically, this number shows the difference between what a company pays for its inventory and the price at which it sells this inventory. This summary number tells you how much profit the company makes selling its products before deducting the expenses of its operation. If the company shows no profit or not enough profit here, it's not worth being in business.

Managers, investors, and other interested parties closely watch the trend of a company's gross profit because it indicates the effectiveness of the company's purchasing and pricing policies. Analysts frequently use this number not only to gauge how well a company manages its product costs internally, but also to gauge how well the firm manages its product costs compared with other companies in the same business.

If profit is too low, a company can do one of two things: find a way to increase sales revenue, or find a way to reduce the cost of the goods it's selling.

To increase sales revenue, the company can raise or lower prices to increase the amount of money it's bringing in. Raising the prices of its product brings in more revenue if the same number of items is sold, but it may bring in less revenue if the price hike turns away customers and fewer items are sold.

Lowering prices to bring in more revenue may sound strange to you, but if a company determines that a price is too high and is discouraging buyers, doing so may increase its volume of sales and, therefore, its gross margin. This scenario is especially true if the company has a lot of *fixed costs* (such as manufacturing facilities, equipment, and labor) that it isn't using to full capacity. The firm can use its manufacturing facilities more effectively and efficiently if it has the capability to produce more product without a significant increase in the *variable costs* (such as raw materials or other factors, like overtime).

A company can also consider using cost-control possibilities for manufacturing or purchasing if its gross profit is too low. The company may find a more efficient way to make the product, or it may negotiate a better contract for raw materials to reduce those costs. If the company purchases finished products for sale, it may be able to negotiate better contract terms to reduce its purchasing costs.

Acknowledging Expenses

Expenses include the items a company must pay for to operate the business that aren't directly related to the sale and production of specific products. Expenses differ from the cost of goods sold, which can be directly traced to the actual sale of a product. Even when a company is making a sizable gross profit, if management doesn't carefully watch the expenses, the gross profit can quickly turn into a net loss.

Expenses make up the second of the two main parts of the income statement; revenues make up the first part.

Advertising and promotion, administration, and research and development are all examples of expenses. Although many of these expenses impact the ability of a company to sell its products, they aren't direct costs of the sales process for individual items. The following are details about the key items that fit into the expenses part of the income statement:

Book II

Accounting and Financial Reports

- ✔ **Advertising and promotion:** For many companies, one of the largest expenses is advertising and promotion. Advertising includes TV and radio ads, print ads, and billboard ads. Promotions include product give-aways (hats, T-shirts, pens with the company logo on it, and so on) or name identification on a sports stadium. If a company helps promote a charitable event and has its name on T-shirts or billboards as part of the event, it must include these expenses in the *Advertising and promotion expense* line item.

- ✔ **Other selling administration expenses:** This category is a catchall for any selling expenses, including salespeople's and sales managers' salaries, commissions, bonuses, and other compensation expenses. The costs of sales offices and any expenses related to those offices also fall into this category.

- ✔ **Other operating expenses:** If a company includes line-item detail in its financial reports, you usually find that detail in the notes to the financial statements. All operating expenses that aren't directly connected to the sale of products fall into the category of other operating expenses, including these expenses:

  - **General office needs:** Administrative salaries and expenses for administrative offices, supplies, machinery, and anything else needed to run the general operations of a company are reported in general office needs. Expenses for human resources, management, accounting, and security also fall into this category.

  - **Royalties:** Any *royalties* (payments made for the use of property) paid to individuals or other companies fall under this umbrella. Companies most commonly pay royalties for the use of patents or copyrights that another company or individual owns. Companies also pay royalties when they buy the rights to extract natural resources from another person's property.

- **Research and product development:** This line item includes any costs for developing new products. Most likely, you find details about research and product development in the notes to the financial statements or in the managers' discussion and analysis. Any company that makes new products has research and development costs because if it isn't always looking for ways to improve its product or introduce new products, it's at risk of losing out to a competitor.

✔ **Interest expenses:** This line item shows expenses paid for interest on long- or short-term debt. You usually find some explanation for the interest expenses in the notes to the financial statements.

✔ **Interest income:** If a company receives interest income for any of its holdings, you see it in this line item. This category includes notes or bonds that the company holds, such as marketable securities, or interest paid by another company to which it loaned short-term cash.

✔ **Depreciation and amortization expenses:** Depreciation on buildings, machinery, or other items, as well as amortization on intangible items, fall into this line item. You have to look in the notes to the financial statements to find more details on depreciation and amortization.

✔ **Insurance expenses:** In addition to insurance expenses for items such as theft, fire, and other losses, companies usually carry life insurance on their top executives and errors and omissions insurance for their top executives and board members. *Errors and omissions insurance* protects executives and board members from being sued personally for any errors or omissions related to their work for the company or as part of their responsibility on the company's board.

✔ **Taxes:** All corporations — in theory, anyway — have to pay income taxes. In the taxes category, you find the amount the company actually paid in taxes. Many companies and their investors complain that corporate income is taxed twice — once directly as a corporation and a second time on the dividends that the shareholders receive. In reality, many corporations can use so many tax write-offs that their tax bill is zero or near zero.

✔ **Other expenses:** Any expenses that don't fit into one of the earlier line items in this list fall into this category. What goes into this category varies among companies, depending on what each company chooses to show on an individual line item and what it groups in other expenses. However, a firm doesn't include expenses relating to operating activities in this category; those expenses go on the line item for other operating expenses. Companies separate operating expenses from non-operating expenses.

Sorting Out the Profit and Loss Types

When you hear earnings or profits reports on the news, most of the time, the reporters are discussing the net profit, net income, or net loss. For readers of financial statements, that bottom-line number doesn't tell the entire story of how a company is doing. Relying solely on the bottom-line number is like reading the last few pages of a novel and thinking that you understand the entire story. All you really know is the end, not how the characters got to that ending.

Because companies have so many different charges or expenses unique to their operations, different profit lines are used for different types of analysis. This section reviews what each of these profit types includes or doesn't include. For example, gross profit is the best number to use to analyze how well a company is managing its sales and the costs of producing those sales, but gross profit gives you no idea how well the company is managing the rest of its expenses.

Using operating profits, which show you how much money a company made after considering all costs and expenses for operating, you can analyze how efficiently the company is managing its operating activities, but you don't get enough detail to analyze product costs.

EBITDA

A commonly used measure to compare companies is *earnings before interest, taxes, depreciation, and amortization,* also known as EBITDA. With this number, analysts and investors can compare profitability among companies or industries because it eliminates the effects of the companies' activities to raise cash outside their operating activities, such as by selling stock or bonds. EBITDA also eliminates any accounting decisions that may impact the bottom line, such as the companies' policies relating to depreciation methods.

Investors reading the financial report can use this line item to focus on the profitability of each company's operations. If a company does include this line item, it appears at the bottom of the expenses section but before line items listing interest, taxes, depreciation, and amortization.

How a firm chooses to raise money can greatly impact its bottom line. Selling equity has no annual costs if dividends aren't paid. Borrowing money means interest costs must be paid every year, so a company will have ongoing required expenses.

EBITDA gives financial report readers a quick view of how well a company is doing without considering its financial and accounting decisions. This number became popular in the 1980s, when leveraged buyouts were common. A *leveraged buyout* takes place when an individual or company buys a controlling interest (which means more than 50 percent) in a company, primarily using debt (up to 70 percent or more of the purchase price). This fad left many businesses in danger of not earning enough from operations to pay their huge debt load.

Today EBITDA is frequently touted by technology companies or other high-growth companies with large expenses for machinery and other equipment. In these situations, the companies like to discuss their earnings before the huge write-offs for depreciation, which can make the bottom line look pretty small. Be aware that a company can use EBITDA as an accounting gimmick to make earnings sound better to the general public or to investors who don't take the time to read the fine print in the annual report.

Firms can get pretty creative when it comes to their income statement groupings. If you don't understand a line item, be sure to look for explanations in the notes to the financial statements. If you can't find an explanation there, call investor relations and ask questions.

Non-operating income or expense

If a company earns income from a source that isn't part of its normal revenue-generating activities, it usually lists this income on the income statement as *non-operating income*. Items commonly listed here include the sale of a building, manufacturing facility, or company division. Other types of non-operating income include interest from notes receivable and marketable securities, dividends from investments in other companies' stock, and rent revenue (if the business subleases some of its facilities).

Companies also group one-time expenses in the non-operating section of the income statement. For example, the severance and other costs of closing a division or factory appear in this area, or, in some cases, the statement has a separate section on discontinuing operations. Other types of expenses include casualty losses from theft, vandalism, or fire; loss from the sale or abandonment of property, plant, or equipment; and loss from employee or supplier strikes.

You usually find explanations for income or expenses from non-operating activities in the notes to the financial statements. Companies need to separate these non-operating activities; otherwise, investors, analysts, and other interested parties can't gauge how well a company is doing with its core operating activities. The *Core operating activities* line item is where you find a company's continuing income. If those core activities aren't raising enough income, the firm may be on the road to significant financial difficulties.

A major gain may make the bottom line look great, but it can send the wrong signal to outsiders, who may then expect similar earnings results the next year. If the company doesn't repeat the results the following year, Wall Street will surely hammer its stock. A major one-time loss also needs special explanation so that Wall Street doesn't downgrade the stock unnecessarily if the one-time non-operating loss won't be repeated in future years.

Whether a gain or a loss, separating non-operating income from operating income and expenses helps avoid sending the wrong signal to analysts and investors about a company's future earnings and growth potential.

Net profit or loss

The bottom line of any income statement is net profit or loss. This number means little if you don't understand the other line items that make up the income statement. Few investors and analysts look solely at net profit or loss to make a major decision about whether a company is a good investment.

Calculating Earnings per Share

In addition to net income, the other number you hear almost as often about a company's earnings results is earnings per share. *Earnings per share* is the amount of net income the company makes per share of stock available on the market. For example, if you own 100 shares of stock in ABC Company and it earns $1 per share, $100 of those earnings are yours unless the company decides to reinvest the earnings for future growth. In reality, a company rarely pays out 100 percent of its earnings; it usually pays out a small fraction of those earnings.

You find the calculation for earnings per share on the income statement after net income, or in a separate statement called the statement of shareholders' equity. The calculation for earnings per share is relatively simple: You divide the net earnings or net income (which you find on the income statement) by the number of outstanding shares (which you can find on the balance sheet).

Basically, earnings per share shows you how much money each shareholder made for each of her shares. In reality, this money doesn't get paid back to the shareholder. Instead, most is reinvested in future operations of the company. The net income or loss is added to the retained earnings number on the balance sheet.

Any dividends declared per share appear on the income statement under the earnings per share information. You find the amount of dividends paid on the statement of cash flows (covered in Book II Chapter 6). The company's board of directors declares dividends either quarterly or annually.

At the bottom of an income statement, you see two numbers:

- ✔ The *basic earnings per share* is a calculation based on the number of shares outstanding at the time the income statement is developed.

- ✔ The *diluted earnings per share* includes other potential shares that may eventually be outstanding. This category includes shares designated for items like stock options (options companies give to employees to buy shares of stock at a set price, usually lower than the market price), *warrants* (shares of stock companies promise to bondholders or preferred shareholders for additional shares of stock at a set price, usually below the stock's market value), and *convertibles* (shares of stock companies promise to a lender who owns bonds that are convertible to stock).

These numbers give you an idea of how much a company earns per share, which you can use to analyze the company's profitability.

Chapter 6

The Statement of Cash Flows

Cash is a company's lifeblood. If a company expects to manage its assets and liabilities and to pay its obligations, it has to know the amount of cash flowing into and out of the business, which isn't always easy to figure out when using accrual accounting. (You can find out more about accrual accounting in Book I Chapter 1.)

The reason accrual accounting makes it hard to figure out how much cash a company actually holds is that cash doesn't have to change hands for the company to record a transaction. The *statement of cash flows* is the financial statement that helps the financial report reader understand a company's cash position by adjusting for differences between cash and accruals. This statement tracks the cash that flows into and out of a business during a specified period of time and lays out the sources of that cash. This chapter explores the basic parts of the statement of cash flows.

Digging into the Statement of Cash Flows

Basically, a statement of cash flows gives the financial report reader a map of the cash receipts, cash payments, and changes in cash that a company holds, minus the expenses that arise from operating the company. In addition, the statement looks at money that flows into or out of the firm through investing and financing activities. As with the income statement (see Book II Chapter 5), companies provide three years' worth of information on the statement of cash flows.

When reading the statement of cash flows, you need to be looking for answers to these three questions:

- Where did the company get the cash needed for operations during the period shown on the statement — from revenue generated, funds borrowed, or stock sold?

- What cash did the company actually spend during the period shown on the statement?

- What was the change in the cash balance during each of the years shown on the statement?

Knowing the answers to these questions helps you determine whether the company is thriving and has the cash needed to continue to grow its operations or the company appears to have a cash-flow problem and may be nearing a point of fiscal disaster. This section shows you how to use the statement of cash flows to find the answers to these questions.

The parts

Transactions shown on the statement of cash flows are grouped in three parts:

- **Operating activities:** This part includes revenue the company takes in through sales of its products or services and expenses the company pays out to carry out its operations.

- **Investing activities:** This part includes the purchase or sale of the company's investments and can include the purchase or sale of long-term assets, such as a building or a company division. Spending on *capital improvements* (upgrades to assets the company holds, such as the renovation of a building) also fits into this category, as does any buying or selling of short-term invested funds.

- **Financing activities:** This part involves raising cash through long-term debt or by issuing new stock. It also includes using cash to pay down debt or buy back stock. Companies include any dividends paid in this section.

Operating activities is the most important section of the statement of cash flows. In reading this section, you can determine whether the company's operations are generating enough cash to keep the business viable.

The formats

Companies can choose between two different formats when preparing their statement of cash flows. Both arrive at the same total but provide different information to get there:

✔ **Direct method:** The Financial Accounting Standards Board (FASB) prefers the direct method, which groups major classes of cash receipts and cash payments. For example, cash collected from customers is grouped separately from cash received on interest-earning savings accounts or from dividends paid on stock the company owns. Major groups of cash payments include cash paid to buy inventory, cash disbursed to pay salaries, cash paid for taxes, and cash paid to cover interest on loans. Figure 6-1 shows you the direct method.

✔ **Indirect method:** Most companies (90 percent) use the indirect method, which focuses on the differences between net income and net cash flow from operations, and allows firms to reveal less than the direct method, leaving their competitors guessing. The indirect method is easier to prepare. Figure 6-2 shows you the indirect method.

Cash flows from operating activities
Cash received from customers
Cash paid to suppliers and employees
Interest received
Interest paid, net of amounts capitalized
Income tax refund received
Income taxes paid
Other cash received (paid)
Net cash provided by (used in) operating activities

Figure 6-1:
The direct
method.

© John Wiley & Son

The direct and indirect methods differ only in the operating activities section of the report. The investing activities and financing activities sections are the same.

Using the indirect method, you just need the information from two years' worth of balance sheets and income statements to make calculations. For example, you can calculate changes in accounts receivable, inventories, prepaid expenses, current assets, accounts payable, and current liabilities by comparing the totals shown on the balance sheet for the current year and the previous year. If a company shows $1.5 million in inventory in 2014 and

$1 million in 2015, the change in inventory using the indirect method is shown easily: "Decrease in Inventory — $500,000." The statement of cash flows for the indirect method summarizes information already given in a different way, but it doesn't reveal any new information.

Figure 6-2:
The indirect method.

Cash flows from operating activities
Net income (loss)
Adjustments to reconcile net income (loss) to net cash provided by (used in) operating activities:
Depreciation and amortization
Provision for deferred taxes
Decrease (increase) in accounts receivable
Decrease (increase) in inventories
Decrease (increase) in prepaid expenses
Increase (decrease) in accounts payable
Increase (decrease) in other current liabilities
Exchange (gain) loss
Net cash provided by (used in) operating activities

© John Wiley & Son

With the direct method, the company has to reveal the actual cash it receives from customers, the cash it pays to suppliers and employees, and the income tax refund it receives. Someone reading the balance sheet and income statement won't find these numbers in other parts of the financial report.

In addition to having to reveal details about the actual cash received or paid to customers, suppliers, employees, and the government, companies that use the direct method must prepare a schedule similar to one used in the indirect method for operating activities to meet FASB requirements. Essentially, companies save no time, must reveal more detail, and must still present the indirect method. Why bother? You can see why you'll most likely see the indirect method used in the vast majority of financial reports you read.

The investing activities and financing activities sections for both the direct and indirect methods look something like Figures 6-3 and 6-4, both of which show the basic line items. Read on to find out what each of these line items includes. If you're interested in finding out about line items that make their way onto the statement only in special circumstances, see "Recognizing the Special Line Items," later in the chapter.

Figure 6-3:
The investing activities section.

> **Cash flows from investing activities**
> Additions (sale) of property, plant, and equipment
> Investments and acquisitions
> Sales of investments
> Other
> Net cash utilized for investing activities

© John Wiley & Son

Figure 6-4:
The financing activities section.

> **Cash flows from financing activities**
> Proceeds from borrowing
> Net proceeds from repayments
> Purchase or sale of common stock
> Stock option transactions
> Dividends paid
> Net cash provided (utilized) by financing activities
> Cash and short-term investments at beginning of the year
> Cash and short-term investments at end of the year

© John Wiley & Son

Checking Out Operating Activities

The operating activities section is where you find a summary of how much cash flowed into and out of the company during the day-to-day operations of the business.

Operating activities is the most important section of the statement of cash flows. If a company isn't generating enough cash from its operations, it isn't going to be in business long. Although new companies often don't generate a lot of cash in their early years, they can't survive that way for long before going bust.

The primary purpose of the operating activities section is to adjust the net income by adding or subtracting entries that were made in order to abide by the rules of accrual accounting that don't actually require the use of cash. This section describes several of the accounts in the operating activities section of the statement and explain how they're impacted by the changes required to revert accrual accounting entries to actual cash flow.

Finding out the importance of cash the hard way

Dot.com babies certainly discovered the importance of cash on hand the hard way. Many newly minted dot.com companies raised millions of dollars in cash in the late 1990s and were able to stay in business for two or three years. But after these companies could no longer raise money from investors or borrow funds, they went bankrupt. Most dot.com companies died when the investor cash dried up in 2000 because they didn't generate enough money from their operations. In fact, more than 850 dot.com companies bit the dust between January 2000 and January 2002.

Depreciation

A company that buys a lot of new equipment or builds new facilities has high depreciation expenses that lower its net income. This fact is particularly true for many high-tech businesses that must always upgrade their equipment and facilities to keep up with their competitors.

The bottom line may not look good, but all those depreciation expenses don't represent the use of cash. In reality, no cash changes hands to pay depreciation expenses. These expenses are actually added back into the equation when you look at whether the company is generating enough cash from its operations because the company didn't actually lay out cash to pay for these expenses.

For example, if the company's net income is $200,000 for the year and its depreciation expenses are $50,000, the $50,000 is added back in to find the net cash from operations, which totals $250,000. Essentially, the firm is in better shape than it looked to be before the depreciation expenses because of this noncash transaction.

Inventory

Another adjustment on the statement of cash flows that usually adds cash to the mix is a decrease in inventory. If a company's inventory on hand is less in the current year than in the previous year, some of the inventory sold in the current year was purchased in the previous year with last year's cash.

On the other hand, if the company's inventory increases from the previous year, then it spent more money on inventory in the current year, and it subtracts the difference from the net income to find its current cash holdings. For example, if inventory decreases by $10,000, the company adds that amount to net income on the statement of cash flows.

Accounts receivable

Accounts receivable is the summary of accounts of customers who buy their goods or services on direct credit from the company. Customers who buy their goods by using credit cards from banks or other financial institutions aren't included in accounts receivable. Payments by outside credit sources are instead counted as cash because the company receives cash from the bank or financial institution. The bank or financial institution collects from those customers, so the company that sells the good or service doesn't have to worry about collecting the cash.

When accounts receivable increase during the year, the company sells more products or services on credit than it collects in actual cash from customers. In this case, an increase in accounts receivable means a decrease in cash available.

The opposite is true if accounts receivable are lower during the current year than the previous year. In this case, the company collects more cash than it adds credit to customers' credit accounts. In this situation, a decrease in accounts receivable results in more cash received, which adds to the net income.

Accounts payable

Accounts payable is the summary of accounts of bills due that haven't yet been paid, which means the company must still lay out cash in a future accounting period to pay those bills.

When accounts payable increase, a company uses less cash to pay bills in the current year than it did in the previous one, so more cash is on hand. This has a positive effect on the cash situation. Expenses incurred are shown on the income statement, which means net income is lower. But in reality, the company hasn't yet laid out the cash to pay those expenses, so an increase is added to net income to find out how much cash is actually on hand.

Conversely, if accounts payable decrease, the company pays out more cash for this liability. A decrease in accounts payable means the company has less cash on hand, and it subtracts this number from net income.

The cash flow from activities section, summed up

To give you a taste of what all these line items look like in the statement of cash flows, see Table 6-1, which rolls together the information from the previous sections.

Table 6-1	Cash Flows from Operating Activities
Line Item	**Cash Received or Spent**
Net income	$200,000
Depreciation	50,000
Increase in accounts receivable	(20,000)
Decrease in inventories	10,000
Decrease in accounts payable	(10,000)
Net cash provided by (used in) operating activities	$230,000

In Table 6-1, the company has $30,000 more in cash from operations than it reported on the income statement, so the company actually generated more cash than you may have thought if you just looked at net income.

If you compare the statements for the toy companies Mattel and Hasbro in 2012 (you can download them from www.mattel.com and www.hasbro.com), you can see that Mattel's net cash flow totaled $1,276 million after adjustments on $777 million net income, whereas Hasbro's net cash was $535 million on $336 million of net income. For Hasbro, depreciation and amortization adjustments added $100 million to the company's net cash position. Mattel added $157 million to its net cash with depreciation and amortization. Mattel increased accounts payable, accrued liabilities, and income taxes by $312 million to hold on to cash. Hasbro decreased its cash with a $22 million decrease in accrued liabilities and accounts payable. It also used $59 million in cash to pay for production costs.

Investigating Investing Activities

The investment activities section of the statement of cash flows, which looks at the purchase or sale of major new assets, is usually a drainer of cash. Consider what this section typically lists:

- ✔ Purchases of new buildings, land, and major equipment
- ✔ Mergers or acquisitions

> ✔ Major improvements to existing buildings
>
> ✔ Major upgrades to existing factories and equipment
>
> ✔ Purchases of new marketable securities, such as bonds or stock

The sale of buildings, land, major equipment, and marketable securities also appears in the investment activities section. When any of these major assets are sold, they're shown as cash generators rather than as cash drainers.

The primary reason to check out the investments section is to see how the company is managing its *capital expenditures* (money spent to buy or upgrade assets) and how much cash it's using for these expenditures. If the company shows large investments in this area, be sure to look for explanations in the management's discussion and analysis and the notes to the financial statements to get more details about the reasons for the expenditures.

If you believe that the firm is making the right choices to grow the business and improve profits, investing in its stock may be worthwhile. If the company is making most of its capital expenditures to keep old factories operating as long as possible, that may be a sign that it isn't keeping up with new technology.

Compare companies in the same industry to see what type of expenditures each lists in investment activities and the explanations for those expenditures in the notes to the financial statements. Comparing a company with one of its peers helps you determine whether the company is budgeting its capital expenditures wisely.

In comparing the statements of Hasbro and Mattel, you can see that Mattel spent more on purchases of tools, dies, molds, property, plant, and equipment. Mattel's spending totaled more than $219 million, whereas Hasbro spent about $112 million.

Book II

Accounting and Financial Reports

Understanding Financing Activities

Companies can't always raise all the cash they need from their day-to-day operations. Financing activities are another means of generating cash. Any cash raised through activities that don't include day-to-day operations appears in the financing section of the statement of cash flows.

Issuing stock

When a company first sells its shares of stock, it shows the money it raises in the financing section of the statement of cash flows. The first time a company sells shares of stock to the general public, this sale is called an *initial public offering* (IPO; see Book II Chapter 3 for more information). Whenever a company decides to sell additional shares to raise capital, all additional sales of stock are called *secondary public offerings*.

Usually, when companies decide to do a secondary public offering, they do so to raise cash for a specific project or group of projects that they can't fund by ongoing operations. The financial department must determine whether it wants to raise funds for these new projects by borrowing money (new debt) or by issuing stock (new equity). If the company already has a great deal of debt and finds that borrowing more is difficult, it may try to sell additional shares to cover the shortfall.

Buying back stock

Sometimes you see a line item in the financing section indicating that a company has bought back its stock. Most often, companies that announce a stock buyback are trying to accomplish one of two goals:

- ✔ Increase the market price of their stock. (If companies buy back their stock, fewer shares remain on the market, thus raising the value of shares still available for purchase.)

- ✔ Meet internal obligations regarding employee stock options, which guarantee employees the opportunity to buy shares of stock at a price that's usually below the price outsiders must pay for the stock.

Sometimes a company buys back stock with the intention of going private (see Book II Chapter 3 for more). In this case, company executives and the board of directors decide that they no longer want to operate under the watchful eyes of investors and the government. Instead, they prefer to operate under a veil of privacy and not to have to worry about satisfying so many company outsiders.

For many firms, an announcement that they're buying back stock is an indication that they're doing well financially and that the executives believe in their company's growth prospects for the future. Because buybacks reduce the number of outstanding shares, a company can make its per-share numbers look better even though a fundamental change hasn't occurred in the business's operations. It may also indicate that the company believes the market value of its stock to be well below the true value of the company, and therefore this makes an excellent investment for excess cash. In that case, you would also expect to see officers and directors buying the company's shares as well.

If you see a big jump in earnings per share, look for an indication of stock buyback in the financing activities section of the statement of cash flows.

Paying dividends

Whenever a company pays dividends, it shows the amount paid to shareholders in the financing activities section. Companies aren't required to pay dividends each year, but they rarely stop paying dividends after the shareholders have gotten used to their dividend checks.

If a company retrenches on its decision to pay dividends, the market price of the stock is sure to tumble. The company's decision not to pay dividends after paying them in the previous quarter or previous year usually indicates that it's having problems, and it raises a huge red flag on Wall Street.

Book II

Accounting and Financial Reports

Incurring new debt

When a company borrows money for the long term, this new debt also appears in the financing activities section. This type of new debt includes the issuance of bonds, notes, or other forms of long-term financing, such as a mortgage on a building.

When you read the statement of cash flows and see that the company has taken on new debt, be sure to look for explanations in the management's discussion and analysis and the notes to the financial statements about how the company is using this debt.

Paying off debt

Debt payoff is usually a good sign, often indicating that the company is doing well. However, it may also be an indication that the company is simply rolling over existing debt into another type of debt instrument.

If you see that the company paid off one debt and took on another debt that costs about the same amount of money, it likely indicates that the firm simply refinanced the original debt. Ideally, that refinancing involves lowering the company's interest expenses. Look for a full explanation of the debt payoff in the notes to the financial statements.

If you compare the financing activities of Mattel and Hasbro, you see that Mattel paid off long-term debt, bought back stock, and paid dividends to deplete its cash holdings. Hasbro also paid dividends and purchased common stock, but it raised cash by taking on short-term borrowings and collecting cash from stock option transactions. Mattel used $410 million of its cash for its financing activities, while Hasbro used $219 million.

When you look at the financing activities on a statement of cash flows for younger companies, you usually see financing activities that raise capital. Their statements include funds borrowed or stock issued to raise cash. Older, more established companies begin paying off their debt and buying back stock when they've generated enough cash from operations.

Recognizing the Special Line Items

Sometimes you see line items on the statement of cash flows that appear unique to a specific company. Businesses use these line items in special circumstances, such as the discontinuation of operations. Companies that have international operations use a line item that relates to exchanging cash among different countries, which is called *foreign exchange*.

Discontinued operations

If a company *discontinues operations* (stops the activities of a part of its business), you usually see a special line item on the statement of cash flows that shows whether the discontinued operations have increased or decreased the amount of cash the company takes in or distributes. Sometimes discontinued operations increase cash because the firm no longer has to pay the salaries and other costs related to that operation.

Other times, discontinued operations can be a one-time hit to profits because the company has to make significant severance payments to laid-off employees and has to continue paying manufacturing and other fixed costs related to those operations. For example, if a company leases space for the discontinued operations, it's contractually obligated to continue paying for that space until the contract is up or the company finds someone to sublease the space.

Foreign currency exchange

Whenever a company has global operations, it's certain to have some costs related to moving currency from one country to another. The U.S. dollar, as well as currencies from other countries, experiences changes in currency exchange rates — sometimes 100 times a day or more.

Each time the dollar exchange rate between two countries changes, moving currency between those countries can result in a loss or a gain. Any losses or gains related to foreign currency exchanges appear on a special line item on the statement of cash flows called *Effect of currency exchange rate changes on cash*. Both Mattel and Hasbro show the effects of currency exchange on their statements in 2007 — Hasbro's net cash decreased by $1 million, and Mattel's increased by $2 million.

Book II

Accounting and Financial Reports

Adding It All Up

This is the big one, the highlight, the bottom line: *Cash and short-term investments at end of year*. This number shows you how much cash or cash equivalents a company has on hand for continuing operations the next year.

Cash equivalents are any holdings that the company can easily change to cash, such as cash, cash in checking and savings accounts, certificates of deposit that are redeemable in less than 90 days, money-market funds, and stocks sold on the major exchanges that can be easily converted to cash.

The top line of the statement starts with net income. Adjustments are made to show the impact on cash from operations, investing activities, and financing. These adjustments convert that net income figure to actual cash available for continuing operations. Remember that this is the cash on hand that the company can use to continue its activities the next year.

If you look at the statement of cash flows for Mattel and Hasbro, you can see that Mattel had about $1,336 million on hand at the end of December 2012 on net earnings of $777 million. Hasbro had about $850 million in cash and cash equivalents at the end of December 2012 on net earnings of $336 million. Mattel's cash on hand was down slightly from 2011, while Hasbro increased its cash holdings.

Chapter 7

Getting a Financial Report Ready

*T*he previous three chapters cover fundamentals of the three primary financial statements of a business. To review briefly:

✔ **Balance sheet:** Summarizes financial condition consisting of amounts for assets, liabilities, and owners' equity at the closing date of the income statement period, and at other times as needed by managers. (Its formal name is the *statement of financial condition*, or *statement of financial position*.) Covered in Book II Chapter 4.

✔ **Income statement:** Summarizes sales revenue and other income (if any) and expenses and losses (if any) for the period. It ends with the bottom-line profit for the period, which most commonly is called *net income* or *net earnings*. (Inside a business a profit performance statement is commonly called the *Profit & Loss,* or *P&L* report.) Covered in Book II Chapter 5.

✔ **Statement of cash flows:** Reports the net cash increase or decrease during the period from the profit-making activities reported in the income statement and the reasons why this key figure is different than bottom-line net income for the period. It also summarizes sources and uses of cash during the period from investing and financing activities. Covered in Book II Chapter 6.

These three statements, plus footnotes to the financials and other content, are packaged into an annual financial report that is distributed to the company's investors and lenders, so they can keep tabs on the business's financial health and performance. Abbreviated versions of their annual reports are distributed quarterly by public companies, as required by federal securities laws. Private companies do not have to provide interim financial reports, though many do. This chapter shines a light on the process of preparing the annual financial report so you can recognize key decisions that must be made before a financial report hits the streets.

Recognizing Top Management's Role

The annual financial report of a business consists of:

- ✔ The three basic financial statements: *income statement*, *balance sheet*, and *statement of cash flows*. This troika of financial statements constitutes the hard core of a financial report. Every financial report should include these three financial statements (well, unless and until different rules are adopted for private companies and owner/managed small businesses).

- ✔ Maybe a *statement of changes in stockholders' (owners') equity*. This statement is not needed when the only changes in the owner's equity during the year are earning profit and paying distributions from profit to owners (these two important items of information are disclosed in the income statement and the statement of cash flows). If there are additional happenings during the year affecting owners' equity, a statement of changes in owners' equity is prepared. This chapter probes into this supplement to the three primary financial statements of a business. (See "Statement of Changes in Owners' Equity" at the end of the chapter.)

- ✔ Additional content, such as photographs of executives, vision statements, highlights of key financial performance measures, letters to stockholders from top management, and more. Public companies provide considerably more additional content than private companies. Much of the additional content falls outside the realm of generally accepted accounting principles and to a large extent is at the discretion of the business.

The business's CEO assisted by his or her top lieutenants play an essential role in the preparation of the financial reports of the company — which they (and outside investors and lenders) should understand. The CEO does (or should) perform certain critical steps before a financial report of the company is released to the outside world:

1. **Confers with the company's chief financial officer and controller (chief accountant) to make sure that the latest accounting and financial reporting standards and requirements have been applied in its financial report.** (A smaller business may consult with a CPA on these matters.) In recent years, we've seen a high degree of flux in accounting and financial reporting standards and requirements. The U.S. and

international rule-making bodies as well as the U.S. federal regulatory agency, the Securities and Exchange Commission (SEC), have been busy to say the least. The movement toward international standards has faced strong headwinds but still is pushing ahead. Furthermore, the initiatives for establishing separate standards for private companies and for small owner-managed businesses have gotten off the ground.

A business and its independent CPA auditors cannot simply assume that the accounting methods and financial reporting practices that have been used for many years are still correct and adequate. A business *must* check carefully whether it is in full compliance with current accounting standards and financial reporting requirements.

2. **Carefully reviews the disclosures to be made in the financial report.** The CEO and financial officers of the business should make sure that the *disclosures* — all information other than the financial statements — are adequate according to financial reporting standards, and that all the disclosure elements are truthful but at the same time, not unnecessarily damaging to the business. Ideally, the disclosures should be written in clear language. Many disclosures seem almost deliberately difficult to read.

This disclosure review can be compared with the concept of *due diligence,* which is done to make certain that all relevant information is collected, that the information is accurate and reliable, and that all relevant requirements and regulations are being complied with. This step is especially important for public corporations whose securities (stock shares and debt instruments) are traded on securities exchanges. Public businesses fall under the jurisdiction of federal securities laws, which require technical and detailed filings with the SEC.

3. **Considers whether the financial statement numbers need *touching up*.** The idea here is to smooth the jagged edges of the company's year-to-year profit gyrations or to improve the business's short-term solvency picture. Although this can be described as putting your thumb on the scale, you can also argue that sometimes the scale is a little out of balance to begin with, and the CEO should approve adjusting the numbers in the financial statements in order to make them jibe better with the normal circumstances of the business.

The third step is a gray area that accountants don't much like to talk about. These topics are rather delicate. Nevertheless, in the "real world" of business, top-level managers have to strike a balance between the interests of their business on the one hand and the interests of its owners (investors) and creditors on the other. For a rough comparison, think of the advertising done by a business. Advertising should be truthful, but businesses have a lot of leeway regarding how to advertise their products, and much advertising uses a lot of hyperbole. Managers exercise the same freedoms in putting together their financial reports. Financial reports may have some hype, and managers may put as much positive spin on bad news as possible without making deceitful and deliberately misleading comments.

Book II

Accounting and Financial Reports

Reviewing the Purposes of Financial Reporting

Business managers, creditors, and investors read financial reports because these reports provide information regarding how the business is doing and where it stands financially. If you read financial information on websites, such as Yahoo! Finance, for instance, keep in mind that the information comes from the financial reports issued by the business. The top-level managers of a business, in reviewing the annual financial report before releasing it outside the business, should keep in mind that a financial report is designed to answer certain basic financial questions:

- ✔ Is the business making a profit or suffering a loss, and how much?
- ✔ How do assets stack up against liabilities?
- ✔ Where did the business get its capital, and is it making good use of the money?
- ✔ What is the cash flow from the profit or loss for the period?
- ✔ Did the business reinvest all its profit or distribute some of the profit to owners?
- ✔ Does the business have enough capital for future growth?

People should read a financial report like a road map — to point the way and check how the trip is going. Managing and putting money in a business is a financial journey. A manager is like the driver and must pay attention to all the road signs; investors and lenders are like the passengers who watch the same road signs. Some of the most important road signs are the ratios between sales revenue and expenses and their related assets and liabilities in the balance sheet.

In short, the purpose of financial reporting is to deliver important information to the lenders and shareowners of the business — information they need and are entitled to receive. Financial reporting is part of the essential contract between a business and its lenders and investors. Although lawyers may not like this, the contract can be stated in a few words:

> *Give us your money, and we'll give you the information you need to know regarding how we're doing with your money.*

Financial reporting is governed by statutory and common law, and it should abide by ethical standards. Unfortunately, financial reporting sometimes falls short of both legal and ethical standards.

Businesses assume that the readers of the financial statements and other information in their financial reports are knowledgeable about business and finance in general, and understand basic accounting terminology and measurement methods. Financial reporting practices, in other words, take a lot for granted about readers of financial reports.

Keeping Current with Accounting and Financial Reporting Standards

Standards and regulatory requirements for accounting and financial reporting don't stand still. For many years, changes in accounting and financial reporting standards moved like glaciers — slowly and not too far. But just like the climate, the activity of the accounting and financial reporting authorities has warmed up. It's hard to keep up with the changes.

Without a doubt, the rash of accounting and financial reporting scandals over the period 1980–2000 (and continuing to a lesser degree) was one reason for the step-up in activity by the standard setters. The Enron accounting fraud brought down a major international CPA firm (Arthur Andersen) and led to passage of the Sarbanes-Oxley Act of 2002, and its demanding requirements on public companies for establishing and reporting on internal controls to prevent financial reporting fraud. Furthermore, CPA auditors have come under increasing pressure to do better audits, especially by the Public Company Accounting Oversight Board, which is an arm of the Securities and Exchange Commission (SEC).

The other reason for the heightened pace of activity by the standard setters is the increasing complexity of doing business. When you look at how business is being conducted these days, you find more and more complexity — for example, the use of financial derivative contracts and instruments. It's difficult to put definite gain and loss values on these financial devices before the final day of reckoning (when the contracts terminate). The legal exposure of businesses has expanded, especially in respect to environmental laws and regulations.

The standard setters should be given credit for their attempts to deal with the problems that have emerged in recent decades and for trying to prevent repetition of the accounting scandals of the past. But the price of doing so has been a rather steep increase in the range and rapidity of changes in accounting and financial reporting standards and requirements. Top-level managers of businesses have to make sure that the financial and accounting officers of the business are keeping up with these changes and make sure that their financial reports follow all current rules and regulations. Managers lean heavily on their chief financial officers and controllers for keeping in full compliance with accounting and financial reporting standards.

It's too early to tell what will happen regarding financial reporting and accounting standards for private companies and for owner-managed small and medium size businesses. The recent establishment of the Private Companies Council (PCC) to recommend standards for private companies has just gotten off the ground at the time of revising this book. The first two alternatives to US GAAP for privately held companies were issued by the FASB on January 16, 2014, due to recommendations from the PCC.

Making Sure Disclosure Is Adequate

The financial statements are the backbone of a financial report. In fact, a financial report is not deserving of the name if financial statements are not included. But a financial report is much more than just the financial statements; a financial report needs *disclosures*. Of course, the financial statements themselves provide disclosure of important financial information about the business. The term disclosures, however, usually refers to *additional* information provided in a financial report.

The CEO of a public corporation, the president of a private corporation, or the managing partner of a partnership has the primary responsibility to make sure that the financial statements have been prepared according to applicable accounting and reporting standards and that the financial report provides adequate disclosure. He or she works with the chief financial officer and controller of the business to make sure that the financial report meets the standard of adequate disclosure. (Many smaller businesses hire an independent CPA to advise them on their financial reports.)

For a quick survey of disclosures in financial reports, the following distinctions are helpful:

✔ Footnotes provide additional information about the figures included in the financial statements. Virtually all financial statements need footnotes to provide additional information for several of the items included in the three financial statements.

✔ Supplementary financial schedules and tables to the financial statements provide more details than can be included in the body of financial statements.

✔ A wide variety of other information is presented, some of which is required if the business is a public corporation subject to federal regulations regarding financial reporting to its stockholders. Other information is voluntary and not strictly required legally or by financial reporting standards that apply to the business.

Footnotes: Nettlesome but needed

Footnotes are attached to the three primary financial statements, and are usually placed at the end of the financial statements. Within the financial statements, you see references to particular footnotes. And at the bottom of each financial statement, you find the following sentence (or words to this effect): "The footnotes are integral to the financial statements." You should read all footnotes for a full understanding of the financial statements, although some footnotes are dense and technical. For one exercise, try reading a footnote that explains how a public corporation puts the value on its management stock options in order to record the expense for this component of management compensation. Then take two aspirin to get rid of your headache.

Footnotes come in two types:

Book II

Accounting and Financial Reports

✔ One or more footnotes are included to identify the major accounting policies and methods that the business uses. (Book II Chapter 8 explains that a business must choose among alternative accounting methods for recording revenue and expenses, and for their corresponding assets and liabilities.) The business must reveal which accounting methods it uses for booking its revenue and expenses. In particular, the business must identify its cost of goods sold and depreciation expense methods. Some businesses have unusual problems regarding the timing for recording sales revenue, and a footnote should clarify their revenue recognition method. Other accounting methods that have a material impact on the financial statements are disclosed in footnotes as well.

✔ Other footnotes provide additional information and details for many assets and liabilities. For example, a business may owe money on many short-term and longer-term debt issues; a footnote presents a schedule of maturity dates and interest rates of the debt issues. Details about stock option plans for executives are the main type of footnote for the capital stock account in the stockholders' equity section of the balance sheet of corporations.

Some footnotes are always required; a financial report would be naked without them. Deciding whether a footnote is needed (after you get beyond the obvious ones disclosing the business's accounting methods) and how to write the footnote is largely a matter of judgment and opinion. The general benchmark is whether footnote information is relevant or not to the investors and creditors of the business. But how relevant? This is the key question. For public companies, keep in mind that the SEC lays down very specific requirements regarding disclosures in the quarterly and annual filings with it.

One problem that most investors face when reading footnotes — and, for that matter, many managers who should understand their own footnotes but find them a little dense — is that footnotes often deal with complex issues (such as lawsuits) and rather technical accounting matters. Here is one footnote that highlights the latter point. The footnote in the 2011 10-K annual report of Caterpillar, Inc., filed with the SEC describing its post-employment benefit plans, runs 11 pages (pages A42-A52). If you are snowbound some evening and have an Internet connection, you might Google this and read your way through this footnote. Actually, it's not that technical, but keeping all the pieces together in your head is very challenging. Caterpillar's post-employment benefit plans footnote is just one of its many footnotes.

For your reading pleasure, here's footnote D in Caterpillar's 2011 annual 10-K report filed with the SEC (page A-12):

> **D. Inventories:** *Inventories are stated at the lower of cost or market. Cost is principally determined using the last-in, first-out (LIFO) method. The value of inventories on the LIFO basis represented about 65% of total inventories at December 31, 2011, and about 70% of total inventories at December 31, 2010 and 2009.*
>
> *If the FIFO (first-in, first-out) method had been in use, inventories would have been $2,422 million, $2,575 million and $3,022 million higher than reported at December 31, 2011, 2010, and 2009, respectively.*

Yes, these dollar amounts are in *millions* of dollars. Caterpillar's inventory cost value for its inventories at the end of 2011 would have been $2,422 million higher if the FIFO accounting method had been used. Of course, it helps to have a basic understanding of the difference between the two accounting methods — LIFO and FIFO — to make sense of this note (see Book II Chapter 8).

You may wonder how different Caterpillar's annual profits would have been if the FIFO cost of goods sold expense accounting method had been in use. A business's managers can ask its accounting department to do this analysis. But as an outside investor, you would have to compute these amounts yourself (assuming you had all the necessary information). Businesses disclose their accounting methods, but they do not disclose how different annual profits would have been if alternative methods had been used.

Other disclosures in financial reports

The following discussion includes a fairly comprehensive list of the various types of disclosures (in addition to footnotes) found in annual financial reports of publicly owned businesses. A few caveats are in order. First, not every public corporation includes every one of the following items, although the disclosures are fairly common. Second, the level of disclosure by private businesses — after you get beyond the financial statements and footnotes — is generally much less than in public corporations. Third, tracking the actual disclosure practices of private businesses is difficult because their annual financial reports are circulated only to their owners and lenders. (A private business keeps its financial report as private as possible, in other words.) A private business may include one or more of the following disclosures, but by and large it is not required to do so (and, in my experience, few do).

In addition to the three financial statements and footnotes to the financials, public corporations typically include the following disclosures in their annual financial reports to their stockholders:

- **Cover (or transmittal) letter:** A letter from the chief executive of the business to the stockholders, which usually takes credit for good news and blames bad news on big government, unfavorable world political developments, a poor economy, or something else beyond management's control.

- **Management's report on internal control over financial reporting:** An assertion by the chief executive officer and chief financial officer regarding their satisfaction with the effectiveness of the internal controls of the business, which are designed to ensure the reliability of its financial reports and to prevent financial and accounting fraud.

- **Highlights table:** A table that presents key figures from the financial statements, such as sales revenue, total assets, profit, total debt, owners' equity, number of employees, and number of units sold (such as the number of vehicles sold by an automobile manufacturer, or the number of "revenue seat miles" flown by an airline, meaning one airplane seat occupied by a paying customer for one mile). The idea is to give the stockholder a financial thumbnail sketch of the business.

Book II

Accounting and Financial Reports

Warren Buffett's annual letter to Berkshire Hathaway shareholders

Warren Buffet's annual letter is one notable exception to the generally self-serving and slanted letter from a business's chief executive officer to its stockholders, which you'll find in most annual financial reports. Warren Buffett is the Chairman of the Board of Berkshire Hathaway, Inc. He has become very well known and is called the "Oracle of Omaha." Mr. Buffett's letters are the epitome of telling it like it is; they are frank, sometimes with brutal honesty, and quite humorous in places. You can go the website of the company (www.berkshirehathaway.com) and download his most recent letter (and earlier ones if you like). You'll learn a lot about his investing philosophy, and the letters are a delight to read even though they're relatively long (20+ pages usually). By the way, the traditional-class shares of Berkshire Hathaway (BRKA) is the most expensive stock listed on the New York Stock Exchange. At the time of this writing (May 2015) a single share cost $219,550.

- **Management discussion and analysis (MD&A):** Deals with the major developments and changes during the year that affected the financial performance and situation of the business. The SEC requires this disclosure to be included in the annual financial reports of publicly owned corporations.

- **Segment information:** A report of the sales revenue and operating profits (before interest and income tax, and perhaps before certain costs that cannot be allocated among different segments) for the major divisions of the organization, or for its different markets (international versus domestic, for example).

- **Historical summaries:** A financial history that extends back three years or longer that includes information from past financial statements.

- **Graphics:** Bar charts, trend charts, and pie charts representing financial conditions; photos of key people and products.

- **Promotional material:** Information about the company, its products, its employees, and its managers, often stressing an overarching theme for the year. Most companies use their annual financial report as an advertising or PR (public relations) opportunity.

- **Profiles:** Information about members of top management and the board of directors. Of course, everyone appears to be well qualified for his or her position. Negative information (such as prior brushes with the law) is not reported. One interesting development in recent years has been that several high level executives have lied about their academic degrees.

- **Quarterly summaries of profit performance and stock share prices:** Shows financial performance for all four quarters in the year and stock price ranges for each quarter (required by the SEC for public companies).

- **Management's responsibility statement:** A short statement indicating that management has primary responsibility for the accounting methods used to prepare the financial statements, for writing the footnotes to the statements, and for providing the other disclosures in the financial report. Usually, this statement appears near the independent CPA auditor's report.

- **Independent auditor's report:** The report from the CPA firm that performed the audit, expressing an opinion on the fairness of the financial statements and accompanying disclosures. Public corporations are required to have audits; private businesses may or may not have their annual financial reports audited. Unfortunately, the wording of audit reports has become more and more difficult to understand. The standards that govern CPA audit reports have mimicked the trend of accounting and financial reporting standards. Audit reports used to be three paragraphs that you could understand with careful reading. Not anymore.

✔ **Company contact information:** Information on how to contact the company, the website address of the company, how to get copies of the reports filed with the SEC, the stock transfer agent and registrar of the company, and other information. Actually, you can take a short cut: Use a web browser such as Google, Safari, or Yahoo!, and simply type in a brief search name for the company you want to find. Your browser calls up the websites for the company.

✔ **No humor allowed:** Annual financial reports have virtually no humor — no cartoons, no one-liners, and no jokes. (Well, the CEO's letter to shareowners may have some humorous comments, even when the CEO doesn't mean to be funny.) Financial reports are written in a somber and serious vein. Maybe companies should lighten up a little. The tone of most annual financial reports is that the fate of the Western world depends on the financial performance of the company. It probably doesn't.

Managers of public corporations rely on lawyers, CPA auditors, and their financial and accounting officers to make sure that everything that should be disclosed in the business's annual financial reports is included, and that the exact wording of the disclosures is not misleading, inaccurate, or incomplete. This is a tall order.

Both federal and state laws, as well as authoritative accounting standards, have to be observed in financial report disclosures. Inadequate disclosure is just as serious as using wrong accounting methods for measuring profit and for determining values for assets, liabilities, and owners' equity. A financial report can be misleading because of improper accounting methods or because of inadequate or misleading disclosure. Both types of deficiencies can lead to nasty lawsuits against the business and its managers.

Putting a Spin on the Numbers (Short of Cooking the Books)

This section discusses two accounting tricks that involve manipulating, or "massaging," the accounting numbers. No endorsement is implied here, but you should be aware of both. In some situations, the financial statement numbers don't come out exactly the way the business prefers. With the connivance of top management, accountants can use certain tricks of the trade — some would say sleight of hand, or shenanigans — to move the numbers closer to what the business prefers. One trick improves the appearance of the *short-term solvency* of the business and the cash balance reported in its balance sheet at the end of the year. The other device shifts some profit from one year to the next to report a smoother trend of net income from year to year.

Not all businesses engage in these accounting machinations — but many do. The extent of use of these unholy schemes is hard to pin down because no business would openly admit to using them. The evidence is convincing, however, that many businesses massage their numbers to some degree. You've probably heard the term *loopholes* applied to income tax. Well, some loopholes exist in financial statement accounting as well.

Window dressing for fluffing up the cash balance and cash flow

Suppose you manage a business and your controller has just submitted for your review the *preliminary,* or first draft, of the year-end balance sheet. Figure 7-1 shows the current assets and current liabilities sections of the balance sheet draft, which is all you need here.

Figure 7-1:
Current assets and current liabilities of a business, before window dressing.

Cash	$0	Accounts payable	$235,000
Accounts receivable	$486,000	Accrued expenses payable	$187,000
Inventory	$844,000	Income tax payable	$58,000
Prepaid expenses	$72,000	Short-term notes payable	$200,000
Current assets	$1,402,000	Current liabilities	$680,000

© John Wiley & Son

Wait — a zero cash balance? How can that be? Maybe your business has been having some cash flow problems and you've intended to increase your short-term borrowing and speed up collection of accounts receivable to help the cash balance. Folks generally don't like to see a zero cash balance — it makes them kind of nervous, to put it mildly, no matter how you try to cushion it. So what do you do to avoid setting off alarm bells?

Your controller is probably aware of a technique called *window dressing,* a very simple method for making the cash balance look better. Suppose your fiscal year-end is October 31. Your controller takes the cash collections from customers paying their accounts receivable that are actually received on November 1, 2, 3, and 4 and records these four days of cash receipts as if these cash collections had been received on October 31. After all, the argument can be made that the customers' checks were in the mail — that money is yours, as far as the customers are concerned.

Window dressing reduces the amount in accounts receivable and increases the amount in cash the same amount — it has no effect on your profit figure for the period. It makes your cash balance look a touch better. Window dressing can also be used to improve other accounts' balances. All of these techniques involve holding the books open — to record certain events that take place after the end of the fiscal year (the ending balance sheet date) to make things look better than they actually were at the close of business on the last day of the year.

Sounds like everybody wins, doesn't it? You look like you've done a better job as manager, and your lenders and investors don't panic. Right? Wrong! Window dressing is deceptive to your creditors and investors, who have every right to expect that the end of your fiscal year as stated on your financial reports is truly the end of your fiscal year.

Window dressing can be a dangerous game to play. Window dressing could be the first step on a slippery slope. A little window dressing today, and tomorrow, who knows — maybe giving the numbers a nudge now will lead to more serious accounting deceptions, or even out-and-out accounting fraud. Moreover, when a business commits some accounting hanky-panky, should the chief executive of the business brief its directors on the accounting manipulation? Things get messy, to say the least!

Also, be aware that window dressing improves cash flow from operating activities, which is an important number in the statement of cash flows that creditors and investors closely watch. Suppose, for example, that a business holds open its cash receipts journal for several days after the close of its fiscal year. The result is that its ending cash balance is reported $3.25 million higher than the business actually had in its checking accounts on the balance sheet date. Also, its accounts receivable balance is reported $3.25 million lower than was true at the end of its fiscal year. This makes cash flow from profit (operating activities) $3.25 million higher, which could be the reason in the decision to do some window dressing.

Sanding the rough edges off the year-to-year profit numbers

Business managers are under tremendous pressure to make profit every year and to keep profit on the up escalator year after year. Managers strive to make their numbers and to hit the milestone markers set for the business. Reporting a loss for the year, or even a dip below the profit trend line, is a red flag that stock analysts and investors view with alarm. Everyone likes to see a steady upward trend line for profit; no one likes to see a profit curve that looks like a roller coaster. Most investors want a smooth journey and don't like putting on their investment life preservers.

Managers can do certain things to deflate or inflate profit (net income) recorded in the year, which are referred to as *profit smoothing* techniques. Other names for these techniques are *income smoothing* and *earnings management*. Profit smoothing is like a white lie told for the good of the business and perhaps for the good of managers as well. Managers know that there is always some noise in the accounting system. Profit smoothing muffles the noise.

The general view in the financial community is that profit smoothing is not nearly as serious as *cooking the books,* or *juggling the books.* These terms refer to deliberate, fraudulent accounting practices such as recording sales revenue that has not happened or not recording expenses that have happened. Nevertheless, profit smoothing is still serious and if carried too far could be interpreted as accounting fraud. Managers have gone to jail for fraudulent financial statements.

Theoretically, having an audit by a CPA firm should root out any significant accounting fraud when the business is knowingly perpetrating the fraud or when it is an innocent victim of fraud against the business. But, in fact, there continue to be many embarrassing cases in which the CPA auditor failed to discover major fraud by or against the business. Several books have been published on this topic, which you can find by using the search words "accounting fraud" or "cooking the books" in your search engine. Check out *Forensic Accounting For Dummies* (John Wiley & Sons, 2011) by Frimette Kass-Shraibman and Vijay S. Sampath.

The pressure on public companies

Managers of publicly owned corporations whose stock shares are actively traded are under intense pressure to keep profits steadily rising. Security analysts who follow a particular company make profit forecasts for the business, and their buy-hold-sell recommendations are based largely on these earnings forecasts. If a business fails to meet its own profit forecast or falls short of stock analysts' forecasts, the market price of its stock shares usually takes a hit. Stock option and bonus incentive compensation plans are also strong motivations for achieving the profit goals set for the business.

The evidence is fairly strong that publicly owned businesses engage in some degree of profit smoothing. Frankly, it's much harder to know whether private businesses do so. Private businesses don't face the public scrutiny and expectations that public corporations do. On the other hand, key managers in a private business may have bonus arrangements that depend on recorded profit. In any case, business investors and managers should know about profit smoothing and how it's done.

Compensatory effects

Most profit smoothing involves pushing some amount of revenue and/
or expenses into years other than those in which they would normally be
recorded. For example, if the president of a business wants to report more
profit for the year, he or she can instruct the chief accountant to accelerate
the recording of some sales revenue that normally wouldn't be recorded until
next year, or to delay the recording of some expenses until next year that
normally would be recorded this year.

Book II Chapter 8 explains that managers choose among alternative accounting methods for several important expenses (and for revenue as well). After
making these key choices, the managers should let the accountants do their
jobs and let the chips fall where they may. If bottom-line profit for the year
turns out to be a little short of the forecast or target for the period, so be it.
This hands-off approach to profit accounting is the ideal way. However,
managers often use a hands-on approach — they intercede (one could say
interfere) and override the normal methods for recording sales revenue or
expenses.

Book II

**Accounting
and Financial
Reports**

Both managers who do profit smoothing and investors who rely on financial
statements in which profit smoothing has been done must understand one
thing: These techniques have robbing-Peter-to-pay-Paul effects. Accountants
refer to these as *compensatory effects.* The effects next year offset and cancel
out the effects this year. Less expense this year is counterbalanced by more
expense next year. Sales revenue recorded this year means less sales revenue recorded next year. Of course, the compensatory effects work the other
way as well: If a business depresses its current year's recorded profit, its
profit next year benefits. In short, a certain amount of profit can be brought
forward into the current year or delayed until the following year.

Two profit histories

Figure 7-2 shows, side by side, the annual profit histories of two businesses
over six years. Steady Flow, Inc. shows a nice smooth upward trend of profit.
Bumpy Ride, Inc., in contrast, shows a zigzag ride over the six years. Both
businesses earned the same total profit for the six years combined — in this
case, $1,050,449. Their total six-year profit performance is the same, down to
the last dollar. Which company would you be more willing to risk your money
in? You'd prefer Steady Flow, Inc. because of the nice and steady upward
slope of its profit history.

Figure 7-2 is not really for two different companies — actually, the two different profit figures for each year are for the same company. The year-by-
year profits shown for Steady Flow, Inc. are the company's *smoothed* profit
amounts for each year, and the annual profits for Bumpy Ride, Inc. are the
actual profits of the same business — the annual profits that were recorded
before smoothing techniques were applied.

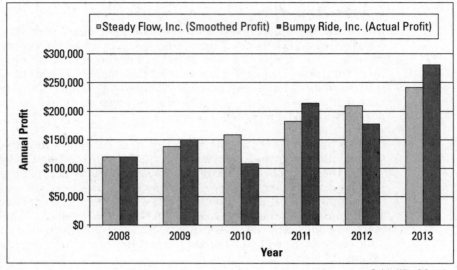

Figure 7-2: Comparison of smoothed and actual profit histories.

For the first year in the series, 2008, no profit smoothing occurred. The two profit numbers are the same; there was no need for smoothing. For each of the next five years, the two profit numbers differ. The difference between actual profit and smoothed profit for the year is the amount that revenue and/or expenses had to be manipulated for the year. For example, in 2009 actual profit would have been a little too high, so the company accelerated the recording of some expenses that should not have been recorded until the following year (2010); it booked those expenses in 2009. In contrast, in 2012, actual profit was running below the target net income for the year, so the business put off recording some expenses until 2013 to make 2012's profit look better. Does all this make you a little uncomfortable? It should.

A business can go only so far in smoothing profit. If a business has a particularly bad year, all the profit-smoothing tricks in the world won't close the gap. And if managers are used to profit smoothing, they may be tempted in this situation to resort to accounting fraud, or cooking the books.

Management discretion in the timing of revenue and expenses

Several smoothing techniques are available for filling the potholes and straightening the curves on the profit highway. Most profit-smoothing techniques require one essential ingredient — management discretion in deciding *when* to record expenses or *when* to record sales.

A common technique for profit smoothing is to delay normal maintenance and repairs, called *deferred maintenance*. Many routine and recurring maintenance costs required for autos, trucks, machines, equipment, and buildings can be put off, or deferred, until later. These costs are not recorded to expense until the actual maintenance is done, so putting off the work means recording the expense is delayed.

Here are a few other techniques used:

✔ A business that spends a fair amount of money for employee training and development may delay these programs until next year so the expense this year is lower.

✔ A company can cut back on its current year's outlays for market research and product development (though this could have serious long-term effects).

✔ A business can ease up on its rules regarding when slow-paying customers are written off to expense as *bad debts* (uncollectible accounts receivable). The business can, therefore, put off recording some of its bad debts expense until next year.

✔ A fixed asset out of active use may have very little or no future value to a business. But instead of writing off the undepreciated cost of the *impaired asset* as a loss this year, the business may delay the write-off until next year.

Keep in mind that most of these costs will be recorded next year, so the effect is to rob Peter (make next year absorb the cost) to pay Paul (let this year escape the cost).

Book II

Accounting and Financial Reports

Financial reporting on the Internet

Most public companies put their financial reports on their websites. For example, you can go to www.cat.com and navigate to Caterpillar's investors' section, where you can locate its SEC filings and its annual report to stockholders. Each company's website is a little different, but usually you can figure out fairly easily how to download its annual and quarterly financial reports.

Alternatively, you can go to the Securities and Exchange Commission website at www.sec.gov. Most public companies make many filings with the SEC, so you have to know which one(s) you want to see. (The annual financial report is form 10-K.) Most company websites take you to their SEC filings with a quick click.

Clearly, managers have a fair amount of discretion over the timing of some expenses, so certain expenses can be accelerated into this year or deferred to next year in order to make for a smoother year-to-year profit trend. But a business does not divulge in its external financial report the extent to which it has engaged in profit smoothing. Nor does the independent auditor comment on the use of profit-smoothing techniques by the business — unless the auditor thinks that the company has gone too far in massaging the numbers and that its financial statements are downright misleading.

Going Public or Keeping Things Private

Suppose you had the inclination (and the time) to compare 100 annual financial reports of publicly owned corporations with 100 annual reports of privately owned businesses (assuming you could assemble 100 private company financial reports). You'd see many differences. Public companies are generally much larger (in terms of annual sales and total assets) than private companies, as you would expect. Furthermore, public companies generally are more complex — concerning employee compensation, financing instruments, multinational operations, federal laws that impact big business, legal exposure, and so on.

At the time of writing, private and public businesses are bound by the same accounting rules for measuring profit and for valuing assets, liabilities, and owners' equity, and for disclosures in their financial reports. (To be more precise, private companies are exempt from a couple of accounting rules but let's not go there.) Many of the accounting and financial reporting standards that have been issued over the last three decades are directed mainly to issues that have come up with public companies; by and large, private companies do not have these accounting issues. As discussed in Book I Chapter 7, the accounting profession has taken initiatives with the goal of recognizing the different information needs from private companies and the different characteristics of the constituents of private companies. The main purpose is to lighten the accounting and financial reporting burden on private companies, which generally don't have the time or the accounting expertise to comply with the large number of complex standards on the books.

Reports from publicly owned companies

Around 10,000 corporations in the United States are publicly owned, and their stock shares are traded on the New York Stock Exchange, NASDAQ, or other electronic stock markets. Publicly owned companies must file annual financial reports with the SEC — the federal agency that makes and enforces the rules for trading in securities (stocks and bonds). These filings are available to the public on the SEC's huge database (see the sidebar "Financial reporting on the Internet").

The annual financial reports of publicly owned corporations include most of the disclosure items I list earlier in the chapter (see the section "Making Sure Disclosure Is Adequate"). As a result, annual reports published by large publicly owned corporations run 30, 40, or 50 pages (or more). As mentioned, the large majority of public companies make their annual reports available on their websites. Many public companies also present condensed versions of their financial reports — see the section "Recognizing condensed versions" later in this chapter.

Annual reports from public companies generally are very well done — the quality of the editorial work and graphics is excellent; the color scheme, layout, and design have good eye appeal. But be warned that the volume of detail in their financial reports is overwhelming. (See the next section for advice on dealing with the information overload in annual financial reports.)

Publicly owned businesses live in a fish bowl. When a company goes public with an *IPO* (initial public offering of stock shares), it gives up a lot of the privacy that a closely held business enjoys. A public company is required to have its annual financial report audited by an independent CPA firm. In doing an audit, the CPA passes judgment on the company's accounting methods and adequacy of disclosure. The CPA auditor has a heavy responsibility to evaluate the client's internal controls to prevent financial reporting fraud.

Reports from private businesses

Compared with their public brothers and sisters, private businesses generally issue less impressive annual financial reports. Their primary financial statements with the accompanying footnotes are pretty much it for most small private businesses. Often, their financial reports may be printed on plain paper and stapled together. A privately held company may have few stockholders, and typically one or more of the stockholders are active managers of the business, who already know a great deal about the business.

Investors in private businesses have one potential advantage compared with public companies. They can request confidential information from managers at the annual stockholders' meetings (which is not practical for a stockholder in a large public corporation). The annual stockholders meeting of a private business is not open to the public, so information can be kept private. Also, major lenders to a private business can demand that certain items of information be disclosed to them on a confidential basis as a condition of the loan.

Up to the present time there has been one set of accounting and financial reporting standards for all businesses, large and small, public and private. However, the blunt truth of the matter is that smaller private companies do not comply fully with all the disclosure requirements that public companies have to comply with. The business and financial communities at large have accepted the "sub par" financial reporting practices of smaller private businesses. Perhaps the recently established Private Company Council (see Book I Chapter 7) will recommend adopting less demanding disclosure rules by private companies. Or, they might leave well enough alone.

A private business may have its financial statements audited by a CPA firm but generally is not required by law to do so. Frankly, CPA auditors cut private businesses a lot of slack regarding disclosure. The stock share market prices of public corporations are extremely important, and full disclosure of information should be made publicly available so that market prices are fairly determined. On the other hand, you could argue that the ownership shares of privately owned businesses are not traded, so there's no urgent need for a complete package of information.

Dealing with Information Overload

As a general rule, the larger a business, the longer its annual financial report. Some financial reports of small, privately owned businesses can be read in 30 minutes to an hour. In contrast, the annual reports of large, publicly owned business corporations are typically 30, 40, or 50 pages (or more . . . note that Caterpillar's 2013 10-K was 352 pages long). You would need two or three hours to do a quick read of the entire annual financial report, without trying to digest its details. This section discusses the typical annual financial report of a large public company.

If you did try to digest all the details of an annual financial report of a public company — a long, dense document not unlike a lengthy legal contract — you would need many hours (perhaps the whole day) to do so. (Also, to get the complete picture, you should read the company's filings with the SEC in conjunction with its annual financial report. Tack on a few more hours for that.) For one thing, there are many, many numbers in an annual financial report — hundreds of numbers at least, and reports for large, diversified, global, conglomerate businesses may have over a thousand.

Browsing based on your interests

How do investors in a business deal with the information overload of annual financial reports? Very few persons take the time to plow through every sentence, every word, every detail, and every number on every page — except for those professional accountants, lawyers, and auditors directly involved in the preparation and review of the financial report. It's hard to say how most managers, investors, creditors, and others interested in annual financial reports go about dealing with the massive amount of information — very little research has been done on this subject.

An annual financial report is like the Sunday edition of a large city newspaper, such as *The New York Times* or the *Los Angeles Times.* Hardly anyone reads every sentence on every page of these Sunday papers, much less every word in the advertisements — most people pick and choose what they want to read. They browse their way through the paper, stopping to read only the particular articles or topics they're interested in. Some people just skim through the paper. Some glance at the headlines. Probably most investors read annual financial reports like they read Sunday newspapers. The complete information is there if you really want to read it, but most readers pick and choose which information they have time to read in depth.

Annual financial reports are designed for *archival purposes,* not for a quick read. Instead of addressing the needs of investors and others who want to know about the profit performance and financial condition of the business — but have only a limited amount of time available — accountants produce an annual financial report that is a voluminous financial history of the business. Accountants leave it to the users of annual reports to extract the main points. Financial statement readers use certain key ratios and other tests to get a feel for the financial performance and position of the business.

Recognizing condensed versions

Here's a well-kept secret: Many public businesses and nonprofit organizations don't send a complete annual financial report to their stockholders or members. They know that few persons have the time or the technical background to read thoroughly the full-scale financial statements, footnotes, and other disclosures in their comprehensive financial reports. So, they present relatively brief summaries that are boiled-down versions of their complete financial reports.

Typically, these summaries — called *condensed financial statements* — do not provide footnotes or the other disclosures that are included in the complete and comprehensive annual financial reports. If you really want to see the official financial report of the organization, you can ask its headquarters to send you a copy (or, for public corporations, you can go to the SEC database — see the sidebar "Financial reporting on the Internet").

Using other sources of business information

Keep in mind that annual financial reports are only one of several sources of information to owners, creditors, and others who have a financial interest in the business. Annual financial reports, of course, come out only once a year — usually two months or so after the end of the company's fiscal (accounting) year. You should keep abreast of developments during the year by reading the quarterly reports of the business. Also, you are advised to follow the businesses you invest in by reading the financial press and watching TV programs. And, it's a good idea to keep up with blogs about the companies on the Internet, subscribe to newsletters, and soon. Financial reports present the sanitized version of events; they don't divulge scandals about the business. You have to find out the negative news about a business by the means just mentioned.

Not everything you may like to know as an investor is included in the annual financial report. For example, information about salaries and incentive compensation arrangements with the top-level managers of the business are disclosed in the *proxy statement,* not in the annual financial report. A proxy statement is the means by which the corporation solicits the vote of stockholders on issues that require stockholder approval — one of which is compensation packages of top-level managers. Proxy statements are filed with the SEC and are available on its database.

Statement of Changes in Owners' Equity

In preparing its financial report, a business needs to decide whether it should include a fourth financial statement in addition to its three primary financial statements (income statement, balance sheet, and statement of cash flows). This additional schedule is called the *statement of changes in owners' equity.* As the name implies, this statement summarizes the activities affecting the business's owners' equity accounts during the period. The balance sheet reports the ending balances of the company's owners' equity accounts but not the activities during the year that caused changes in these accounts.

You find this statement in the financial reports of almost all public companies. Many (most?) smaller private companies, on the other hand, do not need to report this statement because the only changes in their owners'

equity accounts are from earning profit (the bottom line in the income statement) and cash distributions from profit (in the financing activities section of
the statement of cash flows). So, the following discussion applies mainly to
larger public companies.

Owners' equity comes from capital invested in the business by the owners,
and profit earned by and retained in the business. The great majority of
public businesses are organized legally as corporations, and their owners
are called stockholders. A corporation issues ownership shares called *capital
stock*. So, *statement of changes in stockholders' equity* is the title used by corporations. (Book II Chapter 3 explains the corporation and other legal types
of business entities.)

Many publicly traded corporations have complex ownership structures often
consisting of two or more classes of capital stock shares; they usually buy
some of their own capital stock shares that are held and not cancelled (called
treasury stock); and they have certain types of gains or losses during the year
that are recorded directly in their stockholders' equity accounts instead of
going through the income statement. This is a rather sneaky way of bypass-
ing the income statement. In this way, the gains or losses do not affect the
bottom-line profit of a business that is reported in its income statement.

In short, public corporations prepare a statement of changes in stockholders'
equity to collect together in one place all the various changes in their owners'
equity accounts during the year. In particular, you have to read this financial
summary to find out whether the business had any gains or losses that are not
reported in its income statement. These special gains and losses are grouped
into an owners' equity account called *accumulated other comprehensive
income.*

The special types of gains and losses reported in the statement of stockholders' equity (instead of the income statement; see Figure 7-3) have to do
with foreign currency translations, unrealized gains and losses from certain
types of securities investments by the business, and changes in liabilities
for unfunded pension fund obligations of the business. Being so technical in
nature, these gains and losses fall into a twilight zone, as it were. The gains
and losses can be tacked on at the bottom of the income statement, or they
can be put in the separate statement of changes in owners' equity — it's up
to the business to make the choice. Most companies opt for the statement of
changes in stockholders' equity on the grounds that their income statements
are crowded with a lot of information already.

The Proctor & Gamble Company's comprehensive example includes everything but the kitchen sink, and it's a real-world illustration. Figure 7-3 is a
typical example of this financial statement, which suggests an important
question: Can the average reader of financial reports understand what's
presented in this statement?

Book II

**Accounting
and Financial
Reports**

The Procter & Gamble Company
Consolidated Statements of Shareholders' Equity

Dollars in millions/Shares in thousands	Common Shares Outstanding	Common Stock	Preferred Stock	Additional Paid-In-Capital	Reserve for ESOP Debt Retirement	Accumulated Other Comprehensive Income/(loss)	Treasury Stock	Retained Earnings	Non-controlling Interest	Total
BALANCE JUNE 30, 2009	$ 2,917,035	$4,007	$ 1,324	$ 61,118	$ (1,340)	$ (3,358)	$ (55,961)	$ 57,309	$283	$ 63,382
Net earnings								12,736	110	12,846
Other comprehensive income:										
Financial statement translation						(4,194)				(4,194)
Hedges and investment securities, net of $520 tax						867				867
Defined benefit retirement plans, net of $465 tax						(1,137)				(1,137)
Total comprehensive income										$ 8,382
Dividends to shareholders:										
Common								(5,239)		(5,239)
Preferred, net of tax benefits								(219)		(219)
Treasury purchases	(96,759)						(6,004)			(6,004)
Employee plan issuances	17,616	1		574			616			1,191
Preferred stock conversions	5,579		(47)	7			40			—
ESOP debt impacts					(10)			27		17
Noncontrolling interest, net					(2)				(69)	(71)
BALANCE JUNE 30, 2010	2,843,471	4,008	1,277	61,697	(1,350)	(7,822)	(61,309)	64,614	324	61,439
Net earnings								11,797	130	11,927
Other comprehensive income:										
Financial statement translation						6,493				6,493
Hedges and investment securities, net of $711 tax						(1,178)				(1,178)
Defined benefit retirement plans, net of $302 tax						453				453
Total comprehensive income										$ 17,695
Dividends to shareholders:										
Common								(5,534)		(5,534)
Preferred, net of tax benefits								(233)		(233)
Treasury purchases	(112,729)						(7,039)			(7,039)
Employee plan issuances	29,729			702			1,033			1,735
Preferred stock conversions	5,266		(43)	6			37			—
ESOP debt impacts					(7)			38		31
Noncontrolling interest, net									(93)	(93)
BALANCE JUNE 30, 2011	2,765,737	4,008	1,234	62,405	(1,357)	(2,054)	(67,278)	70,682	361	68,001
Net earnings								10,756	148	10,904
Other comprehensive income:										
Financial statement translation						(5,990)				(5,990)
Hedges and investment securities, net of $438 tax						721				721
Defined benefit retirement plans, net of $993 tax						(2,010)				(2,010)
Total comprehensive income										$ 3,625
Dividends to shareholders:										
Common								(5,883)		(5,883)
Preferred, net of tax benefits								(256)		(256)
Treasury purchases	(61,826)						(4,024)			(4,024)
Employee plan issuances	39,546			550			1,665			2,215
Preferred stock conversions	4,576		(39)	6			33			—
ESOP debt impacts								50		50
Noncontrolling interest, net					220				87	307
BALANCE JUNE 30, 2012	$ 2,748,033	$4,008	$ 1,195	$ 63,181	$(1,357)	$(9,333)	$(69,604)	$ 75,349	$ 596	$64,035

© John Wiley & Sons, Inc.

Figure 7-3: Example of statement of changes in stockholders' equity.

Reading a statement of changes in stockholders' equity in an annual financial report can be heavy lifting. The professionals — stock analysts, money and investment managers, and so on — carefully read through and dissect this statement, or at least they should. The average, nonprofessional investor faces an uphill climb in reading this statement. Hopefully you can understand the major items.

Chapter 8

Accounting Alternatives

*T*his chapter explains that when recording revenue, expenses, and other transactions of a business, the accountant generally must choose among different methods for capturing the economic reality of the transactions. You might think that accountants are in unified agreement on the exact ways for recording business transactions, but this isn't the case. An old joke is that when two economists get together there are three economic opinions. It's not that different in accounting.

The financial statements reported by a business are just one version of its financial history and performance. A different accountant for the business undoubtedly would have presented a different version. The income statement and balance sheet of a business depend on which particular accounting methods the accountant chooses. Moreover, on orders from management the financial statements could be tweaked to make them look better. Some businesses can (and do!) put spin on their financial statements.

It's one thing to be generally aware that financial statements depend on the choice of accounting methods used to prepare the statements. It's quite another to see the effects in action. This chapter presents two opposing versions of the financial statements for a business. It explains the reasons for the differences in its revenue, expenses, assets, liabilities, and owners' equity. And it explains the main accounting alternatives for two major expenses of businesses that sell products — cost of goods sold and depreciation.

Accounting for the economic activity of a business can be compared to judging a beauty contest. There might be agreement among the judges that all the contestants are good-looking, but ranking the contestants is sure to vary from judge to judge. Beauty is in the eye of the beholder, as they say.

Setting the Stage

The dollar amounts reported in the financial statements of a business are not simply "facts" that depend only on good bookkeeping. Here's why different accountants record transactions differently. The accountant

✔ Must make choices among different accounting methods for recording the amounts of revenue and expenses.

✔ Can select between pessimistic or optimistic estimates and forecasts when recording certain revenue and expenses.

✔ Has some wiggle room in implementing accounting methods, especially regarding the precise timing of when to record sales and expenses.

✔ Can carry out certain tactics at year-end to put a more favorable spin on the financial statements, usually under the orders or tacit approval of top management.

The popular notion is that accounting is an exact science and that the amounts reported in the financial statements are true and accurate down to the last dollar. When people see an amount reported to the last digit in a financial statement, they naturally get the impression of exactitude and precision. However, in the real world of business the accountant has to make many arbitrary choices between alternative ways for recording revenue and expenses, and for recording changes in their corresponding assets and liabilities. (Book II Chapter 2 explains that revenue and expenses are coupled with assets and liabilities.)

It's always possible that the accountant doesn't fully understand the transaction being recorded, or relies on misleading information, with the result that the entry for the transaction is wrong. And, bookkeeping processing slip-ups happen. The term *error* generally refers to honest mistakes; there is no intention of manipulating the financial statements. Unfortunately, a business may not detect accounting mistakes, and therefore its financial statements end up being misleading to one degree or another.

Taking Financial Statements with a Grain of Salt

Suppose you have the opportunity and the ready cash to buy a going business. Of course, you should consider many factors in deciding your offering price. The company's most recent financial statements would be your main source of information in reaching a decision — not the *only* source, of course, but the most important source for financial information about the business.

You should employ an independent CPA who has a professional credential in business valuation. The CPA could also examine the company's record-keeping and accounting system, to determine whether the accounts of the business are complete, accurate, and in conformity with the applicable accounting standards. The CPA should also test for possible fraud and any accounting shenanigans in the financial statements. As the potential buyer of the business you can't be too careful. You don't want the seller of the business to play you for a sucker.

Only one set of financial statements is included in a business's financial report: one income statement, one balance sheet, and one statement of cash flows. A business does not provide a second, alternative set of financial statements that would have been generated if the business had used different accounting methods and if the business had not tweaked its financial statements. The financial statements would have been different if alternative accounting methods had been used to record sales revenue and expenses and if the business had not engaged in certain end-of-period maneuvers to make its financial statements look better.

Book II

Accounting and Financial Reports

Taking an alternative look at the company's financial statements

Everyone who has a financial stake in a business should understand and keep in mind the bias or tilt of the financial statements they're reading. Using a baseball analogy, the version of financial statements in your hands may be in left field, right field, or center field. All versions are in the ballpark of general accounting standards, which define the playing field but don't dictate that every business has to play straight down the middle. In their financial reports, businesses don't comment on whether their financial statements as a whole are liberal, conservative, or somewhere in between. However, a business does have to disclose in the footnotes to its statements its major accounting methods. (Book II Chapter 7 discusses getting a financial report ready for release.)

As the potential buyer of a business, you have to decide on what the business is worth. Generally speaking, the two most important factors are the profit performance of the business (reported in its income statement) and the composition of assets, liabilities, and owners' equity of the business (reported in its balance sheet). For instance, how much would you pay for a business that has never made a profit and whose liabilities are more than its assets?

There's no simple formula for calculating the market value for a business based on its profit performance and financial condition. But, quite clearly, the profit performance and financial condition of a business are dominant factors in setting its market value.

Figure 8-1 presents a comparison that you never see in real-life financial reporting. The Actual column in Figure 8-1 presents the income statement and balance sheet reported by the business. The Alternative column reveals an income statement for the year and the balance sheet at year-end that the business could have reported (but didn't) if it had used alternative but acceptable accounting methods.

The dollar amounts in the Alternative column are the amounts that would have been recorded using different accounting methods. You don't particularly need the statement of cash flows here, because cash flow from profit (operating activities) is the same amount under both accounting scenarios and the cash flows from investing and financing activities are the same.

The business in our example adopted accounting methods that maximized its recorded profit, which recognize profit as soon as possible. Some businesses go the opposite direction. They adopt conservative accounting methods for recording profit performance, and they wouldn't think of tinkering with their financial statements at the end of the year, even when their profit performance falls short of expectations and their financial condition has some trouble spots. The Alternative column in Figure 8-1 reports the results of conservative accounting methods that could have been used by the business (but were not). As you see in Figure 8-1, using the alternative accounting methods results in less favorable measures of profit and financial condition.

Now, you may very well ask, "Where in the devil did the numbers for the alternative financial statements come from?" The dollar amounts in the Alternative column are best estimates of what conservative numbers would be for this business — a company that has been in business for several years, has made a profit most years, and has not gone through bankruptcy. Both the actual and the alternative financial statements are hypothetical but realistic and are not dishonest or deceitful.

Spotting significant differences

It's a little jarring to see a second set of numbers for the bedrock financial statements, such as the income statement and balance sheet. Both sets of accounting numbers are true and correct, yet different. Financial report users have been conditioned to accept one version for these two financial statements without thinking about what alternative financial statements would look like. Seeing an alternative scenario takes a little time to get used to, like learning how to drive on the left side of the road in Great Britain. There's always an alternative set of numbers lurking in the shadows, even though you don't get to see them.

Typical Product Business, Inc.
(In thousands of dollars)

Two Income Statements for Year Ended December 31, 2015

	Actual	Alternative	Difference
Sales Revenue	$26,000	$25,775	($225)
Cost of Goods Sold Expense	$14,300	$14,580	($280)
Gross Margin	$11,700	$11,195	
Operating Expenses	$8,700	$8,830	($130)
Operating Earnings	$3,000	$2,365	
Interest Expense	$400	$400	$0
Earnings Before Income Tax	$2,600	$1,965	
Income Tax Expense	$910	$615	$295
Net Income	$1,690	$1,350	($340)

Two Balance Sheets at December 31, 2015

Assets	Actual	Alternative	Difference
Cash	$2,165	$2,165	$0
Accounts Receivable	$2,600	$2,255	($345)
Inventory	$3,450	$2,750	($700)
Prepaid Expenses	$600	$550	($50)
Current Assets	$8,815	$7,720	
Property Plant and Equipment	$12,450	$12,225	($225)
Accumulated Depreciation	$6,415	$7,435	($1,020)
Net of depreciation	$6,035	$4,790	
Total Assets	$14,850	$12,510	($2,340)

Liabilities and Owners' Equity	Actual	Alternative	Difference
Accounts Payable	$765	$765	$0
Accrued Expenses Payable	$900	$1,002	$102
Income Tax Payable	$115	$78	($37)
Short-term Notes Payable	$2,250	$2,250	$0
Current Liabilities	$4,030	$4,095	
Long-term Notes Payable	$2,000	$2,000	$0
Owners' Equity:			
Invested Capital	$3,250	$3,250	$0
Retained Earnings	$5,570	$3,165	($2,405)
Total owners' equity	$8,820	$6,415	
Total Liabilities and Owners' Equity	$14,850	$12,510	($2,340)

Figure 8-1: Actual versus alternative income statement and balance sheet for a company.

Book II

Accounting and Financial Reports

© John Wiley & Sons, Inc.

The differences in revenue and expenses don't look that big, until you get to the bottom line. Net income is $340,000 lower in the alternative scenario, which is 20 percent smaller. Suppose that in putting a market value on the business, you use the earnings multiple method. Suppose you are willing to pay six times the most recent annual profit of the business. Using the actual financial statements, you would offer $10.14 million for the business ($1.69 million net income × 6 = $10.14 million). If the alternative accounting methods was used, you would offer only $8.1 million ($1.35 million net income × 6 = $8.1 million). If the business had used the more conservative accounting methods, you would offer $2.04 million less for the business!

The balance sheet differences look more sizable, and they are. Accounts receivable and inventory are significantly lower in the alternative scenario. And, the book value of its fixed assets (original cost minus accumulated depreciation) is significantly smaller. In both scenarios the actual condition and usability of its fixed assets (space in its buildings, output of its machinery and equipment, future miles of its trucks, and so on) are the same. In the alternative scenario these key assets of the business just have a much lower reported value.

You probably noticed that the company's retained earnings balance is $2,405,000 lower in the alternative scenario. Its retained earnings balance is 43 percent smaller! This much less profit would have been recorded over the years if the business had used the alternative accounting methods. Keep in mind that it took all the years of its existence to accumulate the $2,405,000 difference. The net income difference for its latest year (2015) is responsible for only $340,000 of the cumulative, total difference in retained earnings.

Explaining the Differences

In the following discussion you need to refer to the Differences column in Figure 8-1. Start by checking the $2,405,000 difference in *retained earnings*. Recall that profit is recorded in this owners' equity account. Because retained earnings is $2,405,000 lower, the cumulative profit of the business would be $2,405,000 lower if it had used the conservative accounting methods.

Remember the following about revenue and expenses:

- ✔ Recording sales revenue increases an asset (or decreases a liability in some cases).
- ✔ Recording an expense decreases an asset or increases a liability.

Therefore, assets are lower and/or liabilities are higher having used the alternative accounting methods, and collectively these differences should equal the difference in retained earnings. In Figure 8-1 total assets are $2,340,000 lower in the alternative scenario. And liabilities are $65,000 higher ($102,000 higher Accrued Expenses Payable minus the $37,000 lower amount of Income Tax Payable = $65,000 higher liabilities). Therefore, the difference in retained earnings checks out:

> $2,340,000 smaller amount of assets + $65,000 higher amount of liabilities = $2,405,000 less net income recorded over the years

The following sections briefly explain each of the differences in Figure 8-1, except the retained earnings difference explained just above. The idea is to give you a basic taste of some of the reasons for the differences.

Accounts receivable and sales revenue

Here are some common reasons why the balance of the accounts receivable asset is lower when conservative accounting methods are adopted:

✔ A business waits a little longer to record sales made on credit, to be more certain that all aspects of delivering products and the acceptance by customers are finalized, and there is little chance of the products being returned by the customers. This delay in recording sales causes its accounts receivable balance to be slightly lower, because at December 31, 2015 credit sales of $345,000 were not yet recorded that were still in the process of final acceptance by the customers. (Of course the cost of goods sold for these sales would not have been recorded either.)

If products are returnable and the deal between the seller and buyer does not satisfy normal conditions for a completed sale, the recording of sales revenue should be postponed until the return privilege no longer exists. For example, some products are sold *on approval,* which means the customer takes the product and tries it out for a few days or longer to see if the customer really wants it.

Businesses should be consistent from year to year regarding when they record sales. For some businesses, the timing of recording sales revenue is a major problem — especially when the final acceptance by the customer depends on performance tests or other conditions that must be satisfied. Some businesses engage in *channel stuffing* by forcing their dealers or customers to take delivery of more products than they wanted to buy. A good rule to follow is to read the company's footnote in its financial statements that explains its revenue recognition method, to see whether there is anything unusual. If the footnote is vague, be careful — be very careful!

✔ A business may be quicker in writing off a customer's past due balance as uncollectible. After it has made a reasonable effort to collect the debt but a customer still hasn't sent a check, a more conservative business writes off the balance as a *bad debts* expense. It decreases the past due accounts receivable balance to zero and records an expense of the same amount. In contrast, a business could wait much longer to write off a customer's past due amount. Both accounting methods end up writing off a customer's debt if it has been outstanding too long — but a company could wait until the last minute to make the write-off entry.

Inventory and cost of goods sold expense

The business in the example sells products mainly to other businesses. A business either manufactures the products its sells or purchases products for resale to customers. At this point it is not too important whether the business manufactures or purchases the products it sells. The costs of its products have drifted upward over time because of inflation and other factors. The business increased its sales prices to keep up with the product cost increases. When product costs change a business must choose which accounting method it uses for recording cost of goods sold expense.

One accounting method takes product costs out of the inventory asset account and records the costs to cost of goods sold expense in the sequence in which the costs were entered in the asset account. This scheme is called the first-in, first-out (FIFO) method. Instead, a business may choose to use the reverse method in which the latest product costs entered in the inventory asset account are selected for recording cost of goods sold expense, which leaves the oldest product costs in the asset account. This method is called the last-in, first-out (LIFO) method. FIFO is being used in the actual scenario, and LIFO is what you see in the alternative scenario in Figure 8-1.

When product costs drift upward over time, the FIFO method yields a lower cost of goods sold expense and a higher inventory asset balance compared with LIFO. Figure 8-1 shows that inventory is $700,000 lower in the alternative accounting scenario and that cost of goods sold expense is $280,000 higher. The $700,000 lower inventory balance is the cumulative effect of using LIFO, including the carry forward effects from previous years.

Some of the $700,000 inventory difference and some of the $280,000 cost of goods expense difference for 2015 are due to differences in how rigorously the business applies the *lower of cost or market* (LCM) rule. Before being sold, products may suffer loss in value due to deterioration, damage, theft, lower replacement costs, and diminished sales demand. A business tests regularly for such product losses and records the losses by decreasing its inventory balance and charging cost of goods sold expense. The LCM test can be applied loosely or tightly. It is applied more strictly in the alternative accounting scenario than in the actual scenario, which results in a larger amount of write-down of inventory (and higher expense).

Fixed assets and depreciation expense

All accountants agree that the costs of long-term operating assets that have limited useful lives to a business should be spread out over those predicted useful lives instead of being charged off entirely to expense in the year of acquisition. These long-lived operating assets are labeled *property, plant and equipment* in Figure 8-1, and less formally are called *fixed assets*. (The cost of land owned by a business is not depreciated because land is a property right that has perpetual life.) The allocation of the cost of a fixed asset over its estimated useful economic life to a business is called *depreciation*. The principle of depreciation is beyond criticism, but the devil is in the details.

The original costs of fixed assets should theoretically include certain costs in addition to their purchase or construction costs. However, in actual practice these fringe costs are not always included in the original cost of fixed assets. For example, it is theoretically correct to include installation costs of putting into place and connecting electrical and other power sources of heavy machinery and equipment. It is correct to include the cost of painting logos on the sides of delivery trucks. The cost of an older building just bought by a business should include the preparatory cleanup costs and the safety inspection cost. But in practice a business may not include such additional costs in the original costs of its fixed assets.

In the actual accounting scenario the business does include these additional costs in the original costs of its fixed assets, which means that the cost balances of its fixed assets are $225,000 higher compared with the alternative, conservative scenario (see Figure 8-1). These additional costs are not expensed immediately but are included in the total amount to be depreciated over future years. Also, in the actual scenario the company uses *straight-line depreciation* (discussed later), which spreads out the cost of a fixed asset evenly over the years of its useful life.

In the alternative conservative scenario the business does not include any costs other than purchase or construction costs in its fixed asset accounts, which means the additional costs are charged to expense immediately. Also, and most importantly, the business uses *accelerated depreciation* (discussed later) for allocating the cost of its fixed assets to expense. Higher amounts are allocated to early years and smaller amounts to later years. The result is that the accumulated depreciation amount in the alternative scenario is $1,020,000 higher, which signals that a lot more depreciation expense has been recorded over the years.

Book II

Accounting and Financial Reports

Accrued expenses payable, income tax payable, and expenses

A typical business at the end of the year has liabilities for certain costs that have accumulated but that will not be paid until sometime after the end of the year — costs that are an outgrowth of the current year's operating activities. These delayed-payment expenses should be recorded and matched against the sales revenue for the year. For example, a business should accrue (calculate and record) the amount it owes to its employees for unused vacation and sick pay. A business may not have received its property tax bill yet, but it should estimate the amount of tax to be assessed and record the proper portion of the annual property tax to the current year. The accumulated interest on notes payable that hasn't been paid yet at the end of the year should be recorded.

Here's another example: Most products are sold with expressed or implied warranties and guarantees. Even if good quality controls are in place, some products sold by a business don't perform up to promises, and the customers want the problems fixed. A business should estimate the cost of these future obligations and record this amount as an expense in the same period that the goods are sold (along with the cost of goods sold expense, of course). It should not wait until customers actually return products for repair or replacement because if it waits to record the cost then some of the expense for the guarantee work would not be recorded until the following year. After being in business a few years, a company can forecast with reasonable accuracy the percent of products sold that will be returned for repair or replacement under the guarantees and warranties offered to its customers. On the other hand, brand new products that have no track record may be a serious problem in this regard.

In the actual scenario the business does not make the effort to estimate future product warranty and guaranty costs and certain other costs that should be accrued. It records these costs on a when-paid basis. It waits until it actually incurs these costs to record an expense. The company has decided that although its liabilities are understated, the amount is not material. In the alternative scenario, on the other hand, the business takes the high road and goes to the trouble of estimating future costs that should be matched against sales revenue for the year. Therefore, its accrued expenses payable liability account is $102,000 higher (see Figure 8-1).

The alternative conservative scenario (see Figure 8-1) assumes that the business uses the same accounting methods for income tax, which gives a lower taxable income and income tax for the year. Accordingly, notice that the income tax expense for the year is $295,000 lower and the year-end balance of income tax payable is lower. A business makes installment payments during the year on its estimated income tax for the year, so only a fraction of the annual income tax is still unpaid at the end of the year. (A business may use different accounting methods for income tax than it does for recording its transactions, which leads to complexities not covered here.)

Wrapping things up

In the business example (Figure 8-1) the accounts payable liability is the same in both scenarios. These short-term operating liabilities are definite amounts for definite services or products that have been received by the business. There are no accounting alternatives in recording accounts payable. Also, cash has the same year-end balance in both scenarios because these transactions are recorded when cash is received and paid out. (Well, a business may do a little "window dressing" to bump up its reported cash balance.) Finally, the accounts not affected by recording revenue and expenses are the same in both accounting scenarios, which are notes payable and owners' invested capital.

The numbers for the alternative, conservative scenario are no more than educated guesses. Businesses keep only one set of books. Even a business itself doesn't know how different its financial statements would be if it had used different accounting methods. Financial report readers can read the footnotes to determine whether liberal or conservative accounting methods are being used. Footnotes are not easy to read. It is very difficult, if not impossible, to determine exactly how much profit would have been and how much different balance sheet amounts would be if alternative accounting methods had been used by a business.

If you own or manage a business, get involved in deciding which accounting methods to use for measuring your profit and how these methods are actually implemented. A manager has to answer questions about his or her financial reports on many occasions, so you should know which accounting methods are used to prepare the financial statements. However, "get involved" should not mean manipulating the amounts of sales revenue and expenses recorded in the year — to make profit look higher, to smooth fluctuations in profit from year to year, or to improve the amounts of assets and liabilities reported in your ending balance sheet. You shouldn't even consider doing these things. (Of course these manipulations go on in the real world. Some people also drive under the influence, but that doesn't mean you should.)

Calculating Cost of Goods Sold Expense and Inventory Cost

Companies that sell products must select which method to use for recording cost of goods sold expense, which is the sum of the costs of the products sold to customers during the period. You deduct cost of goods sold from sales revenue to determine *gross margin* — the first profit line on the income statement (refer to Figure 8-1). Cost of goods sold is a very important figure; if gross margin is wrong, bottom-line profit (net income) is wrong.

A business can choose between two opposite methods for recording its cost of goods sold and the cost balance that remains in its inventory asset account:

✔ The first-in, first-out (FIFO) cost sequence

✔ The last-in, first-out (LIFO) cost sequence

Other methods are acceptable, but these two are the primary options.

Product costs are entered in the inventory asset account in the order the products are acquired, but they are not necessarily taken out of the inventory asset account in this order. The FIFO and LIFO terms refer to the order in which product costs are *taken out* of the inventory asset account. You may think that only one method is appropriate; however, accounting standards permit these two alternatives.

The choice between the FIFO and LIFO accounting methods does *not* depend on the actual physical flow of products. Generally speaking, products are delivered to customers in the order the business bought or manufactured the products — one reason being that a business does not want to keep products in inventory too long because the products might deteriorate or show their age. So, products generally move out of inventory in a first-in, first-out sequence. Nevertheless, a business may choose the last-in, first-out accounting method. Read on.

FIFO

With the FIFO method, you charge out product costs to cost of goods sold expense in the chronological order in which you acquired the goods. The procedure is that simple. It's like the first people in line to see a movie get in the theater first. The ticket-taker collects the tickets in the order in which they were bought.

Suppose that you acquire four units of a product during a period, one unit at a time, with unit costs as follows (in the order in which you acquire the items): $100, $102, $104, and $106, for a total of $412. By the end of the period, you have sold three of these units. Using FIFO, you calculate the cost of goods sold expense as follows:

$$\$100 + \$102 + \$104 = \$306$$

In short, you use the first three units to calculate cost of goods sold expense.

The cost of the ending inventory asset, then, is $106, which is the cost of the most recent acquisition. The $412 total cost of the four units is divided between $306 cost of goods sold expense for the three units sold and the $106 cost of the one unit in ending inventory. The total cost has been accounted for; nothing has fallen between the cracks.

FIFO has two things going for it:

Book II

Accounting and Financial Reports

✔ Products generally move out of inventory in a first-in, first-out sequence: The earlier acquired products are delivered to customers before later acquired products are delivered, so the most recently purchased products are the ones still in ending inventory to be delivered in the future. Using FIFO, the inventory asset reported in the balance sheet at the end of the period reflects recent purchase (or manufacturing) costs, which means the balance in the asset is close to the current *replacement costs* of the products.

✔ When product costs are steadily increasing, many (but not all) businesses follow a first-in, first-out sales price strategy and hold off raising sales prices as long as possible. They delay raising sales prices until they have sold their lower-cost products. Only when they start selling from the next batch of products, acquired at a higher cost, do they raise sales prices. Favor the FIFO cost of goods sold expense method when a business follows this basic sales pricing policy, because both the expense and the sales revenue are better matched for determining gross margin. Sales pricing is complex and may not follow such a simple process, but the main point is that many businesses use a FIFO-based sales pricing approach. If your business is one of them, use the FIFO expense method to be consistent with your sales pricing.

LIFO

Remember the movie ticket-taker mentioned earlier? Think about that ticket-taker going to the *back* of the line of people waiting to get into the next showing and letting them in first. The later you bought your ticket, the sooner you get into the theater. This is what happens in the LIFO method, which stands for *last-in, first-out.* The people in the front of a movie line wouldn't stand for it, of course, but the LIFO method is acceptable for determining the cost of goods sold expense for products sold during the period.

The main feature of the LIFO method is that it selects the *last* item you purchased, and then works backward until you have the total cost for the total number of units sold during the period. What about the ending inventory — the products you haven't sold by the end of the year? Using the LIFO method, the earliest cost remains in the inventory asset account (unless all products are sold and the business has nothing in inventory).

Using the same example from the preceding section, assume that the business uses the LIFO method. The four units, in order of acquisition, had costs of $100, $102, $104, and $106. If you sell three units during the period, the LIFO method calculates the cost of goods sold expense as follows:

$$\$106 + \$104 + \$102 = \$312$$

The ending inventory cost of the one unit not sold is $100, which is the oldest cost. The $412 total cost of the four units acquired less the $312 cost of goods sold expense leaves $100 in the inventory asset account. Determining which units you actually delivered to customers is irrelevant; when you use the LIFO method, you always count backward from the most recent unit you acquired.

Here are the two main arguments in favor of the LIFO method:

✔ Assigning the most recent costs of products purchased to the cost of goods sold expense makes sense because you have to replace your products to stay in business, and the most recent costs are closest to the amount you will have to pay to replace your products. Ideally, you should base your sales prices not on original cost but on the cost of replacing the units sold.

✔ During times of rising costs, the most recent purchase cost maximizes the cost of goods sold expense deduction for determining taxable income, and thus minimizes income tax. In fact, LIFO was invented for income tax purposes. True, the cost of inventory on the ending balance sheet is lower than recent acquisition costs, but the taxable income effect is more important than the balance sheet effect.

But here are the reasons why LIFO is problematic:

✔ Unless you are able to base sales prices on the most recent purchase costs or you raise sales prices as soon as replacement costs increase — and most businesses would have trouble doing this — using LIFO depresses your gross margin and, therefore, your bottom-line net income.

✔ The LIFO method can result in an ending inventory cost value that's seriously out of date, especially if the business sells products that have very long lives. For instance, for several years, Caterpillar's LIFO-based inventory has been billions less than what it would have been under the FIFO method.

✔ Unscrupulous managers can use the LIFO method to manipulate their profit figures if business isn't going well. They deliberately let their inventory drop to abnormally low levels, with the result that old, lower product costs are taken out of inventory to record cost of goods sold expense. This gives a one-time boost to gross margin. These "LIFO liquidation gains" — if sizable in amount compared with the normal gross profit margin that would have been recorded using current costs — have to be disclosed in the footnotes to the company's financial statements. (Dipping into old layers of LIFO-based inventory cost is necessary when a business phases out obsolete products; the business has no choice but to reach back into the earliest cost layers for these products. The sales prices of products being phased out usually are set low, to move the products out of inventory, so gross margin is not abnormally high for these products.)

Book II

Accounting and Financial Reports

If you sell products that have long lives and for which your product costs rise steadily over the years, using the LIFO method has a serious impact on the ending inventory cost value reported on the balance sheet and can cause the balance sheet to look misleading. Over time, the current cost of replacing products becomes further and further removed from the LIFO-based inventory costs. In our business example (Figure 8-1) the 2015 balance sheet may very well include products with 2003, 1997, or 1980 costs. As a matter of fact, the product costs reported for inventory could go back even further.

Note: A business must disclose in a footnote with its financial statements the difference between its LIFO-based inventory cost value and its inventory cost value according to FIFO. However, not many people outside of stock analysts and professional investment managers read footnotes very closely. Business managers get involved in reviewing footnotes in the final steps of getting annual financial reports ready for release (see Book II Chapter 7). If your business uses FIFO, ending inventory is stated at recent acquisition costs, and you do not have to determine what the LIFO value would have been.

Many products and raw materials have very short lives; they're regularly replaced by new models (you know, with those "New and Improved!" labels) because of the latest technology or marketing wisdom. These products aren't around long enough to develop a wide gap between LIFO and FIFO, so the accounting choice between the two methods doesn't make as much difference as with long-lived products.

Another serious problem with LIFO has emerged recently. For several years there have been continuing and serious efforts towards developing one unified set of global accounting and financial reporting standards. How this will all turn out is anyone's guess. More problems have arisen that anyone would have predicted. In any case, the international standards group does not approve LIFO. This position does not seem, at this time, open to negotiation. So, LIFO may become obsolete if international accounting standards are adopted.

One last note: FIFO and LIFO are not the only games in town. Businesses use other methods for cost of goods sold and inventory, including average cost methods, retail-price based methods, and so on. There is no space here to go into these other methods. FIFO and LIFO dominate.

Recording Depreciation Expense

In theory, depreciation expense accounting is straightforward enough: You divide the cost of a fixed asset (except land) among the number of years that the business expects to use the asset. In other words, instead of having a huge lump-sum expense in the year that you make the purchase, you charge a fraction of the cost to expense for each year of the asset's lifetime. Using this method is much easier on your bottom line in the year of purchase, of course.

Theories are rarely as simple in real life as they are on paper, and this one is no exception. Do you divide the cost *evenly* across the asset's lifetime, or do you charge more to certain years than others? Furthermore, when it eventually comes time to dispose of fixed assets, the assets may have some disposable, or *salvage,* value. In theory, only cost minus the salvage value should be depreciated. But in actual practice most companies ignore salvage value and the total cost of a fixed asset is depreciated. Moreover, how do you estimate how long an asset will last in the first place? Do you consult an accountant psychic hot line?

As it turns out, the IRS runs its own little psychic business on the side, with a crystal ball known as the Internal Revenue Code. Okay, so the IRS can't tell you that your truck is going to conk out in five years, seven months, and two days. The Internal Revenue Code doesn't give you predictions of how long your fixed assets will *last*; it only tells you what kind of time line to use for income tax purposes, as well as how to divide the cost along that time line.

Hundreds of books have been written on depreciation, but the book that really counts is the Internal Revenue Code. Most businesses adopt the useful lives allowed by the income tax law for their financial statement accounting; they don't go to the trouble of keeping a second depreciation schedule for financial reporting. Why complicate things if you don't have to? Why keep one depreciation schedule for income tax and a second for preparing your financial statements? That said, it may be a different story for some large companies.

The IRS rules offer two depreciation methods that can be used for particular classes of assets. Buildings must be depreciated just one way, but for other fixed assets you can take your pick:

Book II

Accounting and Financial Reports

✔ **Straight-line depreciation:** With this method, you divide the cost evenly among the years of the asset's estimated lifetime. Buildings have to be depreciated this way. Assume that a building purchased by a business costs $390,000, and its useful life — according to the tax law — is 39 years. The depreciation expense is $10,000 (1/39 of the cost) for each of the 39 years. You may choose to use the straight-line method for other types of assets. After you start using this method for a particular asset, you can't change your mind and switch to another depreciation method later.

✔ **Accelerated depreciation:** Actually, this term is a generic catchall for several different kinds of methods. What they all have in common is that they're *front-loading* methods, meaning that you charge a larger amount of depreciation expense in the early years and a smaller amount in the later years. The term *accelerated* also refers to adopting useful lives that are shorter than realistic estimates. (Very few automobiles are useless after five years, for example, but they can be fully depreciated over five years for income tax purposes.)

The *salvage value* of fixed assets (the estimated disposal values when the assets are taken to the junkyard or sold off at the end of their useful lives) is ignored in the calculation of depreciation for income tax. Put another way, if a fixed asset is held to the end of its entire depreciation life, then its original cost will be fully depreciated, and the fixed asset from that time forward will have a zero book value. (Recall that *book value* is equal to original cost minus the balance in the accumulated depreciation account.)

Fully depreciated fixed assets are grouped with all other fixed assets in external balance sheets. All these long-term resources of a business are reported in one asset account called *property, plant and equipment* (instead of the term *fixed assets*). If all its fixed assets were fully depreciated, the balance sheet of a company would look rather peculiar — the cost of its fixed assets would be offset by its accumulated depreciation. Keep in mind that the cost of land (as opposed to the structures on the land) is not depreciated. The original cost of land stays on the books as long as the business owns the property.

The straight-line depreciation method has strong advantages: It's easy to understand, and it stabilizes the depreciation expense from year to year.

Nevertheless, many business managers and accountants favor an accelerated depreciation method in order to minimize the size of the checks they have to write to the IRS in the early years of using fixed assets. This lets the business keep the cash, for the time being, instead of paying more income tax. Keep in mind, however, that the depreciation expense in the annual income statement is higher in the early years when you use an accelerated depreciation method, and so bottom-line profit is lower. Many accountants and businesses like accelerated depreciation because it paints a more conservative picture of profit performance in the early years. Fixed assets may lose their economic usefulness to a business sooner than expected. If this happens, using the accelerated depreciation method would look very wise in hindsight.

Except for brand-new enterprises, a business typically has a mix of fixed assets — some in their early years of depreciation, some in their middle years, and some in their later years. There is a balancing-out effect among the different vintages of fixed assets being depreciated. Therefore, the overall depreciation expense for the year using accelerated depreciation may not be too different than what the straight-line depreciation amount would be. A business does *not* have to disclose in its external financial report what its depreciation expense would have been if it had been using an alternative method. Readers of the financial statements cannot tell how much difference the choice of accounting methods would have caused in depreciation expense that year.

Scanning Revenue and Expense Horizons

Recording sales revenue and other income can present some hairy accounting problems. As a matter of fact, the — accounting rule-making authorities — rank revenue recognition as a major problem area. A good part of the reason for putting revenue recognition high on the list of accounting problems is that many high profile financial accounting frauds have involved recording bogus sales revenue that had no economic reality. Sales revenue accounting presents challenging problems in some situations. But the accounting for many key expenses is equally important. Frankly, it's difficult to measure expenses on a year-by-year basis.

Here are a few major expense accounting issues to pay attention to:

✔ **Asset impairment write-downs:** Inventory shrinkage, bad debts, and depreciation by their very nature are asset write-downs. Other asset write-downs are required when an asset becomes *impaired,* which means that it has lost some or all of its economic utility to the business and has little or no disposable value. An asset write-down reduces the book (recorded) value of an asset (and at the same time records an expense or loss of the same amount).

✔ **Employee-defined benefits pension plans and other post-retirement benefits:** The U.S. accounting rule on this expense is extremely complex. Several key estimates must be made by the business, including, for example, the expected rate of return on the investment portfolio set aside for these future obligations. This and other estimates affect the amount of expense recorded. In some cases, a business uses an unrealistically high rate of return in order to minimize the amount of this expense. Using unrealistically optimistic rates of investment return is a pernicious problem at the present time.

✔ **Certain discretionary operating expenses:** Many operating expenses involve timing problems and/or serious estimation problems. Furthermore, some expenses are discretionary in nature, which means how much to spend during the year depends almost entirely on the discretion of managers. Managers can defer or accelerate these expenses in order to manipulate the amount of expense recorded in the period. For this reason, businesses filing financial reports with the SEC are required to disclose certain of these expenses, such as repairs and maintenance expense, and advertising expense. (To find examples, go to the Securities and Exchange Commission website at www.sec.gov.)

Book II

Accounting and Financial Reports

✔ **Income tax expense:** A business can use different accounting methods for some of the expenses reported in its income statement than it uses for calculating its taxable income. Oh, boy! The hypothetical amount of taxable income, as if the accounting methods used in the income statement were used in the tax return, is calculated; then the income tax based on this hypothetical taxable income is figured. This is the income tax expense reported in the income statement. This amount is reconciled with the actual amount of income tax owed based on the accounting methods used for income tax purposes. A reconciliation of the two different income tax amounts is provided in a technical footnote schedule to the financial statements.

✔ **Management stock options:** A *stock option* is a contract between an executive and the business that gives the executive the option to purchase a certain number of the corporation's capital stock shares at a fixed price (called the *exercise* or *strike* price) after certain conditions are satisfied. Usually a stock option does not vest until the executive has been with the business for a certain number of years. The question is whether the granting of stock options should be recorded as an expense. This issue had been simmering for some time. The U.S. rule-making body finally issued a pronouncement that requires a value measure be put on stock options when they are issued and that this amount be recorded as an expense.

You could argue that management stock options are simply an arrangement between the stockholders and the privileged few executives of the business, by which the stockholders allow the executives to buy shares at bargain prices. The granting of stock options does not reduce the assets or increase the liabilities of the business, so you could argue that stock options are not a direct expense of the business; instead, the cost falls on the stockholders. Allowing executives to buy stock shares at below-market prices increases the number of shares over which profit has to be spread, thus decreasing earnings per share. Stockholders have to decide whether they are willing to do this; the granting of management stock options must be put to a vote by the stockholders.

Please don't think that the short list above does justice to all the expense accounting problems of businesses. U.S. businesses — large and small, public and private — operate in a highly developed and very sophisticated economy. One result is that expense accounting has become very complicated and confusing.

Book III

Day-to-Day Bookkeeping

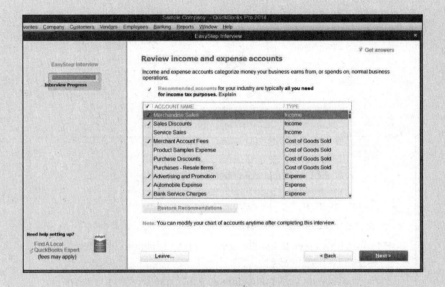

In this book . . .

- ✔ Track inventory and keep your business supplied
- ✔ Monitor payments due, and learn how to handle bad debt
- ✔ Learn new ways to handle payroll responsibilities, including collecting and paying taxes
- ✔ Figure worker's compensation as well as an employer's share of Social Security and Medicare

Chapter 1

Buying and Tracking Your Purchases

*I*n order to make money, your business must have something to sell. Whether you sell products or offer services, you have to deal with costs directly related to the goods or services being sold. Those costs primarily come from the purchase or manufacture of the products you plan to sell or the items you need in order to provide the services.

All companies must keep careful watch over the cost of the products to be sold or services to be offered. Ultimately, your company's profits depend on how well you manage those costs because, in most cases, costs increase over time rather than decrease. How often do you find a reduction in the price of needed items? Doesn't happen often. If costs increase but the price to the customer remains unchanged, the profit you make on each sale is less.

In addition to the costs to produce products or services, every business has additional expenses associated with purchasing supplies needed to run the business. The bookkeeper has primary responsibility for monitoring all these costs and expenses as invoices are paid and for alerting company owners or managers when vendors increase prices. This chapter covers how to track purchases and their costs, manage inventory, and buy and manage supplies as well as pay the bills for the items your business buys.

Keeping Track of Inventory

Products to be sold are called *inventory*. As a bookkeeper or accountant, you use two accounts to track inventory:

- ✔ **Purchases:** Where you record the actual purchase of goods to be sold. This account is used to calculate the *Cost of Goods Sold,* which is an item on the income statement (see Book II Chapter 5 for more on the income statement).

- ✔ **Inventory:** Where you track the value of inventory on hand. This value is shown on the balance sheet as an asset in a line item called *Inventory* (see Book II Chapter 4 for more on the balance sheet).

Companies track physical inventory on hand by using one of two methods:

- ✔ **Periodic inventory:** Conducting a physical count of the inventory in the stores and in the warehouse. This count can be done daily, monthly, yearly, or for any other period that best matches your business needs. (Many stores close for all or part of a day when they must count inventory.)

- ✔ **Perpetual inventory:** Adjusting inventory counts as each sale is made. In order to use this method, you must manage your inventory by using a computerized accounting system that's tied into your point of sale (usually cash registers).

Even if you use a perpetual inventory method, periodically doing a physical count of inventory to be sure those numbers match what's in your computer system is a good idea. Because theft, damage, and loss of inventory aren't automatically entered in your computer system, those losses don't show up until you do a physical count of the inventory you have on hand in your business.

When preparing your income statement at the end of an accounting period (whether that period is for a month, a quarter, or a year), you need to calculate the Cost of Goods Sold in order to calculate the profit made. To do so, you must first find out how many items of inventory were sold. You start with the amount of inventory on hand at the beginning of the month (called Beginning Inventory), as recorded in the Inventory account, and add the amount of purchases, as recorded in the Purchases account, to find the Goods Available for Sale. Then you subtract the Ending Inventory on hand at the end of the month, which is determined by counting remaining inventory.

Here's how you calculate the number of goods sold:

Beginning Inventory + Purchases = Goods Available for Sale

Goods Available for Sale – Ending Inventory = Goods Sold

After you determine the number of goods sold, you compare that number to the actual number of items sold by the company during that accounting period, which is based on sales figures collected through the month. If the numbers don't match, you have a problem. The mistake may be in the inventory count, or items may be unaccounted for because they've been misplaced or damaged and discarded. In the worst-case scenario, you may have a problem with theft by customers or employees. These differences are usually tracked within the accounting system in a line item called *Inventory Shrinkage.*

Entering initial cost

When your company first receives inventory, you enter the initial cost of that inventory into the bookkeeping system based on the shipment's invoice. In some cases, invoices are sent separately, and only a packing slip is included in the order. If that's the case, you should still record the receipt of the goods because the company incurs the cost from the day the goods are received and must be sure it will have the money to pay for the goods when the invoice arrives and the bill comes due. (You track outstanding bills in the Accounts Payable account.)

Entering the receipt of inventory is a relatively easy entry in the bookkeeping system. For example, if your company buys $1,000 of inventory to be sold, you make the following record in the books:

	Debit	**Credit**
Purchases	$1,000	
Accounts Payable		$1,000

The Purchases account increases by $1,000 to reflect the additional costs, and the Accounts Payable account increases by the same amount to reflect the amount of the bill that needs to be paid in the future.

When inventory enters your business, in addition to recording the actual costs, you need more detail about what was bought, how much of each item was bought, and what each item cost. You also need to track

- ✔ How much inventory you have on hand.
- ✔ The value of the inventory you have on hand.
- ✔ When you need to order more inventory.

Tracking these details for each type of product bought can be a nightmare, especially if you're trying to keep the books for a retail store, because you

Book III

Day-to-Day Bookkeeping

need to set up a special Inventory journal with pages detailing purchase and sale information for every item you carry. (See Book I Chapter 4 for the scoop on journals.)

However, computerized accounting simplifies this process of tracking inventory. Details about inventory can be entered initially into your computer accounting system in several ways:

✔ If you pay by check or credit card when you receive the inventory, you can enter the details about each item on the check or credit card form.

✔ If you use purchase orders, you can enter the detail about each item on the purchase order, record receipt of the items when they arrive, and update the information when you receive the bill.

✔ If you don't use purchase orders, you can enter the detail about the items when you receive them and update the information when you receive the bill.

To give you an idea of how this information is collected in a computerized accounting software program, Figure 1-1 shows you how to enter the details in QuickBooks. This particular form is for the receipt of inventory with a bill, but similar information is collected on the software program's check, credit card, and purchase order forms.

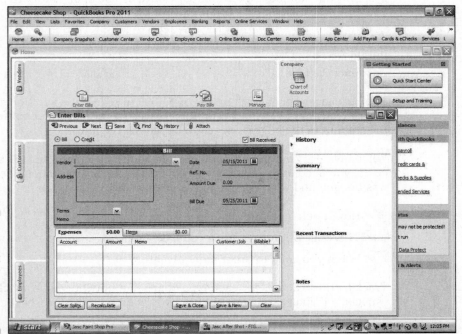

Figure 1-1: You record the receipt of inventory by using the "Enter Bills" forms.

Image courtesy of Intuit

Notice that on the form in Figure 1-1, you record not only the name of the vendor, the date received, and the payment amount but also details about the items bought, including the quantity and cost. When you load each item into the computerized accounting system, you can easily track cost detail over time.

Figure 1-2 shows how you initially set up an inventory item in the computerized accounting system. Note that in addition to the item name, two descriptions are added to the system: One is an abbreviated version you can use on purchase transactions, and the other is a longer description that shows on customer invoices (sales transactions). You can input a cost and sales price if you want, or you can leave them at zero and enter the cost and sales prices with each transaction.

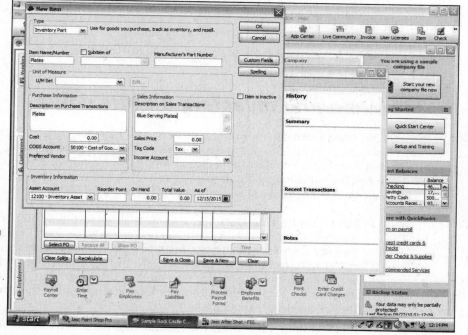

Figure 1-2: Setting up an Inventory Item with QuickBooks.

Image courtesy of Intuit

Book III

Day-to-Day Bookkeeping

If you have a set contract purchase price or sales price on an inventory item, it saves time to enter it on this form so you don't have to enter the price each time you record a transaction. But, if the prices change frequently, it's best to leave the space blank so you don't forget to enter the updated price when you enter a transaction.

Notice in Figure 1-2 that information about inventory on hand and when inventory needs to be reordered can also be tracked by using this form. To be sure your store shelves are never empty, for each item you can enter a number that indicates at what point you want to reorder inventory. In Figure 1-2, you can indicate the "Reorder Point" in the section called "Inventory Information." (A nice feature of QuickBooks is that it gives you an inventory reminder when inventory reaches the reorder point.)

After you complete and save the form that records the receipt of inventory in QuickBooks, the software automatically

- Adjusts the quantity of inventory you have in stock
- Increases the asset account called Inventory
- Lowers the quantity of items on order (if you initially entered the information as a purchase order)
- Averages the cost of inventory on hand
- Increases the Accounts Payable account

Managing inventory and its value

After you record the receipt of inventory, you have the responsibility of managing the inventory you have on hand. You also must know the value of that inventory. You may think that as long as you know what you paid for the items, the value isn't difficult to calculate. Well, accountants can't let it be that simple, so there are actually five different ways to value inventory:

- **LIFO (Last In, First Out):** You assume that the last items put on the shelves (the newest items) are the first items to be sold. Retail stores that sell nonperishable items, such as tools, are likely to use this type of system. For example, when a hardware store gets new hammers, workers probably don't unload what's on the shelves and put the newest items in the back. Instead, the new tools are just put in the front, so they're likely to be sold first.

- **FIFO (First In, First Out):** You assume that the first items put on the shelves (the oldest items) are sold first. Stores that sell perishable goods, such as food stores, use this inventory valuation method most often. For example, when new milk arrives at a store, the person stocking the shelves unloads the older milk, puts the new milk at the back of the shelf, and then puts the older milk in front. Each carton of milk (or other perishable item) has a date indicating the last day it can be sold, so food stores always try to sell the oldest stuff first, while it's still sellable. (They try, but how many times have you reached to the back of a food shelf to find items with the longest shelf life?)

- **Averaging:** You average the cost of goods received, so you don't have to worry about which items are sold first or last. This method of inventory is used most often in any retail or services environment where prices are constantly fluctuating and the business owner finds that an average cost works best for managing his Cost of Goods Sold.

- **Specific Identification:** You maintain cost figures for each inventory item individually. Retail outlets that sell big-ticket items, such as cars, which often have a different set of extras on each item, use this type of inventory valuation method.

- **LCM (Lower of Cost or Market):** You set inventory value based on whichever is lower: the amount you paid originally for the inventory item (its cost), or the current market value of the item. Companies that deal in precious metals, commodities, or publicly traded securities often use this method because the prices of their products can fluctuate wildly, sometimes even in one day.

After you choose an inventory valuation method, you need to use the same method each year on your financial reports and when you file your taxes. If you decide you want to change the method, you need to explain the reasons for the change to both the IRS and to your financial backers because the change impacts the value of your company and your profit margins. If you're running a company that's incorporated and has sold stock, you want to explain the change to your stockholders as well. You also have to go back and show how the change in inventory method impacts your prior financial reporting and adjust your profit margins in previous years to reflect the new inventory valuation method's impact on your long-term profit history.

Figuring out the best method for you

You may be wondering why which inventory valuation method you use matters so much. The key to the choice is the impact on your bottom line as well as the taxes your company will pay.

FIFO, because it assumes the oldest (and most likely the lowest priced) items are sold first, results in a low Cost of Goods Sold number. Because Cost of Goods Sold is subtracted from sales to determine profit, a low Cost of Goods Sold number produces a high profit.

The opposite is true for LIFO, which uses cost figures based on the last price (and most likely the highest price) paid for the inventory. Using the LIFO method, the Cost of Goods Sold number is high, which means a larger sum is subtracted from sales to determine profit. Thus, the profit margin is low. The good news, however, is that the tax bill is low, too.

The Averaging method gives a business the best picture of what's happening with inventory costs and trends. Instead of constantly dealing with the ups and downs of inventory costs, this method smoothes out the numbers used to calculate a business's profits. Cost of Goods Sold, taxes, and profit margins for this method fall between those of LIFO and FIFO. If you're operating a business in which inventory prices are constantly going up and down, Averaging is definitely the method you should choose.

QuickBooks uses the Averaging method to calculate Cost of Goods Sold and Inventory line items on its financial reports, so if you choose this method, you can use QuickBooks and the financial reports it generates. However, if you choose to use one of the other four inventory methods, you can't use the QuickBooks financial report numbers. Instead, you have to print out a report of purchases and calculate the accurate numbers to use on your financial reports for the Cost of Goods Sold and Inventory accounts.

Check with your accountant to see which inventory method he or she thinks is best for you given the type of business you're operating.

Comparing the methods

To show you how much of an impact inventory valuation can have on profit margin, this section compares three of the most common methods: FIFO, LIFO, and Averaging. The example assumes that Company A bought the inventory in question at different prices on three different occasions. Beginning Inventory is valued at $500 (that's 50 items at $10 each).

Here's the calculation for determining the number of items sold:

Beginning Inventory + Purchases = Goods Available for Sale

Goods Available for Sale – Ending Inventory = Items Sold

50 + 500 = 550

550 – 75 = 475

Here's what the company paid to purchase the inventory:

Date	Quantity	Unit Price
April 1	150	$10
April 15	150	$25
April 30	200	$30

Using Averaging

Here's an example of how you use the Averaging method to calculate the Cost of Goods Sold:

Beginning Inventory	50	$500
Purchases	150@$10	$1,500
	150@$25	$3,750
	200@$30	$6,000
Total Inventory	550	$11,750
Average Inventory Cost	$11,750 ÷ 550 = $21.36	
Cost of Goods Sold	475 × $21.36 = $10,146	
Ending Inventory	75@$21.36 = $1,602	

Remember, the Cost of Goods Sold number appears on the income statement and is subtracted from Sales. The Ending Inventory number shows up as an asset on the balance sheet. The placement of these items on an income statement or balance sheet is true for all three inventory valuation methods.

Using FIFO

Here's an example of how you calculate the Cost of Goods Sold by using the FIFO method. With this method, you assume that the first items received are the first ones sold, and because the first items received here are those in Beginning Inventory, it starts with them:

Beginning Inventory	50@$10	$500
Next in – April 1	150@$10	$1,500
Then – April 15	150@$25	$3,750
Then – April 30	125@$30	$3,750
Cost of Goods Sold	475	$9,500
Ending Inventory	75@$30	$2,250

Note: Only 125 of the 200 units purchased on April 30 are used in the FIFO method. Because this method assumes that the first items into inventory are the first items sold (or taken out of inventory), the first items used are those in beginning inventory and then those purchased on April 1. Then the April 15 items are used, and finally the remaining needed items are taken from those bought on April 30. Because 200 were bought on April 30 and only 125 were needed, 75 of the items bought on April 30 would be the ones left in ending inventory.

Using LIFO

Here's an example of how you calculate the Cost of Goods Sold with the LIFO method. With this method, you assume that the last items received are the

Book III

Day-to-Day Bookkeeping

first ones sold, and because the last items received were those purchased on April 30, it starts with them:

April 30	200@$30	$6,000
Next April 15	150@$25	$3,750
Then April 1	125@$10	$1,250
Cost of Goods Sold	475	$11,000
Ending Inventory	75@$10	$750

Note: Because LIFO assumes the last items to arrive are sold first, the Ending Inventory includes the 25 remaining units from the April 1 purchase plus the 50 units in Beginning Inventory.

Here's how the use of inventory under the LIFO method impacts the company profits. Assume the items are sold to the customers for $40 per unit, which means total sales of $19,000 for the month (that's $40 × 475 units sold). This example just looks at the *Gross Profit,* which is the profit from Sales before considering expenses incurred for operating the company. Book II Chapter 2 talks more about profit. Gross Profit is calculated by the following equation:

Sales – Cost of Goods Sold = Gross Profit

Looking at all three side by side

Table 1-1 shows a comparison of Gross Profit for the three methods used in this example scenario.

Table 1-1 **Comparison of Gross Profit Based on Inventory Valuation Method**

Income Statement Line Item	FIFO	LIFO	Averaging
Sales	$19,000	$19,000	$19,000
Cost of Goods Sold	$9,500	$11,000	$10,146
Gross Profit	$9,500	$8,000	$8,854

Looking at the comparisons of gross profit, you can see that inventory valuation can have a major impact on your bottom line. LIFO is likely to give you the lowest profit because the last inventory items bought are usually the most expensive. FIFO is likely to give you the highest profit because the first items bought are usually the cheapest. And the profit produced by the Averaging method is likely to fall somewhere in between the two.

Practice: Working with Inventory and Calculating Cost of Goods Sold

Q. If you purchase goods with cash and plan to sell them to customers, which accounts does your purchase impact?

a. Purchases and Cash

b. Purchases and Accounts Payable

c. Inventory and Cash

d. Inventory and Accounts Payable

A. The answer is a), Purchases and Cash. You enter a debit to the Purchases account, which increases the balance in the account and shows the additional expense. You enter a credit to the Cash account, which decreases the balance in that account.

Q. A hardware store owner purchased hammers several times during the month of April. (He doesn't have a warehouse, so all new goods purchased are put on the store shelves.):

Date	Quantity	Per-Hammer Price
April 1	150	$5.00
April 10	150	$7.50
April 20	200	$8.00

He started the month with 50 hammers worth $250. At the end of the month, when he counts what's left on the shelf, he has 75 units. What's the value of his Ending Inventory, and what was the Cost of Goods Sold?

A. To calculate inventory value, you start with the number of inventory at the beginning of the month. Then add the purchases made during the month. That total gives you the number of goods he had available for sale. Then you subtract the amount of inventory left on the shelf. The inventory left on the shelf is the Ending Inventory, and the difference between goods available for sale and ending inventory is the Cost of Goods Sold. The Ending Inventory is the value that goes in the asset account Inventory shown on the Balance Sheet, and the Cost of Goods shown would be an expense on the Income Statement.

Here's how you calculate the Cost of Goods sold and Ending Inventory by using the Averaging method:

Beginning Inventory	50	$250.00
Purchases	150 @ $5.00	$750.00
	150 @ $7.50	$1,125.00
	200 @ $8.00	<u>$1,600.00</u>
Total Goods Available for Sale		$3,725.00
Average Cost per Unit	($3,725/550) $6.77	
Ending Inventory	(75 × $6.77) $507.75	
Cost of Goods Sold	(550–75 = 475 goods sold × $6.77) $3,215.75	

1. If you keep track of the amount of inventory you have on hand by counting how much product is on your store shelves and in your warehouse, you have

a. A perpetual inventory system

b. A periodic inventory system

c. A physical inventory system

d. A counting inventory system

2. If your inventory is counted each time you ring up a sale on your register, you have

a. A perpetual inventory system

b. A periodic inventory system

c. A physical inventory system

d. A counting inventory system

3. If you work in a grocery store and carefully place the newest loaves of bread at the back of the shelf and bring the older loaves of bread to the front of the shelf, what type of inventory system does your store probably use?

a. FIFO

b. LIFO

c. Averaging

d. Specific Identification

4. If you work at a car dealership and you must track the sale of a car by using the original invoice price, what type of inventory system does your dealership probably use?

a. FIFO

b. LIFO

c. Averaging

d. Specific Identification

5. Harry's Hardware started the month with 25 wrenches on the shelf with an average per-unit value of $3.25. During the month, Harry made these additional purchases:

April 1	100 wrenches @ $3.50
April 10	100 wrenches @ $3.75
April 20	150 wrenches @ $4.00

At the end of the month, he had 100 wrenches on the shelf. Calculate the value of the ending inventory and the cost of goods sold by using the Averaging method.

Solve It

6. With the info for Harry's Hardware in Question 5, use the FIFO method to calculate the value of the Ending Inventory and the Cost of Goods Sold.

Solve It

7. With the info for Harry's Hardware in Question 5, use the LIFO method to calculate the value of the Ending Inventory and the Cost of Goods Sold

Solve It

Buying and Monitoring Supplies

In addition to inventory, all businesses must buy supplies (such as paper, pens, and paper clips) that are used to operate the business. Supplies that aren't bought in direct relationship to the manufacturing or purchasing of goods or services for sale fall into the category of *expenses*.

When it comes to monitoring the supplies you use, just how closely you want to watch things depends on your business needs. The expense categories you establish may be as broad as "Office Supplies" and "Retail Supplies," or you may want to set up accounts for each type of supply used. Each additional account is just one more thing that needs to be managed and monitored in the accounting system, so determine whether keeping a very detailed record of supplies is worth your time.

Your best bet is to carefully track supplies that make a big dent in your budget with an individual account. For example, if you anticipate paper usage will be very high, monitor that usage with a separate account called "Paper Expenses."

Note: Many companies don't use the bookkeeping system to manage their supplies. Instead, they designate one or two people as office managers or supply managers and keep the number of accounts used for supplies to a minimum. Other businesses decide they want to monitor supplies by department or division and set up a supply account for each one. That puts the burden of monitoring supplies in the hands of the department or division managers.

Staying on Top of Your Bills

Eventually, you have to pay for both the inventory and the supplies you purchase for your business. In most cases, the bills are posted to the Accounts Payable account when they arrive, and they're paid when due. The following sections cover some important bill paying considerations.

Keeping tasks separate

A large chunk of the cash paid out of your Cash account (see Book I Chapters 4 and 5 for more information on the Cash account and handling cash, respectively) is in the form of the checks sent out to pay bills due in Accounts Payable, so you need to have careful controls over the five key functions of Accounts Payable:

✔ Entering the bills to be paid into the accounting system

✔ Preparing checks to pay the bills

✔ Signing checks to pay the bills

✔ Sending out payment checks to vendors

✔ Reconciling the checking account

In your business, the person who enters the bills to be paid into the system likely also prepares the payment checks, but the other tasks should be done by someone else. You should never allow the person who prepares the check to review the bills to be paid and sign the checks, unless of course that person's you, the business owner. The person signing the checks should carefully review what's being paid, verify that proper management approvals for the payment are shown on that paperwork, and confirm that the amount being paid is accurate. You should also separate responsibilities to be sure that the person who reconciles your checking account isn't preparing or signing checks. (Book I Chapter 5 talks more about cash control and the importance of separating duties.)

Developing a system for Accounts Payable

Properly managing Accounts Payable can save your company a lot of money by avoiding late fees or interest and by taking advantage of discounts offered for paying early. If you're using a computerized accounting system, the bill due date and any discount information should be entered at the time you receive the inventory or supplies (refer to Figure 1-1 to see how you record this information).

If you're working with a paper system rather than a computerized accounting system, you need to set up some way to be sure you don't miss bill due dates. Many companies use two accordion files: one that's set up by the month, and the other that's set up by the day. When a bill first comes in, it's put into the first accordion file according to the month in which it's due. On the first day of that month, the Accounts Payable clerk pulls all the bills due that month and puts them in the daily accordion file based on the date the bill is due. Payment checks are then mailed in time to arrive in the vendor's office by the due date. Another method is to have bill payment set up with your bank. Your bank then automatically sends the remittance at the time you specify.

Book III

Day-to-Day Bookkeeping

Paying early if it benefits you

In some cases, companies offer a discount if their bills are paid early. For example, if the terms are stated as "2% 10 Net 30," that means that if the bill is paid in 10 days, the vendor company can take a 2 percent discount; otherwise, the amount due must be paid in full in 30 days. In addition, many companies state that interest or late fees will be charged if a bill isn't paid in 30 days.

Suppose the total amount due for a bill is $1,000. If the company pays the bill in ten days, it can take a 2 percent discount, or $20. That may not seem like much, but if your company buys $100,000 of inventory and supplies in a month and each vendor offers a similar discount, you can save $1,000 in that month. Over the course of a year, discounts on purchases can save your business a significant amount of money and improve your profits.

Practice: Calculating Discounts

Suppose a company receives a bill for $100,000 on March 31 that is stamped "2% 10 Net 30." What does that designation mean, and when should the bill be paid?

The stamp "2% 10 Net 30" means that the company can take a 2 percent discount if it pays the bill by April 10 (that is, within 10 days); otherwise, the full amount is due if paid between April 11 and April 30 (within 30 days). To calculate the discount, you multiply the total amount of the invoice by 2 percent and then subtract that amount from the bill total to find the discounted amount due.

$$\$100,000 \times 2\% = \$2,000$$

So the company saves $2,000 if it pays the bill by April 10.

Suppose a company receives a bill for $500,000 on March 31 that is stamped "3% 10 Net 30." What does that designation mean, and when should the bill be paid?

Book III

Day-to-Day Bookkeeping

Solve it:

_____

_____

_____

Suppose a company receives a bill for $100,000 on March 31 that's stamped "2% 15 Net 45." What does that designation mean, and when should the bill be paid?

Solve it:

_____

_____

_____

Answers to Problems on Buying and Tracking Your Purchases

1 b), A periodic inventory system.

2 a), A perpetual inventory system.

3 a), FIFO. A grocery store would want the first product in (oldest item) to be the first product out (first sold).

4 d), Specific Identification. A car dealership usually wants to maintain a specific identification system because each car in the inventory likely has different options and will have a different cost.

5 Here's how you calculate the ending inventory and cost of goods sold by using the averaging method:

Beginning Inventory	25 @ $3.25	$81.25
April 1	100 wrenches @ $3.50	$350.00
April 10	100 wrenches @ $3.75	$375.00
April 20	150 wrenches @ $4.00	$600.00
Total Goods Available for Sale	375 wrenches	$1,406.25
Average Cost per Unit	$1,406.25/375	$3.75
Ending Inventory	100 @ $3.75	$375.00
Cost of Goods Sold	275 @ $3.75	$1,031.25

6 Here's how you calculate the ending inventory and cost of goods sold by using the FIFO method:

Beginning Inventory	25 wrenches @ $3.25	$81.25
Next in: April 1	100 wrenches @ $3.50	$350.00
April 10	100 wrenches @ $3.75	$375.00
April 20	50 wrenches @ $4.00	$200.00
Cost of Goods Sold	$1,006.25	
Ending Inventory	100 wrenches @ $4.00	$400.00

7 Here's how you calculate the ending inventory and cost of goods sold by using the LIFO method:

First Sold purchased	April 20: 150 @ $4.00	$600.00	
Next Sold purchased	April 10: 100 @ $3.75	$375.00	
Next Sold purchased	April 1: 25 @ $3.50	$87.50	
Cost of Goods Sold	$1,062.50		
Ending Inventory			
	75 from April 1	$262.50	purchase @ $3.50
	25 from Beginning	$81.25	Inventory @ $3.25
		$343.75	

8 The stamp means that the company can receive a 3 percent discount if it pays the bill in 10 days by April 10 and no discount if it pays the bill between April 11 and April 30. The discount will be $15,000 if paid by April 10. So the bookkeeper or accountant should pay the bill by April 10 to take advantage of the discount.

9 The stamp means that the company can receive a 2 percent discount if it pays the bill in 15 days by April 15 and no discount if the bill is paid between April 16 and May 30. The discount will be $2,000 if paid by April 15. So the bookkeeper or accountant should pay the bill by April 15 to take advantage of the discount.

Chapter 2

Counting Your Sales

. . . .

In This Chapter

▶ Taking in cash

▶ Discovering the ins and outs of store credit

▶ Managing discounts for best results

▶ Staying on top of returns and allowances

▶ Monitoring payments due and dealing with bad debt

. . . .

*E*very business loves to take in money, and that means you, the book-keeper or accountant, have a lot to do to make sure sales are properly tracked and recorded in the books. In addition to recording the sales themselves, you must track customer accounts, discounts offered to customers, and customer returns and allowances.

If the company sells products on store credit, you have to carefully monitor customer accounts in Accounts Receivable, including monitoring whether customers pay on time and alerting the sales team if customers are behind on their bills and future purchases on credit need to be denied. Some customers never pay, and in that case, you must adjust the books to reflect nonpayment as a bad debt.

This chapter reviews the basic responsibilities that fall to a business's book-keeping and accounting staff for tracking sales, making adjustments to those sales, monitoring customer accounts, and notifying management of slow-paying customers.

Collecting on Cash Sales

Most businesses collect some form of cash as payment for the goods or services they sell. *Cash receipts* include more than just bills and coins; checks and credit cards also are considered cash sales for the purpose of bookkeeping. In fact, with electronic transaction processing (that's when a customer's credit card is swiped through a machine), a deposit is usually made to the business's checking account the same day (sometimes within just seconds of the transaction, depending on the type of system the business sets up with the bank).

The only type of payment that doesn't fall under the umbrella of a cash payment is purchases made on store credit. *Store credit* means credit offered to customers directly by your business rather than through a third party, such as a bank credit card or loan. This type of sale is discussed in the section "Selling on Credit" later in this chapter.

Discovering the value of sales receipts

Modern businesses generate sales slips in one of three ways: by the cash register, by the credit card machine, or by hand (written out by the salesperson). Whichever of these three methods you choose to handle your sales transactions, the sales receipt serves two purposes:

✔ Gives the customer proof that the item was purchased on a particular day at a particular price in your store in case he needs to exchange or return the merchandise.

✔ Gives the store a receipt that can be used at a later time to enter the transaction into the company's books. At the end of the day, the receipts also are used to *prove out* (show that they have the right amount of cash in the register based on the sales transactions during the day) the cash register and ensure that the cashier has taken in the right amount of cash based on the sales made. (Book I Chapter 5 talks more about how cash receipts can be used as an internal control tool to manage your cash.)

You're probably familiar with cash receipts, but just to show you how much useable information can be generated for the bookkeeper on a sales receipt, here's a sample receipt from a sale at a bakery:

Sales Receipt 4/25/2015

Item	Quantity	Price	Total
White Serving Set	1	$40	$40
Cheesecake, Marble	1	$20	$20
Cheesecake, Blueberry	1	$20	$20
			$80.00
Sales Tax @ 6%			$4.80
			$84.80
Cash Paid			$90.00
Change			$5.20

You've probably never thought about how much bookkeeping information is included on a sales receipt, but receipts contain a wealth of information that's collected for your company's accounting system. A look at a receipt tells you the amount of cash collected, the type of products sold, the quantity of products sold, and how much sales tax was collected.

Unless your company uses some type of computerized system at the point of sale (which is usually the cash register) that's integrated into the company's accounting system, sales information is collected throughout the day by the cash register and printed out in a summary form at the end of the day. At that point, you enter the details of the sales day in the books.

If you don't use your computerized system to monitor inventory, you use the data collected by the cash register to simply enter into the books the cash received, total sales, and sales tax collected. Although in actuality, you'd have many more sales and much higher numbers at the end of the day, here's what an entry in the Cash Receipts journal would look like for the receipt:

	Debit	*Credit*
Cash in Checking	$84.80	
Sales		$80.00
Sales Tax Collected		$4.80

Cash receipts for 4/25/2011

Book III

Day-to-Day Bookkeeping

In this example entry, Cash in Checking is an asset account shown on the balance sheet (see Book II Chapter 4 for more about balance sheets), and its value increases with the debit. The Sales account is a revenue account on the income statement (see Book II Chapter 5 for more about income statements), and its balance increases with a credit, showing additional revenue. (Book I Chapter 1 introduces debits and credits.) The Sales Tax Collected account is a Liability account that appears on the balance sheet, and its balance increases with this transaction.

Businesses pay sales tax to state and local government entities either monthly or quarterly depending on rules set by the states, so your business must hold the money owed in a liability account to be certain you're able to pay the taxes collected from customers when they're due. Book V Chapter 4 talks more about tax reporting and payment.

Recording cash transactions in the books

If you're using a computerized accounting system, you can enter more detail from the day's receipts and track inventory sold as well. Most of the computerized accounting systems do include the ability to track the sale of inventory. Figure 2-1 shows you the QuickBooks Sales receipt form that you can use to input data from each day's sales.

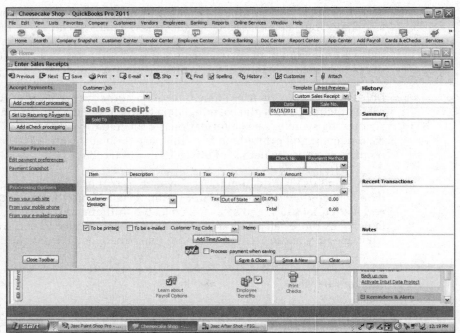

Figure 2-1: Example of a sales receipt in QuickBooks.

In addition to the information included in the Cash Receipts journal, note that QuickBooks also collects information about the items sold in each transaction. QuickBooks then automatically updates inventory information, reducing the amount of inventory on hand when necessary. When the inventory number falls below the reorder number you set, QuickBooks alerts you to pass the word on to whoever is responsible for ordering to order more inventory.

If the sales receipt in Figure 2-1 were for an individual customer, you'd enter his or her name and address in the "Sold To" field. At the bottom of the receipt, you can see a section asking whether you want to print or email the receipt; you can print the receipt and give it to the customer or email it to the customer if the order was made by phone or Internet. The bottom of the receipt also has a place to mark whether the item should be charged to a credit card. (For an additional fee, QuickBooks allows you to process credit card receipts when saving an individual cash receipt.)

If your company accepts credit cards, expect sales revenue to be reduced by the fees paid to credit card companies. Usually, you face monthly fees as well as fees per transaction; however, each company sets up individual arrangements with its bank regarding these fees. Sales volume impacts how much you pay in fees, so when researching bank services, be sure to compare credit card transaction fees to find a good deal.

Practice: Recording Sales in the Books

Q. How do you record the following transaction in your books?

Sales Receipt 2/15/2015

Item	Quantity	Price	Total
Pecan Pie	1	$35.00	$35.00
Cheesecake	1	$35.00	$35.00
Pound Cookies	1	$10.00	$10.00
Subtotal Sales			$80.00
Sales Tax @ 7%			$5.60
Total Sales			$85.60
Cash Paid			$90.00
Change			$4.40

A. The key numbers you need to use are Total Sales, Subtotal Sales, and Sales Tax. Here's what the bookkeeping entry looks like:

	Debit	Credit
Cash in Checking	$85.60	
Sales		$80.00
Sales Tax Collected		$5.60

Cash receipts for 2/25/2015

You record the information from this entry in your Sales journal (see Book I Chapter 4). Note that you enter a debit to the Cash in Checking account and a credit to the Sales and Sales Tax Collected accounts. Equal amounts are posted to both the debits and the Credits. That should always be true; your bookkeeping entries should always be in balance. These entries would increase the amount in all three accounts. To understand more about how debits and credits work, (re)read Book I Chapter 1.

When you work for a company, you typically get a summary of total sales for the day and may not necessarily need to add up each receipt, depending on the types of cash registers used in your store. The entry into your books in that case would most likely be a total of cash sales on a daily basis.

Book III

Day-to-Day Bookkeeping

1. How do you record the following transaction in your books if you're the book-keeper for a hardware store?

Sales Receipt 2/25/2015

Item	Quantity	Price	Total
Hammer	1	$15.00	$15.00
Paint Brushes	5	$5.00	$25.00
Paint	2 gallons	$10.00	$20.00
			$60.00
Sales Tax @ 7%			$4.20
Total Sale			$64.20
Paid by Visa Credit Card			$64.20

2. How do you record the following transaction in your books if you're a bookkeeper for an office supply store?

Sales Receipt 3/05/2015

Item	Quantity	Price	Total
Paper	2 boxes	$15.00	$30.00
Print Cartridge	1	$25.00	$25.00
Hanging Files	2 boxes	$10.00	$20.00
			$75.00
Sales Tax @ 6%			$4.50
Total Sale			$79.50
Paid by Personal Check			$79.50

Selling on Credit

Many businesses decide to sell to customers on *direct credit,* meaning credit offered by the business and not through a bank or credit card provider. This approach offers more flexibility in the type of terms you can offer your customers, and you don't have to pay bank fees. However, it involves more work for you, the bookkeeper, and more risk if a customer doesn't pay what he or she owes.

If you accept a customer's bank-issued credit card for a sale and the customer doesn't pay the bill, you get your money, and the bank is responsible for collecting from the customer and takes the loss if he or she doesn't pay. That's not the case if you decide to offer credit to your customers directly. If a customer doesn't pay, your business takes the loss.

Deciding whether to offer store credit

The decision to set up your own store credit system depends on what your competition is doing. For example, if you run an office supply store and all other office supply stores allow store credit to make it easier for their customers to get supplies, you probably need to offer store credit to stay competitive.

If you want to allow your customers to buy on store credit, the first thing you need to do is set up some ground rules. You have to decide

- How you plan to check a customer's credit history
- What the customer's income level needs to be to be approved for credit
- How long you give the customer to pay the bill before charging interest or late fees

Book III

Day-to-Day Bookkeeping

The harder you make it to get store credit and the stricter you make the bill-paying rules, the less chance you have of a taking a loss. However, you may lose customers to a competitor with lighter credit rules. For example, you may require a minimum income level of $50,000 and make customers pay in 30 days if they want to avoid late fees or interest charges. Your sales staff reports that these rules are too rigid because your direct competitor down the street allows credit on a minimum income level of $30,000 and gives customers 60 days to pay before late fees and interest charges.

Now you have to decide whether you want to change your credit rules to match the competition's. But, if you do lower your credit standards to match your competitor, you may end up with more customers who can't pay on time or at all because you've qualified customers for credit at lower income levels and given them more time to pay. If you loosen your qualification criteria and bill-paying requirements, you have to carefully monitor your customer accounts to be sure they're not falling behind.

The key risk you face is selling product for which you're never paid. For example, if you allow customers 30 days to pay and cut them off from buying goods if their accounts fall more than 30 days behind, the most you can lose is the amount purchased over a two-month period (60 days). But if you give customers more leniency, allowing them 60 days to pay and cutting them off after payment's 30 days late, you're faced with three months (90 days) of purchases for which you may never be paid.

Recording store credit transactions in the books

When sales are made on store credit, you have to enter specific information into the accounting system. In addition to inputting information regarding cash receipts (see "Collecting on Cash Sales" earlier in this chapter), you update the customer accounts to be sure each customer is billed and the money is collected. You debit the Accounts Receivable account, an asset account shown on the Balance Sheet (see Book II Chapter 4), which shows money due from customers.

Here's how a journal entry of a sale made on store credit looks:

	Debit	Credit
Accounts Receivable	$84.80	
Sales		$80.00
Sales Tax Collected		$4.80

Cash receipts for 4/25/2015

In addition to making this journal entry, you enter the information into the customer's account so that accurate bills can be sent out at the end of the month. When the customer pays the bill, you update the individual customer's record to show that payment has been received and enter the following into the bookkeeping records:

	Debit	Credit
Cash	$84.80	
Accounts Receivable		$84.80

Payment from S. Smith on invoice 123.

If you're using QuickBooks, you enter purchases on store credit by using an invoice form like the one in Figure 2-2. Most of the information on the invoice form is similar to the sales receipt form (see "Collecting on Cash Sales"), but the invoice form also has space to enter a different address for shipping (the "Ship To" field) and includes payment terms (the "Terms" field). For the sample invoice form shown in Figure 2-2, you can see that payment is due in 30 days.

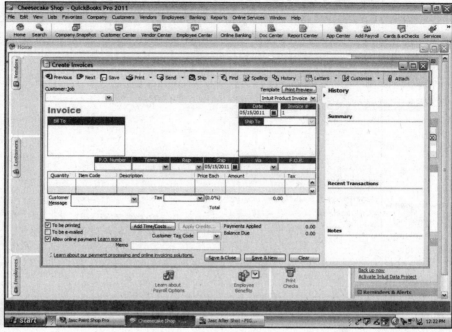

Figure 2-2:
QuickBooks
sales
invoice for
purchases
made on
store credit.

Book III

Day-to-Day Bookkeeping

QuickBooks uses the information on the invoice form to update the following accounts:

- ✔ Accounts Receivable
- ✔ Inventory
- ✔ The customer's account
- ✔ Sales Tax Collected

Based on this data, when it comes time to bill the customer at the end of the month, QuickBooks generates statements for all customers with outstanding invoices with a little prompting from you (see Figure 2-3). You can easily generate statements for specific customers or all customers on the books.

When you receive payment from a customer, here's what happens:

1. You enter the customer's name on the customer payment form (shown in Figure 2-4).

2. QuickBooks automatically lists all outstanding invoices.

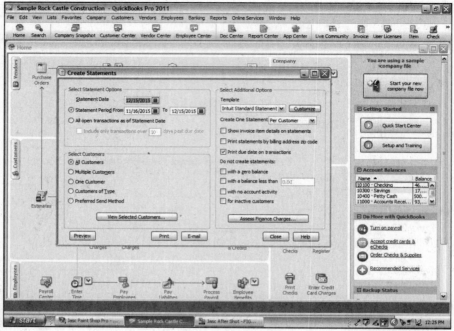

Figure 2-3:
Generating
statements
for
customers
with
QuickBooks.

3. You select the invoice or invoices paid.

4. QuickBooks updates the Accounts Receivable account, the Cash
   account, and the customer's individual account to show that payment
   has been received.

If your company uses a point of sale program that's integrated into the computerized accounting system, recording store credit transactions is even
easier for you. Sales details feed into the system as each sale is made, so you
don't have to enter the detail at the end of day. These point of sale programs
save a lot of time, but they can get very expensive — usually at least $500 for
just one cash register.

Even if customers don't buy on store credit, point of sale programs provide
businesses with an incredible amount of information about their customers
and what they like to buy. This data can be used in the future for direct marketing and special sales to increase the likelihood of return business.

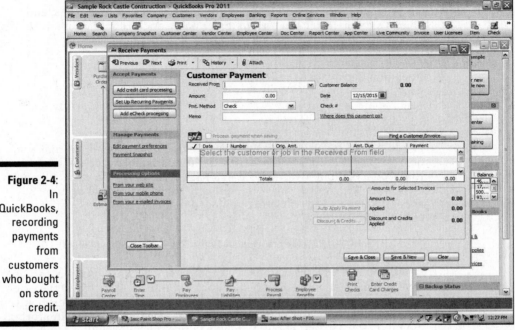

Figure 2-4: In QuickBooks, recording payments from customers who bought on store credit.

Book III

Day-to-Day Bookkeeping

Practice: Sales on Store (Direct) Credit

Q. Suppose you're the bookkeeper for a bakery that allows customers to buy on store credit. How do you record the following sales transaction in your books?

Sales Receipt #456, 2/15/2015, First Baptist Church, Account #10356

Item	Quantity	Price	Total
Pecan Pie	1	$35.00	$35.00
Cheesecake	1	$35.00	$35.00
Pound Cookies	1	$10.00	$10.00
			$80.00
Sales Tax @ 7%			$5.60
Total Sale			$85.60

A. The key numbers you need to use are Total Sales, Subtotal Sales, and Sales Tax. You also need the customer name and account number. Here's what the bookkeeping entry looks like:

	Debit	*Credit*
Accounts Receivable	$85.60	
Sales		$80.00
Sales Tax Collected		$5.60

Credit receipts for 2/25/2015

In addition to recording the sales transaction in your Sales Journal, you also need to record the transaction in the customer's account, whether that's on a computer worksheet, in a paper journal, or on cards for each customer. Whichever way your company tracks individual customer accounts, here's the entry that you need to make to the account of the First Baptist Church:

2/15/2015 Baked Goods — Sales Receipt #456 $85.60

When you record a transaction in a customer's account, you want to be sure you have enough identifying information to be able to find the original sales transaction in case the customer questions the charge when you send the bill at the end of the month. The upcoming section "Monitoring Accounts Receivable" shows you how to use this information to bill and collect from your customers.

3. Suppose you're the bookkeeper for a hardware store that allows customers to buy on store credit. How do you record the following sales transaction in your books?

Sales Receipt 2/25/2015, Joe Tester, Account #789			
Item	**Quantity**	**Price**	**Total**
Hammer	1	$15.00	$15.00
Paint Brushes	5	$5.00	$25.00
Paint	2 gallons	$10.00	$20.00
			$60.00
Sales Tax @ 7%			$4.20
Total Sale			$64.20

4. Suppose you're the bookkeeper for an office supply store that allows customers to buy on store credit. How do you record the following sales transaction in your books?

Sales Receipt 3/05/2015, Sue's Insurance Agency, Account #156			
Item	*Quantity*	*Price*	*Total*
Paper	2 boxes	$15.00	$30.00
Print Cartridge	1	$25.00	$25.00
Hanging Files	2 boxes	$10.00	$20.00
			$75.00
Sales Tax @ 6%			$4.50
Total Sale			$79.50

Proving Out the Cash Register

To ensure that cashiers don't pocket a business's cash, at the end of each day, cashiers must *prove out* the amount in cash, checks, and charges they took in during the day.

Book III

Day-to-Day Bookkeeping

This process of proving out a cash register actually starts at the end of the previous day, when a cashier and his manager agree to the amount of cash left in the cash register drawer. Cash sitting in cash registers or cash drawers is recorded as part of the Cash on Hand account.

You monitor cash by knowing exactly how much cash was in the register at the beginning of the day and then checking how much cash is left at the end of the day. You should count the cash at the end of the day as soon as all sales transactions have been completed and print out a summary of all transactions. In many companies, the sales manager actually cashes out the register at night with the cashiers and gives you the copy of the completed cash-out form. Here's one example of a cash-out form:

Cash Register: _____	Date: _____	
Receipts	*Sales*	*Cash in Register*
Beginning Cash	_____	_____
Cash Sales	_____	_____

(continued)

(continued)

Receipts	Sales	Cash in Register
Credit Card Sales	_____	_____
Store Credit Sales	_____	_____
Total Sales	_____	_____
Minus Sales on Credit	_____	_____
Total Cash Received	_____	_____
Total Cash that Should Be in Register		_____
Actual Cash in Register		_____
Difference		_____

A store manager reviews the cashier's cash register summary (produced by the actual register) and compares it to the cash-out form. If the ending cash (the amount of cash remaining in the register) doesn't match the cash-out form, the cashier and the manager try to pinpoint the mistake. If they can't find a mistake, they fill out a cash-overage or cash-shortage form. Some businesses charge the cashier directly for any shortages, while others take the position that the cashier will be fired after a certain number of shortages of a certain dollar amount (say, three shortages of more than $10). Some states have laws against deducting a shortage from an employee's pay.

The store manager decides how much cash to leave in the cash drawer or register for the next day and deposits the remainder. He does this task for each of his cashiers and then deposits all the cash and checks from the day in a night deposit box at the bank. He sends a report with details of the deposit to the bookkeeper so that the data makes it into the accounting system. The bookkeeper enters the data on the Cash Receipts form (see Figure 2-1 earlier in the chapter) if a computerized accounting system is being used or into the Cash Receipts journal if the books are being kept manually.

Book IV Chapter 3 covers proving out the cash in detail.

Practice: Proving Out

Q. Suppose you began the day with $100 in the register and ended the day with $264.50 in the register. Is the ending cash total in the following cash summary correct?

Sales Summary for 3/05/2015

Item	Quantity	Price	Total
Paper	10 boxes	$15.00	$150.00
Print Cartridges	5	$25.00	$125.00
Hanging Files	7 boxes	$10.00	$70.00
Envelopes	10 boxes	$7.00	$70.00
Pens	20 boxes	$8.00	$160.00
			$575.00
Sales Tax @ 6%			$34.50
Total Cash Sales			$159.50
Total Credit Card Sales			$200.00
Total Store Credit Sales			$250.00
Total Sales			$609.50

A. Complete the following cash-out form:

Cash Register: Sales Summary   Date: 3/5/2015

Receipts	Sales	Cash in Register
Beginning Cash		$100.00
Cash Sales	$159.50	
Credit Card Sales	$200.00	
Store Credit Sales	$250.00	
Total Sales	$609.50	
Minus Sales on Credit	($450.00)	
Total Cash Received		$159.50
Total Cash that Should be in Register		$259.50
Actual Cash in Register		$264.50
Difference		Overage of $5.00

So in this example, with the cash remaining in the cash register, the cashier actually took in $5 more than needed, most likely from an error in giving change.

5. Suppose the cash register had $100 at the beginning of the day and $316.10 at the end of the day. Use the following cash register summary to fill out the blank cash-out form and determine whether the ending cash total in the summary is correct.

Cash Register: Sales Summary   Date: 3/15/2015

Item	Quantity	Price	Total
Paper	20 boxes	$15.00	$300.00
Print Cartridges	10	$25.00	$250.00
Envelopes	10 boxes	$7.00	$70.00
Pens	20 boxes	$8.00	$160.00
			$780.00
Sales Tax @ 6%			$46.80
Total Cash Sales			$226.80
Total Credit Card Sales			$200.00
Total Store Credit Sales			$400.00
Total Sales			$826.80

Cash Register: Sales Summary   Date: 3/15/2015

Receipts	Sales	Cash in Register
Beginning Cash	____	____
Cash Sales	____	____
Credit Card Sales	____	____
Store Credit Sales	____	____
Total Sales	____	____
Minus Sales on Credit	____	____
Total Cash Received	____	____
Total Cash that Should Be in Register		____
Actual Cash in Register		____
Difference		____

Tracking Sales Discounts

Most business offer discounts at some point in time to generate more sales. Discounts are usually in the form of a sale with 10 percent, 20 percent, or even more off purchases.

When you offer discounts to customers, it's a good idea to track your sales discounts in a separate account so that you can keep an eye on how much you discount sales in each month. If you find you're losing more and more money to discounting, look closely at your pricing structure and competition to find out why you frequently need to lower your prices to make sales. You can track discount information very easily by using the data found on a standard sales register receipt. The following receipt from a bakery includes sales discount details:

Sales Receipt 4/25/2015

Item	Quantity	Price	Total
White Serving Set	1	$40	$40
Cheesecake, Marble	1	$20	$20
Cheesecake, Blueberry	1	$20	$20
			$80.00
Sales Discount @ 10%			(8.00)
			$72.00
Sales Tax @ 6%			4.32
			$76.32
Cash Paid			$80.00
Change			$3.68

Book III

Day-to-Day Bookkeeping

From this example, you can see clearly that stores take in less cash when offering discounts. When recording the sale in the Cash Receipts journal, you record the discount as a debit. This debit increases the Sales Discount account, which is subtracted from the Sales account to calculate the Net Sales. (Book II Chapter 5 walks you through all these steps and calculations in the discussion of preparing the income statement.) Here's what the bakery's entry for this particular sale looks like in the Cash Receipts journal:

	Debit	Credit
Cash in Checking	$76.32	
Sales Discounts	$8.00	
Sales		$80.00
Sales Tax Collected		$4.32

Cash receipts for 4/25/2015

If you use a computerized accounting system, add the sales discount as a line item on the sales receipt or invoice, and the system automatically adjusts the sales figures and updates your Sales Discount account.

Practice: Recording Discounts

Q. How do you record the following sales transaction?

Sales Receipt 2/15/2015

Item	Quantity	Price	Total
Pecan Pie	1	$35.00	$35.00
Cheesecake	1	$35.00	$35.00
Pound Cookies	1	$10.00	$10.00
			$80.00
Sales Discount @ 10%			(8.00)
			$72.00
Sales Tax @ 7%			$5.04
Total Sales			$77.04
Cash Paid			$80.00
Change			$2.96

A. Here's what the bookkeeping entry looks like:

	Debit	Credit
Cash in Checking	$77.04	
Sales Discount	$8.00	
Sales		$80.00
Sales Tax Collected		$5.04

Cash receipts for 2/15/2015

Note that in this situation, the Cash in Checking amount is actually less than the sales amount to compensate for the lost revenue for the sales discount. Yet when you total the debit and credit entries, they're equal — both total to $85.04.

6. How do you record the following transaction in your books?

Sales Receipt 3/05/2015

Item	Quantity	Price	Total
Paper	2 boxes	$15.00	$30.00
Print Cartridge	1	$25.00	$25.00
Hanging Files	2 boxes	$10.00	$20.00
			$75.00
Sales Discount @ 20%			$15.00
			$60.00
Sales Tax @ 6%			$3.60
Total Cash Sale			$63.60

7. How do you record the following credit transaction in your books?

Sales Summary for 3/05/2015

Item	Quantity	Price	Total
Paper	10 boxes	$15.00	$150.00
Print Cartridges	5	$25.00	$125.00
Hanging Files	7 boxes	$10.00	$70.00
Envelopes	10 boxes	$7.00	$70.00
Pens	20 boxes	$8.00	$160.00
			$575.00
Sales Discount @20%			$115.00
			$460.00
Sales Tax @ 6%			$27.60
Total Cash Sales			$162.60
Total Credit Card Sales			$150.00
Total Store Credit Sales			$175.00
Total Sales			$487.60

Recording Sales Returns and Allowances

Most stores deal with *sales returns* on a regular basis. Customers commonly return items they've purchased because the item is defective, because they've changed their minds, or for any other reason. Instituting a no-return policy is guaranteed to produce very unhappy customers, so to maintain good customer relations, you should allow sales returns.

Sales allowances (sales incentive programs) are becoming more popular with businesses. Sales allowances are most often in the form of a gift card. A gift card that's sold is actually a liability for the company because the company has received cash, but no merchandise has gone out; therefore, the company has to keep track of how much is yet to be sold without receiving additional cash. For that reason, gift card sales are entered in a Gift Card liability account. When a customer makes a purchase at a later date with the gift card, the Gift Card liability account is reduced by the purchase amount.

Accepting sales returns can be a more complicated process than accepting sales allowances. Usually, a business posts a set of rules for returns that may include stipulations like the following:

✔ Returns are only allowed within 30 days of purchase.

✔ You must have a receipt to return an item.

✔ If you return an item without a receipt, you can receive only store credit.

You can set up whatever rules you want for returns. For internal control purposes, the key to returns is monitoring how your staff handles them. In most cases, you should require a manager's approval on returns. Also, be sure your staff pays close attention to how the customer originally paid for the item being returned. You certainly don't want to give a customer cash if she paid on store credit — that's just handing over your money! After a return is approved, the cashier either returns the amount paid by cash or credit card. Customers who bought the items on store credit don't get any money back. That's because they didn't pay anything when they purchased the item but expected to be billed later. Instead, the cashier fills out a form so that the amount of the original purchase can be subtracted from the customer's store credit account.

You use the information collected by the cashier who handled the return to input the sales return data into the books. For example, if a customer returns a $40 item that was purchased with cash, you record the cash refund in the Cash Receipts Journal like this:

	Debit	Credit
Sales Returns and Allowances	$40.00	
Sales Taxes Collected @ 6%	$2.40	
Cash in Checking		$42.40

To record return of purchase, 4/30/2015

If the item had been bought with a discount, you'd list the discount as well and adjust the price to show that discount.

In this journal entry, the following is true:

- ✔ The Sales Returns and Allowances account increases. This account normally carries a debit balance and is subtracted from Sales when preparing the income statement, thereby reducing revenue received from customers.

- ✔ The debit to the Sales Tax Collected account reduces the amount in that account because sales tax is no longer due on the purchase.

- ✔ The credit to the Cash in Checking account reduces the amount of cash in that account.

Practice: Tracking Sales Returns and Allowances

Q. A customer returns a blouse she bought with cash for $40. She has a receipt showing when she made the original purchase; the sales tax is 6 percent. How do you record that transaction in the books?

A. Here's how you record the transaction:

	Debit	Credit
Sales Returns and Allowances	$40.00	
Sales Taxes Collected	$2.40	
Cash in Checking		$42.40

8. A customer returns a pair of pants he bought on a credit card for $35. He has a receipt showing when he made the original purchase; the sales tax is 6 percent. How do you record that transaction in the books?

9. A customer returns a toy she bought with cash for $25. She has a receipt for the purchase; the sales tax is 6 percent. How do you record that transaction in the books?

Book III

Day-to-Day Bookkeeping

Monitoring Accounts Receivable

Making sure customers pay their bills is a crucial responsibility of the book-keeper. Before sending out the monthly bills, you should prepare an *Aging Summary Report* that lists all customers who owe money to the company and how old each debt is. If you keep the books manually, you collect the necessary information from each customer account. If you keep the books in a computerized accounting system, you can generate this report automatically. Either way, your Aging Summary Report should look similar to this example report:

Aging Summary: As of May 1, 2015

Customer	Current	31–60 Days	61–90 Days	>90 Days
S. Smith	$84.32	$46.15		
J. Doe			$65.78	
H. Harris	$89.54			
M. Man				$125.35
Totals	$173.86	$46.15	$65.78	$125.35

The Aging Summary quickly tells you which customers are behind in their bills. In the case of this example, customers are cut off from future purchases when their payments are more than 60 days late, so J. Doe and M. Man aren't able to buy on store credit until their bills are paid in full.

Give a copy of your Aging Summary to the sales manager so he can alert staff to problem customers. He can also arrange for the appropriate collections procedures. Each business sets up its own collections process, but usually it starts with a phone call, followed by letters, and possibly even legal action, if necessary.

Practice: Aging Summary

 Q. The following list shows five customers who bought on credit from the office supply store and had not yet paid their bills as of 3/31/2015. Prepare an Aging Summary report as of March 31 for all outstanding customer accounts.

Customer	Date of Purchase	Amount Purchased
Sue's Insurance Company	3/5/2015	$79.50
Joe Tester	2/25/2015	$64.20
First Baptist Church	2/15/2015	$85.60
	3/15/2015	$67.20
Jane Doe	1/15/2015	$49.50
Harry Man	12/23/2015	$89.20

A. Here's what the Aging Summary report looks like:

Aging Summary: As of March 31, 2014				
Customer	Current	31–60 Days	61–90 Days	>90 Days
Sue's Insurance	$79.50			
Joe Tester		$64.20		
First Baptist Church	$67.20	$85.60		
Jane Doe			$49.50	
Harry Man				$89.20
Totals	$146.70	$149.80	$49.50	$89.20

Book III

Day-to-Day Bookkeeping

10. Use the information from the following account list to set up an Aging Summary as of 4/30/2015:

Customer	Date of Purchase	Amount Purchased
Sarah Smith	4/5/2015	$37.85
Joe James	3/15/2015	$63.20
Manny's Restaurant	3/20/2015	$135.20
	4/15/2015	$128.75
Harry Harris	2/25/2015	$49.50
Maury Man	1/5/2015	$89.20

Accepting Your Losses

You may encounter a situation in which your business never gets paid by a customer, even after an aggressive collections process. In this case, you have no choice but to write off the purchase as a *bad debt* and accept the loss.

Most businesses review their Aging Reports every 6 to 12 months and decide which accounts need to be written off as bad debt. Accounts written off are tracked in a General Ledger account called *Bad Debt.* (See Book I Chapter 3 for more information about the General Ledger.) The Bad Debt account appears as an expense account on the income statement. When you write off a customer's account as bad debt, the Bad Debt account increases, and the Accounts Receivable account decreases.

To give you an idea of how you write off an account, assume that a customer never pays the $105.75 it owes. Here's what your journal entry looks like for this debt:

	Debit	*Credit*
Bad Debt	$105.75	
Accounts Receivable		$105.75

In a computerized accounting system, you enter the information by using a customer payment form and allocate the amount due to the Bad Debt expense account.

Answers to Counting Your Sales

1 Here's what the transaction entry looks like:

	Debit	*Credit*
Cash in Checking	$64.20	
Sales		$60.00
Sales Tax Collected		$4.20
Cash receipts for 2/25/2015		

2 Here's what the transaction entry looks like:

	Debit	*Credit*
Cash in Checking	$79.50	
Sales		$75.00
Sales Tax Collected		$4.50
Cash receipts for 3/5/2015		

3 Here's what the transaction entry looks like:

	Debit	Credit
Accounts Receivable	$64.20	
Sales		$60.00
Sales Tax Collected		$4.20

Credit receipts for 2/25/2015

4 Here's what the transaction entry looks like:

	Debit	Credit
Accounts Receivable	$79.50	
Sales		$75.00
Sales Tax Collected		$4.50

Credit receipts for 3/5/2015

5 Here's how you complete the cash out form.

Cash Register: Jane Doe	Date: 3/15/2015	
Receipts	**Sales**	**Cash in Register**
Beginning Cash		$100.00
Cash Sales	$226.80	
Credit Card Sales	$200.00	
Store Credit Sales	$400.00	
Total Sales	$826.80	
Minus Sales on Credit	$600.00	
Total Cash Received		$226.80
Total Cash that Should be in Register		$326.80
Actual Cash in Register		$316.10
Difference		Shortage of $10.70

6 Here's what the transaction entry looks like:

	Debit	Credit
Cash in Checking	$63.60	
Sales Discount	$15.00	
Sales		$75.00
Sales Tax Collected		$3.60

Cash receipts for 3/5/2015

7 Here's what the transaction entry looks like:

	Debit	Credit
Cash in Checking	$312.60	
Accounts Receivable	$175.00	
Sales Discount	$115.00	
Sales		$575.00
Sales Tax Collected		$27.60

Cash receipts for 3/5/2015

8 Here's what the transaction entry looks like:

	Debit	Credit
Sales Returns and Allowances	$35.00	
Sales Taxes Collected	$2.10	
Cash in Checking		$37.10

Even though the customer is receiving a credit on his credit card, you show this refund by crediting your "Cash in Checking" account. Remember that when a customer uses a credit card, the card is processed by the bank and cash is deposited in the store's checking account.

9 Here's what the transaction entry looks like:

	Debit	Credit
Sales Returns and Allowances	$25.00	
Sales Taxes Collected	$1.50	
Cash in Checking		$26.50

10 Here's what the Aging Summary report looks like:

Aging Summary: As of April 30, 2015

Customer	Current	31–60 Days	61–90 Days	>90 Days
Sarah Smith	$37.85			
Joe James		$63.20		
Manny's Restaurant	$128.75	$135.20		
Harry Harris			$49.50	
Maury Man				$89.20
Totals	$166.60	$198.40	$49.50	$89.20

Chapter 3

Employee Payroll and Benefits

. . . .

In This Chapter

▶ Planning for your pay structure

▶ Figuring net pay and collecting and depositing employee taxes

▶ Keeping track of benefits

▶ Preparing and recording payroll

▶ Finding new ways to deal with payroll responsibilities

. . . .

*U*nless your business has only one employee (you, the owner), you'll most likely hire employees, and that means you'll have to pay them, offer benefits, and manage a payroll.

Responsibilities for hiring and paying employees usually are shared between the human resources staff and the bookkeeping staff. As the bookkeeper, you must be sure that all government tax-related forms are completed and handle all payroll responsibilities, including paying employees, collecting and paying employee taxes, collecting and managing employee benefit contributions, and paying benefit providers. This chapter examines the various employee staffing issues that bookkeepers need to be able to manage.

Setting the Stage for Staffing: Making Payroll Decisions

After you decide that you want to hire employees for your business, you must be ready to deal with a lot of government paperwork. In addition to paperwork, you face many decisions about how to pay employees and who will be responsible for maintaining the paperwork required by state, local, and federal government entities.

Knowing what needs to be done to satisfy government bureaucracies isn't the only issue you must consider before the first person is hired; you also must decide how frequently you will pay employees and what type of wage and salary scales you want to set up.

Completing government forms

Even before you hire your first employee, you need to start filing government forms related to hiring. If you plan to hire staff, you must first apply for an Employer Identification Number, or EIN. Government entities use this number to track your employees, the money you pay them, and any taxes collected and paid on their behalf.

Before employees start working for you, they must fill out forms, including the W-4 (tax withholding form) and I-9 (citizenship verification form). The following sections explain each of these forms as well as the EIN.

Employer Identification Number (EIN)

Every company must have an EIN to hire employees. If your company is incorporated, which means you've filed paperwork with the state and become a separate legal entity, you already have an EIN. Otherwise, you must complete and submit Form SS-4 to get an EIN.

Luckily, the government offers two ways to submit the necessary information and obtain an EIN. You used to be able to call and complete the form by telephone, but beginning in 2014, the IRS began referring refer all domestic EIN requests received by toll-free phones to the EIN Online Assistant. You access the Assistant by going to www.irs.gov, entering "EIN" in the Search feature, and following instructions for applying for an EIN online. You get your EIN immediately after completing the application. You can also download Form SS-4 at www.irs.gov/pub/irs-pdf/fss4.pdf and submit it by fax or by mail.

In addition to tracking pay and taxes, state entities use the EIN number to track the payment of unemployment taxes and workers' compensation taxes, both of which the employer must pay. Book III Chapter 4 talks more about them.

W-4

Every person you hire must fill out a W-4 form called the "Employee's Withholding Allowance Certificate." You've probably filled out a W-4 at least once in your life if you've ever worked for someone else. You can download this form and make copies for your employees at www.irs.gov/pub/irs-pdf/fw4.pdf.

This form tells you, the employer, how much to take out of your employees' paychecks in income taxes. On the W-4, employees indicate whether they're married or single. They can also claim additional allowances if they have children or other major deductions that can reduce their tax bills. The amount of income taxes you need to take out of each employee's check depends on how many allowances he or she claimed on the W-4.

It's a good idea to ask employees to fill out a W-4 immediately, but you can allow them to take the form home if they want to discuss allowances with a spouse or accountant. If an employee doesn't complete a W-4, you must take income taxes out of his check based on the highest possible amount for that person. The section "Collecting Employee Taxes" later in this chapter talks more about this.

An employee can always fill out a new W-4 to reflect life changes that impact tax deductions. For example, if the employee was single when he started working for you and gets married a year later, he can fill out a new W-4 and claim his spouse, lowering the amount of taxes that must be deducted from his check. Another common life change that can reduce an employee's tax deduction is the birth or adoption of a baby.

I-9

All employers in the United States must verify that any person they intend to hire is a U.S. citizen or has the right to work in the United States. As an employer, you verify this information by completing and keeping on file an I-9 form from the U.S. Citizenship and Immigration Services (USCIS). The new hire fills out Section 1 of the form by providing information about his name and address, birth history, Social Security number, and U.S. Citizenship or work permit.

You then fill out Section 2, which requires you to check for and copy documents that establish identity and prove employment eligibility. For a new hire who's a U.S. citizen, you must review one picture ID (usually a driver's license but maybe a military ID, student ID, or other state ID) and an ID that proves employment authorization, such as a Social Security card, birth certificate, or citizen ID card. A U.S. passport can serve as both a picture ID and proof of employment eligibility. Instructions provided with the form list all acceptable documents you can use to verify work eligibility. Although a photocopy of the ID proof is not required, it is a good idea to keep a copy of the information in the employee's file just in case there is an immigration audit in the future.

You can download the form and its instructions from the U.S. Citizenship and Immigration Services Web site at `www.uscis.gov/files/form/i-9.pdf`.

Keeping time with time sheets

For each employee who's paid hourly, you need to have some sort of time sheet to keep track of work hours. These time sheets are usually completed by the employees and approved by their managers. Completed and approved time sheets are then sent to the bookkeeper so that checks can be calculated based on the exact number of hours worked.

Picking pay periods

Deciding how frequently you'll pay employees is an important point to work out before hiring staff. Most businesses chose one or more of these four pay periods:

- ✔ **Weekly:** Employees are paid every week, and payroll must be done 52 times a year.
- ✔ **Biweekly:** Employees are paid every two weeks, and payroll must be done 26 times a year.
- ✔ **Semimonthly:** Employees are paid twice a month, commonly on the 15th and the last day of the month, and payroll must be done 24 times a year.
- ✔ **Monthly:** Employees are paid once a month, and payroll must be done 12 times a year.

You can choose to use any of these pay periods, and you may even decide to use more than one type. For example, some companies will pay hourly employees (employees paid by the hour) weekly or biweekly and pay salaried employees (employees paid by a set salary regardless of how many hours they work) semimonthly or monthly. Whatever your choice, decide on a consistent pay period policy and be sure to make it clear to employees when they're hired.

Determining wage and salary types

You have a lot of leeway regarding the level of wages and salary you pay your employees, but you still have to follow the rules laid out by the U.S. Department of Labor. When deciding on wages and salaries, you have to first categorize your employees. Employees fall into one of two categories:

✔ **Exempt employees** are exempt from the Fair Labor Standards Act (FLSA), which sets rules for minimum wage, equal pay, overtime pay, and child labor laws. Executives, administrative personnel, managers, professionals, computer specialists, and outside salespeople can all be exempt employees. They're normally paid a certain amount per pay period with no connection to the number of hours worked. Often, exempt employees work well over 40 hours per week without extra pay. Prior to rules from the Department of Labor effective in 2004, only high-paid employees fell in this category; today, however, employees making as little as $23,660 can be placed in the exempt category.

✔ **Nonexempt** employees must be hired according to rules of the FLSA, meaning that companies with gross sales of over $500,000 per year must pay a minimum wage per hour of $7.25. Smaller companies must comply with minimum wage rules if they engage in interstate commerce or in the production of goods for commerce, such as having employees who work in transportation or communications or who regularly use the mail or telephones for interstate communications.

For new employees who are under the age of 20 and need training, an employer can pay as little as $4.25 for the first 90 days. Also, any nonexempt employee who works over 40 hours in a seven-day period must be paid time and one-half for the additional hours. Minimum wage doesn't have to be paid in cash. The employer can pay some or all of the wage in room and board provided it doesn't make a profit on any non-cash payments. Also, the employer can't charge the employee to use its facilities if the employee's use of a facility is primarily for the employer's benefit.

Book III

Day-to-Day Bookkeeping

The federal government adjusted the minimum wage law in 2009. Some states do have higher minimum wage laws, so be sure to check with your state department of labor to be certain you're meeting state wage guidelines. You can get a quick overview of states with higher minimum wage rates at www.dol.gov/whd/minwage/america.htm.

If you plan to hire employees who are under the age of 18, you must pay attention to child labor laws. Federal and state laws restrict what kind of work children can do, when they can do it, and how old they have to be to do it, so be sure you become familiar with the laws before hiring employees who are younger than 18. For minors below the age of 16, work restrictions are even tighter than for teens aged 16 and 17. (You can hire your own child without worrying about these restrictions.)

You can get a good summary of all labor laws at the Business Owner's Toolkit online at http://csi.toolkit.tst.cch.com/text/P05_0000.asp.

Exempt or nonexempt

You're probably wondering how to determine whether to hire exempt or nonexempt employees. Of course, most businesses would prefer to exempt all their employees from the overtime laws. You don't have a choice if your employees earn less than $23,660 per year or $455 per week. All employees lower than this earning range must be paid overtime if they work more than 40 hours in a week. These employees are nonexempt employees — in other words, not exempt from the Fair Labor Practices Act, which governs who must be paid overtime.

You have more flexibility with employees earning more than $23,660 per year. You can classify employees who work as executives, administrative personnel, professionals, computer specialists, and outside salespeople as exempt. Also, those who perform office or nonmanual work earning over $100,000 per year can be exempt. Blue-collar workers in manual labor positions can't be exempt employees and must be paid overtime. Also police, firefighters, paramedics, and other first responders can't be exempt employees and must be paid overtime.

To help you figure out whether or not you can hire exempt employees, go to the Fair Labor Standards Act Advisor (www.dol.gov/elaws/esa/flsa/scope/screen9.asp.)

Collecting Employee Taxes

In addition to following wage and salary guidelines set for your business (see the earlier section "Setting the Stage for Staffing: Making Payroll Decisions"), you, the bookkeeper, must also be familiar with how to calculate the employee taxes that must be deducted from each employee's paycheck when calculating payroll. These taxes include Social Security; Medicare; and federal, state, and local withholding taxes.

Sorting out Social Security tax

Employers and employees share the Social Security tax equally: Each must pay 6.2 percent (0.062) toward Social Security up to a cap of $118,500 for 2015 per year per person (as of this writing). After an employee earns $118,500 for 2015 no additional Social Security taxes are taken out of his check. The federal government adjusts the cap each year based on salary level changes in the marketplace. Essentially, the cap gradually increases as salaries increase.

The calculation for Social Security taxes is relatively simple. For example, for an employee who makes $1,000 per pay period, you calculate Social Security tax this way:

$$\$1,000 \times 0.062 = \$62$$

The bookkeeper deducts $62 from this employee's gross pay, and the company pays the employer's share of $62. Thus, the total amount submitted in Social Security taxes for this employee is $124.

Making sense of Medicare tax

Employees and employers also share Medicare taxes, which are 1.45 percent each. However, unlike Social Security taxes, the federal government places no cap on the amount that must be paid in Medicare taxes. So even if someone makes $1 million per year, 1.45 percent is calculated for each pay period and paid by both the employee and the employer. Here's an example of how you calculate the Medicare tax for an employee who makes $1,000 per pay period:

$1,000 \times 0.0145 = $14.50

The bookkeeper deducts $14.50 from this employee's gross pay, and the company pays the employer's share of $14.50. Thus, the total amount submitted in Medicare taxes for this employee is $29.

In addition for individuals with wages or self-employment income over $200,000, there is a 0.9 percent Medicare tax.

Figuring out federal withholding tax

Deducting federal withholding taxes is a much more complex task for bookkeepers than deducting Social Security or Medicare taxes. Not only do you have to worry about an employee's tax rate, but you also must consider the number of withholding allowances the employee claimed on her W-4 and whether she's married or single. For example, the first $9075 of an unmarried person's income (the first $18,150 for a married couple filing jointly) is taxed at 10 percent. Other tax rates depending on income are 15 percent, 25 percent, 28 percent, 33 percent, 35 percent and 39.6%.

Trying to figure out taxes separately for each employee based on his or her tax rate and number of allowances would be an extremely time-consuming task, but luckily, you don't have to do that. The IRS publishes tax tables in Publication 15, Employer's Tax Guide, that let you just look up an employee's tax obligation based on the taxable salary and withholdings. You can access the IRS Employer's Tax Guide online at www.irs.gov/publications/p15/index.html. You'll find the links to income tax withholding tables in Chapter 17 of the online version of Publication 15.

The IRS's tax tables give you detailed numbers up to ten withholding allowances. Table 3-1 shows a sample tax table with only seven allowances because of space limitations. But even with seven allowances, you get the idea — just match the employee's wage range with the number of allowances he or she claims, and the box where they meet contains the amount of that employee's tax obligation. For example, if you're preparing a paycheck for an employee whose taxable income is $1,000 per pay period, and he claims three withholding allowances — one for himself, one for his wife, and one for his children — the amount of federal income taxes you deduct from his pay is $113.

Table 3-1		Portion of an IRS Tax Table for Employers						
If Wages Are:		**And the Number of Allowances Claimed Is:**						
At Least	**But Less Than**	**1**	**2**	**3**	**4**	**5**	**6**	**7**
1,000	1,010	149	131	113	95	83	72	62
1,010	1,020	151	134	116	98	85	74	63
1,020	1,030	154	136	118	100	86	75	65

Settling up state and local withholding taxes

In addition to the federal government, most states have income taxes, and some cities even have local income taxes. You can find all state tax rates and forms online at www.payroll-taxes.com/PayrollTaxes/00000103.htm. If your state or city has income taxes, they need to be taken out of each employee's paycheck.

Determining Net Pay

Net pay is the amount a person is paid after subtracting all tax and benefit deductions. In other words, after all deductions are subtracted from a person's gross pay, you're left with the net pay.

After you figure out all the necessary taxes to be taken from an employee's paycheck, you can calculate the check amount. Here's the equation and an example of how you calculate the net pay amount:

Gross pay – (Social Security + Medicare + Federal withholding tax + State withholding tax + Local withholding tax) = Net pay

1,000 – (62 + 14.50 + 148 + 45 + 0) = 730.50

This net pay calculation doesn't include any deductions for benefits. Many businesses offer their employees health, retirement, and other benefits but expect the employees to share a portion of those costs. The fact that some of these benefits are tax deductible and some are not makes a difference in when you deduct the benefit costs. If an employee's benefits are tax deductible and taken out of the check before federal withholding taxes are calculated, the federal tax rate may be lower than if the benefits were deducted after calculating federal withholding taxes. Many states follow the federal government's lead on tax deductible benefits, so the amount deducted for state taxes will be lower as well. For example, the federal government allows employers to consider health insurance premiums as nontaxable, so the states do so also. The later section "Surveying Your Benefits Options" covers benefits and taxation.

Practice: Payroll Tax Calculations

Book III

Day-to-Day Bookkeeping

Q. Mary earns $1,000 per week and claims one withholding deduction. Calculate her Social Security, Medicare, and federal withholding taxes. Then calculate her paycheck after taxes have been taken out. (Use Table 3-1 earlier in the chapter.)

A. Here's how Mary's calculations work out:

Social Security	1000×0.062	=	$62.00
Medicare	1000×0.0145	=	$14.50
Federal withholding		=	$149.00
Paycheck minus taxes	$1,000 – $62.00 – $14.50		
	– $149.00	=	$774.50

1. Carl earns $1,015 per week and claims four withholding deductions. Calculate his Social Security, Medicare, and federal withholding taxes. Then calculate his paycheck after taxes have been taken out. (Use Table 3-1 earlier in the chapter.)

2. Karen earns $1,025 per week and claims two withholding deductions. Calculate her Social Security, Medicare, and federal withholding taxes. Then calculate her paycheck after taxes have been taken out. (Use Table 3-1 earlier in the chapter.)

3. Tom earns $1,020 per week and claims seven withholding deductions. Calculate his Social Security, Medicare, and federal withholding taxes. Then calculate his paycheck after taxes have been taken out. (Use Table 3-1 earlier in the chapter.)

Surveying Your Benefits Options

Benefits include programs that you provide your employees to better their lives, such as health insurance and retirement savings opportunities. Most benefits are *tax-exempt,* which means that the employee isn't taxed for them. However, some benefits are taxable, so the employee has to pay taxes on the money or the value of the benefits received. This section reviews the different tax-exempt and taxable benefits you can offer your employees.

Tax-exempt benefits

Most benefits are *tax-exempt,* or not taxed. Healthcare and retirement benefits are the most common of this type of benefit. In fact, accident and health benefits and retirement benefits make up the largest share of employers' pay toward employees' benefits. Luckily, not only are these benefits tax-exempt, but anything an employee pays toward them can also be deducted from the gross pay, so the employee doesn't have to pay taxes on that part of his salary or wage.

For example, if an employee's share of health insurance is $50 per pay period and he makes $1,000 per pay period, his taxable income is actually $1,000 minus the $50 health insurance premium contribution, or $950. As the bookkeeper, you calculate taxes on $950 rather than $1,000 in this situation.

The money that an employee contributes to the retirement plan you offer is tax deductible, too. For example, if an employee contributes $50 per pay period to your company's 401(k) retirement plan, that $50 can also be subtracted from the employee's gross pay before you calculate net pay. So if an employee contributes $50 to both health insurance and retirement, the $1,000 taxable pay is reduced to only $900 taxable pay. (According to the tax table for that pay level, his federal withholding taxes are only $123, a savings of $25 over a taxable income of $1,000, or 25 percent of his health and retirement costs. Not bad.)

You can offer myriad other tax-exempt benefits to employees, as well, including

✔ **Adoption assistance:** You can provide up to $13,400 per child that an employee plans to adopt without having to include that amount in gross income for the purposes of calculating federal withholding taxes. The value of this benefit must be included when calculating Social Security and Medicare taxes, however.

✔ **Athletic facilities:** You can offer your employees the use of a gym on premises your company owns or leases without having to include the value of the gym facilities in gross pay. In order for this benefit to qualify as tax-exempt, the facility must be operated by the company primarily for the use of employees, their spouses, and their dependent children.

✔ **Dependent care assistance:** You can help your employees with dependent care expenses, which can include children and elderly parents, provided you offer the benefit to make it possible for the employee to work.

✔ **Education assistance:** You can pay employees' educational expenses up to $5,250 without having to include that payment in gross income.

✔ **Employee discounts:** You can offer employees discounts on the company's products without including the value of the discounts in their gross pay, provided the discount isn't more than 20 percent less than what's charged to customers. If you only offer this discount to high-paid employees, the value of these discounts must be included in gross pay of those employees.

✔ **Group term life insurance:** You can provide group term life insurance up to a coverage level of $50,000 to your employees without including the value of this insurance in their gross pay. Premiums for coverage above $50,000 must be added to calculations for Social Security and Medicare taxes.

✔ **Meals:** Meals that have little value (such as coffee and doughnuts) don't have to be reported as taxable income. Also, occasional meals brought in so employees can work late also don't have to be reported in employees' income.

✔ **Moving expense reimbursements:** If you pay moving expenses for employees, you don't have to report these reimbursements as employee income as long as the reimbursements are for items that would qualify as tax-deductible moving expenses on an employee's individual tax return. Employees who have been reimbursed by their employers can't deduct the moving expenses that the employer paid.

Taxable benefits

You may decide to provide some benefits that are taxable. These include the personal use of a company automobile, life insurance premiums for coverage over $50,000, and benefits that exceed allowable maximums. For example, if you pay $10,250 toward an employee's education expenses, $5,000 of that amount must be reported as income because the federal government's cap is $5,250.

Book III

Day-to-Day Bookkeeping

Dealing with cafeteria plans

Cafeteria plans are benefit plans that offer employees a choice of benefits based on cost. Employees can pick and choose from those benefits and put together a benefit package that works best for them within the established cost structure.

For example, a company tells its employees that it will pay up to $5,000 in benefits per year and values its benefit offerings this way:

Health insurance	$4,600
Retirement	$1,200
Child care	$1,200
Life insurance	$800

Joe, an employee, then picks from the list of benefits until he reaches $5,000. If Joe wants more than $5,000 in benefits, he pays for the additional benefits with a reduction in his paycheck.

The list of possible benefits may be considerably longer, but in this case, if Joe chooses health insurance, retirement, and life insurance, the total cost is $6,600. Because the company pays up to $5,000, Joe needs to co-pay $1,600, a portion of which is taken out of each paycheck. If Joe gets paid every two weeks for a total of 26 paychecks per year, the deduction for benefits from his gross pay is $61.54 ($1,600 ÷ 26).

Cafeteria plans are becoming more popular among larger businesses, but some employers decide not to offer their benefits this way. Primarily, this decision comes because managing a cafeteria plan can be much more time-consuming for the bookkeeping and human resources staff. Many small business employers that do choose to offer a cafeteria plan for benefits do so by outsourcing benefit management services to an outside company that specializes in managing cafeteria plans.

Preparing Payroll and Posting It in the Books

After you know the details about your employees' withholding allowances and their benefit costs (both of which are covered earlier in the chapter), you can calculate the final payroll and post it to the books.

Calculating payroll for hourly employees

When you're ready to prepare payroll for nonexempt employees, the first thing you need to do is collect time records from each person being paid hourly. Regardless of whether your company uses time clocks, time sheets, or some other method to produce the required time records, the manager of each department usually reviews the time records for each employee he supervises and then sends those time records to you, the bookkeeper.

With time records in hand, you have to calculate gross pay for each employee. For example, if a nonexempt employee worked 45 hours and is paid $12 an hour, you calculate gross pay like so:

40 regular hours × $12 per hour = $480

5 overtime hours × $12 per hour × 1.5 overtime rate = $90

$480 + $90 = $570

In this case, because the employee isn't exempt from the FLSA (see "Determining wage and salary types" earlier in this chapter), overtime must be paid for any hours worked over 40 in a seven-day workweek. This employee worked five hours more than the 40 hours allowed, so he needs to be paid at time plus one-half for those extra hours.

Doling out funds to salaried employees

In addition to employees paid based on hourly wages, you also must prepare payroll for salaried employees. Paychecks for salaried employees are relatively easy to calculate — all you need to know are their base salaries and their pay period calculations. For example, if a salaried employee makes $30,000 per year and is paid twice a month (totaling 24 pay periods), that employee's gross pay is $1,250 for each pay period.

Totaling up for commission checks

Running payroll for employees paid based on commission can involve the most-complex calculations because of the variety of commission scenarios available. To show you a number of variables, this section calculates various commission checks based on a salesperson who sells $60,000 worth of products during one month.

- **Straight commission:** For a salesperson on a straight commission of 10 percent, you calculate pay by using this formula:

    Total amount sold × Commission percentage = Gross pay

    $60,000 × 0.10 = $6,000

- **Base salary plus commission:** For a salesperson with a guaranteed base salary of $2,000 plus an additional 5 percent commission on all products sold, you calculate pay by using this formula:

    Base salary + (Total amount sold × Commission percentage) = Gross pay

    $2,000 + ($60,000 × 0.05) = $5,000

Although this employee may be happier having a base salary he can count on each month, he actually makes less with a base salary because the commission rate is so much lower. By selling $60,000 worth of products, he made only $3,000 in commission at 5 percent. Without the base pay, he would've made 10 percent on the $60,000 or $6,000, so he actually got paid $1,000 less with a base pay structure that includes a lower commission pay rate.

But the base-salary setup isn't always less lucrative. If the same salesperson has a slow sales month of just $30,000 worth of products sold, his pay is

    $30,000 × 0.10 = $3,000 on straight commission of 10 percent

    $30,000 × 0.05 = $1,500 plus $2,000 base salary, or $3,500

For a slow month, the salesperson makes more money with the base salary than with the higher straight commission rate.

- **Higher commissions on higher levels of sales:** This type of pay system encourages salespeople to keep their sales levels over a certain level — in this example, $30,000 — to get the best commission rate.

- **Graduated commission scale:** With a *graduated commission scale,* a salesperson can make a straight commission of 5 percent on his first $10,000 in sales, 7 percent on his next $20,000, and finally 10 percent on anything over $30,000. Here's what his gross pay calculation looks like using this commission pay scale:

    ($10,000 × 0.05) + ($20,000 × 0.07) + (<u>$30,000 × 0.10</u>) = $4,900 Gross pay

Determining base salary plus tips

One other type of commission pay system involves a base salary plus tips. (See the preceding section for more on figuring commission pay.) This method is common in restaurant settings in which servers receive between $2.13 and $5 per hour plus tips.

Businesses that pay less than minimum wage must prove that their employees make at least minimum wage when tips are accounted for. Today, that's relatively easy to prove because most people pay their bills with credit cards and include tips on their bills. Businesses can then come up with an average tip rate by using that credit card data.

Employees must report tips to their employers on an IRS Form 4070, Employee's Report of Tips to Employer, which is part of IRS Publication 1244, Employees Daily Record of Tips and Report to Employer. The publication provides details about what the IRS expects you and your employees to do if they work in an environment where tipping is common.

If your employees receive tips and you want to supply the necessary paperwork, you can find Publication 1244 included with this book or download the document at www.irs.gov/pub/irs-pdf/p1244.pdf.

As an employer, you must report an employee's gross taxable wages based on salary plus tips. Here's how you calculate gross taxable wages for an employee whose earnings are based on tips and wages:

Base wage + Tips = Gross taxable wages

($3 × 40 hours per week) + $300 = $420

If your employees are paid using a combination of base wage plus tips, you must be sure that your employees are earning at least the minimum wage rate of $7.25 per hour. Checking this employee's gross wages, the hourly rate earned is $10.50 per hour:

Hourly wage = $10.50 ($420 ÷ 40)

Taxes due are calculated on the base wage plus tips, so the check you prepare for the employee in this example is for the base wage minus any taxes due.

Book III

Day-to-Day Bookkeeping

Practice: Payroll Preparation

Q. Suppose Jack, who is paid weekly, earns $12 per hour and worked 48 hours last week. How do you calculate his gross paycheck before deductions?

A. You separate the amount of timed work at regular pay, 40 hours, from the time worked at overtime pay, 8 hours. Then you calculate the gross paycheck this way:

40 hours regular pay × $12 per hour = $480

8 hours overtime pay × $ 12 per hour × 1.5 overtime rate = $144

$480 + $144 = $624

Q. If Ann earns $3.00 per hour plus $5 per hour in tips, what is her gross paycheck, and what is the total pay you use to calculate her taxes?

A. You calculate her paycheck based on her hourly pay.

$3 × 40 hours work = $120

You figure up her taxes based on her pay plus tips, or $8 per hour.

$8 × 40 hours = $320

4. Suppose John, who gets paid biweekly, earns $15 per hour. He worked 40 hours in the first week of the pay period and 45 hours in the second week of the pay period. How much was his gross pay before deductions?

5. Suppose Mary Ann, who gets paid biweekly, earns $13 per hour. She worked 42 hours in the first week and 46 hours in the second week of the pay period. How much is her gross pay before deductions?

6. Suppose Bob makes $30,000 per year and is paid semimonthly. He is an exempt employee. How much is his gross pay each pay period?

7. Suppose Ginger makes $42,000 per year and is paid monthly. She is an exempt employee. How much is her gross pay each pay period?

8. Jim earns a base salary of $1,500 plus 3 percent commission. He is paid monthly. What is his gross paycheck if he has $75,000 in sales?

9. Sally earns $4.00 per hour plus $7 per hour in tips. If she works 40 hours, what is her gross paycheck, and what is the total pay you use to calculate her taxes?

10. Betty earns $2.50 per hour plus $8 per hour in tips. If she works 40 hours, what is her weekly gross paycheck, and what is the total pay you use to calculate her taxes?

Finishing the Job

After calculating paychecks for all your employees, you prepare the payroll, make up the checks, and post the payroll to the books. In addition to Cash, many accounts are impacted by payroll, including the following:

- ✔ Accrued Federal Withholding Payable, which is where you record the liability for future federal tax payments

- ✔ Accrued State Withholding Payable, which is where you record the liability for future state tax payments

- ✔ Accrued Employee Medical Insurance Payable, which is where you record the liability for future medical insurance premiums

- ✔ Accrued Employee Elective Insurance Payable, which is where you record the liability for miscellaneous insurance premiums, such as life or accident insurance

When you post the payroll entry, you indicate the withdrawal of money from the Cash account as well as record liabilities for future cash payments that will be due for taxes and insurance payments. Just for the purposes of giving you an example of the proper setup for a payroll journal entry, the total payroll is assumed to be $10,000 with $1,000 set aside for each type of withholding payable. In reality, your numbers will be much different, and your payables will probably never all be the same. Here's what your journal entry for posting payroll should look like:

Payroll Posting Journal Entry

	Debit	Credit
Salaries and Wages Expense	$10,000	
Accrued Federal Withholding Payable		$1,000
Accrued State Withholding Payable		$1,000
Accrued Medical Insurance Payable		$1,000
Accrued Elective Insurance Payable		$1,000
Cash		$6,000

To record payroll for May 27, 2015

In this entry, you increase the expense account for salaries and wages as well as all the accounts in which you accrue future obligations for taxes and employee insurance payments. You decrease the amount of the Cash account; when cash payments are made for the taxes and insurance payments in the future, you post those payments in the books. Here's an example of the entry you would post to the books after making the federal withholding tax payment:

Book III

Day-to-Day Bookkeeping

Federal Witholding Tax Posting

	Debit	Credit
Accrued Federal Withholding Payable	$	
Cash in Checking		$

To record the payment of May 2015 federal taxes for employees

Depositing Employee Taxes

Federal taxes must be deposited through EFTPS, the Electronic Federal Tax Payment System. You can enroll and set up an account at https://www.eftps.com/eftps/. After you are enrolled, you can make your payments online or by using their voice response system at 1-800-555-3453. (If your total quarterly liability is less than $2,500, you can submit the balance due with your Form 941 by using Form 941-V.) Most states have also gone to online systems for depositing taxes.

For the purposes of tax payments collected from employees for the federal government, you must complete Form 941. This form summarizes the tax payments made on behalf of employees. You can get instructions and a copy of Form 941 online at www.irs.gov/pub/irs-pdf/f941.pdf (for the form) and www.irs.gov/pub/irs-pdf/i941.pdf (for the instructions). Book III Chapter 4 talks more about the various forms employers must file.

During the first year as an employer, your company will have to make monthly deposits of employee taxes. Monthly payments must be made by the 15th day of the month following when the taxes were taken. For example, taxes collected from employees in April must be paid by May 15. If the date the deposit is due falls on a weekend or bank holiday, the payment is due on the next day the banks are open.

As your business gets larger, you'll need to make more frequent deposits. Large employers that accumulate taxes of $100,000 or more in a day must deposit the funds on the next banking day.

Outsourcing Payroll and Benefits Work

Given all that's required of you to prepare payroll, you may think that your small company would be better off to outsource the work of payroll and benefits. Maybe so. Many companies *outsource* the work (contract with an outside company to handle those functions) because it's such a specialized area and requires extensive software to manage both payroll and benefits.

If you don't want to take on payroll and benefits alone but don't want to send them to an outside company, you can also pay for a monthly payroll service from the software company that provides your accounting software. For example, QuickBooks provides various levels of payroll services for as low as $25 a month depending on the services you require. The QuickBooks payroll features include calculating earnings and deductions, printing checks or making direct deposits, providing updates to the tax tables, and supplying data necessary to complete all government forms related to payroll. The advantage of doing payroll in-house in this manner is that the payroll can then be more easily integrated into the company's books.

Answers to Problems on Employee Payroll and Benefits

1   Here's how Carl's calculations work out:

Social Security	$1,015 × .062	=	$62.93
Medicare	$1,015 × .0145	=	$14.72
Federal Withholding		=	$98.00
Paycheck after taxes	$1,015 − $62.93 − $14.72 − $98	=	$839.35

2   Here's how Karen's calculations work out:

Social Security	$1,025 × .062	=	$63.55
Medicare	$1,025 × .0145	=	$14.86
Federal Withholding		=	$136.00
Paycheck after taxes	$1,025 − $63.55 − $14.86 − $136	=	$810.59

3   Here's how Tom's calculations work out:

Social Security	$1,020 × .062	=	$63.24
Medicare	$1,020 × .0145	=	$14.79
Federal Withholding		=	$65.00
Paycheck after taxes	$1,020 − $63.24 − $14.79 − $65	=	$876.97

4   Here's how you calculate John's paycheck:

Regular hours	80 × $15	=	$1,200.00
Overtime hours	5 × $15 × 1.5	=	$112.50
Gross pay		=	$1,312.50

5   Here's how you calculate Mary Ann's paycheck:

Regular hours	80 × $13	=	$1,040.00
Overtime hours	8 × $13 × 1.5	=	$156.00
Gross pay		=	$1,196.00

6   Bob's gross semimonthly pay is $1,250 (or $30,000/24).

7   Ginger's gross monthly pay is $3,500 (or $42,000/12).

Book III

Day-to-Day Bookkeeping

8 Jim's gross paycheck is $3,750: $1,500 + $2,250 ($75,000 × .03) = $3,750.

9 Sally's gross paycheck: $4 × 40 = $160

Pay for tax calculation: $11 × 40 = $440

10 Betty's gross paycheck: $2.50 × 40 = $100

Pay for tax calculation: $10.50 × 40 = $420

Chapter 4

Employer-Paid Taxes and Government Payroll Reporting

In This Chapter

▶ Tallying up the employer's share of Social Security and Medicare

▶ Filing and paying unemployment taxes

▶ Figuring out workers' compensation

▶ Keeping accurate employee records

You may think that employees will make your job as a business owner easier, but you're wrong on that one. It's really a mixed bag. Although employees help you keep your business operating and enable you to grow, they also add a lot of government paperwork.

After your company hires employees, you need to complete regular reports for the government regarding the taxes you must pay toward the employees' Social Security and Medicare, as well as unemployment taxes. Most states require employers to buy workers' compensation insurance based on employees' salaries and wages. Some states do provide exemptions for small businesses or certain types of workers. Others do allow employers to self-insure. For more details about how this is handled in your state, go to www.cutcomp.com/depts.htm.

This chapter reviews the federal, state, and local government reporting requirements for employers as well as the records you, the bookkeeper, must keep in order to complete these reports. You also find out how to calculate the various employee taxes and how to buy workers' compensation insurance.

This chapter looks at the employer side of these taxes, as well as other employer-paid government taxes. Book III Chapter 3 shows you how to calculate the employee side of Social Security and Medicare taxes.

Paying Employer Taxes on Social Security and Medicare

In the United States, both employers and employees must contribute to the Social Security and Medicare systems. In fact, employers share equally with employees the tax obligation for both Social Security and Medicare.

As discussed in greater detail in Book III Chapter 3, the employer and the employee each must pay 6.2 percent of an employee's compensation for Social Security up to a salary of $118,500 in 2011.

The percentage both the employer and employee pay toward Medicare is 1.45 percent. There is no salary cap related to the amount that must be paid toward Medicare, so even if your employee makes $1 million (don't you wish your business was that successful?), you still must pay Medicare taxes on that amount.

In addition for individuals with wages or self-employment income over $200,000, there is a 0.9 percent Medicare tax.

When you finish calculating payroll checks, you calculate the employer's portion of Social Security and Medicare. When you post the payroll to the books, the employer's portion of Social Security and Medicare are set aside in an accrual account.

Filing Form 941

Each quarter you must file federal Form 941, Employer's Quarterly Federal Tax Return, which details the number of employees that received wages, tips, or other compensation for the quarter.

Table 4-1 tells what months are reported during each quarter and when the report is due:

Table 4-1	Filing Requirements for Form 941
Months in Quarter	*Report Due Date*
January, February, March	On or before April 30
April, May, June	On or before July 31
July, August, September	On or before October 31
October, November, December	On or before January 31

Form 941 is revised frequently, so be sure you're using the newest version. The newest form usually requires more detail than older versions, so you definitely don't want to be working from an old form or you may find yourself in big trouble.

The following key information must be included on Form 941:

- ✔ Number of employees who received wages, tips, or other compensation in the pay period
- ✔ Total of wages, tips, and other compensation paid to employees
- ✔ Total tax withheld from wages, tips, and other compensation
- ✔ Taxable Social Security and Medicare wages
- ✔ Taxable Social Security tips
- ✔ Taxable wages and tips subject to additional Medicare tax withholding
- ✔ Total paid out to employees in sick pay
- ✔ Adjustments for tips and group-term life insurance
- ✔ Amount of income tax withholding
- ✔ Amount of tax liability per month
- ✔ Total deposits made for the quarter

Knowing how often to file

As an employer, you file Form 941 on a quarterly basis, but you probably have to pay taxes more frequently. Most new employers start out making monthly deposits for taxes due by depositing money online using the IRS's Electronic Federal Tax Payment System (EFTPS). For more information on EFTPS, go to www.eftps.gov.

Employers on a monthly payment schedule (usually small companies) must deposit all employment taxes due by the 15th day of the following month. For example, the taxes for the payroll in April must be paid by May 15th. Larger employers must pay taxes more frequently. For example, employers whose businesses accumulate $100,000 or more in taxes due on any day during a deposit period must deposit those taxes on the next banking day. If you hit $100,000 due when you're a monthly depositor, you must start paying taxes semiweekly for at least the remainder of the current tax year.

Book III

Day-to-Day Bookkeeping

After you become a semiweekly payer, you must deposit your taxes on Wednesday or Friday, depending on your payday:

> ✔ **If you pay employees on Wednesday, Thursday, or Friday,** you must deposit the taxes due by the next Wednesday.

> ✔ **If you pay employees on Saturday, Sunday, Monday, or Tuesday,** you must deposit the taxes due by the next Friday.

However you're required to pay your payroll-based taxes, one thing you definitely don't want to do is underpay. Interest and penalty charges for late payment can make your tax bite even higher — and you're probably convinced it's high enough already. If you find it hard to accurately estimate your quarterly tax payment, your best bet is to pay a slightly higher amount in the first and second month of a quarter. Then, if you've paid a bit more than needed, you can cut back the payment for the third month of the quarter. This strategy lets you avoid the possibility of underpaying in the first two months of a quarter and risking interest and penalty charges.

Completing Unemployment Reports and Paying Unemployment Taxes

If you ever faced unemployment, you were relieved to get a weekly check — meager as it may have been — while you looked for a job. Did you realize that unemployment compensation was partially paid by your employer? In fact, an employer pays a share of unemployment compensation based on its record of firing or laying off employees. So think for a moment of your dear employees and your own past experiences, and you'll see the value of paying toward unemployment compensation.

The fund that used to be known simply as Unemployment is now known as the Federal Unemployment Tax (FUTA) fund. Employers contribute to the fund, but states also collect taxes to fill their unemployment fund coffers.

For FUTA, employers pay a federal rate of 6.0 percent on the first $7,000 that each employee earns. Luckily, you don't have to just add the state rate on top of that; the federal government allows you to subtract up to 5.4 percent of the first $7,000 per employee, if that amount is paid to the state. Essentially, the amount you pay to the state can serve as a credit toward the amount you must pay to the federal government.

Each state sets its own unemployment tax rate. Many states also charge additional fees for administrative costs and job-training programs. You can check out the full charges for your state at payroll-taxes.com, but to give you an idea of how taxes vary state to state, check out the sampling shown in Table 4-2.

Table 4-2	Sampling of Unemployment Tax Rates		
State	*Percentage Range*	*For a Salary Up To*	*New Employer Percentage*
California	1.5 to 6.2	$7,000	3.4
Florida	0.24 to 5.4	$8,000	2.7
Nevada	0.25 to 5.4	$27,800	2.95
New York	2.025 to 9.825	$10,500	4.025
Rhode Island	1.69 to 9.79	$21,200	2.74

The percentage an employer must pay isn't a set amount but instead is a percentage range. The employee income amount on which this percentage is charged also varies from state to state. The percentage range is based on the company's employment history and how frequently its employees collect unemployment.

Examining how states calculate the FUTA tax rate

States use four different methods to calculate how much you may need to pay in FUTA taxes:

- **Benefit ratio formula:** The state looks at the ratio of benefits collected by former employees to your company's total payroll over the past three years. States also adjust your rate depending on the overall balance in the state unemployment insurance fund.

- **Benefit wage formula:** The state looks at the proportion of your company's payroll that's paid to workers who become unemployed and receive benefits, and then divides that number by your company's total taxable wages.

- **Payroll decline ratio formula:** The state looks at the decline in your company's payrolls from year to year or from quarter to quarter.

- **Reserve ratio formula:** The state keeps track of your company's balance in the unemployment reserve account, which gives a cumulative representation of its use by your former employees that were laid off and paid unemployment. This record keeping dates back from the date you were first subject to the state unemployment rate. The reserve account is calculated by adding up all your contributions to the account and then subtracting total benefits paid. This amount is then divided by your company's total payroll. The higher the reserve ratio, the lower the required contribution rate.

These formulas can be very complicated, so your best bet is to meet with your state's unemployment office to review how your company's unemployment rate will be set. In addition to getting a better idea of what may impact your FUTA tax rate, you can also discuss how best to minimize that rate.

Calculating FUTA tax

After you know what your rate is, calculating the actual FUTA tax you owe isn't difficult.

Consider a new company that's just getting started in Florida; it has ten employees, and each employee makes more than $7,000 per year. For state unemployment taxes, the new employer rate of 2.7 percent on the first $7,000 of income will be used. The federal FUTA is the same for all employers — 6.0 percent in 2015. Here's how you calculate the FUTA tax for this company:

State unemployment taxes:

$7,000 × 0.027 = $189 per employee

$189 × 10 employees = $1,890

Federal unemployment taxes:

$7,000 × 0.060 = $420

$434 × 10 employees = $4,200

The company doesn't have to pay the full federal amount because it can take up to a 5.4-percent credit for state taxes paid ($7,000 × 0.054 = $378). Because in this example state taxes in Florida are only 2.7 percent of $7,000, this employer can subtract the full amount of Florida FUTA taxes from the federal FUTA tax:

$4,340 − $1,890 = $2,450

So this company only needs to pay $2,450 to the federal government in FUTA taxes. Any company paying more than $378 per employee to the state is only able to reduce its federal bill by the maximum of $378 per employee. So every employer pays at least $56 per employee into the federal FUTA pool.

Each year, you must file IRS Form 940, Employer's Annual Federal Unemployment (FUTA) Tax Return. You can find Form 940 with its instructions online at www.irs.gov/pub/irs-pdf/f940.pdf.

You can pay taxes for Form 940 by using the same coupon (Form 8109) used to pay Form 941 taxes (see "Filing Form 941" earlier in this chapter for an explanation). Most employers pay unemployment taxes quarterly, but if the amount you must pay is less than $250 in any one quarter, you can wait until at least $250 is due. For example, if you owe $125 in federal unemployment taxes in one quarter, you can wait two quarters before making the payment.

Note that FUTA is paid only on the first $7,000 in wages, the greatest liability is usually going to be for the first quarter of the year, unless it is a seasonal business or one with a lot of turnover.

Filing and paying unemployment taxes to state governments

States collect their unemployment taxes on a quarterly basis, and many states allow you to pay your unemployment taxes online. Check with your state to find out how to file and make unemployment tax payments.

Skipping out on state taxes isn't a good idea. If you don't pay your state taxes, you may end up with a lien filed against your business. You may also end up facing penalties and interest charges for late payments. And if the state has to take you to court to collect back taxes, you'll have to pay court and processing costs in addition to the back taxes, penalties, and interest.

Unfortunately, the filing requirements for state unemployment taxes are much more difficult to complete than those for federal taxes (see the discussion of Federal Form 940 in the preceding section). States require you to detail each employee by name and Social Security number because that's how unemployment records are managed at the state level. The state must know how much an employee was paid each quarter in order to determine his or her unemployment benefit, if the need arises. Some states also require you to report the number of weeks an employee worked in each quarter because the employee's unemployment benefits are calculated based on the number of weeks worked.

Each state has its own form and filing requirements. Some states require a detailed report as part of your quarterly wage and tax reports. Other states allow a simple form for state income tax and a more detailed report with your unemployment tax payment.

Florida doesn't have an income tax, so only unemployment information needs to be filed. Eight other states — Alaska, Nevada, New Hampshire, South Dakota, Tennessee, Texas, Washington, and Wyoming — have no income tax on wages. (New Hampshire and Tennessee do have a state income tax on dividends and interest, however.)

Book III

Day-to-Day Bookkeeping

Practice: Calculating FUTA Tax

1. Using Table 4-2 earlier in the chapter, calculate the FUTA taxes for a new employer in the state of California. He has ten employees who earn more than $20,000 each.

2. Using Table 4-2, calculate the FUTA taxes for a new employer in the state of Nevada. He has ten employees. Eight earn $20,000 each, one earns $24,000, and one earns $30,000.

3. Using Table 4-2, calculate the FUTA taxes for a new employer in the state of New York. He has ten employees who earn more than $30,000 each.

4. Using Table 4-2, calculate the FUTA taxes for a new employer in the state of Rhode Island. He has ten employees. Eight workers earn $14,000. One earns $24,000, and one earns $30,000.

Carrying Workers' Compensation Insurance

Taxes aren't the only thing you need to worry about when figuring out your state obligations after hiring employees. Every state (except Texas) requires employers to carry *workers' compensation insurance,* which covers costs of lost income, medical expenses, vocational rehabilitation, and, if applicable, death benefits for your employees in case they're injured on the job. Texas doesn't require this insurance but permits employees injured on the job to sue their employers in civil court to recoup the costs of injuries. Again, some states have exemptions for very small employers (less than 3 to 5 employees), some states exempt certain types of workers (executives or administrative), and some states allow the employer to self-insure.

Each other state sets its own rules regarding how much medical coverage you must provide. If the injury also causes the employee to miss work, the state determines what percentage of the employee's salary you must pay and how long you pay that amount. If the injury results in the employee's death, the state also sets the amount you must pay toward funeral expenses and the amount of financial support you must provide the employee's family.

The state also decides who gets to pick the physician that will care for the injured employee; options are the employer, the employee, the state agency, or a combination of these folks. Most states allow either the employer or the injured employee to choose the physician.

Additionally, each state makes up its own rules about how a company must insure itself against employee injuries on the job. Some states create state-based workers' compensation funds to which all employers must contribute. Other states allow you the option of participating in a state-run insurance program or buying insurance from a private company. A number of states permit employers to use HMOs, PPOs, or other managed-care providers to handle workers' claims. If your state doesn't have a mandatory state pool, you'll find that shopping around for the best private rates doesn't help you much. States set the requirements for coverage, and premiums are established by either a national rating bureau called the National Council on Compensation Insurance (NCCI) or a state rating bureau. For the lowdown on NCCI and workers' compensation insurance, visit www.ncci.com.

You may find lower rates over the long-term if your state allows you to buy private workers' compensation insurance. Many private insurers give discounts to companies with good safety standards in place and few past claims. So the best way to keep your workers' compensation rates low is to encourage safety and minimize your company's claims.

Your company's rates are calculated based on risks identified in two areas:

- ✔ **Classification of the business:** These classifications are based on historic rates of risk in different industries. For example, if you operate a business in an industry that historically has a high rate of employee injury, such as a construction business, your base rate for workers' compensation insurance is higher than that of a company in an industry without a history of frequent employee injury, such as an office that sells insurance.

- ✔ **Classification of the employees:** The NCCI publishes classifications of over 700 jobs in a book called the *Scopes Manual.* Most states use this manual to develop the basis for their classification schedules. For example, businesses that employ most workers at desk jobs pay less in workers' compensation than businesses with a majority of employees operating heavy machinery because more workers are hurt operating heavy machinery than working at desks.

Be careful how you classify your employees. Many small businesses pay more than needed for workers' compensation insurance because they misclassify employees. Be sure you understand the classification system and properly classify your employee positions before applying for workers' compensation insurance. Be sure to read the information on the NCCI website before classifying your employees.

When computing insurance premiums for a company, the insurer (whether the state or a private firm) looks at employee classifications and the rate of pay for each employee. For example, consider the position of a secretary who earns $25,000 per year. If that job classification is rated at 29 cents per $100 of income, the workers' compensation premium for that secretary is $72.50.

Most states allow you to exclude any overtime paid when calculating workers' compensation premiums. You may also be able to lower your premiums by paying a *deductible* on claims. A deductible is the amount you have to pay before the insurance company pays anything. Deductibles can lower your premium by as much as 25 percent, so consider that route as well to keep your upfront costs low.

Maintaining Employee Records

One thing that's abundantly clear when you consider all the state and federal filing requirements for employee taxes is that you must keep very good employee records. Otherwise, you'll have a hard time filling out all the necessary forms and providing quarterly detail on your employees and your payroll. The best way to track employee information with a manual bookkeeping system is to set up an employee journal and create a separate journal page for each employee. (Book I Chapter 4 gets into how to set up journals.)

The detailed individual records you keep on each employee should include this basic information, most of which is collected or determined as part of the hiring process:

- Name, address, phone number, and Social Security number
- Department or division within the company
- Start date with the company
- Pay rate
- Pay period (weekly, biweekly, semimonthly, or monthly)
- Whether hourly or salaried
- Whether exempt or nonexempt
- W-4 withholding allowances
- Benefits information
- Payroll deductions
- All payroll activity

If an employee asks to change the number of withholding allowances and file a new W-4 or asks for benefits changes, his or her record must be updated to reflect such changes.

The personal detail that doesn't change each pay period should appear at the top of the journal page. Then, you divide the remaining information into at least seven columns. Here's a sample of what an employee's journal page may look like:

Name: _____

SS#:_____

Address: _____

Tax Info: Married, 2 WH

Pay Information: $8 hour, nonexempt, biweekly

Benefits: None

The following sample journal page contains only seven columns: date of check, taxable wages, Social Security tax, Medicare tax, benefits withholding, federal withholding, and net check amount. (In many states, you'd include an eighth column for state withholding, but the state tax in the sample is zero because this particular employee works in a nonincome tax state.)

Date	Taxable Wages	Fed SS	Medicare	Benefits Withholding	Federal Withholding	Check
4/8/2015	$640	39.68	9.28	8.62	56	526.42
4/22/2015	$640	38.68	9.28	8.62	56	526.42

You may want to add other columns to your employee journal to keep track of things such as

- **Non-taxable wages:** This designation can include items such as health or retirement benefits that are paid before taxes are taken out.

- **Benefits:** If the employee receives benefits, you need at least one column to track any money taken out of the employee's check to pay for those benefits. In fact, you may want to consider tracking each benefit in a separate column.

- **Sick time**

- **Vacation time**

Clearly, these employee journal sheets can get very lengthy very quickly. That's why many small businesses use computerized accounting systems to monitor both payroll and employee records. Figure 4-1 shows you how a new employee is added to the QuickBooks system.

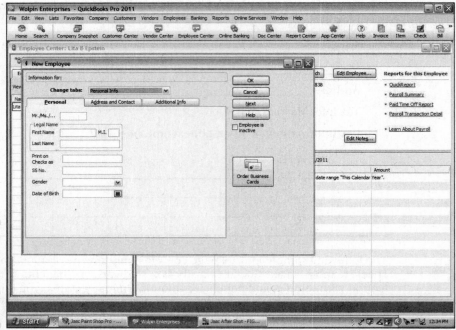

Figure 4-1:
New
employee
personal
and contact
information.

Image courtesy of Intuit

Answers to Problems on Employer-Paid Taxes and Government Payroll Reporting

1 You first calculate state unemployment taxes by multiplying 3.4 percent by $7,000, which is the maximum amount of salary upon which the employer must pay unemployment taxes. Then multiply that number by 10 (because the employees all earn higher than the maximum): $.034 \times 7,000 \times 10 = \$2,380$.

FUTA taxes are (.06 X $7,000 X10) – credit for CA taxes (.054 X $7,000 X 10) = $420, or FUTA taxes are $7,000 X .006 = $420

2 You first calculate state unemployment taxes for the eight employees earning $20,000 by multiplying $20,000 × .0295 × 8 = $4,720 (or $590 per employee).

For the two employees earning more than $24,000, the calculation is $24,000 × .0295 × 2 = $1,416. For the $30,000 employee, the tax is $27,800 × 2.95% = $820.10. Totals is $6,248.10.

Because the maximum FUTA credit is $378 per employee and the employer pays more than that per employee, you can subtract $378 × 10 employees, or $3,780, from the amount due the federal government on FUTA (.062 × $7,000 × 10) − $3,780 = $560.

Because the employer paid his state unemployment taxes on time he is entitled to the full credit of 5.4 percent, so his net FUTA rate is .006 or .6 percent. His FUTA tax is $7,000 × .006 × 8 = $336.

Amount due Nevada: $4,720 + $708 + $820.10 = $6,248.10

3 You first calculate the state unemployment taxes by multiplying $10,500 × .04025 × 10 = $4,226.25 (or $42.26 per employee)

FUTA taxes are $7,000 × .006 × 10 = $420.10

4 You first calculate state unemployment taxes for the eight employees earning $14,000 by multiplying $14,000 × .0274 × 8 = $3,068.80 (or $383.60 per employee).

$16,000 × .0274 = $438.40

$21,200 × .0274 = $580.88

Total Rhode Island taxes are $3,068.80 + $438.40 + $580.88 = $4,088.08

Because the employer paid his Rhode Island unemployment taxes on time he qualifies for the full credit of 5.4 percent, so his net FUTA tax rate is .006.

FUTA tax due is $7,000 × .006 × X 10 = $420.00

Book III

Day-to-Day Bookkeeping

Book IV

Preparing for Year's End

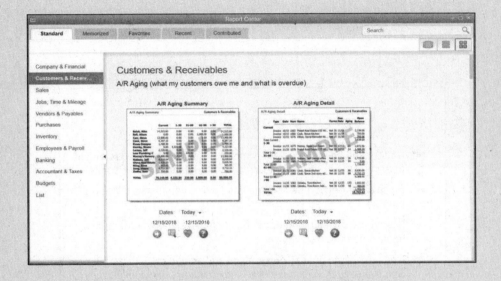

In this book . . .

- ✔ Understand how depreciation impacts both the income statement and your tax bill, and how to record depreciation in your books

- ✔ Review different types of loans and how to calculate and record interest

- ✔ Learn how to prove out (or verify) the accuracy of your financial books and records

- ✔ Find out how to post all corrections and adjustments to the General Ledger after you make them in the appropriate journal

- ✔ Learn how to find and correct errors, and know how to delete accounts

- ✔ Review the types of adjustments you need to make to your books before preparing the financial statements

Chapter 1

Depreciating Your Assets

- -

In This Chapter

▶ Understanding depreciation and why you do it

▶ Exploring depreciation methods

▶ Looking at depreciation's tax impact

▶ Pulling together depreciation schedules

▶ Entering depreciation expenses in the books

- -

*A*ll businesses use equipment, furnishings, and vehicles that last more than a year. Any asset that has a lifespan of more than a year is called a *fixed* asset. They may last longer than other assets, but even fixed assets eventually get old and need replacing.

And because your business should match its expenses with its revenue, you don't want to write off the full expense of a fixed asset in one year. After all, you'll certainly be making use of the asset for more than one year.

Imagine how bad your income statement would look if you wrote off the cost of a $100,000 piece of equipment in just one year? It would sure look as if your business wasn't doing well. Imagine the impact on a small business — $100,000 could eat up its entire profit or maybe even put it in the position of reporting a loss.

Instead of writing off the full amount of a fixed asset in one year, you use an accounting method called depreciation to write off the asset as it gets used up. This chapter introduces you to the various ways you can depreciate your assets and explain how to calculate depreciation, how depreciation impacts both the income statement and your tax bill, and how to record depreciation in your books.

Defining Depreciation

You may think of depreciation as something that happens to your car as it loses value. In fact, most new cars depreciate 20 to 30 percent or even more as soon as you drive them off the lot. But when you're talking about accounting, the definition of depreciation is a bit different.

Essentially, accountants use depreciation as a way to allocate the costs of a fixed asset over the period in which the asset is useable to the business. You, the bookkeeper, record the full transaction when the asset is bought, but the value of the asset is gradually reduced by subtracting a portion of that value as a depreciation expense each year. Depreciation expenses don't involve the exchange of cash; they're solely done for accounting purposes. Most companies enter depreciation expenses into the books once a year just before preparing their annual reports, but others calculate depreciation expenses monthly or quarterly.

One key reason to write off assets is to lower your tax bill, so the IRS gets involved in depreciation, too. As a business owner, you can't write off the cost of all major purchases in one year. Instead the IRS has strict rules about how you can write off assets as tax-deductible expenses. The section "Tackling Taxes and Depreciation" later in this chapter talks more about the IRS's rules.

Knowing what you can and can't depreciate

Businesses don't depreciate all assets. Low-cost items or items that aren't expected to last more than one year are recorded in expense accounts rather than asset accounts. For example, office supplies are expense items and not depreciated, but that office copier, which you'll use for more than one year, is recorded in the books as a fixed asset and depreciated each year.

Lifespan isn't the deciding factor for depreciation, however. Some assets that last many years are never depreciated. One good example is land; you can always make use of land, so its value never depreciates. You also can't depreciate any property that you lease or rent, but if you make improvements to leased property, you can depreciate the cost of those improvements. In that case, you write off the lease or rent as an expense item and depreciate the lease improvements over their estimated useful life.

You can't depreciate any items that you use outside your business, such as your personal car or home computer, but if you use these assets for both personal needs and business needs, you can depreciate a portion of them based on the percentage of time or other measurement that proves how much you use the car or computer for business. For example, the portion of a car that can be depreciated is based on the miles driven for business versus the miles driven for personal use. If you drive your car a total of 12,000 miles in a year and have records showing that 6,000 of those miles were for business purposes, you can depreciate 50 percent of the cost of the car. That percentage is allocated over the anticipated useful life of the car.

Another example of depreciation of a dual-usage asset is a room in your home designated exclusively for your business. You may be able to depreciate a portion of your home's cost as part of your business expenses. The amount you can depreciate is based on the portion of your home used for business.

Figuring out the useful life of a fixed asset

You're probably wondering how you figure out the useful life of a fixed asset. Well, the IRS has done the dirty work for you by creating a chart that spells out the recovery periods allowed for business equipment (see Table 1-1). Recovery periods are the anticipated useful lifespan of a fixed asset. For example, cars have a five-year recovery period because the IRS anticipates that they'll have a useful lifespan of five years. Though the car will probably run longer than that, you're not likely to continue using that car for business purposes after the first five years. You're more likely to trade it in and get a new car.

Table 1-1   Depreciation Recovery Periods for Business Equipment

Property Class Recovery Period	Business Equipment
3-year property	Tractor units and horses over 12 years old (or race horses over 2 years old)
5-year property	Cars, taxis, buses, trucks, computers, office machines (faxes, copiers, calculators, and so on), research equipment, and cattle
7-year property	Office furniture and fixtures
10-year property	Water transportation equipment, single-purpose agricultural or horticultural structures, and fruit- or nut-bearing vines and trees
15-year property	Land improvements, such as shrubbery, fences, roads, and bridges
20-year property	Farm buildings that are not agricultural or horticultural structures
27.5-year property	Residential rental property, not including the value of land
39-year property	Nonresidential real property, such as office buildings, stores, or warehouses, not including the value of land

Book IV

Preparing for Year's End

You can use the IRS chart to determine your fixed asset's useful life, or you can develop a chart that makes more sense for your business. For example, if you run a trucking company, you may determine that your trucks get used up more quickly than those used by a business for occasional deliveries. Although the IRS says that five years is the normal useful life for a truck, you may determine that trucks in your business are only useable for three years. You may need to justify the shorter useful life to the IRS, so be sure that you have the data to back up your decision.

Most accountants use the IRS estimates of useful life unless there's something unique about the way the business uses its fixed assets.

Delving into cost basis

In order to calculate depreciation for an asset, you need to know the cost basis of that asset. The equation for cost basis is:

Cost of the fixed asset + Sales tax + Shipping and delivery costs + Installation charges + Other costs = Cost basis

- **Cost of the fixed asset:** What you paid for the equipment, furniture, structure, vehicle, or other asset.

- **Sales tax:** What you were charged in sales tax to buy the fixed asset.

- **Shipping and delivery:** Any shipping or delivery charges you paid to get the fixed asset.

- **Installation charges:** Any charges you paid in order to have the equipment, furniture, or other fixed asset installed on your business's premises.

- **Other costs:** Any other charges you need to pay to make the fixed asset usable for your business. For example, if you buy a new computer and need to set up certain hardware in order to use that computer for your business, those setup costs can be added as part of the cost basis of the fixed asset (the computer).

Reducing the Value of Assets

After you decide on the useful life of an asset and calculate its cost basis (see the preceding sections), you have to decide how to go about reducing the asset's value according to accounting standards.

Evaluating your depreciation options

When calculating depreciation of your assets each year, you have a choice of four methods: Straight-Line, Sum-of-Years-Digits, Declining Balance, and Units of Production. This section explains these methods as well as the pros and cons of using each one.

To show you how the methods handle assets differently, the first year's depreciation expense is calculated using the purchase of a truck on January 1, 2015, with a cost basis of $25,000. This assumes that the truck can be sold in five years for $5,000, called the *salvage* value. The example shows you how to use the salvage value as part of the calculations for three of the depreciation methods. The fourth method covered here, Units of Production, is used primarily in manufacturing, so the truck example doesn't work. But you'll still get the idea of how to use that method, don't worry.

Straight-Line

When depreciating assets using the Straight-Line method, you spread the cost of the asset evenly over the number of years the asset will be used. Straight-Line is the most common method used for depreciation of assets, and it's also the easiest one to use. Another advantage of this method is that you can use it for both accounting purposes and tax purposes. (If you use any of the other methods, you have to keep separate depreciation records — one for your financial reports and one for the tax man.)

The formula for calculating Straight-Line depreciation is:

> (Cost of fixed asset – Salvage) ÷ Estimated useful life = Annual depreciation expense

For the truck in this example, the cost basis is $25,000, the salvage value is $5,000, and the IRS estimate of useful life of five years is being used. With these figures, the calculation for finding the annual depreciation expense of this truck based on the Straight-Line depreciation method is:

> ($25,000 – $5,000) ÷ 5 = $4,000

Each year, the business's Income Statement should include $4,000 as a depreciation expense for this truck. You add this $4,000 depreciation expense to the accumulated depreciation account for the truck. This accumulated depreciation account is shown below the truck's original value on the Balance Sheet. You subtract the accumulated depreciation from the cost basis of the truck to show a net asset value, which is the value remaining on the truck.

Sum-of-Years-Digits

If you think your asset loses a greater portion of its useful life in the early years, you can speed up its depreciation by using the *Sum-of-Years-Digits (SYD) method*. This method allows you to write off higher depreciation expenses in the earlier years of useful life and lower depreciation in later years. When you use Sum-of-Years-Digits, you assume that the fixed asset will be used less in later years.

One big disadvantage of writing off assets quickly is that the higher depreciation expense lowers your business's net income.

Sum-of-Years-Digits requires a three-step calculation:

1. **Find the SYD using this formula, with** n representing the number of years of estimated useful life remaining as of the start of the fiscal year:

   $n(n+1) \div 2 = \text{SYD}$

2. **Find the applicable fraction using this formula:** $n \div \text{SYD} = $ Applicable fraction

3. **Calculate the depreciation expense using this formula:**

   (Cost – Salvage value) $\times$ Applicable fraction = Depreciation expense

   To calculate the first year of the depreciation expense on the truck, this formula works like so: **SYD:** $5(5+1) \div 2 = 15$

   Applicable fraction: $5 \div 15 = \frac{1}{3}$
   Depreciation expense: $\$20,000 \times \frac{1}{3} = \$6,666.67$

The depreciation expense written off during the truck's first year of life is $2,666.67 higher than it is when it's calculated using the Straight-Line depreciation method. If you do the same calculation for the remaining years of useful life, you get the following results:

Year 2: $5,333.33

Year 3: $4,000.00

Year 4: $2,666.67

Year 5: $1,333.33

By Year 3, $16,000 has been written off, 80 percent of the depreciable amount for the truck.

Double-Declining Balance

The Double-Declining Balance method of depreciation allows you to write off an asset even more quickly than the Sum-of-Years-Digits (see the preceding section). This method is ideal for assets whose primary usefulness is in the early years of life.

You calculate the depreciation using the Declining Balance method using this formula:

2 × (1 ÷ Estimated useful life) × Book value at the beginning of the year = Depreciation expense

The calculation for the truck's depreciation expense using the Declining Balance method is:

2 × (1 ÷ 5) × $25,000 = $10,000

As you can see, the depreciation expense for the first year of using the truck is $10,000. If you do the same calculation for the remaining years of useful life, you get the following results:

Year 2: $6,000

Year 3: $3,600

Year 4: $400

Year 5: $0

Eighty percent of the value of the truck is written off in the first two years. Clearly, the Double-Declining Balance method of depreciation reduces the value of an asset even faster than the Sum-of-Years-Digits.

Units of Production

The Units of Production (UOP) method of depreciation works well primarily in a manufacturing environment because it calculates depreciation based on the number of units produced in a year. Companies whose machinery usage varies greatly each year depending on the market and the number of units needed for sale make use of this depreciation method.

The formula for calculating depreciation using Units of Production is a two-step process:

1. **Find the UOP rate using this formula:**

   (Cost – Salvage value) ÷ Estimated number of units to be produced during estimated useful life = UOP rate

2. **Find the depreciation expense using this formula:**

   Units produced during the year × UOP rate = Depreciation expense

You only need to use the Units of Production depreciation method if you're manufacturing the products you sell and if the usage of your equipment fluctuates widely from year to year.

Tackling Taxes and Depreciation

Depreciation calculations for tax purposes are a completely different animal than the calculations used to record depreciation for accounting purposes. You can use Straight-Line depreciation to calculate your depreciation expense for tax purposes, but most businesses prefer to write off the highest expense legally permissible and reduce their tax bills by the greatest amount.

In addition to Straight-Line depreciation, two other acceptable IRS methods for writing off assets are: Section 179 and Modified Accelerated Cost Recovery System (MACRS). The big advantage of the Section 179 Deduction is that you can write off up to 100 percent of the cost basis of qualifying property. (The next section talks more about what qualifies.) If the property doesn't qualify, most businesses choose to use MACRS rather than Straight-Line depreciation.

Section 179

Section 179, which gets its name from a section of the tax code, is a great boon for companies. Businesses can write off up to $25,000 in newly purchased property that qualifies for the deduction up to 100 percent of the cost basis of the property. This amount could be increased if Congress changes the law. In 2014, companies were allowed up to $500,000 for the Section 179 deduction. It was unknown at the time of this writing whether this would be extended in 2015 and beyond.

The primary reason for this part of the tax code is to encourage businesses to buy new property in order to stimulate the economy. That's why only certain types of property are included, and there are limits on the amount that can be deducted for some types of property.

Basically, Section 179's qualifying property includes tangible property such as machines, equipment, and furniture. In addition, some storage facilities qualify, as do some single-purpose agricultural and horticultural structures. All cars and SUVs between 6,000 and 14,000 pounds can't be fully written off under Section 179. You also can't write off property held for the production of income (such as rental property), most real property, property acquired as a gift or inheritance, and property held outside the United States.

You can get full details about Section 179 by ordering a copy of IRS Publication 946, How to Depreciate Property, from the IRS or accessing it online at `www.irs.gov/pub/irs-pdf/p946.pdf`. Be sure to work with your accountant to determine what's eligible and how much of the cost basis is eligible for the Section 179 deduction.

MACRS

The most common type of depreciation write-off used by businesses is Modified Accelerated Cost Recovery System, or MACRS. The recovery period shown in Table 1-1 is the basis for this depreciation method. After you know what type of property you have (three-year, five-year, and so on), you use the MACRS table in IRS Publication 946, "How to Depreciate Property," to figure out the depreciation expense you can write off. Luckily, you can leave MACRS calculations for your accountant to do when she prepares your business tax forms.

Setting Up Depreciation Schedules

In order to keep good accounting records, you need to track how much you depreciate each of your assets in some form of a schedule. After all, your financial statements include only a total value for all your assets and a total accumulated depreciation amount. Most businesses maintain depreciation schedules in some type of spreadsheet program that exists outside their accounting systems. Usually, one person is responsible for managing assets and their depreciation. However, in a large company, these tasks can turn into full-time jobs for several people.

The best way to keep track of depreciation is to prepare a separate schedule for each asset account that you depreciate. For example, set up depreciation schedules for buildings, furniture and fixtures, office equipment, and so on. Your depreciation schedule should include all the information you need to determine annual depreciation, such as the original purchase date, original cost basis, and recovery period. You can add columns to track the actual depreciation expenses and calculate the current value of each asset. Here's a sample depreciation schedule for vehicles:

Date Put in Service	Description	Cost	Recovery Period	Annual Depreciation
1/5/2013	Black car	$30,000	5 years	$5,000
1/1/2014	Blue truck	$25,000	5 years	$4,000

If you use a different method of depreciation for tax purposes (see "Tackling Taxes and Depreciation"), you should prepare schedules for tax purposes as well.

Depreciation can be more than just a mathematical exercise. Keeping track of depreciation is a good way to monitor the age of your assets and know when you should plan for their replacement. As your assets age, they'll incur greater repair costs, so keeping depreciation schedules can help you plan repair and maintenance budgets as well.

Recording Depreciation Expenses

Recording a depreciation expense calls for a rather simple entry into your accounting system.

After calculating your depreciation expense, no matter which method you used to calculate that expense, here is how you would record a depreciation expense of $4,000:

	Debit	Credit
Depreciation Expense	$4,000	
Accumulated Depreciation: Vehicles		$4,000

The Depreciation Expense account increases by the debit, and the Accumulated Depreciation: Vehicles account increases by the credit. On the income statement, you subtract the Depreciation Expense from sales, and on the balance sheet, you subtract the Accumulated Depreciation: Vehicles from the value of Vehicles.

Chapter 2

Paying and Collecting Interest

- -

In This Chapter

▶ Understanding interest calculations

▶ Making the most of interest income

▶ Calculating loan interest

- -

*F*ew businesses are able to make major purchases without taking out loans. Whether loans are for vehicles, buildings, or other business needs, businesses must pay *interest,* a percentage of the amount loaned, to whoever loans them the money.

Some businesses loan their own money and receive interest payments as income. In fact, a savings account can be considered a type of loan because by placing your money in the account, you're giving the bank the opportunity to loan that money to others. So the bank pays you for the use of your money by paying interest, which is a type of income for your company.

This chapter reviews different types of loans and how to calculate and record interest expenses for each type. In addition, it talks about how you calculate and record interest income in your business's books.

Deciphering Types of Interest

Any time you make use of someone else's money, such as a bank, you have to pay interest for that use — whether you're buying a house, a car, or some other item you want. The same is true when someone else is using your money. For example, when you buy a bond or deposit money in a money market account, you're paid interest for allowing the use of your money while it's on deposit.

The financial institution that has your money will likely combine your money with that of other depositors and loan it out to other people to make more interest than it's paying you. That's why when the interest rates you have to pay on loans are low, the interest rates you can earn on savings are even lower.

Banks actually use two types of interest calculations:

- **Simple interest** is calculated only on the principal amount of the loan.
- **Compound interest** is calculated on the principal and on interest earned.

Simple interest

Simple interest is, maybe not surprisingly, simple to calculate. Here's the formula for calculating simple interest:

Principal × interest rate × n = interest

To show you how interest is calculated, assume someone deposited $10,000 in the bank in a money market account earning 3 percent (0.03) interest for 3 years. So, the interest earned over 3 years is $10,000 × .03 × 3 = $900.

Compound interest

Compound interest is computed on both the principal and any interest earned. You must calculate the interest each year and add it to the balance before you can calculate the next year's interest payment, which will be based on both the principal and interest earned.

Here's how you would calculate compound interest:

Principal × interest rate	= interest for year one
(Principal + interest earned) × interest rate	= interest for year two
(Principal + interest earned) × interest rate	= interest for year three

You repeat this calculation for all years of the deposit or loan. The one exception could be with a loan. If you pay the total interest due each month or year (depending on when your payments are due), there would be no interest to compound.

To show you how this impacts earnings, calculate the three-year deposit of $10,000 at 3 percent (0.03):

$10,000 × .03	= $300 — Year One interest
($10,000 + 300) × .03	= $309 — Year Two Interest
($10,000 + 300 +309) × .03	= $318.27 — Year Three Interest
Total Interest Earned	= $927.27

You can see that you'd earn an extra $27.27 during the first three years of that deposit if the interest is compounded. When working with much larger sums or higher interest rates for longer periods of time, compound interest can make a big difference in how much you earn or how much you pay on a loan.

Ideally, you want to find a savings account, certificate deposit, or other savings instrument that earns compound interest. But if you want to borrow money, look for a simple interest loan.

Also, not all accounts that earn compound interest are created equally. Watch carefully to see how frequently the interest is compounded. The preceding example shows a type of account for which interest is compounded annually. But if you can find an account where interest is compounded monthly, the interest you earn will be even higher. Monthly compounding means that interest earned will be calculated each month and added to the principle each month before calculating the next month's interest, which results in a lot more interest than a bank that compounds interest just once a year.

Handling Interest Income

The income that your business earns from its savings accounts, certificates of deposits, or other investment vehicles is called *interest income*. As the bookkeeper, you're rarely required to calculate interest income using the simple interest or compounded interest formulas described in the earlier sections of this chapter. In most cases, the financial institution sends you a monthly, quarterly, or annual statement that has a separate line item reporting interest earned.

When you get your monthly statement, you then reconcile the books. *Reconciliation* is a process in which you prove out whether the amount the bank says you have in your account is equal to what you think you have in your account. Book IV Chapter 3 talks more about reconciling bank accounts. The first step in the reconciliation process involves recording any interest earned or bank fees in the books so that your balance matches what the bank shows. Figure 2-1 shows you how to record $25 in Interest Income.

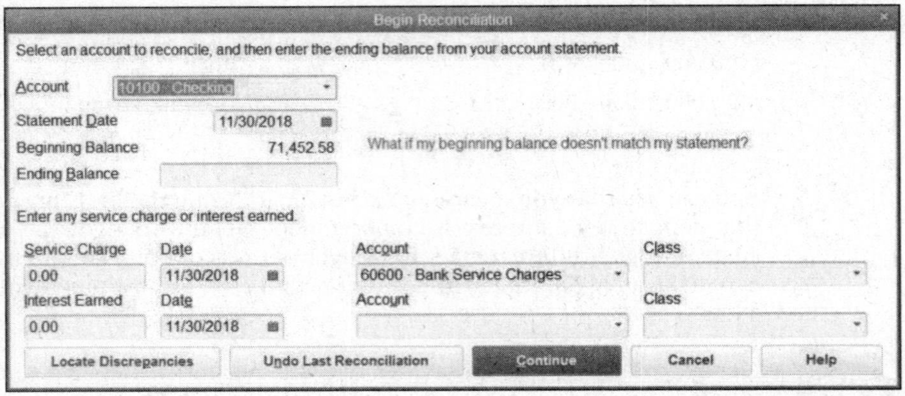

Figure 2-1:
In
QuickBooks,
you enter
interest
income
at the
beginning of
the account
reconcil-
iation
process.

Image courtesy of Intuit

If you're keeping the books manually, a journal entry to record interest would look similar to this:

	Debit	**Credit**
Cash	XXXX	
Interest Income		XXXX

To record interest income from American Savings Bank.

When preparing financial statements, you show Interest Income on the income statement in a section called Other Income. Other Income includes any income your business earned that was not directly related to your primary business activity — selling your goods or services.

Delving into Loans and Interest Expenses

Businesses borrow money for both *short-term periods* (periods of less than 12 months) and *long-term periods* (periods of more than one year). Short-term debt usually involves some form of credit-card debt or line-of-credit debt. Long-term debt can include a 5-year car loan, 20-year mortgage, or any other type of debt that is paid over more than one year.

Short-term debt

Any money due in the next 12-month period is shown on the balance sheet as short-term or current debt. Any interest paid on that money is shown as an Interest Expense on the income statement.

In most cases, you don't have to calculate your interest due. The financial institution sending you a bill gives you a breakdown of the principal and interest to be paid.

How credit-card interest is calculated

For example, when you get a credit-card bill at home, a line always shows you new charges, the amount to pay in full to avoid all interest, and the amount of interest charged during the current period on any money not paid from the previous bill. If you don't pay your credit in full, interest on most cards is calculated using a daily periodic rate of interest, which is compounded each day based on the unpaid balance. Yes, credit cards are a type of compounded interest. When not paid in full, interest is calculated on the unpaid principal balance plus any unpaid interest. Table 2-1 shows what a typical interest calculation looks like on a credit card.

Table 2-1	**Credit-Card Interest Calculation**				
	Avg. Daily Balance	*Daily Periodic Rate*	*Corresponding Annual Rate*	*Finance Charges*	
Daily Rate	*Transaction Fees*				
Purchases	$XXX	0.034076%	12.40%	$XXX	$XXX
Cash	$XXX	0.0452%	16.49%	$XXX	$XXX

On many credit cards, you start paying interest on new purchases immediately, if you haven't paid your balance due in full the previous month. When opening a credit-card account for your business, be sure you understand how interest is calculated and when the bank starts charging on new purchases. Some issuers give a grace period of 20 to 30 days before charging interest, while others don't give any type of grace period at all.

In Table 2-1, the Finance Charges include the daily rate charged in interest based on the daily periodic rate plus any transaction fees. For example, if you take a cash advance from your credit card, many credit-card companies charge a transaction fee of 2 to 3 percent of the total amount of cash taken. This fee can be true when you transfer balances from one credit card to another. Although the company entices you with an introductory rate of

1 or 2 percent to get you to transfer the balance, be sure to read the fine print. You may have to pay a 3 percent transaction fee on the full amount transferred, which makes the introductory rate much higher.

Using credit lines

As a small business owner, you get better interest rates using a line of credit with a bank rather than a credit card. Interest rates are usually lower on lines of credit. Typically, a business owner uses a credit card for purchases, but if he can't pay the bill in full, he draws money from his line of credit rather than carry over the credit-card balance.

When the money is first received from the credit line, you record the cash receipt and the liability. Just to show you how this transaction works, record the receipt of a credit line of $1,500. Here is what the journal entry would look like:

	Debit	Credit
Cash	1,500	
Credit Line Payable		1,500

To record receipt of cash from credit line.

In this entry, you increase the Cash account and the Credit Line Payable account balances. If you're using a computerized accounting program, you record the transaction using the deposit form, as shown in Figure 2-2.

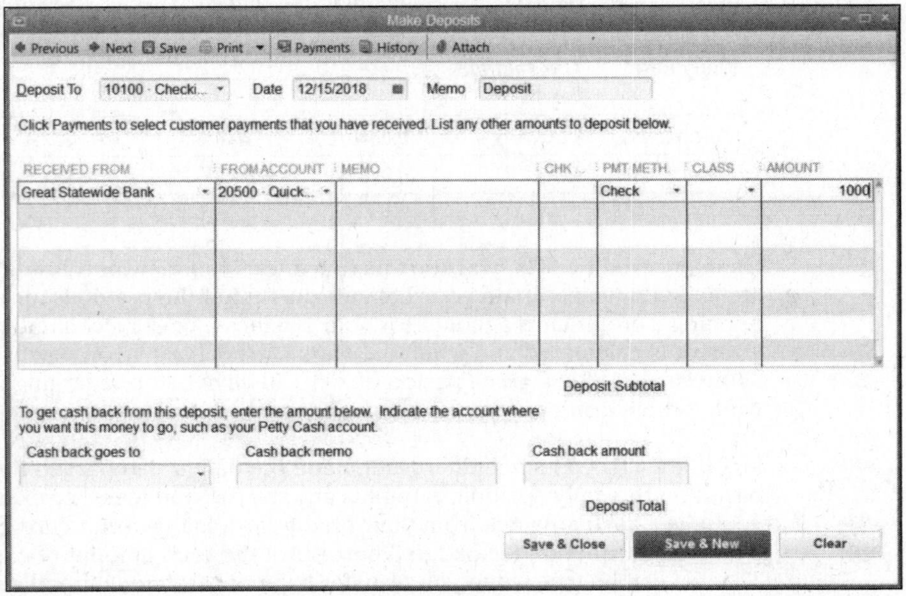

Figure 2-2: Recording receipt of cash from credit line.

Image courtesy of Intuit

When you make your first payment, you must record the use of cash, the amount paid on the principal of the loan, and the amount paid in interest. Here is what that journal entry looks like:

	Debit	*Credit*
Credit Line Payable	150	
Interest Expense	10	
Cash		160

To make monthly payment on credit line.

This journal entry reduces the amount due in the Credit Line Payable account, increases the amount paid in the Interest Expense account, and reduces the amount in the Cash account.

If you're using a computerized system, you simply complete a check form and indicate which accounts are impacted by the payment, and the system updates the accounts automatically. Figure 2-3 shows you how to record a loan payment in QuickBooks.

As you can see in Figure 2-3, at the same time that you prepare the check for printing, you can add the accounts that are impacted by that payment by splitting the detail expense information. $150 of that payment should be recorded in the Bank Credit Card Payable account, and $10 should be recorded as Interest Expense. The top of the check indicates which account will be used to pay the bill. QuickBooks can then print the check and update all affected accounts. You don't need to do any additional postings to update your books.

Book IV

Preparing for Year's End

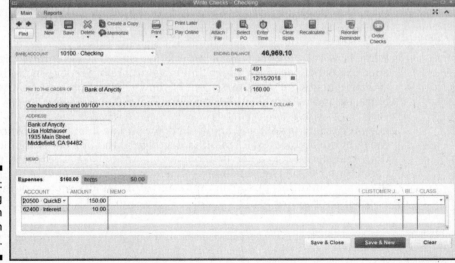

Figure 2-3: Recording a loan payment in QuickBooks.

Image courtesy of Intuit

Long-term debt

Most companies take on some form of debt that will be paid over a period of time that is longer than 12 months. This debt may include car loans, mortgages, or promissory notes. A *promissory note* is a written agreement where you agree to repay someone a set amount of money at some point in the future at a particular interest rate. It can be monthly, yearly, or some other term specified in the note. Most installment loans are types of promissory notes.

Recording a debt

When the company first takes on the debt, it's recorded in the books in much the same way as a short-term debt:

	Debit	*Credit*
Cash	XXX	
Notes Payable		XXX

To record receipt of cash from American Bank promissory note.

Payments are also recorded in a manner similar to short-term debt:

	Debit	*Credit*
Notes Payable	XXX	
Interest Expense	XXX	
Cash		XXX

To record payment on American Bank promissory note.

You record the initial long-term debt and make payments the same way in QuickBooks as you do for short-term debt.

While how you enter the initial information isn't very different, a big difference exists between how short- and long-term debt are shown on the financial statements. All short-term debt is shown in the Current Liability section of the balance sheet.

Long-term debt is split and shown in different line items. The portion of the debt due in the next 12 months is shown in the Current Liabilities section, which is usually a line item named something like "Current Portion of Long-Term Debt." The remaining balance of the long-term debt due beyond the next 12 months appears in the Long-Term Liability section of the balance sheet as Notes Payable.

Major purchases and long-term debt

Sometimes a long-term liability is set up at the same time as you make a major purchase. You may pay some portion of the amount due in cash as a down payment and the remainder as a note. To show you how to record such a transaction, assume that a business has purchased a truck for $25,000, made a down payment of $5,000, and took a note at an interest rate of 6 percent for $20,000. Here's how you record this purchase in the books:

	Debit	Credit
Vehicles	25,000	
Cash		5,000
Notes Payable – Vehicles		20,000

To record payment for the purchase of the blue truck.

You then record payments on the note in the same way as any other loan payment:

	Debit	Credit
Notes Payable – Vehicles	XXX	
Interest Expense	XXX	
Cash		XXX

To record payment on note for blue truck.

When recording the payment on a long-term debt for which you have a set installment payment, you may not get a breakdown of interest and principal with every payment. For example, many times when you take out a car loan, you get a coupon book with just the total payment due each month. Each payment includes both principal and interest, but you don't get any break-down detailing how much goes toward interest and how much goes toward principal.

Separating principal and interest

Why is this lack of separation a problem for recording payments? Each payment includes a different amount for principal and for interest. At the beginning of the loan, the principal is at its highest amount, so the amount of interest due is much higher than later in the loan payoff process when the balance is lower. Many times in the first year of notes payable on high-price items, such as a mortgage on a building, you're paying more interest than principal.

In order to record long-term debt for which you don't receive a breakdown each month, you need to ask the bank that gave you the loan for an amortiza-tion schedule. An *amortization schedule* lists the total payment, the amount of each payment that goes toward interest, the amount that goes toward principal, and the remaining balance to be paid on the note.

Some banks provide an amortization schedule automatically when you sign all the paperwork for the note. If your bank can't give you one, you can easily get one online using an amortization calculator. You can find one online at www.amortization-calc.com.

Using that calculator, Table 2-2 lists the principal/interest breakdown for the first six months of payment on the truck in a six-month amortization chart. You can see from Table 2-2 that the amount paid to principal on a long-term note gradually increases, while the amount of interest paid gradually decreases as the note balance is paid off. The calculator did calculate payments for all 60 months, but they're not all shown here here.

Table 2-2   Six-Month Amortization Chart for Truck Payments

Total Payment	Principal	Interest	Remaining Note Balance
$386.66	$286.66	100.00	$19,713.34
$386.66	$288.09	98.57	$19,425.25
$386.66	$289.53	97.13	$19.135.72
$386.66	$290.98	95.68	$18,844.75
$386.66	$292.43	94.23	$18,552.32
$386.66	$293.89	92.77	$18,258.42

Looking at the six-month amortization chart, here's what you would need to record in the books for the first payment on the truck:

	Debit	Credit
Notes Payable – Vehicles	286.66	
Interest Expense	100.00	
Cash		386.66

To record payment on note for blue truck.

In reading the amortization chart in Table 2-2, notice how the amount paid toward interest is slightly less each month as the balance on the note still due is gradually reduced. Also, the amount paid toward the principal of that note gradually increases as less of the payment is used to pay interest.

By the time you start making payments for the final year of the loan, interest costs drop dramatically because the balance is so much lower. For the first payment of Year 5, the amount paid in interest is $22.47, and the amount paid on principal is $364.19. The balance remaining after that payment is $4,128.34.

As you lower your principal balance, much less of your payment goes toward interest and much more goes toward reducing principal. That's why many financial specialists advice you to pay down principal as fast as possible if you want to reduce the term of a loan.

Book IV

Preparing for Year's End

Chapter 3

Proving Out the Cash

. . . .

In This Chapter

▶ Counting your company's cash

▶ Finalizing the cash journals

▶ Balancing out your bank accounts

▶ Posting cash-related adjustments

. . . .

All business owners — whether the business is a small, family-owned candy store or a major international conglomerate — like to periodically test how well their businesses are doing. They also want to be sure that the numbers in their accounting systems actually match what's physically in their stores and offices. After they check out what's in the books, these business owners can prepare financial reports to determine the company's financial success or failure during the last month, quarter, or year. This process of verifying the accuracy of your cash is called *proving out*.

The first step in proving out the books involves counting the company's cash and verifying that the cash numbers in your books match the actual cash on hand at a particular point in time. This chapter explains how you can test to be sure the cash counts are accurate, finalize the cash journals for the accounting period, prove out the bank accounts, and post any adjustments or corrections to the General Ledger.

Why Prove Out the Books?

You're probably thinking that proving out the books sounds like a huge task that takes lots of time. You're right — it's a big job, but it's also a very necessary one to do periodically so you can be sure that what's recorded in your accounting system realistically measures what's actually going on in your business.

With any accounting system, mistakes can be made, and, unfortunately, any business can fall victim to incidents of theft or embezzlement. The only way to be sure that none of these problems exist in your business is to periodically prove out the books. The process of proving out the books is a big part of the accounting cycle, discussed in detail in Book I Chapter 1. The first three steps of the accounting cycle — recording transactions, making journal entries, and posting summaries of those entries to the General Ledger — involve tracking the flow of cash throughout the accounting period. All three steps are part of the process of recording a business's financial activities throughout the entire accounting period. The rest of the steps in the accounting cycle are conducted at the end of the period and are part of the process of proving out the accuracy of your books. They include running a trial balance (see Book IV Chapter 5), creating a worksheet (see Book IV Chapter 5), adjusting journal entries (see Book IV Chapter 6), creating financial statements (refer to Book II Chapters 4 and 5), and closing the books (see Book V Chapter 6). Most businesses prove out their books every month.

Of course, you don't want to shut down your business for a week *while* you prove out the books, so you should select a day during each accounting period on which you'll take a financial snapshot of the state of your accounts. For example, if you're preparing monthly financial reports at the end of the month, you test the amount of cash your business has on hand as of that certain time and day, such as 6 p.m. on June 30 after your store closes for the day. The rest of the testing process — running a trial balance, creating a worksheet, adjusting journal entries, creating financial statements, and closing the books — is based on what happened before that point in time. When you open the store and sell more products the next day and buy new things to run your business, those transactions and any others that follow the point in time of your test become part of the next accounting cycle.

Making Sure Ending Cash Is Right

Testing your books starts with counting your cash. Why start with cash? Because the accounting process starts with transactions, and transactions occur when cash exchanges hands either to buy things you need to run the business or to sell your products or services. Before you can even begin to test whether the books are right, you need to know if your books have captured what's happened to your company's cash and if the amount of cash shown in your books actually matches the amount of cash you have on hand.

You've heard the well-worn expression, "Show me the money!" Well, in business, that idea is the core of your success. Everything relies on your cash profits that you can take out of your business or use to expand your business.

Book III Chapter 2 discusses how a business proves out the cash taken in by each of its cashiers. That daily process gives a business good control of the point at which cash comes into the business from customers who buy the company's products or services. It also measures any cash refunds that were given to customers who returned items. But the points of sale and return aren't the only times cash comes into or goes out of the business.

If your business sells products on store credit (see Book III Chapter 2), some of the cash from customers is actually collected at a later point in time by the bookkeeping staff responsible for tracking customer credit accounts. And when your business needs something, whether products to be sold or supplies needed by various departments, you must pay cash to vendors, suppliers, and contractors. Sometimes cash is paid out on the spot, but many times the bill is recorded in the Accounts Payable account and paid at a later date. All these transactions involve the use of cash, so the amount of cash on hand in the business at any one time includes not only what's in the cash registers but also what's on deposit in the company's bank accounts. You need to know the balances of those accounts and test those balances to be sure they're accurate and match what's in your company's books. The section "Reconciling Bank Accounts" later in this chapter talks more about how to do that.

So your snapshot in time includes not only the cash on hand in your cash registers but also any cash you may have in the bank. Some departments may also have petty cash accounts, which means you total that cash as well. The total cash figure is what you show as an asset named "Cash" on the first line of your company's financial statement, the *balance sheet.* The balance sheet shows all that the company owns (its assets) and owes (its liabilities) as well as the equity the owners have in the company. Book II Chapter 4 talks more about the balance sheet and how you prepare one.

The actual cash you have on hand is just one tiny piece of the cash moving through your business during the accounting period. The true detail of what cash has flowed into and out of the business is in your cash journals. Closing those are the next step in the process of figuring out how well your business did.

Book IV

Preparing for Year's End

Closing the Cash Journals

As explained in Book I Chapter 4, if you keep the books manually, you can find a record of every transaction that involves cash in one of two cash journals: the Cash Receipts journal (cash that comes into the business) and the Cash Disbursements journal (cash that goes out of the business).

If you use a computerized accounting system, you don't have these cash journals, but you have many different ways to find out the same detailed information that they contain. You can run reports of sales by customer, by item, or by sales representative. Figure 3-1 shows the types of sales reports that QuickBooks can automatically generate for you. You can also run reports that show you all the company's purchases by vendor or by item as well as list any purchases still on order. Figure 3-2 shows the various purchase reports that QuickBooks can automatically run for you. These reports can be run by the week, the month, the quarter, or the year, or you can customize the reports to show a particular period of time that you're analyzing. For example, if you want to know what sales occurred between June 5 and 10, you can run a report specifying the exact dates.

In addition to the sales and purchase reports shown in Figures 3-1 and 3-2, you can generate other transaction detail reports including customers and receivables; jobs, time, and mileage; vendors and payables; inventory; employees and payroll; and banking (see the options listed on the left side of Figure 3-1). One big advantage of a computerized accounting system when you're trying to prove out your books is the number of different ways you can develop reports to check for accuracy in your books if you suspect an error.

Figure 3-1: Using Quick-Books, you can easily generate reports showing your company's cash receipts organized by customer, items sold, or sales representative.

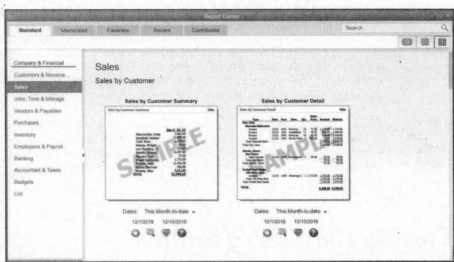

Image courtesy of Intuit

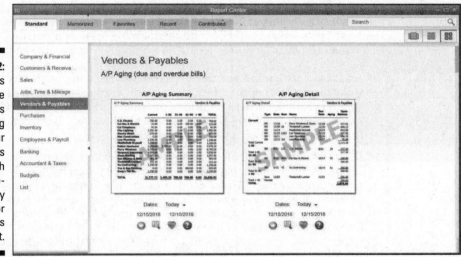

Image courtesy of Intuit

Figure 3-2: QuickBooks can produce reports showing your company's cash disbursements by vendor or by items bought.

Finalizing cash receipts

If all your books are up-to-date, when you summarize the Cash Receipts journal on whatever day and time you choose to prove out your books, you should come up with a total of all cash received by the business at that time. Unfortunately, in the real world of bookkeeping, things don't come out so nice and neat. In fact, you probably wouldn't even start entering the transactions from that particular day into the books until the next day, when you enter the cash reports from all cashiers and others who handle incoming cash (such as the accounts receivable staff who collect money from customers buying on credit) into the Cash Receipts journal.

After entering all the transactions from the day in question, the books for the period you're looking at may still be incomplete. Sometimes, adjustments or corrections must be made to the ending cash numbers. For example, monthly credit-card fees and interest received from the bank may not yet be recorded in your cash journals. As the bookkeeper, you must be sure that all bank fees related to cash receipts as well as any interest earned are recorded in the Cash Receipts journal before you summarize the journals for the period you're analyzing.

Remembering credit-card fees

When your company allows customers to use credit cards, you must pay fees to the bank that processes these transactions, which is probably the same bank that handles all your business accounts. These fees actually lower the amount you take in as cash receipts, so the amount you record as a cash receipt must be adjusted to reflect those costs of doing business. Monthly credit-card fees vary greatly depending upon the bank you're using, but here are some of the most common fees your company may be charged:

- **Address verification service (AVS) fee** is a fee companies pay if they want to avoid accepting fraudulent credit card sales. Businesses that use this service take orders by phone or email and therefore don't have the credit card in hand to verify a customer's signature. Banks charge this fee for every transaction that's verified.

- **Discount rate** is a fee all companies that use credit cards must pay; it's based on a percentage of the sale or return transaction. The rate your company may be charged varies greatly depending on the type of business you conduct and the volume of your sales each month. Companies that use a terminal to swipe cards and electronically send transaction information usually pay lower fees than companies that use paper credit-card transactions because the electronic route creates less work for the bank and eliminates the possibility of key-entry errors by employees.

- **Secure payment gateway fee,** which allows the merchant to process transactions securely, is charged to companies that transact business over the Internet. If your business sells products online, you can expect to pay this fee based on a set monthly amount.

- **Customer support fee** is charged to companies that want bank support for credit-card transactions for 24 hours a day, 365 days a year. Companies such as mail-order catalogs that allow customers to place orders 24 hours a day look for this support. Sometimes companies even want this support in more than one language if they sell products internationally.

- **Monthly minimum fee** is the least a business is required to pay for the ability to offer its customers the convenience of using credit cards to buy products. This fee usually varies between $10 and $30 per month.

Even if your company doesn't generate any credit-card sales during a month, you're still required to pay this minimum fee. As long as enough sales are generated to cover the fee, you shouldn't have a problem. For example, if the fee is $10 and your company pays 2 percent per sale in discount fees, you need to sell at least $500 worth of products each month to cover that $10 fee. When deciding whether to accept credit cards as a payment option, be sure you're confident that you'll generate enough business through credit-card sales to cover that fee. If not, you may find that accepting credit cards costs you more than the sales you generate by offering that convenience.

- ✔ **Transaction fee** is a standard fee charged to your business for each credit-card transaction you submit for authorization. You pay this fee even if the cardholder is denied and you lose the sale.

- ✔ **Equipment and software fees** are charged to your company based on the equipment and computer software you use in order to process credit-card transactions. You have the option of buying or leasing credit-card equipment and related software.

- ✔ **Chargeback and retrieval fees** are charged if a customer disputes a transaction.

When deciding whether to accept credit cards as a form of payment, you must consider what your competition is doing. If all your competitors offer the convenience of using credit cards and you don't, you may lose sales if customers take their business elsewhere.

Reconciling your credit-card statements

Each month, the bank that handles your credit-card sales will send you a statement listing

- ✔ All your company's transactions for the month.

- ✔ The total amount your company sold through credit-card sales.

- ✔ The total fees charged to your account.

If you find a difference between what the bank reports was sold on credit cards and what the company's books show regarding credit-card sales, it's time to play detective and find the reason for the difference. In most cases, the error involves the charging back of one or more sales because a customer disputes the charge. In this case, the Cash Receipts journal is adjusted to reflect that loss of sale, and the bank statement and company books should match up.

For example, suppose $200 in credit-card sales was disputed. The original entry of the transaction in the books should look like this:

	Debit	Credit
Sales	$200	
Cash		$200

To reverse disputed credit sales recorded in June.

This entry reduces the total Sales for the month as well as the amount of the Cash account. If the dispute is resolved and the money is later retrieved, the sale is then reentered when the cash is received.

You also record any fees related to credit-card fees in the Cash Disbursements journal. For example, if credit-card fees for the month of June total $200, the entry in the books should look like this:

	Debit	*Credit*
Credit-Card Fees	$200	
Cash		$200

To record credit-card fees for the month of June.

Summarizing the Cash Receipts journal

When you're sure that all cash receipts as well as any corrections or adjustments to those receipts have been properly entered in the books (see the previous two sections), you summarize the Cash Receipts journal as explained in detail in Book I Chapter 4. After summarizing the Cash Receipts journal for the accounting period you're analyzing, you know the total cash that was taken into the business from sales as well as from other channels.

In the Cash Receipts journal, sales usually appear in two columns:

- ✔ **Sales:** The cash shown in the Sales column is cash received when the customer purchases the goods using cash, check, or bank credit card.

- ✔ **Accounts Receivable:** The Accounts Receivable column is for sales in which no cash was received when the customer purchased the item. Instead, the customer bought on credit and intends to pay cash at a later date. (Book III Chapter 2 talks more about Accounts Receivable and collecting money from customers.)

After you add all receipts to the Cash Receipts journal, entries for items bought on store credit can be posted to the Accounts Receivable journal and the individual customer accounts. You then send bills to customers that reflect all transactions from the month just closed as well as any payments still due from previous months. Billing customers is a key part of the closing process that occurs each month.

In addition to the Sales and Accounts Receivable columns, your Cash Receipts journal should have at least two other columns:

- ✔ **General:** The General column lists all other cash received, such as owner investments in the business.

- ✔ **Cash:** The Cash column contains the total of all cash received by the business during an accounting period.

Finalizing cash outlays

After you close the Cash Receipts journal (see "Summarizing the Cash Receipts journal"), the next step is to close the Cash Disbursements journal. Any adjustments related to outgoing cash receipts, such as bank credit-card fees, should be added to the Cash Disbursements journal.

Before you close the journal, you must also be certain that any bills paid at the end of the month have been added to the Cash Disbursements journal.

Bills that are related to financial activity for the month being closed but that haven't yet been paid have to be *accrued,* which means recorded in the books, so they can be matched to the revenue for the month. These accruals are only necessary if you use the accrual accounting method. If you use the cash-basis accounting method, you only need to record the bills when cash is actually paid. For more on the accrual and cash-basis methods, flip to Book I Chapter I.

You accrue bills yet to be paid in the Accounts Payable account. For example, suppose your company prints and mails fliers to advertise a sale during the last week of the month. A bill for the fliers totaling $500 hasn't been paid yet. Here's how you enter the bill in the books:

	Debit	Credit
Advertising	$500	
Accounts Payable		$500

To accrue the bill from Jack's printing for June sales flyers.

This entry increases advertising expenses for the month and increases the amount due in Accounts Payable. When you pay the bill, the Accounts Payable account is debited (to reduce the liability), and the Cash account is credited (to reduce the amount in the cash account). You make the actual entry in the Cash Disbursements journal when the cash is paid out.

When proving out the cash, you should also review any accounts in which expenses are accrued for later payment, such as Sales Taxes Collected, to be sure all accrual accounts are up-to-date. These tax accounts are actually liability accounts for taxes that will need to be paid in the future. If you use the accrual accounting method, the expenses related to these taxes must be matched to the revenues collected for the month they're incurred.

Book IV

Preparing for Year's End

Using a Temporary Posting Journal

Some companies use a Temporary Posting journal to record payments that are made without full knowledge of how the cash outlay should be posted to the books and which accounts will be impacted. For example, a company using a payroll service probably has to give that service a certain amount of cash to cover payroll even if it's not yet known exactly how much is needed for taxes and other payroll-related costs.

In this payroll example, cash must be disbursed, but transactions can't be entered into all affected accounts until the payroll is done. Suppose a company's payroll is estimated to cost $15,000 for the month of May. The company sends a check to cover that cost to the payroll service and posts the payment to the Temporary Posting journal, and after the payroll is calculated and completed, the company receives a statement of exactly how much was paid to employees and how much was paid in taxes. After the statement arrives, allocating the $15,000 to specific accounts such as Payroll Expenses or Tax Expenses, that information is posted to the Cash Disbursements journal.

If you decide to keep a Temporary Posting journal to track cash coming in or going out, before summarizing your Cash Disbursements journal and closing the books for an accounting period, be sure to review the transactions listed in this journal that may need to be posted in the Cash Disbursements journal.

Reconciling Bank Accounts

Part of proving out cash involves checking that what you have in your bank accounts actually matches what the bank thinks you have in those accounts. This process is called *reconciling* the accounts.

Before you tackle reconciling your accounts with the bank's records, it's important to be sure that you've made all necessary adjustments to your books. When you make adjustments to your cash accounts, you identify and correct any cash transactions that may not have been properly entered into the books. You also make adjustments to reflect interest income or payments, bank fees, and credit-card chargebacks.

If you've done everything right, your accounting records should match the bank's records when it comes to how much cash you have in your accounts. The day you close your books probably isn't the same date as the bank sends its statements, so do your best at balancing the books internally without actually reconciling your checking account. Correcting any problems during the process of proving out, will minimize problems you may face reconciling the cash accounts when that bank statement actually does arrive.

You've probably reconciled your personal checking account at least a few times over the years, and you'll be happy to hear that reconciling business accounts is a similar process. Table 3-1 shows one common format for reconciling your bank account:

Table 3-1	Bank Reconciliation			
Transactions	*Beginning Balance*	*Deposits*	*Disbursements*	*Ending Balance*
Balance per bank statement	$	$	$	$
Deposits in transit (not shown on statement)		$		$
Outstanding checks			($)	($)
Total	$	$	$	$
Balance per checkbook or Cash in Checking (should be the same)				$

Tracking down errors

Ideally, your balance and the bank's balance adjusted by transactions not yet shown on the statement should match. If they don't, you need to find out why.

✓ **If the bank balance is higher than your balance,** check to be sure that all the deposits listed by the bank appear in the Cash account in your books. If you find that the bank lists a deposit that you don't have, you need to do some detective work to figure out what that deposit was for and add the detail to your accounting records. Also, check to be sure that all checks have cleared. Your balance may be missing a check that should have been listed in outstanding checks.

✓ **If the bank balance is lower than your balance,** check to be sure that all checks listed by the bank are recorded in your Cash account. You may have missed one or two checks that were written but not properly recorded. You also may have missed a deposit that you have listed in your Cash account and you thought the bank already should have shown as a deposit, but it was not yet on the statement. If you notice a missing deposit on the bank statement, be sure you have your proof of the deposit and check with the bank to be sure the cash is in the account.

Book IV

Preparing for Year's End

✔ **If all deposits and checks are correct but you still see a difference,** your only option is to check your math and make sure all checks and deposits were entered correctly.

Sometimes, you have to decide whether rooting out every little difference is really worth the time it takes. If it's just a matter of pennies, you probably don't need to waste your time trying to find the error, and you can just adjust the balance in your books. But if the difference is a significant amount for your business, you should try to track it down. You never know exactly what accounts are impacted by an error or how that difference may impact your profit or loss.

Using a computerized system

If you use a computerized accounting system, reconciliation should be much easier than keeping your books manually. In QuickBooks, for example, when you start the reconciliation process, a screen pops up in which you can add the ending bank statement balance and any bank fees or interest earned. Figure 3-3 shows you that screen. This example adds $60,000 as the ending balance and $60 in bank fees. (The bank fees are automatically added to the bank fees expense account.)

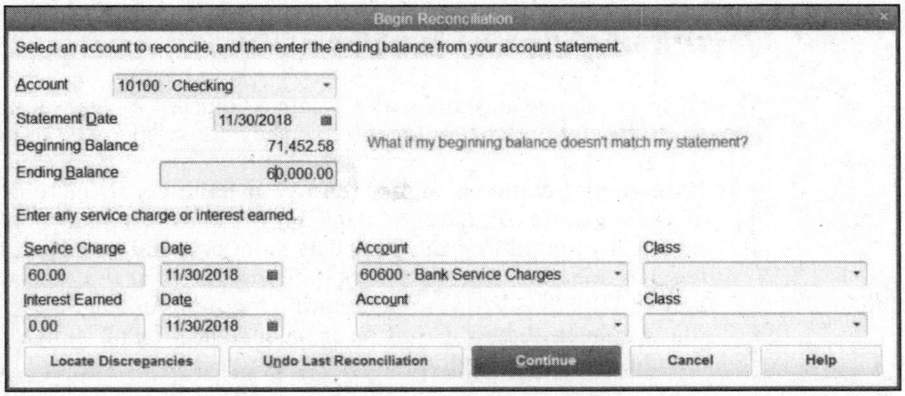

Figure 3-3: Indicate the bank's ending balance and any bank service charges or interest earned on a particular account.

Begin Reconciliation

Select an account to reconcile, and then enter the ending balance from your account statement.

Account	10100 · Checking
Statement Date	11/30/2018
Beginning Balance	71,452.58
Ending Balance	60,000.00

What if my beginning balance doesn't match my statement?

Enter any service charge or interest earned.

Service Charge	Date	Account	Class
60.00	11/30/2018	60600 · Bank Service Charges	
Interest Earned	Date	Account	Class
0.00	11/30/2018		

Locate Discrepancies   Undo Last Reconciliation   Continue   Cancel   Help

Image courtesy of Intuit

After you click Continue, you get a screen that lists all checks written since the last reconciliation as well as all deposits. You put a check mark next to the checks and deposits that have cleared on the bank statement, as in Figure 3-4, and then click Reconcile Now.

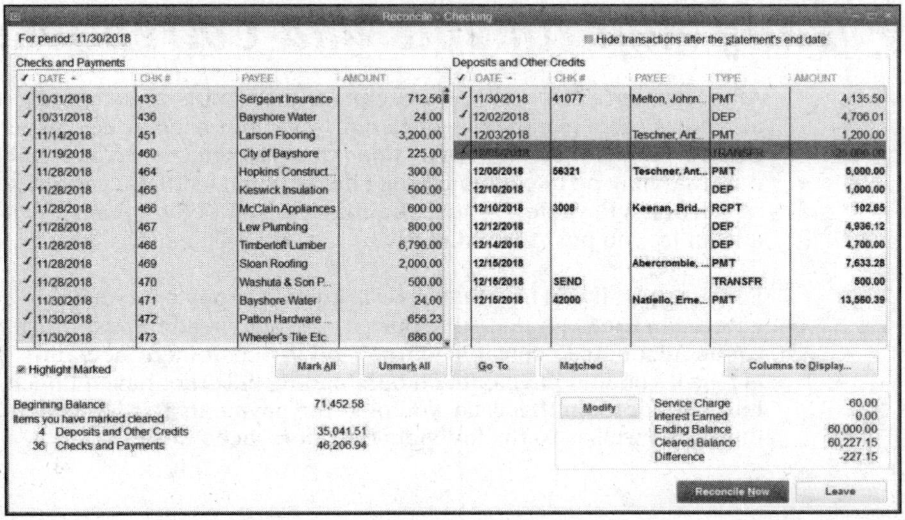

Figure 3-4:
Put a check
mark next to
checks and
deposits
that have
cleared the
account
and click
Reconcile
Now.

Image courtesy of Intuit

QuickBooks automatically reconciles the accounts and provides reports that indicate any differences. It also provides a *reconciliation summary,* shown in Figure 3-5, that includes the beginning balance, the balance after all cleared transactions have been recorded, and a list of all uncleared transactions. QuickBooks also calculates what your check register should show when the uncleared transactions are added to the cleared transactions.

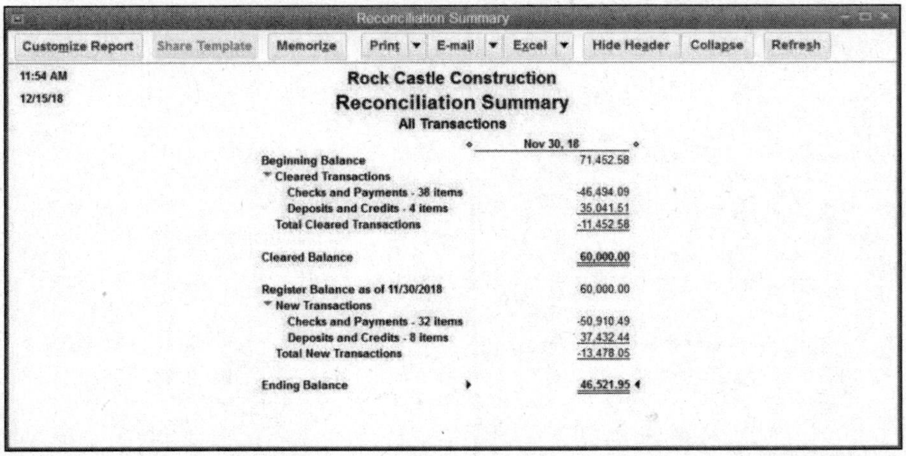

Figure 3-5:
After
reconciling
your
accounts,
QuickBooks
automati-
cally
provides a
reconcili-
ation
summary.

Image courtesy of Intuit

Posting Adjustments and Corrections

After you close out the Cash Receipts and Cash Disbursements journals as well as reconcile the bank account with your accounting system, you post any adjustments or corrections that you uncover to any other journals that may be impacted by the change, such as the Accounts Receivable or Accounts Payable. If you make changes that don't impact any journal accounts, you post them directly to the General Ledger.

For example, if you find that several customer payments haven't been entered in the Cash Receipts journal, you also need to post those payments to the Accounts Receivable journal and the customers' accounts. The same is true if you find payments on outstanding bills that haven't been entered into the books. In this case, you post the payments to the Accounts Payable journal as well as to the individual vendors' accounts.

Chapter 4

Closing the Journals

As the old saying goes, "The devil is in the details." When it comes to your bookkeeping, especially if you keep your books manually, those details are in the journals you keep. And those small details can get you every time.

If you use a computerized accounting system to do your books, you don't need to close out your journals, but you can still run a series of reports to verify that all the information in the computer accounting system matches what you have on paper. This chapter talks briefly about how to do that.

This chapter focuses primarily on how to prove out your journals and close them at the end of an accounting period. (Book IV Chapter 3 looks at this process for cash journals in particular, if you're interested.) You also find out how to post all corrections and adjustments to the General Ledger after you make them in the appropriate journal. (To find out how to set up your journals, flip to Book I Chapter 4.)

Prepping to Close: Checking for Accuracy and Tallying Things Up

As you prepare to close the books, you first need to total what is in your journals, which is called *summarizing the journals*. During the process, it's a good idea to look for blatant errors and be sure that the entries accurately reflect the transactions during the accounting period.

Even the smallest error in a journal can cause a lot of frustration when you try to run a trial balance and close out your books, so it's best to do a thorough search for errors as you close out each journal for the month. It's much easier to find an error at this point in the closing process than to try to track it back through all your various accounts.

Paying attention to initial transaction details

Do a quick check to be sure the transaction details in your journals are accurate. Book IV Chapter 3 tells you how to do this type of check with the cash journals, but when you follow the rules of accrual accounting, not all transactions involve cash.

In accrual accounting, noncash transactions can include customer purchases made on store credit (which you track in the Accounts Receivable journal) and bills you will pay in the future (which you track in the Accounts Payable journal). You may also have created other journals to track transactions in your most active accounts, and you probably also keep details about sales in the Sales journal and payroll in the Payroll journal.

In the Payroll journal, make sure that all payrolls for the month have been added with all the proper details about salaries, wages, and taxes. Also verify that you've recorded all employer taxes that need to be paid. These taxes include the employer's portion of Medicare and Social Security as well as unemployment taxes. (Book III Chapter 4 talks more about employer tax obligations.)

Summarizing journal entries

The first step in checking for accuracy in your journals is summarizing them, explained in Book I Chapter 4, which is primarily totaling all the columns in the journal. This summary process gives you totals for the accounts being tracked by each journal. For example, summarizing the Accounts Receivable journal gives you a grand total of all transactions for that period that involved customer credit accounts. Figure 4-1 shows a summary of an Accounts Receivable journal.

The Accounts Receivable journal includes transactions from the Sales journal (where customer purchases on store credit first appear) and the Cash Receipts journal (where customers' payments toward their store credit accounts first appear) as well as any credit memos for customer returns.

The example in Figure 4-1 is only a few lines long, but, in most companies, the Accounts Receivable journal is very active with transactions posted every day the store is open during the month. When you summarize the Accounts Receivable journal, you get a *closing balance,* a balance that shows the total of all financial activity recorded in that journal. Figure 4-1 shows a closing balance of $2,240, which is the amount outstanding from customers.

Figure 4-1: A sample Accounts Receivable journal summary.

		Cheesecake Shop			
		Accounts Receivable			
		March 2015			
Date	Description	Ref. #	Debit	Credit	Balance
	Opening Balance				$2,000
3/31	From Cash Receipts Journal	Journal P2		$500	$1,500
3/31	From Sales Journal	Journal P3	$800		$2,300
3/31	Credit Memo 124 (General Journal)	Journal P3		$60	$2,240
	March Closing Balance				$2,240

Image courtesy of Intuit

REMEMBER

Each transaction in the journal should have a reference number next to it, which tells you where the detail for that transaction first appears in the books. You may need to review this information later when you're proving out the books. When you check for errors in the journal, you may need to review the original source information used to enter some transactions in order to double-check that entry's accuracy.

In addition to the Accounts Receivable journal, you also have individual journal pages for each customer; these pages detail each customer's purchases on store credit and any payments made toward those purchases. At the end of an accounting period, prepare an *Aging Summary* detailing all outstanding customer accounts. This report shows you what money is due from customers and how long it has been due. (Book III Chapter 2 talks more about managing customer accounts.)

For the purpose of proving out the books, the aging report is a quick summary that ensures that the customer accounts information matches what's in the Accounts Receivable journal.

Table 4-1 shows what an aging summary would look like for the time period.

Book IV

Preparing for Year's End

Table 4-1	Aging Summary: Accounts Receivable as of March 31, 2015			
Customer	*Current*	*31–60 Days*	*61–90 Days*	*>90 Days*
S. Smith	$300			
J. Doe	$100	$300	$200	
H. Harris	$500	$240		
M. Man	$400	$200		
Total	$1,300	$740	$200	

In this sample Accounts Receivable Aging Summary, the total amount outstanding from customers matches the balance total in the Accounts Receivable journal. Therefore, all customer accounts have been accurately entered in the books, and the bookkeeper shouldn't encounter any errors related to customer accounts when running a trial balance, explained in Book IV Chapter 5.

If you find a difference between the information in your journal and your aging summary, review your customer account transactions to find the problem. An error may be the result of

✔ Recording a sales transaction without recording the details of that transaction in the customer's account.

✔ Recording a purchase directly into the customer's account without adding the purchase amount to the Accounts Receivable journal.

✔ Recording a customer's payment in the customer's account without recording the cash receipt in the Accounts Receivable journal.

✔ Recording a customer's payment in the Accounts Receivable journal without recording the cash receipt in the customer's account record.

The process of summarizing and closing out the Accounts Payable journal is similar to that of the Accounts Receivable journal. For Accounts Payable, you can prepare an aging summary for your outstanding bills as well.

That summary should look something like Table 4-2.

Table 4-2	Aging Summary: Accounts Payable as of March 31, 2015			
Vendor	**Current**	**31–60 Days**	**61–90 Days**	**>90 Days**
American Bank	$150			
Carol's Realty	$800			
Helen's Paper Goods		$250		
Henry's Bakery Supplies		$500		
Plates Unlimited	$400	$200		
Total	$1,350	$950		

The total of outstanding bills on the Accounts Payable Aging Summary should match the total shown on the Accounts Payable journal summary for the accounting period. If yours match, you're ready for a trial balance. If they don't, you must figure out the reason for the difference before closing out the Accounts Payable journal. The problem may be the result of

✔ Recording a bill due in the Accounts Payable journal without recording it in the vendor's account.

✔ Recording a bill due in the vendor's account without recording it in the Accounts Payable journal.

✔ Making a payment to the vendor without recording it in the Accounts Payable journal.

✔ Making a payment to the vendor and recording it in the Accounts Payable journal but neglecting to record it in the vendor's account.

Correct any problems you find before closing out the journal. If you know that you may be working with incorrect data, you don't want to try to do a trial balance because you know that balance will be filled with errors and you won't be able to generate accurate financial reports. Also, if you know errors exist, it's likely the books won't balance anyway, so it's just a wasted exercise to do a trial balance.

Analyzing summary results

You may be wondering how you can find problems in your records by just reviewing a page in a journal. Well, that skill comes with experience and practice. As you summarize your journals each month, you'll become familiar with the expected level of transactions and the types of transactions that occur month after month. If you don't see a transaction that you expect to find, take the time to research the transaction to find out why it's missing. It's possible that the transaction didn't take place, but it's also possible that someone forgot to record it.

For example, suppose that when summarizing the Payroll journal, you notice that the payroll for the 15th of the month seems lower than normal. As you check your details for that payroll, you find that the amount paid to hourly employees was recorded, but someone didn't record the amount paid to salaried employees. For that particular payroll, the payroll company experienced a computer problem after running some checks and as a result sent the final report on two separate pages. The person who recorded the payroll numbers didn't realize there was a separate page for salaried employees, so the final numbers entered into the books didn't reflect the full amount paid to employees.

As you close the books each month, you'll get an idea of the numbers you can expect for each type of journal. After a while, you'll be able to pick out problems just by scanning a page — no detailed research required!

Planning for cash flow

The process you go through each month as you prepare to close your books helps you plan for future cash flow. Reviewing the Accounts Receivable and Accounts Payable Aging Summaries tells you what additional cash you can expect from customers during the next few months and how much cash you'll need in order to pay bills for the next few months.

If you notice that your Accounts Payable Aging Summary indicates that more and more bills are slipping into past-due status, you may need to find another source for cash, such as a credit line from the bank. For example, the Accounts Payable Aging Summary reveals that three key vendors — Helen's Paper Goods, Henry's Bakery Supplies, and Plates Unlimited — haven't been paid on time.

Late payments can hurt your business's working relationship with vendors; they may refuse to deliver goods unless cash is paid upfront. And if you can't get the raw materials you need, you may have trouble filling customer orders on time. The lesson here is to act quickly and find a way to improve cash flow before your vendors cut you off. (For more on Accounts Payable management, check out Book III Chapter 1.)

You may also find that your Accounts Receivable Aging Summary reveals that certain previously good customers are gradually becoming slow or nonpaying customers. For example, J. Doe's account is past due, and at least some portion of his account is overdue by more than 60 days. The bookkeeper dealing with these accounts may need to consider putting a hold on that account until payment is received in full. (For more on Accounts Receivable management, check out Book III Chapter 2.)

Posting to the General Ledger

An important part of closing your books is posting to the General Ledger any corrections or adjustments you find as you close the journals. This type of posting consists of a simple entry that summarizes any changes you found.

For example, suppose you find that a customer purchase was recorded directly in the customer's account record but not in the Accounts Receivable journal. You have to research how that transaction was originally recorded. If the only record was a note in the customer's account, both the Sales account and the Accounts Receivable account are affected by the mistake, and the correcting entry looks like this:

	Debit	*Credit*
Accounts Receivable	$100	
Sales		$100

To record sale to J. Doe on 3/15/2015 — corrected 3/31/2015.

If you find this type of error, the Sales transaction record for that date of sale isn't accurate, which means that someone bypassed your standard bookkeeping process when recording the sale. You may want to research that part of the issue as well because there may be more than just a recording problem behind this incident. Someone in your company may be allowing customers to take product, purposefully not recording the sale appropriately in your books, and pocketing the money instead. It's also possible that a salesperson recorded a sale for a customer that never took place. If that's the case and you bill the customer, he would likely question the bill, and you'd find out about the problem at that point.

The process of proving out your journals, or any other part of your bookkeeping records, is a good opportunity to review your internal controls as well. As you find errors during the process of proving out the books, keep an eye out for ones (probably similar errors that appear frequently) that may indicate bigger problems than just bookkeeping mistakes. Repeat errors may call for additional staff training to be sure your bookkeeping rules are being followed to a T. Or such errors may be evidence that someone in the company is deliberately recording false information. Whatever the explanation, you need to take corrective action. (Book I Chapter 5 covers internal controls in depth.)

Book IV

Preparing for Year's End

Checking Out Computerized Journal Records

Although you don't have to close out journal pages if you keep your books using a computerized accounting system, running a spot-check (at the very least) of what you have in your paper records versus what you have on your computer is a smart move. Simply run a series of reports using your computerized accounting system and then check to be sure that those computer records match what you have in your files.

For example, in QuickBooks, go to the Report Navigator and click on Vendors & Payables. The first section of the navigator page, shown in Figure 4-2, is called A/P Aging (due and overdue bills). This section offers three possible reports: Summary, which shows how much is due for each vendor; Detail, which gives a list of bills due and overdue; and an Accounts Payable Graph that illustrates your outstanding bills.

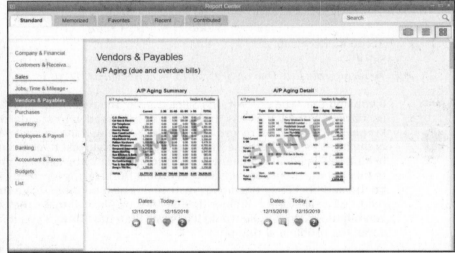

Figure 4-2: QuickBooks lets you run reports concerning vendors and payables that tell you how much money your company owes to others.

Figure 4-3 shows you the kind of detail you get when you select the Detail report. The Detail report is divided into

✔ Current bills

✔ Bills overdue by 1 to 30 days

✔ Bills overdue by 31 to 60 days

✔ Bills overdue by 61 to 90 days

✔ Bills overdue by more than 90 days

Figure 4-3: When you run an Accounts Payable Detail report in QuickBooks, you get a listing of all outstanding bills, the dates they were received, and the dates they're due.

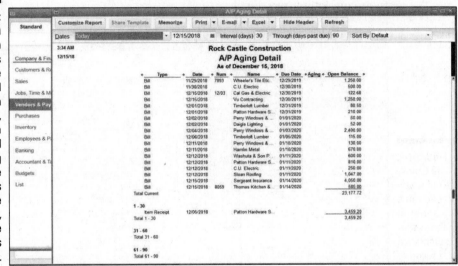

Image courtesy of Intuit

 Obviously, anything in the last two columns — overdue by more than 60 days — is bad news. You can expect a supplier or vendor whose bills appear in these columns to soon cut you off from additional credit until your account is up to date.

In addition to locating your bill-paying problem areas, you can also use the information in the Detail report to verify that the paper bills you have waiting to be paid in vendor files match what you have on your computer. You don't need to check each and every bill, but it's a good idea to do a spot-check of several bills. The goal is to verify the accuracy of your records as well as make sure that no one's entering and paying duplicate or nonexistent bills.

 When it comes to cash flow out of the business, keep tight controls on who can actually sign checks and how the information that explains those checks is recorded. Book I Chapter 5 talks more about the importance of separating duties to protect each aspect of your bookkeeping system from corruption.

Book IV

Preparing for Year's End

You can also run reports showing the information recorded in your Accounts Receivable account. Figure 4-4 shows you a list of possible reports to run from the Customers & Receivables page. In addition to the Summary, Detail, and Accounts Receivable Graph, you can also run a report for Open Invoices, which lists outstanding customer invoices or statements, and Collections, which lists not only overdue customers but also how much they owe and their contact information.

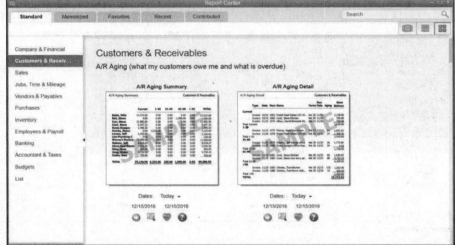

Figure 4-4: In Quick-Books, you can run a series of reports that summarize customer accounts.

Image courtesy of Intuit

Again, running spot-checks on a few customer accounts to be sure your paper records of their accounts match the information in your computerized system is a good idea. There's always a chance that a customer's purchase was entered in error in the computer, and you could end up sending the bill to the wrong person.

Some companies double-check their Accounts Receivable bookkeeping for accuracy by sending surveys to customers periodically (usually twice a year) to see if their accounts are correct. If you choose to do this, include with the customer's bill a postage-paid card asking if the account is correct and giving the customer room to indicate any account problems before mailing the card back to your company. In most cases, a customer who has been incorrectly billed will contact you soon after getting that bill — especially if he or she has been billed for more than anticipated.

In addition to keeping actual accounts, such as Accounts Payable or Accounts Receivable, your computerized accounting system keeps a journal of all your company's transactions. This journal contains details about all your transactions over a specified time period and the accounts that were impacted by each transaction. Figure 4-5 is a sample computerized journal page.

Figure 4-5: A computerized accounting system keeps a journal of all transactions, which you can review during the closing process.

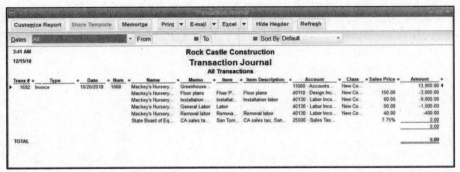

Image courtesy of Intuit

If you need to be reminded of how you recorded a transaction into your computerized accounting system, run the Journal report by date, isolating all transactions that took place at a particular time. Running a report by date can be a helpful tool if you're trying to locate the source of an error in your books; if you find a questionable transaction, you can open the detail of that transaction and see how it was entered and where you can find the original source material.

Book IV

Preparing for Year's End

Chapter 5

Checking Your Accuracy

· ·

In This Chapter

▶ Putting your balances on trial

▶ Finding and correcting errors

▶ Preparing a worksheet

▶ Generating reports from your computerized system

· ·

*A*fter you close out all your journals and do your darndest to catch any and all errors (flip to Book IV Chapter 5 for instructions on how to do this), the time comes to test your work. If you've entered all double-entry transactions in the books correctly, the books balance out, and your trial's a success!

Unfortunately, few bookkeepers get their books to balance on the first try. And in some cases, the books balance, but errors still exist. This chapter explains how you do a trial balance of your books and gives tips on finding any errors that may be lurking. You also find out how to take your first step to developing financial reports (explored in Book II's chapters), by creating a worksheet.

Working with a Trial Balance

When you first start entering transactions in a dual-entry accounting system, you may think, "This is a lot of work, and I don't know how I'm ever going to use all this information." You enter all your transactions using debits and credits without knowing whether they'll actually produce useful financial information that you can use to gauge how well your business is doing. It's not until after you close your journals and prepare your first set of financial reports that you truly see the value of double-entry accounting.

The first step toward useable reports that help you interpret your financial results is doing a trial balance. Basically, a *trial balance* is a worksheet prepared manually or spit out by your computer accounting system that lists all the accounts in your General Ledger at the end of an accounting period (whether that's at the end of a month, the end of a quarter, or the end of a year).

Conducting your trial balance

If you've been entering transactions manually, you create a trial balance by listing all the accounts with their ending debit or credit balances. (Book I Chapter 1 talks more about debits and credits.) After preparing the list, you total both the debit and credit columns. If the totals at the bottom of the two columns are the same, the trial is a success, and your books are in balance.

The primary purpose of the trial balance is to prove that, at least mathematically, your debits and credits are equal. If any errors exist in your calculations or in how you summarized the journals or posted the summaries to the General Ledger, they're uncovered in the trial balance when the columns don't come out equal. Also, if you entered any transactions out of balance, you see the mistake when you add the columns of the trial balance.

The four basic steps to developing a trial balance are as follows:

1. **Prepare a worksheet with three columns: one for account titles, one for debits, and one for credits.**

2. **Fill in all the account titles and record their balances in the appropriate debit or credit columns.**

3. **Total the debit and credit columns.**

4. **Compare the column totals.**

Figure 5-1 shows a sample trial balance for a company as of May 31, 2015. Note that the debit column and the credit column both equal $57,850, making this a successful trial balance.

A successful trial balance is no guarantee that your books are totally free of errors; it just means that all your transactions have been entered in balance. You still may have errors in the books related to how you entered your transactions, including:

- You forgot to put a transaction in a journal or in the General Ledger.
- You forgot to post a journal entry to the General Ledger.
- You posted a journal entry twice in either the General Ledger or in the journal itself.
- You posted the wrong amount.
- You posted a transaction to the wrong account.

Trial Balance Cheesecake Shop 5/31/2014		
Account	Debit	Credit
Cash	$ 2,500.00	
Petty Cash	$ 500.00	
Accounts Receivable	$ 1,000.00	
Inventory	$ 1,200.00	
Equipment	$ 5,050.00	
Vehicle	$ 25,000.00	
Furniture	$ 5,600.00	
Accounts Payable		$ 2,200.00
Loans Payable		$ 29,150.00
Capital		$ 5,000.00
Sales		$ 20,000.00
Sales Discounts	$ 1,000.00	
Purchases	$ 8,000.00	
Purchase Discounts		$ 1,500.00
Credit Card Fees	$ 125.00	
Advertising	$ 1,500.00	
Bank Service Charges	$ 120.00	
Insurance Expenses	$ 100.00	
Interest Expense	$ 125.00	
Legal and Accounting Expense	$ 300.00	
Office Expense	$ 250.00	
Payroll Taxes Expense	$ 350.00	
Postage Expense	$ 75.00	
Rent Expense	$ 800.00	
Salaries & Wages Expense	$ 3,500.00	
Supplies	$ 300.00	
Telephone Expenses	$ 200.00	
Utilites Expenses	$ 255.00	
Totals	$ 57,850.00	$ 57,850.00

Figure 5-1:
A sample
trial
balance.

© John Wiley & Sons, Inc.

If, by chance, the errors listed here slip through the cracks, there's a good chance that someone will notice the discrepancy when the financial reports are prepared.

Even with these potentially lurking errors, the trial balance is a useful tool and the essential first step in developing your financial reports.

Book IV

**Preparing for
Year's End**

Dealing with trial balance errors

If your trial balance isn't correct, you need to work backwards in your closing process to find the source of the mathematical error. When you need to find errors after completing a trial balance that fails, follow these four basic steps to identify and fix the problem. And remember, this is why all bookkeepers and accountants work with pencils, not pens — pencils make erasing mistakes and making corrections much easier.

1. **Check your math.** Keep your fingers crossed, and add up your columns again to be sure the error isn't just one of addition. That's the simplest kind of error to find. Correct the addition mistake and re-total your columns.

2. **Compare your balances.** Double-check the balances on the trial balance worksheet by comparing them to the totals from your journals and your General Ledger. Be sure you didn't make an error when transferring the account balances to the trial balance. Correcting this type of problem isn't very difficult or time-consuming. Simply correct the incorrect balances, and add up the trial balance columns again.

3. **Check your journal summaries.** Double-check the math in all your journal summaries, making sure that all totals are correct and that any totals you posted to the General Ledger are correct. Running this kind of a check, of course, is somewhat time-consuming, but it's still better than rechecking all your transactions. If you do find errors in your journal summaries, correct them, reenter the totals correctly, change the numbers on the trial balance worksheet to match your corrected totals, and retest your trial balance.

4. **Check your journal and General Ledger entries.** Unfortunately, if Steps 1, 2, and 3 fail to fix your problem, all that's left is to go back and check your actual transaction entries. The process can be time-consuming, but the information in your books isn't useful until your debits equal your credits.

If this step is your last resort, scan through your entries looking specifically for ones that appear questionable. For example, if you see an entry for office supplies that's much larger or much smaller than you normally expect, check the original source material for that entry to be sure it's correct. If you carefully proved out the Accounts Payable and Accounts Receivable journals as explained in Book IV Chapters 3 and 4, you can concentrate your efforts on accounts with separate journals. After you find and correct the error or errors, run another trial balance. If things still don't match up, repeat the steps listed here until your debits and credits equal out.

You can always go back and correct the books and do another trial balance before you prepare the financial reports. Don't close the books for the accounting period until the financial reports are completed and accepted.

Testing Your Balance Using Computerized Accounting Systems

If you use a computerized accounting system, your trial balance is automatically generated for you. Because the system allows you to enter only transactions that are in balance, the likelihood that your trial balance won't be successful is pretty slim. But that doesn't mean your accounts are guaranteed error-free.

Remember the saying, "Garbage in, garbage out"? If you make a mistake when you enter transaction data into the system, even if the data's in balance, the information that comes out will also be in error. Although you don't have to go through the correction steps covered in the earlier section "Dealing with trial balance errors" to reach a successful trial balance, you still may have errors lurking in your data.

In QuickBooks, the trial balance report is the first report on the Report Navigator's Accountant & Taxes page, shown in Figure 5-2. In addition to the trial balance, you can request a report showing the General Ledger, transaction detail by account, journal detail, voided transactions, and transactions by date.

Your business's accountant is likely to use many of the report options on the Accountant & Taxes page to double-check that your transactions were entered correctly and that no one is playing with the numbers. In particular, the accountant may use a report option called *Audit Trail,* which reveals what changes impacted the company's books during an accounting period and who made those changes.

Although it doesn't match the trial balance done manually in Figure 5-1, the QuickBooks trial balance shown in Figure 5-3 gives you an idea of what a computerized accounting trial balance looks like.

Book IV

Preparing for Year's End

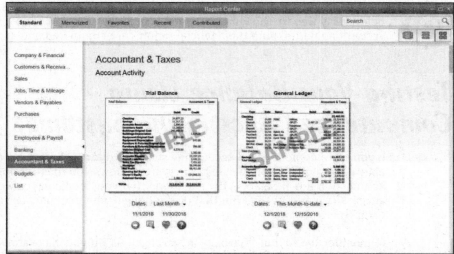

Figure 5-2:
The Accountant & Taxes page of the QuickBooks Report Navigator provides the option of creating many useful reports.

Figure 5-3:
A sample trial balance report produced by QuickBooks.

Trial Balance

Rock Castle Construction
Trial Balance
As of November 30, 2018

	Nov 30, 18	
	Debit	Credit
10100 · Checking	55,354.24	
10300 · Savings	43,410.19	
10400 · Petty Cash	500.00	
11000 · Accounts Receivable	83,547.91	
12000 · Undeposited Funds	0.00	
12100 · Inventory Asset	27,872.63	
12800 · Employee Advances	770.00	
13100 · Pre-paid Insurance	0.00	
13400 · Retainage Receivable	5,418.02	
15000 · Furniture and Equipment	34,326.00	
15100 · Vehicles	78,936.91	
15200 · Buildings and Improvements	325,000.00	
15300 · Construction Equipment	15,300.00	
16900 · Land	90,000.00	
17000 · Accumulated Depreciation		110,344.60
18700 · Security Deposits	1,720.00	
20000 · Accounts Payable		58,345.02
20500 · QuickBooks Credit Card		25.00
20600 · CalOil Credit Card		436.80
24000 · Payroll Liabilities:24010 · Federal Withholding		841.00
24000 · Payroll Liabilities:24020 · FICA Payable		1,293.78
24000 · Payroll Liabilities:24030 · AEIC Payable	0.00	
24000 · Payroll Liabilities:24040 · FUTA Payable	0.00	
24000 · Payroll Liabilities:24050 · State Withholding		191.21
24000 · Payroll Liabilities:24060 · SUTA Payable	0.00	
24000 · Payroll Liabilities:24070 · State Disability Payable		82.57
24000 · Payroll Liabilities:24080 · Worker's Compensation		805.83
24000 · Payroll Liabilities:24100 · Emp. Health Ins Payable		75.00

Developing a Financial Statement Worksheet

After your accounts successfully pass a trial balance test (see "Conducting your trial balance" earlier in this chapter), you can then take your first stab at creating *financial statements,* including balance sheets and income statements. The first step in producing these statements is using the information from the trial balance and its corrections to develop a *worksheet* that includes the initial trial balance, the accounts that would be shown on a balance sheet, and finally the accounts that would normally be shown on an income statement.

You create the worksheet that includes these seven columns:

✓ **Column 1:** Account list

✓ **Columns 2 and 3:** Trial balance (one column for debits, one column for credits)

✓ **Columns 4 and 5:** Balance sheet (one column for debits, one column for credits)

✓ **Columns 6 and 7:** Income statement (one column for debits, one column for credits)

In Figure 5-4, you can see a sample of a worksheet developed from trial balance numbers. Note that the numbers of the trial balance are transferred to the appropriate financial statement; for example, the Cash account, which is an asset account, is shown in the debit column of the balance sheet (see Book II Chapter 4 for more on the balance sheet).

After you transfer all the accounts to their appropriate balance sheet or income statement columns, you total the worksheet columns. Don't panic when you see that the totals at the bottom of your columns aren't equal — it's because the net income hasn't been calculated yet. However, the difference between the debits and credits in both the balance sheet and the income statement totals should be the same. That amount should represent the net income that will appear on the income statement. (See Book II Chapter 5 for more on the income statement.)

In Figure 5-4, the $4,500 difference for the balance sheet is shown as a credit, representing an increase in Retained Earnings. The Retained Earnings account reflects the profits that have been reinvested into the company's assets in order to grow the company. You can find more about Retained Earnings in Book II Chapter 4.

Book IV

Preparing for Year's End

Trial Balance						
	Trial Balance		Balance Sheet		Income Statement	
Account	Debit	Credit	Debit	Credit	Debit	Credit
Cash	2,500.00		2,500.00			
Petty Cash	500.00		500.00			
Accounts Receivable	1,000.00		1,000.00			
Inventory	1,200.00		1,200.00			
Equipment	5,050.00		5,050.00			
Vehicle	25,000.00		25,000.00			
Furniture	5,600.00		5,600.00			
Accounts Payable		2,200.00		2,200.00		
Loans Payable		29,150.00		29,150.00		
Capital		5,000.00		5,000.00		
Sales		20,000.00				20,000.00
Sales Discounts	1,000.00				1,000.00	
Purchases	8,000.00				8,000.00	
Purchase Discounts		1,500.00				1,500.00
Credit Card Fees	125.00				125.00	
Advertising	1,500.00				1,500.00	
Bank Service Charges	120.00				120.00	
Insurance Expenses	100.00				100.00	
Interest Expenses	125.00				125.00	
Legal and Accounting Expenses	300.00				300.00	
Office Expenses	250.00				250.00	
Payroll Taxes Expenses	350.00				350.00	
Postage Expenses	75.00				75.00	
Rent Expenses	800.00				800.00	
Salaries & Wages Expenses	3,500.00				3,500.00	
Supplies	300.00				300.00	
Telephone Expenses	200.00				200.00	
Utilites Expenses	255.00				255.00	
Net Income				4500.00	4,500.00	
Totals	57,850.00	57,850.00	40,850.00	40,850.00	21,500.00	21,500.00

Figure 5-4: This sample worksheet shows the first step in developing a company's financial statements.

Image courtesy of Intuit

In some incorporated companies, part of the earnings are taken out in the form of *dividends* paid to stockholders. Dividends are a portion of the earnings divided up among stockholders. The board of directors of the corporation set a certain amount per share to be paid to stockholders.

Many other small companies that haven't incorporated pay out earnings to their owners using a *Drawing account,* which tracks any cash taken out by the owners. Each owner should have his or her own Drawing account so that you have a history of how much each owner withdraws from the company's resources.

Replacing Worksheets with Computerized Reports

If you use a computerized accounting system, you don't have to create a worksheet at all. Instead, the system gives you the option of generating many different types of reports to help you develop your income statement and balance sheet.

One of the advantages of your computerized system's reports is that you can easily look at your numbers in many different ways. For example, Figure 5-5 shows the Company & Financial Report Navigator from QuickBooks. Notice that you can generate so many different reports that the entire list doesn't even fit on one computer screen! To get the report you want, all you need to do is click on the report title.

Figure 5-5:
The Company & Financial Report Navigator page in QuickBooks gives you access to many key financial reports.

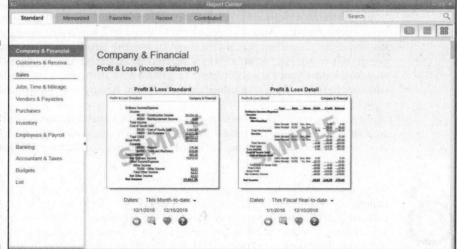

Book IV

Preparing for Year's End

Image courtesy of Intuit

You can generate a number of different reports within the following categories:

- ✔ **Profit & Loss (income statement):** Some key reports in this section include

    - A standard report that shows how much the company made or lost during a specific period of time

    - A detail report that includes all the year-to-date transactions

    - A report that compares year-to-date figures with the previous year (provided you kept the accounts using the computerized system in the previous year)

- ✔ **Income & Expenses:** Some key reports in this section include

    - Income by customer (both a summary and a detailed report)

    - Expenses by vendor (both a summary and a detailed report)

- ✔ **Balance Sheet & Net Worth:** Some key reports in this section include

    - A standard balance sheet showing a summary of assets, liabilities, and equity

    - A detail report of assets, liabilities, and equity

    - A report that compares the assets, liabilities, and equity levels with those of the previous year

- ✔ **Cash Flow:** Some key reports in this section include

    - A statement of cash flows for the year

    - A forecast of cash flows during the next few weeks or months based on money due in accounts receivable and money to be paid out in accounts payable

Computerized accounting systems provide you with the tools to manipulate your company's numbers in whatever way you find useful for analyzing your company's results. And if a report isn't quite right for your needs, you can customize it. For example, if you want to see the profit and loss results for a particular week during an accounting period, you can set the dates for only that week and generate the report. You can also produce a report looking at data for just one day, one month, one quarter, or any combination of dates.

You can also take the time to custom design reports that meet your company's unique financial information needs. Many companies customize reports to collect information by department or division. You're only limited by your imagination!

As you work with your computerized system, you'll be asked for information not easily found using standardized reports. The first few times you pull that information together, you may need to do so manually. But as you get used to your computerized accounting system and its report functions, you'll be able to design customized reports that pull together information in just the way you need it.

Chapter 6

Adjusting the Books

During an accounting period, your bookkeeping duties focus on your business's day-to-day transactions. When it comes time to report those transactions in financial statements, you must make some adjustments to your books. Your financial reports are supposed to show your company's financial health, so your books must reflect any significant change in the value of your assets, even if that change doesn't involve the exchange of cash.

If you use cash-basis accounting, these adjustments aren't necessary because you only record transactions when cash changes hands. Accrual and cash-basis accounting are discussed in Book I Chapter 1.

This chapter reviews the types of adjustments you need to make to the books before preparing the financial statements, including calculating asset depreciation, dividing up prepaid expenses, updating inventory numbers, dealing with bad debt, and recognizing salaries and wages not yet paid. You also find out how to add and delete accounts.

Adjusting All the Right Areas

Even after testing your books using the trial balance process gone over in Book IV Chapter 5, you still need to make some adjustments before you're able to prepare accurate financial reports with the information you have. These adjustments don't involve the exchange of cash but rather involve recognizing the use of assets, loss of assets, or future asset obligations that aren't reflected in day-to-day bookkeeping activities.

The key areas in which you likely need to adjust the books include

- ✔ **Asset depreciation:** To recognize the use of assets during the accounting period.

- ✔ **Prepaid expenses:** To match a portion of expenses that were paid at one point during the year, but benefits from that payment are used throughout the year, such as an annual insurance premium. The benefit should be apportioned out against expenses for each month.

- ✔ **Inventory:** To update inventory to reflect what you have on hand.

- ✔ **Bad debts:** To acknowledge that some customers will never pay and to write off those accounts.

- ✔ **Unpaid salaries and wages:** To recognize salary and wage expenses that have been incurred but not yet paid.

Depreciating assets

The largest noncash expense for most businesses is *depreciation*. Depreciation is an accounting exercise that's important for every business to undertake because it reflects the use and aging of assets. Older assets need more maintenance and repair and also need to be replaced eventually. As the depreciation of an asset increases and the value of the asset dwindles, the need for more maintenance or replacement becomes apparent. (For more on depreciation and why you do it, check out Book IV Chapter 1.)

The time to actually make this adjustment to the books is when you close the books for an accounting period. (Some businesses record depreciation expenses every month to more accurately match monthly expenses with monthly revenues, but most business owners only worry about depreciation adjustments on a yearly basis, when they prepare their annual financial statements.)

Depreciation doesn't involve the use of cash. By accumulating depreciation expenses on an asset, you're reducing the value of the asset as shown on the balance sheet (see Book II Chapter 4 for the lowdown on balance sheets).

Readers of your financial statements can get a good idea of the health of your assets by reviewing your accumulated depreciation. If a financial report reader sees that assets are close to being fully depreciated, he knows that you'll probably need to spend significant funds on replacing or repairing those assets sometime soon. As he evaluates the financial health of the company, he takes that future obligation into consideration before making a decision to loan money to the company or possibly invest in it.

Usually, you calculate depreciation for accounting purposes using the *Straight-Line depreciation method.* This method is used to calculate an amount to be depreciated that will be equal each year based on the anticipated useful life of the asset. For example, suppose your company purchases a car for business purposes that costs $25,000. You anticipate that car will have a useful lifespan of five years and will be worth $5,000 after five years. Using the Straight-Line depreciation method, you subtract $5,000 from the total car cost of $25,000 to find the value of the car during its five-year useful lifespan ($20,000). Then divide $20,000 by 5 to find your depreciation expense for the car ($4,000 per year). When adjusting the assets at the end of each year in the car's five-year lifespan, your entry to the books should look like this:

	Debit	*Credit*
Depreciation Expense	$4,000	
Accumulated Depreciation: Vehicles		$4,000

To record depreciation for Vehicles.

This entry increases depreciation expenses, which appear on the income statement (see Book II Chapter 5). The entry also increases Accumulated Depreciation, which is the use of the asset and appears on the balance sheet directly under the Vehicles asset line. The Vehicles asset line always shows the value of the asset at the time of purchase.

You can speed up depreciation if you believe that the asset will not be used evenly over its lifespan — in other words, if the asset will be used more heavily in the early years of ownership. Book IV Chapter 1 covers alternative depreciation.

If you use a computerized accounting system, you may or may not need to make this adjustment at the end of an accounting period. If your system is set up with an asset management feature, depreciation is automatically calculated, and you don't have to worry about it. Check with your accountant (he or she is the one who would set up the asset management feature) before calculating and recording depreciation expenses.

Allocating prepaid expenses

Most businesses have to pay certain expenses at the beginning of the year even though they will benefit from that expense throughout the year. Insurance is a prime example of this type of expense. Most insurance companies require you to pay the premium annually at the start of the year even though the value of that insurance protects the company throughout the year.

For example, suppose your company's annual car insurance premium is $1,200. You pay that premium in January in order to maintain insurance coverage throughout the year. Showing the full cash expense of your insurance when you prepare your January financial reports would greatly reduce any profit that month and make your financial results look worse than they actually are. That's no good.

Instead, you record a large expense such as insurance or prepaid rent as an asset called *Prepaid Expenses,* and then you adjust the value of that asset to reflect that it's being used up. Your $1,200 annual insurance premium is actually valuable to the company for 12 months, so you calculate the actual expense for insurance by dividing $1,200 by 12, giving you $100 per month. At the end of each month, you record the use of that asset by preparing an adjusting entry that looks like this:

	Debit	Credit
Insurance Expenses	$100	
Prepaid Expenses		$100

To record insurance expenses for March.

This entry increases insurance expenses on the income statement and decreases the asset Prepaid Expenses on the balance sheet. No cash changes hands in this entry because cash was laid out when the insurance bill was paid, and the asset account Prepaid Expenses was increased in value at the time the cash was paid.

QuickBooks enables you to set up automatic monthly entries for these recurring types of adjustments.

Counting inventory

Inventory is a balance sheet asset that needs to be adjusted at the end of an accounting period. During the accounting period, your company buys inventory and records those purchases in a Purchases account without indicating any change to inventory. When the products are sold, you record the sales in the Sales account but don't make any adjustment to the value of the inventory. Instead, you adjust the inventory value at the end of the accounting period because adjusting with each purchase and sale would be much too time-consuming.

Here are the steps for making proper adjustments to inventory in your books:

1. **Determine the inventory remaining.** In addition to calculating ending inventory using the purchases and sales numbers in the books, you

should also do a physical count of inventory to be sure that what's on the shelves matches what's in the books.

2. **Set a value for that inventory.** The value of ending inventory varies depending on your method of valuing inventory.

3. **Adjust the number of pieces remaining in inventory in the Inventory Account and adjust the value of that account based on the information collected in Steps 1 and 2.**

If you track inventory using your computerized accounting system, the system makes adjustments to inventory as you record sales. At the end of the accounting period, the value of your company's ending inventory should be adjusted in the books already. Although the work's already done for you, you should still do a physical count of the inventory to be sure that your computer records match the physical inventory at the end of the accounting period.

Allowing for bad debts

No company likes to accept the fact that it will never see the money owed by some of its customers, but, in reality, that's what happens to most companies that sell items on store credit. When your company determines that a customer who has bought products on store credit will never pay for them, you record the value of that purchase as a *bad debt*. (For an explanation of store credit, check out Book III Chapter 2.)

At the end of an accounting period, you should list all outstanding customer accounts in an *aging report* (see Book III Chapter 2), which shows which customers owe how much and for how long. After a certain amount of time, you have to admit that some customers simply aren't going to pay. Each company sets its own determination of how long it wants to wait before tagging an account as a bad debt. For example, your company may decide that when a customer is six months late with a payment, you're unlikely to ever see the money.

After you determine that an account is a bad debt, you should no longer include its value as part of your assets in Accounts Receivable. Including its value doesn't paint a realistic picture of your situation for the readers of your financial reports. Because the bad debt is no longer an asset, you adjust the value of your Accounts Receivable to reflect the loss of that asset.

You can record bad debts in a couple of ways:

✔ **By customer:** Some companies identify the specific customers whose accounts are bad debts and calculate the bad debt expense each accounting period based on specified customers' accounts.

> ✔ **By percentage:** Other companies look at their bad-debts histories and develop percentages that reflect those experiences. Instead of taking the time to identify each specific account that will be a bad debt, these companies record bad debt expenses as a percentage of their Accounts Receivable.

However you decide to record bad debts, you need to prepare an adjusting entry at the end of each accounting period to record bad debt expenses. Here's an adjusting entry to record bad debt expenses of $1,000:

	Debit	Credit
Bad Debt Expense	$1,000	
Accounts Receivable		$1,000

To write off customer accounts.

You can't have bad debt expenses if you don't sell to your customers on store credit. You only need to worry about bad debt if you offer your customers the convenience of buying your products on store credit.

If you use a computerized accounting system, check the system's instructions for how to write off bad debts. To write off a bad debt using QuickBooks:

1. **Open the screen where you normally record customer payments, and instead of entering the amount received in payment, enter "$0."**

2. **Place a check mark next to the amount being written off.**

3. **Click Discount and Credits tab on the Customer Payment screen.**

4. **On the discount tab (Figure 6-1), type the amount of the discount.**

5. **Select Bad Debt Expense from the Discount Account menu.**

6. **Click Done and verify that the discount is applied and no payment is due (see Figure 6-2).**

Recognizing unpaid salaries and wages

Not all pay periods fall at the end of a month. If you pay your employees every two weeks, you may end up closing the books in the middle of a pay period, meaning that, for example, employees aren't paid for the last week of March until the end of the first week of April.

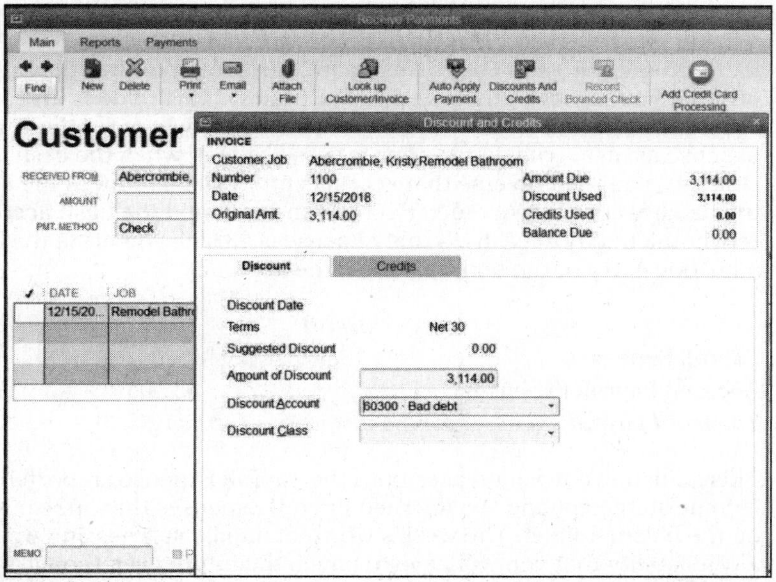

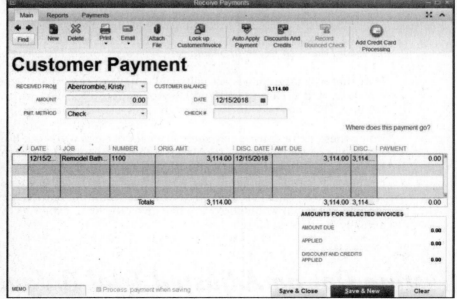

Figure 6-1: In QuickBooks, you record bad debts on the Discount and Credits page, which is part of the Customer Payment function.

Image courtesy of Intuit

Figure 6-2: After you record a bad debt in QuickBooks, the discount appears, indicating that $0 is due.

Image courtesy of Intuit

Book IV

Preparing for Year's End

When your pay period hits before the end of the month, you need to make an adjusting entry at month's end to record the payroll expense that has been incurred but not yet paid. You estimate the amount of the adjustment based on what you pay every two weeks. The easiest thing to do is just accrue the expense of half of your payroll (which means you enter the anticipated expense as an accrual in the appropriate account; when the cash is actually paid out, you then reverse that accrual entry, which reduces the amount in the liability account, Accrued Payroll expenses, and the Cash account, to reflect the outlay of cash). If that expense is $3,000, you make the following adjusting entry to the books to show the accrual:

	Debit	Credit
Payroll Expenses	$3,000	
Accrued Payroll Expenses		$3,000

To record payroll expenses for the last week of March.

This adjusting entry increases both the Payroll Expenses reported on the income statement and the Accrued Payroll Expenses that appear as a liability on the balance sheet. The week's worth of unpaid salaries and wages is actually a liability that you will have to pay in the future even though you haven't yet spent the cash. When you finally do pay out the salaries and wages, you reduce the amount in Accrued Payroll Expenses with the following entry:

	Debit	Credit
Accrued Payroll Expenses	$3,000	
Cash		$3,000

To record the cash payment of salaries and wages for the last week of March.

Note that when the cash is actually paid, you don't record any expenses; instead, you decrease the Accrued Payroll Expense account, which is a liability. The Cash account, which is an asset, also decreases.

Doing these extra entries may seem like a lot of extra work, but if you didn't match the payroll expenses for March with the revenues for March, your income statements wouldn't reflect the actual state of your affairs. Your revenues at the end of March would look very good because your salary and wage expenses weren't fully reflected in the income statement, but your April income statement would look very bad given the extra expenses that were actually incurred in March.

Testing Out an Adjusted Trial Balance

Book IV Chapter 5 explains why and how you run a trial balance on the accounts in your General Ledger. Adjustments to your books call for another trial balance, the *adjusted trial balance,* to ensure that your adjustments are correct and ready to be posted to the General Ledger.

You track all the adjusting entries on a worksheet similar to the one shown in Book IV Chapter 5. You only need to do this worksheet if you're doing your books manually. It's not necessary if you're using a computerized accounting system. The key difference in the worksheet for the Adjusted Trial Balance is that four additional columns must be added to the worksheet for a total of 11 columns. Columns include

- **Column 1:** Account titles.

- **Columns 2 and 3:** Unadjusted Trial Balance. The trial balance before the adjustments are made with Column 2 for debits and Column 3 for credits.

- **Columns 4 and 5:** Adjustments. All adjustments to the trial balance are listed in Column 4 for debits and Column 5 for credits.

- **Columns 6 and 7:** Adjusted Trial Balance. A new trial balance is calculated that includes all the adjustments. Be sure that the credits equal the debits when you total that new Trial Balance. If they don't, find any errors before adding entries to the balance sheet and income statement columns.

- **Columns 8 and 9:** Balance sheet. Column 8 includes all the Balance Sheet accounts that have a debit balance, and Column 9 includes all the Balance Sheet accounts with a credit balance.

- **Columns 10 and 11:** Income statement. Column 10 includes all the Income Statement accounts with a debit balance, and Column 11 includes all the Income Statement accounts with a credit balance.

When you're confident that all the accounts are in balance, post your adjustments to the General Ledger so that all the balances in the General Ledger include the adjusting entries. With the adjustments, the General Ledger will match the financial statements you prepare.

Book IV

Preparing for Year's End

Changing Your Chart of Accounts

After you finalize your General Ledger for the year, you may want to make changes to your Chart of Accounts, which lists all the accounts in your accounting system. (For the full story on the Chart of Accounts, see Book I Chapter 2.) You may need to add accounts if you think you need additional ones or delete accounts if you think they will no longer be needed.

You should only delete accounts from your chart of accounts at the end of the year. If you delete an account in the middle of the year, your annual financial statements will not reflect the activities in that account prior to its deletion. So even if you decide halfway through the year to no longer use an account, you should leave it on the books until the end of the year, and then delete it. You can add accounts to your Chart of Accounts throughout the year, but if you decide to add an account in the middle of the year in order to more closely track certain assets, liabilities, revenues, or expenses, you may need to adjust some related entries.

Suppose you start the year out tracking paper expenses in the Office Supplies Expenses account, but paper usage and its expense keeps increasing, so you decide to track the expense in a separate account beginning in July.

First, you add the new account, Paper Expenses, to your Chart of Accounts. Then you prepare an adjusting entry to move all the paper expenses that were recorded in the Office Supplies Expenses account to the Paper Expenses account. In the interest of space and to avoid boring you, the adjusting entry below is an abbreviated one. In your actual entry, you would probably detail the specific dates paper was bought as an office supplies expense rather than just tally one summary total.

	Debit	*Credit*
Paper Expenses	$1,000	
Office Supplies Expenses		$1,000

To move expenses for paper from the Office Supplies Expenses account to the Paper Expenses account.

Moving beyond the catch-all Miscellaneous Expenses account

When new accounts are added to the Chart of Accounts, the account most commonly adjusted is the Miscellaneous Expenses account. In many cases, you may expect to incur an expense only one or two times during the year, therefore making it unnecessary to create a new account specifically for that expense. But after a while, you find that your "rare" expense is adding up, and you'd be better off with a designated account, meaning that it's time to create some adjusting entries to move expenses out of the Miscellaneous Expenses account.

For example, suppose you think you'll only need to rent a car for the business one time before you buy a new vehicle, so you enter the rental cost in the books as a Miscellaneous Expense. However, after renting cars three times, you decide to start a Rental Expense account mid-year. When you add the Rental Expense account to your Chart of Accounts, you need to use an adjusting entry to transfer any expenses incurred and recorded in the Miscellaneous Expense account prior to the creation of the new account.

Book V
Accounting and Managing Your Business

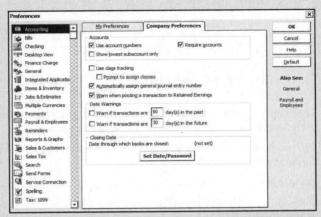

Image credit Intuit

In this book . . .

- Learn how to record all costs correctly so that profit can be determined each period, and understand how to analyze profit

- Plan and prepare for your business's future, control its actual performance to reach its financial goals

- Understand the importance of measuring costs

- Recognize a business's legal structure, and know what taxes need to be paid when

- Know the process of closing the books at year-end and beginning a new accounting cycle for the next year

Chapter 1

Managing Profit

· ·

In This Chapter

▶ Facing up to the profit-making function of business managers

▶ Scoping the field of managerial accounting

▶ Centering on profit centers

▶ Making internal P&L reports useful

▶ Analyzing profit for fun and more profit

· ·

As a manager, you get paid to make profit happen. That's what separates a manager from the other employees at a business. Of course, a manager should be a motivator, innovator, consensus builder, lobbyist, and maybe sometimes a babysitter, but the hard-core purpose of your job is to make and improve profit. No matter how much your staff loves you (or do they love those donuts you bring in every Monday?), if you don't meet your profit goals, you're facing the unemployment line.

Competition in most industries is fierce, and you can never take profit performance for granted. Changes take place all the time — changes initiated by the business and changes from outside forces. Maybe a new superstore down the street is causing your profit to fall off, and you figure that you'll have a huge sale to draw customers, complete with splashy ads on TV and a clown in the store. Whoa, not so fast. First make sure that you can afford to cut prices and spend money on advertising and still turn a profit. Maybe price cuts and the clown's balloon creations would keep your cash register singing, but making sales does not guarantee that you make a profit. Profit is a two-sided challenge: Profit comes from making sales *and* controlling expenses.

This chapter focuses on the fundamental factors that drive profit — the *levers of profit*. Business managers need a sure-handed grip on these profit handles. One of the purposes of accounting is to provide this critical information to the managers. Externally reported income statements don't provide all the information that business managers need for sustainable profit performance. Managers need to thoroughly understand their external income statements and also need to look deeper into the bowels of the business.

Helping Managers: The Fourth Vital Task of Accounting

As this book surely has made clear, bookkeeping and accounting serve critical functions in a business.

- ✔ A business needs a dependable recordkeeping and bookkeeping system for operating in a smooth and efficient manner. Strong internal accounting controls are needed to minimize errors and fraud.

- ✔ A business must comply with a myriad tax laws, and it depends on its chief accountant (controller) to make sure that all its tax returns are prepared on time and correctly.

- ✔ A business prepares financial statements that should conform with established accounting and financial reporting standards, which are reported on a regular basis to its creditors and external shareowners.

- ✔ Accounting should help managers in their decision-making, control, and planning. This branch of accounting is generally called *managerial* or *management accounting*.

This is the first of three chapters devoted to managerial accounting. This chapter pays particular attention to reporting profit to managers and providing the essential information needed for plotting profit strategy and controlling profit performance. It also explains how managers can use accounting information in analyzing how they make profit and why profit changes from one period to the next. Book V Chapter 2 concentrates on financial planning and budgeting, and Book V Chapter 3 examines the methods and problems of determining product costs (generally called *cost accounting*).

Designing and monitoring the accounting recordkeeping system, complying with complex federal and state tax laws, and preparing external financial reports put heavy demands on the time and attention of the accounting department of a business. Even so, managers' special needs for additional accounting information should not be given second-level priority or done by default. The chief accountant (controller) has the responsibility of ensuring that the accounting information needs of managers are served with maximum usefulness. Managers should demand this information from their accountants.

Following the organizational structure

In a small business, there often is only one manager in charge of profit. As businesses get larger two or more managers have profit responsibility. The first rule of managerial accounting is to follow the organizational structure:

to report relevant information for which each manager is responsible. (This principle is logically referred to as *responsibility accounting.*) If a manager is in charge of a product line, for instance, the controller reports the sales and expenses for that product line to the manager in charge.

Two types of organizational business units are of primary interest to managerial accountants:

- ✔ **Profit centers:** These are separate, identifiable sources of sales revenue and expenses so that a measure of profit can be determined for each. A profit center can be a particular product or a product line, a particular location or territory in which a wide range of products are sold, or a channel of distribution. Rarely is the entire business managed as one conglomerate profit center, with no differentiation of its various sources of sales and profit.

- ✔ **Cost centers:** Some departments and other organizational units do not generate sales, but they have costs that can be identified to their operations. Examples are the accounting department, the headquarters staff of a business, the legal department, and the security department. The managers responsible for these organizational units need accounting reports that keep them informed about the costs of running their departments. The managers should keep their costs under control, of course, and they need informative accounting reports to do this.

Note: The term *center* is simply a convenient word to include a variety of types of organizational sub-groups, such as centers, departments, divisions, territories, and other monikers.

Centering on profit centers

This chapter concentrates on accounting for managers of profit centers. The type of accounting information needed by the managers of cost centers is relatively straightforward. They need a lot of detailed information, including comparisons with last period and with the budgeted targets for the current period. Not to suggest that the design of cost center reports is a trivial matter. Sorting out significant cost variances and highlighting these cost problems for management attention is very important. But the spotlight of this chapter is on profit analysis techniques using accounting information for managers with profit responsibility.

Note: Large businesses commonly create relatively autonomous units within the organization that, in addition to having responsibility for their profit and cost centers, also have broad authority and control over investing in assets and raising capital for their assets. These organization units are called, quite logically, *investment centers*. Basically, an investment center is a mini business within the larger conglomerate. Discussing investment centers is beyond the scope of this chapter.

From a one-person sole proprietorship to a mammoth business organization like General Electric or IBM, one of the most important tasks of managerial accounting is to identify each source of profit within the business and to accumulate the sales revenue and the expenses for each of these sources of profit. Can you imagine an auto dealership, for example, not separating revenue and expenses between its new car sales and its service department? For that matter an auto dealer may earn more profit from its financing operations (originating loans) than from selling new and used cars.

Even small businesses may have a relatively large number of different sources of profit. In contrast, even a relatively large business may have just a few mainstream sources of profit. There are no sweeping rules for classifying sales revenue and costs for the purpose of segregating sources of profit — in other words, for defining the profit centers of a business. Every business has to sort this out on its own. The controller (chief accountant) can advise top management regarding how to organize the business into profit centers. But the main job of the controller is to identify the profit centers that have been (or should be) established by management and to make sure that the managers of these profit centers get the accounting information they need. Of course managers should know how to use the information.

Internal Profit Reporting

External financial statements, including the income statement (also called the profit report) comply with well-established rules and conventions. In contrast, the format and content of internal accounting reports to managers is a wide-open field. If you could sneak a peek at the internal financial reports of several businesses, you would be probably surprised at the diversity among the businesses. All businesses include sales revenue and expenses in their internal P&L (profit and loss) reports. Beyond this broad comment, it's very difficult to generalize about the specific format and level of detail included in P&L reports, particularly regarding how operating expenses are reported.

Designing internal profit (P&L) reports

Profit performance reports prepared for a business's managers typically are called a *P&L* (profit and loss). These reports should be prepared as frequently as managers need them, usually monthly or quarterly — perhaps even weekly or daily in some businesses. A P&L report is prepared for the manager in charge of each profit center; these confidential profit reports do not circulate outside the business. The P&L contains sensitive information that competitors would love to get hold of.

Accountants are not in the habit of preparing brief, summary-level profit reports. Accountants tend to err on the side of providing too much detailed data and information. Their mantra is to give managers more information, even if the information is not asked for. Managers are very busy people, and they don't have spare time to waste, whether for reading long rambling emails or multi-page profit reports with too much detail. Profit reports should be compact for a quick read. If a manager wants more back-up detail they can request it as time permits. Ideally, the accountant should prepare a profit *main page* that would fit one computer screen, although this may be a smidgeon too small as a practical matter. In any case, keep it brief.

Businesses that sell products deduct the cost of goods sold expense from sales revenue, and then report *gross margin* (alternatively called *gross profit*) — both in their externally reported income statements and in their internal P&L reports to managers. However, internal P&L reports have a lot more detail about sources of sales and the components of cost of goods sold expense. This chapter uses the example of a business that sells products. Businesses that sell products manufactured by other businesses generally fall into one of two types: *retailers* that sell products to final consumers, and *wholesalers* (distributors) that sell to retailers. The following discussion applies to both. Also, this chapter lays the foundation for companies that manufacture products, discussed in Book V Chapter 2.

There's a need for short-and-to-the-point, or quick-and-dirty profit models that managers can use for decision-making analysis and plotting profit strategy. Short meaning one page or even smaller than one full page. Like on one computer monitor screen, for instance, with which the manager can interact and test the critical factors that drive profit. For example: If sales price were decreased 5 percent to gain 10 percent more sales volume, what would happen to profit? Managers of profit centers need a tool to quickly answer such questions. Later in the chapter the section "Presenting a Profit Analysis Template" introduces just such a profit analysis template for managers.

Reporting operating expenses

Below the gross margin line in an internal P&L statement, reporting practices vary from company to company. There is no standard pattern. One question looms large: How should the *operating expenses* of a profit center be presented in its P&L report? There's no authoritative answer to this question. Different businesses report their operating expenses differently in their internal P&L statements. One basic choice for reporting operating expenses is between the *object of expenditure basis* and the *cost behavior basis*.

Reporting operating expenses on object of expenditure basis

By far the most common way to present operating expenses in a profit center's P&L report is to list them according to the *object of expenditure basis*. This means that expenses are classified according to what is purchased (the object of the expenditure) — such as salaries and wages, commissions paid to salespersons, rent, depreciation, shipping costs, real estate taxes, advertising, insurance, utilities, office supplies, telephone costs, and so on. To do this, the operating expenses of the business have to be recorded in such a way that these costs can be traced to each of its various profit centers. For example, employee salaries of persons working in a particular profit center are recorded as belonging to that profit center.

The object of expenditure basis for reporting operating costs to managers of profit centers is practical. And this information is useful for management control because, generally speaking, controlling costs focuses on the particular items being bought by the business. For example, a profit center manager analyzes wages and salary expense to decide whether additional or fewer personnel are needed relative to current and forecast sales levels. A manager can examine the fire insurance expense relative to the types of assets being insured and their risks of fire losses. For cost control purposes the object of expenditure basis works well. But there is a downside. This method for reporting operating costs to profit center managers obscures the all-important factor in making profit: *margin*. Managers absolutely need to know margin, as explained in the following sections.

Separating operating expenses further on their behavior basis

The first and usually largest *variable* expense of making sales is the cost of goods sold expense (for companies that sell products). In addition to cost of goods sold, an obvious variable expense, businesses also have other expenses that depend either on the volume of sales (quantities sold) or the dollar amount of sales (sales revenue). And virtually all businesses have *fixed* expenses that are not sensitive to sales activity — at least, not in the short run. Therefore, it makes sense to take operating expenses classified according to object of expenditure and further classify each expense into either variable or fixed. There would be a variable or fixed tag on each expense.

The principal advantage of separating operating expenses between variable and fixed is that margin can be reported. *Margin* is the residual amount after all variable expenses of making sales are deducted from sales revenue. In other words, margin equals profit after all variable costs are deducted from sales revenue but before fixed costs are deducted from sales revenue. Margin is compared with total fixed costs for the period. This head-to-head comparison of margin against fixed costs is critical. The next section comes back to this important point.

Although it's hard to know for sure — because internal profit reporting practices of businesses are not publicized or generally available — probably the large majority of companies do not attempt to classify operating expenses as variable or fixed. Yet for making profit decisions, managers absolutely need to know the variable versus fixed nature of their operating expenses.

Presenting a Profit Analysis Template

Figure 1-1 presents a profit analysis template for a profit center example. After arguing for the separation of fixed and variable expenses, you shouldn't be surprised to see in Figure 1-1 operating expenses are divided according to how they behave relative to sales activity. There are just four lines for expenses — cost of goods sold (a variable expense), two variable operating expenses, and fixed operating expenses. No further details for sales revenue and expenses are included in this profit model, in order to keep the template as brief (and therefore, as useful) as possible.

	Year Ended December 31, 2015		Year Ended December 31, 2014	
Sales volume	100,000 units		97,500 units	
	Per Unit	Totals	Per Unit	Totals
Sales revenue	$100.00	$10,000,000	$98.00	$9,555,000
Cost of goods sold expense	$60.00	$6,000,000	$61.50	$5,996,250
Gross margin	$40.00	$4,000,000	$36.50	$3,558,750
Revenue-driven operating expenses	8.50%	$850,000	8.00%	$764,400
Volume-driven operating expenses	$6.50	$650,000	$6.00	$585,000
Margin	$25.00	$2,500,000	$22.66	$2,209,350
Fixed operating expenses		$1,000,000		$925,000
Operating earnings		$1,500,000		$1,284,350

Figure 1-1: Profit analysis template for a profit center.

© John Wiley & Sons

Conceivably, a template such as shown in Figure 1-1 could be the first, top-level page for the formal P&L reports to managers. The following pages would have more detailed information for each line in the profit template. The additional information for each variable and fixed expense would be presented according to the object of expenditure basis. For example, depreciation on the profit center's fixed assets would be one of many items listed in the *fixed expenses* category. The amount of commissions paid to salespersons would be listed in the *revenue-driven expenses* category.

The example shown in Figure 1-1 is for one year. As mentioned earlier, profit reports are prepared as frequently as needed by managers, monthly in most cases. Interim P&L reports may be abbreviated versions of the annual report. Keep in mind that this example is for just one slice of the total business, which has other profit centers each with its own profit profile.

The profit template shown in Figure 1-1 includes *sales volume,* which is the total number of units of product sold during the period. Of course, the accounting system of a business has to be designed to accumulate sales volume information for the P&L report of each profit center. Generally speaking, keeping track of sales volume for products is possible, unless the business sells a huge variety of different products. When a business cannot come up with a meaningful measure of sales volume, it still can classify its operating costs between variable and fixed, although it loses the ability to use per-unit values in analyzing profit and has to rely on other techniques.

Separating variable and fixed expenses

For a manager to analyze a business's profit behavior thoroughly, she needs to know which expenses are *variable* and which are *fixed* — in other words, which expenses change according to the level of sales activity in a given period, and which don't. The title of each expense account often gives a pretty good clue. For example, the cost of goods sold expense is variable because it depends on the number of units of product sold, and sales commissions are variable expenses. On the other hand, real estate property taxes and fire and liability insurance premiums are fixed for a period of time. Managers should always have a good feel for how their operating expenses behave relative to sales activity.

Variable expenses

Virtually every business has *variable expenses,* which move up and down in tight proportion with changes in sales volume or sales revenue, like soldiers obeying orders barked out by their drill sergeant. Here are examples of common variable expenses:

- The cost of goods sold expense, which is the cost of products sold to customers
- Commissions paid to salespeople based on their sales
- Franchise fees based on total sales for the period, which are paid to the franchisor
- Transportation costs of delivering products to customers via FedEx, UPS, and freight haulers (railroads and trucking companies)
- Fees that a retailer pays when a customer uses a credit or debit card

Cost of goods sold is usually (but not always) the largest variable expense of a business that sells products, as you would suspect. Other variable expenses are referred to as *operating* expenses, which are the costs of making sales and running the business. The sizes of variable operating expenses, relative to sales revenue, vary from industry to industry. Delivery costs of Walmart and Costco, for instance, are minimal because their customers take the products they buy with them. (Walmart and Costco employees generally don't even help carry purchases to their customers' vehicles.) Other businesses deliver products to their customers' doorsteps, so that expense is obviously much higher (and depending on which delivery service the company uses — FedEx or UPS versus the U.S. Postal Service, for example).

Fixed expenses

Fixed operating expenses include many different costs that a business is obligated to pay and cannot decrease over the short run without major surgery on the human resources and physical facilities of the business.

As an example of fixed expenses, consider the typical self-service car wash business — you know, the kind where you drive in, put some coins in a box, and use the water spray to clean your car. Almost all the operating costs of this business are fixed; rent on the land, depreciation of the structure and the equipment, and the annual insurance premium don't depend on the number of cars passing through the car wash. The main variable expenses are the water and the soap, and perhaps the cost of electricity.

Fixed expenses are the costs of doing business that, for all practical purposes, are stuck at a certain amount over the short term. Fixed expenses do not react to changes in the sales level. Here are some more examples of fixed operating expenses:

- ✔ Gas and electricity costs to heat, cool, and light the premises
- ✔ Employees' salaries and benefits
- ✔ Real estate property taxes
- ✔ Annual audit fee (if the business has its financial statements audited)
- ✔ General liability and officers' and directors' insurance premiums

If you want to decrease fixed expenses significantly, you need to downsize the business (lay off workers, sell off property, and so on). When looking at the various ways for improving profit, significantly cutting down on fixed expenses is generally the last-resort option. Refer to the section "Know your options for improving profit" later in the chapter. A business should be careful not to overreact to a temporary downturn in sales by making drastic reductions in its fixed costs, which it may regret later if sales pick up again.

Stopping at operating earnings

In Figure 1-1, the profit template terminates at the *operating earnings* line; it does not include interest expense or income tax expense. Interest expense and income tax expense are business-wide types of expenses, which are the responsibility of the financial executive(s) of the business. Generally, interest and income tax expenses are not assigned to profit centers, unless a profit center is a rather large and autonomous organizational division of the business that has responsibility for its own assets, finances, and income tax.

The measure of profit before interest and income tax is commonly called *operating earnings* or *operating profit.* It also goes by the name *earnings before interest and tax,* or EBIT. It is not and should not be called *net income,* because this term is reserved for the final bottom-line profit number of a business, after all expenses (including interest and income tax) are deducted from sales revenue.

Focusing on margin — the catalyst of profit

Figure 1-1 includes a very important line of information: *margin* — both *margin per unit* and *total margin. Margin* is your operating profit before fixed expenses are deducted. Don't confuse this number with *gross margin,* which is profit after the cost of goods sold expense is subtracted from sales revenue but before any other expenses are deducted. (See the sidebar "Different uses of the term *margin.*")

With the information in Figure 1-1 in hand, you can dig into the reasons that margin per unit increased from $22.66 in fiscal year 2012 to $25.00 in fiscal year 2013. Two favorable changes occurred: The sales price per unit increased, and the product cost decreased — no small achievement, to be sure! However, the gain in the gross profit per unit was offset by unfavorable changes in both variable operating expenses. The profit center manager must keep on top of these changes.

As a manager, your attention should be riveted on margin per unit, and you should understand the reasons for changes in this key profit driver from period to period. A small change in unit margin can have a big impact on operating earnings. (See the section "Don't underestimate the impact of small changes in sales price" later in the chapter.)

Different uses of the term *margin*

Gross margin, also called *gross profit,* equals sales revenue minus the cost of goods sold expense. Gross margin does not reflect other variable operating expenses that are deducted from sales revenue. In contrast, the term *margin* refers to sales revenue less *all* variable expenses. Some people use the term *contribution margin* instead of just *margin* to stress that margin contributes toward the recovery of fixed expenses (and to profit after fixed expenses are covered). However, the prefix *contribution* is not really necessary. Why use two words when one will do?

As a general rule, businesses that sell products report gross margin in their external income statements (although some don't). However, they do not disclose their variable and fixed operating expenses. They report expenses according to an object of expenditure basis, such as "marketing, administrative, and general expenses." The broad expense categories reported in external income statements include both variable and fixed cost components. Therefore, the margin of a business (sales revenue after all variable expenses but before fixed expenses) is not reported in its external income statement. Managers carefully guard information about margins. They don't want competitors to know the margins of their business.

Further complicating the issue, unfortunately, is that newspaper reporters frequently use the term *margin* when referring to operating earnings. Inside the world of accounting, however, the term margin means profit after all variable expenses are deducted from sales revenue but before fixed expenses are deducted. So, be careful when you see the term margin: It may refer to gross margin, to what accountants mean by margin, or to operating earnings (used in the press).

Answering Critical Profit Questions

Suppose you are the manager of a profit center, and you have just received your P&L report for the latest year. The first, or top, page of the report is the same as Figure 1-1. There are many more pages to your annual P&L with a lot more details about sales and expenses, but concentrate on the first page here. So, refer to Figure 1-1 as you go along. You should immediately ask yourself two questions:

- ✔ How did I make $1.5 million profit (operating earnings before interest and income tax) in 2015?

- ✔ Why did my profit increase $215,650 over last year ($1,500,000 in 2015 – $1,284,350 in 2016 = $215,650 profit increase)?

How did you make profit?

Actually, you can answer this profit question three ways (see Figure 1-1 for data):

- **Answer # 1: You earned total margin that is more than fixed expenses.**

  You earned $25 profit margin per unit and sold 100,000 units; therefore:

  $25 unit margin × 100,000 units sales volume = $2,500,000 margin

  Your profit center is charged with $1 million fixed expenses for the year; therefore:

  $2,500,000 margin – $1,000,000 fixed operating expenses = $1,500,000 operating profit

- **Answer # 2: Your sales volume exceeded your break-even point.**

  Your break-even point is the sales volume at which total margin exactly equals total fixed expenses. Your break-even point for 2015 was:

  $1,000,000 total fixed expenses for year ÷ $25 margin per unit = 40,000 units sales volume break-even point

  Your actual sales volume for the year was 100,000 units, or 60,000 units in excess of your break-even point. Each unit sold in excess of break-even generated $25 "pure" profit because the first 40,000 units sold covered your fixed expenses. Therefore:

  60,000 units sold in excess of break-even × $25 margin per unit = $1,500,000 operating profit

- **Answer # 3: Your high sales volume diluted fixed expenses per unit to below your margin per unit.**

  The average fixed expenses per unit sold for the year is:

  $1,000,000 total fixed expenses ÷ 100,000 units sold = $10 fixed expenses per unit sold

  Your margin per unit was $25; so operating earnings per unit were $15 ($25 margin per unit – $10 fixed expenses per unit = $15 operating earnings per unit). Therefore:

  $15 operating earnings per unit × 100,000 units sales volume = $1,500,000 operating earnings

Each answer is valid. In certain situations, one method of analysis is more useful than another. If you were thinking of making a large increase in fixed operating expenses, for example, you should pay attention to the effect on your break-even point; Answer #2 is useful in this situation. If you were thinking of changing sales prices, Answer #1, which focuses on margin per unit, is very relevant. (See the later section "Using the Profit Template for Decision-Making Analysis.") Likewise, if you're dealing with changes in product cost or variable operating expenses that affect unit margin, Answer #1 is very helpful.

Answer #3 is useful to focus on the *full cost* of a product. In the example, the sales price is $100 per unit (refer back to good ol' Figure 1-1). The total of variable costs per unit is $75 (which includes product cost and the two variable operating costs per unit). The average fixed cost per unit sold is $10, which added to the $75 variable cost per unit gives $85 full cost per unit. Subtracting the full cost per unit from the $100 sales price gives the $15 profit per unit (before interest and income tax expenses are considered).

How did you increase profit?

In your profit center report (our old friend, Figure 1-1), note that your total fixed expenses increased from $925,000 last year to $1 million in 2015, a $75,000 increase. Of course, you should investigate the reasons for your fixed expense increases. These fixed costs are your responsibility as manager of the profit center. You definitely should know which of these costs were higher than last year, and the reasons for the increases.

In any case, you were able to increase margin more than enough to cover the fixed costs increases and to boost profit. In fact, your margin increased $290,650 over last year ($2,500,000 margin in 2015 – $2,209,350 margin in 2014 = $290,650 margin increase). How did you do this?

This question can be answered more than one way. In my view, the most practical method is to calculate the effect of changes in *sales volume* and the *margin per unit*. Being the superb manager that you are, to say nothing of your marketing genius, your profit center increased sales volume over last year. Furthermore, you were able to increase margin per unit, which is even more impressive. The profit impact of each change is determined as follows (refer to Figure 1-1 for data):

- ✔ **Sales volume change impact on profit:**

  $25 margin per unit × 2,500 units sales volume increase = $62,500 increase in margin

- ✔ **Margin per unit change impact on profit:**

  $2.34 increase in margin per unit × 97,500 units sales volume last year = $228,150 increase in margin

Even if your sales volume had stayed the same, the $2.34 increase in your margin per unit (from $22.66 to $25) would have increased margin $228,150. And by selling 2,500 more units than last year, you increased margin $62,500. Quite clearly, the major factor was the significant increase in your margin per unit. You were able to increase this key profit driver by more than 10 percent (10.3 percent to be precise). However, you may not be able to repeat this performance in the coming year; you may have to increase sales volume to boost profit next year.

Taking a Closer Look at the Lines in the Profit Template

As the previous sections should make clear, profit center managers depend heavily on the information in their P&L reports. They need to thoroughly understand these profit reports. Therefore, this section spends some time walking through each element of the profit template. Flip back to your dear old pal Figure 1-1 as you go along.

Sales volume

Sales volume, the first line in the profit template, is the total number of units sold during the period, net of any returns by customers. Sales volume should include only units that actually brought in revenue to the business. In general, businesses do a good job in keeping track of the sales volumes of their products (and services). These are closely monitored figures in, for example, the automobile and personal computer industries.

Now here's a nagging problem: Some businesses sell a huge variety of products. No single product or product line brings in more than a fraction of the total sales revenue. For instance, McGuckin Hardware, a general hardware store in Boulder, carries more than 100,000 products according to its advertising. The business may keep count of customer traffic or the number of individual sales made over the year, but it probably does not track the quantities sold for each and every product it sells. The section "Closing with a Boozy Example" explores this issue later in the chapter.

Sales revenue

Sales revenue is the net amount of money received by the business from the sales of products during the period. Notice the word *net* here. The business in our example, like most, offers its customers many incentives to buy its products and to pay quickly for their purchases. The amount of sales revenue in Figure 1-1 is not simply the list prices of the products sold times the number of units sold. Rather, the sales revenue amount takes into account deductions for rebates, allowances, prompt payment discounts, and any other incentives offered to customers that reduce the amount of revenue received by the business. (The manager can ask that these revenue offsets be included in the supplementary layer of schedules to the main page of the P&L report.)

Cost of goods sold

Cost of goods sold is the cost of the products sold during the period. This expense should be net of discounts, rebates, and allowances the business receives from its vendors and suppliers. The cost of goods sold means different things for different types of businesses:

✔ To determine product costs, manufacturers add together three costs:

- The costs of raw materials
- Labor costs
- Production overhead costs

Accounting for the cost of manufactured products is a major function of *cost accounting,* discussed in Book V Chapter 3.

✔ For retailers and distributors, product cost basically is purchase cost. However, refer to Book II Chapter 8, which explains the differences between the FIFO and LIFO methods for releasing inventory costs to the cost of goods sold expense. The profit center manager should have no doubts about which cost of goods sold expense accounting method is being used. For that matter, the manager should be aware of any other costs that are included in total product cost (such as inbound freight and handling costs in some cases).

Dealing with inventory shrinkage

One common problem is where to put the loss from *inventory shrinkage,* which refers to losses from shoplifting by customers, physical deterioration of products as they sit in inventory, employee theft of products, damage caused in the handling and storage of products, and so on. The amount of inventory shrinkage can be included in the cost of goods sold expense, or it may be included in volume-driven operating expenses. A manager definitely should know which other costs have been placed in the cost of goods sold expense, in addition to the product cost of units sold during the period.

Variable operating expenses

In the profit analysis template (Figure 1-1), variable operating expenses are divided into two types: revenue-driven expenses and volume-driven expenses.

Revenue-driven expenses are those that depend primarily on the dollar amount of sales revenue. This group of variable operating expenses includes commissions paid to salespersons based on the dollar amount of their sales, credit card fees paid by retailers, franchise fees based on sales revenue, and any other cost that depends directly on the amount of sales revenue. Notice in Figure 1-1 that these operating expenses are presented as a *percent* of sales price in the per-unit column. In the example these costs equal 8.5 percent, or $8.50 per $100 of sales revenue in 2015 (versus only 8.0 percent in 2014).

Volume-driven expenses are driven by and depend primarily on the number of units sold, or the total quantity of products sold during the period (as opposed to the dollar value of the sales). These expenses include delivery and transportation costs paid by the business, packaging costs, and any costs that depend primarily on the size and weight of the products sold.

Most businesses have both types of variable operating expenses. However, one or the other may be so minor that it would not be useful to report the cost as a separate item. Only the dominant type of variable operating expense would be presented in the profit analysis template; the one expense would absorb the other type — which is good enough for government work, as they say.

Fixed operating expenses

Managers may view fixed operating expenses as an albatross around the neck of the business. In fact, these costs provide the infrastructure and support for making sales. The main characteristic of fixed operating costs is that they do not decline when sales during the period fall short of expectations. A business commits to many fixed operating costs for the coming period. For all practical purposes these costs cannot be decreased much over the short run. Examples of fixed costs are wages of employees on fixed salaries (from managers to maintenance workers), real estate taxes, depreciation and rent on the buildings and equipment used in making sales, and utility bills.

Certain fixed costs can be matched with a particular profit center. For example, a business may advertise a specific product, and the fixed cost of the advertisement can be matched against revenue from sales of that product. A major product line may have its own employees on fixed salaries or its own delivery trucks on which depreciation is recorded. A business may purchase specific liability insurance covering a particular product it sells.

Dealing with a shortcoming

The profit analysis template shown in Figure 1-1 and the techniques for analyzing profit explained in the section "Answering Critical Profit Questions" hinge on the separation of variable and fixed operating costs. The classification between variable and fixed operating expenses is not needed for external financial statements and income tax returns. Operating expenses are reported on the object of expenditure basis in external financial reports and tax returns, so the accounting systems of many businesses do not tag operating expense accounts as fixed or variable. As a result, variable versus fixed information for operating expenses is not readily available

from the accounting system. What's a manager to do?

Well, here's a practical solution: As the profit center manager, you can tell your accountant whether an operating expense is variable or fixed. Give your classification of the operating expenses in your profit center to the accountant, and stress that you want this classification in the profit template for your profit center. This may be extra work for your accountant, but the variable versus fixed classification of operating expense is of great value for your management decision-making, control, and planning.

In contrast, you cannot directly couple company-wide fixed operating expenses to particular products, product lines, or other types of profit units in the organizational structure of a business. General administrative expenses (such as the CEO's annual salary and corporate legal expenses) are incurred on an entity-as-a-whole basis and cannot be connected directly with any particular profit center. A business may, therefore, allocate these fixed costs among its different profit centers. The fixed costs that are handed down from headquarters, if any, are included in *fixed operating expenses* in Figure 1-1.

Using the Profit Template for Decision-Making Analysis

The profit template (refer to the ever-helpful Figure 1-1) is very useful for decision-making analysis. To demonstrate, suppose that you're under intense competitive pressure to lower the sales price of one product you sell. This product is one "slice" of the total activity reported in Figure 1-1. Suppose that during the year (2015) you sold 1,000 units of the product at a $100 sales price, and the unit costs of this product are the same as in Figure 1-1.

Your competitors are undercutting your sales price, so you're thinking of cutting the sales price 10 percent next year, or $10 per unit. You predict that the price reduction will boost sales volume 25 percent and increase your market share. Seems like a good idea — or does it? You should run some numbers before making a final decision, just to be sure. Answer #1 in the earlier section *How did you make profit?* is the best method for this analysis. For the year just ended, this product generated $25,000 margin:

$25 margin per unit × 1,000 units sold = $25,000.00 margin

Assuming your prediction about sales volume at the lower price is correct and sales volume increases to 1,250 units, and assuming that the variable costs for the product remain the same, next year you would earn $19,812.50 margin:

$15.85 margin per unit × 1,250 units sold = $19,812.50 margin

Cutting the sales price $10 reduces the margin per unit $9.15. (The revenue-driven operating expense would drop $.85 per unit with the $10.00 sales price decrease.) Therefore, the new margin per unit would be $15.85 per unit. That's a 37 percent drop in margin per unit. A 25 percent gain in sales volume cannot make up for the 37 percent plunge in margin per unit. You'd need a much larger sales volume increase just to keep margin the same as in 2015, and even more sales to increase margin next year. You'd better think twice about dropping the sales price.

You may gain a larger market share, but your margin would drop from $25,000.00 to $19,812.50 on this product if you go ahead with the sales price cut. Is the larger market share worth this much sacrifice of margin? That's why you get paid the big bucks: to make decisions like this. Your controller can only help you do the analysis and calculate the impact on profit before you make a final decision.

Another factor to consider is this: Fixed expenses (people, warehouse space, distribution channels, and so on) provide the *capacity* to make sales and carry on operations. A small increase in sales volume, such as selling 250 more units of the product in question, should not push up the total fixed expenses of your profit center (unless you are already bursting at the seams). On the other hand, a major sales volume increase across the board would require additional capacity, and your fixed expenses would have to be increased.

This sales price reduction decision is just one example of the many decisions business managers have to deal with day in and day out. The profit analysis template is a useful — indeed an invaluable — analysis framework for many decisions facing business managers.

Tucking Away Some Valuable Lessons

The profit analysis template shown in Figure 1-1 offers managers several important lessons. Like most tools, the more you use it the more you learn. The following sections summarize some important lessons from the template.

Recognize the leverage effect caused by fixed operating expenses

Suppose sales volume had been 10 percent higher or lower in 2015, holding other profit factors the same. Would profit have been correspondingly 10 percent higher or lower? The intuitive, knee-jerk reaction answer is yes, profit would have been 10 percent higher or lower. Wouldn't it? Not necessarily. *Margin* would have been 10 percent higher or lower — $250,000 higher or lower ($25 margin per unit × 10,000 units = $250,000).

The $250,000 change in margin would carry down to operating earnings *unless* fixed expenses would have been higher or lower at the different sales volume. The very nature of fixed expenses is that these costs do not change with relatively small changes in sales volume. In all likelihood, fixed expenses would have been virtually the same at a 10 percent higher or lower sales level.

Therefore, operating earnings would have been $250,000 higher or lower. On the base profit of $1.5 million, the $250,000 swing equals a 17 percent shift in profit. Thus, a 10 percent swing in sales volume causes a 17 percent swing in profit. This wider swing in profit is called the *operating leverage* effect. The idea is that a business makes better use of its fixed expenses when sales go up; its fixed expenses don't increase with the sales volume increase. Of course, the downside is that fixed expenses don't decrease when sales volume drops.

Don't underestimate the impact of small changes in sales price

Recall that in the example the sales price is $100, and revenue-driven variable expenses are 8.5 percent of sales revenue (refer to Figure 1-1). Suppose the business had sold the product for $4 more or less than it did, which is only a 4 percent change — pretty small it would seem. This different sales price would have changed its margin per unit $3.66 net of the corresponding change in the revenue-driven variable expenses per unit. ($4 sales price change × 8.5 percent = $.34 per unit, which netted against the $4 sales price change = $3.66 change in margin per unit.)

Therefore, the business would have earned total margin $366,000 higher or lower than it did at the $100 sales price. ($3.66 change in margin per unit × 100,000 units sales volume = $366,000 shift in margin.) Fixed expenses are not sensitive to sales price changes and would have been the same, so the $366,000 shift in margin would carry down to profit.

The $366,000 swing in profit, compared with the $1.5 million baseline profit in the example, equals a 24 percent swing in profit. A 4 percent change in sales price causes a 24 percent change in profit. Recall that a 10 percent change in sales volume causes just a 17 percent change in profit. When it comes to profit impact, sales price changes dominate sales volume changes.

The moral of the story is to protect margin per unit above all else. Every dollar of margin per unit that's lost — due to decreased sales prices, increased product cost, or increases in other variable costs — has a tremendously negative impact on profit. Conversely, if you can increase the margin per unit without hurting sales volume, you reap very large profit benefits.

Know your options for improving profit

Improving profit boils down to three critical factors, listed in order from the most effective to the least effective:

- Increasing margin per unit
- Increasing sales volume
- Reducing fixed expenses

Say you want to improve your profit from the $1.5 million you earned in 2015 to $1.8 million next year, which is a $300,000 or 20 percent increase. Okay, so how are you going to increase profit $300,000? Here are your basic options:

- Increase your margin per unit $3, which would raise total margin $300,000 based on the 100,000 units sales volume.

- Sell 12,000 additional units at the present margin per unit of $25, which would raise your total margin by $300,000. (12,000 additional units × $25 = $300,000 additional margin.)

- Use a combination of these two strategies: Increase both the margin per unit and sales volume such that the combined effect is to improve total margin $300,000.

- Reduce fixed expenses $300,000.

The last alternative may not be very realistic. Reducing your direct fixed expenses $300,000, on a base of $1,000,000, would be drastic and probably would reduce your capacity to make sales and carry out the operations in your part of the business. Perhaps you could do a little belt-tightening in your fixed expenses area, but in all likelihood you would have to turn to the other alternatives for increasing your profit.

The second approach is obvious — you just need to set a sales goal of increasing the number of products sold by 12,000 units. (How you motivate your already overworked sales staff to accomplish that sales volume goal is up to you.) But how do you go about the first approach, increasing the margin per unit by $3?

The simplest way to increase margin per unit by $3 would be to decrease your product cost per unit $3. Or you could attempt to reduce sales commissions from $8.50 per $100 of sales to $5.50 per $100 — which may hurt the motivation of your sales force, of course. Or you could raise the sales price about $3.38 (remember that 8.5 percent comes off the top for sales commission, so only $3 would remain to improve the unit margin). Or you could combine two or more such changes so that your unit margin next year would increase $3.

Closing with a Boozy Example

Some years ago, let's say a group of people pooled their capital and opened a liquor store in a rapidly growing area. In their estimation, the business had a lot of promise. During their planning stage — in addition to location analysis and competition analysis, of course — they should have run some critical numbers through a basic profit model like Figure 1-1 in order to estimate the annual sales revenue they would need to break even. Of course, they wanted to do better than break even, but the break-even sales level is a key point of reference.

Starting up any business involves making commitments to a lot of fixed expenses. Leases are signed, equipment is purchased, people are hired, and so on. All this puts a heavy fixed cost burden on a new business. The business needs to make sales and generate margin from the sales that is enough to cover its fixed expenses before it can break into the profit column. So, they should have estimated their fixed expenses for the first year. Next, they should have estimated their profit margin on sales. Here there is a slight problem, but one that is not difficult to deal with.

During their open house for the new store, there were a large number of different beers, wines, and spirits available for sale. Quite literally, the business sold thousands of distinct products. The store also sold many products like soft drinks, ice, corkscrews, and so on. Therefore, the business did not have an easy-to-define sales volume factor (the number of units sold) for analyzing profit. In the liquor store example, the sales volume factor, the number of units sold during the period, won't work. So, a modification is made. *Total sales revenue* is used for the measure of sales volume, not the number of units (bottles) sold.

The next step, then, is to determine the *average margin as a percent of sales revenue*. A liquor store's average gross margin (sales revenue less cost of goods sold) is about 25 percent. The other variable operating expenses of the liquor store probably run about 5 percent of sales. So, the average margin would be 20 percent of sales (25 percent gross margin less 5 percent variable operating expenses). Suppose the total fixed operating expenses of the liquor store were $100,000 per month (for rent, salaries, electricity, and so on), which is $1.2 million per year. So, the store needs $6 million in annual sales to break even:

$1,200,000 annual fixed expenses ÷ 20% average margin =
$6,000,000 annual sales revenue to break even

Selling $6 million of product a year means moving a *lot* of booze. The business needs to sell another $1 million to provide $200,000 of operating earnings (at the 20 percent average margin) — to pay interest expense and income tax and leave enough net income for the owners who invested capital in the business and who expect a decent return on their investment.

Chapter 2

Budgeting

. . . .

. . . .

A business can't open its doors each day without having a pretty good idea of what to expect. And it can't close its doors at the end of the day not knowing what happened. Recall the Boy Scouts' motto: "Be prepared." A business should follow that dictum: It should plan and be prepared for its future, and it should control its actual performance to reach its financial goals.

Business managers can wait for results to be reported to them on a "look back" basis, and then wing it from there. Or, they can look ahead and carefully plan profit, cash flows, and financial condition of the business, to chart its course into the future. The plan provides invaluable benchmarks; actual results can be compared against the plan to detect when things go off course.

Planning the financial future of a business and comparing actual performance against the plan are the essences of *business budgeting*. Budgeting is not an end to itself but rather a means or tool of financial planning and control.

But keep in mind that budgeting costs time and money. The business manager should put budgeting to the classic technique: the cost versus benefit test. Frankly, budgeting may not earn its keep and could actually cause serious problems that contradict the very reasons for doing it.

Budgeting offers important benefits, but a business may decide not to go to the effort of full-scale budgeting. Some businesses can get away with a minimal budgeting strategy. However, a business should not throw out the budgeting baby with the bathwater. Certain techniques used in budgeting are very useful even when a business doesn't do formal budgeting.

Exploring the Reasons for Budgeting

The financial statements included in the financial reports of a business are prepared *after the fact*; they're based on transactions that have already taken place. Budgeted financial statements, on the other hand, are prepared *before the fact* and reflect future transactions that are expected to take place based on the business's strategy and financial goals. Budgeted financial statements are not shared outside the business; they are strictly for internal management use.

Business budgeting requires setting specific goals and developing the detailed plans necessary to achieve them. Business budgeting should be built on realistic forecasts for the coming period. *Realistic* means attainable and probable. (In larger organizations managers may set their budget objectives too low and easy, in order to achieve them.) A business budget is an integrated plan of action — not simply a few trend lines on a financial chart. Budgeting is much more than slap-dashing together a few figures. A budget is an integrated financial plan put down on paper — or, more likely these days, entered in computer spreadsheets. (There are several good budgeting software programs on the market today; your CPA or other consultant can advise you on which ones are best for your business.)

Business managers don't (or shouldn't) just look out the window and come up with budget numbers. Budgeting is not pie-in-the-sky wishful thinking. Business budgeting — to have practical value — must start with a broad-based critical analysis of the most recent actual performance and position of the business by the managers who are responsible for the results. Then the managers decide on specific and concrete goals for the coming year. (Budgets can be done for more than one year, but the first stepping stone into the future is the budget for the coming year — see the sidebar "Taking it one game at a time.")

In short, budgeting demands a fair amount of managers' time and energy. Budgets should be worth this time and effort. So why should a business go to the trouble of budgeting? Business managers budget and prepare budgeted financial statements for three main reasons: modeling, planning, and control.

Taking it one game at a time

A company generally prepares one-year budgets, although many businesses also develop budgets for two, three, and five years out. Whenever you reach out beyond a year, what you're doing becomes more tentative and iffy. Making forecasts and estimates for the next 12 months is tough enough. A one-year budget is more definite and detailed in comparison to longer-term budgets. As they say in the sports world, a business should take it one game (or year) at a time. Looking down the road beyond one year is a good idea, to set long-term goals and to develop long-term strategy. But long-term planning is different than short-term budgeting.

Modeling reasons for budgeting

Business managers should make detailed analyses to determine how to improve the financial performance and condition of their business. The status quo is usually not good enough; business managers are paid to improve things — not to simply rest on their past accomplishments. For this reason managers should develop good *models* of profit, cash flow, and financial condition for their business. Models are blueprints or schematics of how things work. A financial model is like a roadmap that clearly marks the pathways to profit, cash flow, and financial condition.

Don't be intimidated by the term *model*. Simply put, a model consists of variables and how they interact. A *variable* is a critical factor that, in conjunction with other factors, determines results. A model is analytical, but not all models are mathematical. But you do have to look at each factor of the model and how it interacts with one or more other factors.

Here's an example of an accounting model — the famous *accounting equation*:

Assets = Liabilities + Owners' equity

This is a very condensed model of the balance sheet. The accounting equation is not detailed enough for budgeting, however. More detail about assets and liabilities is needed for budgeting purposes.

Book V Chapter 1 presents a profit template for managers (see Figure 1-1 from that chapter). This template is, at its core, a model. It includes the critical variables that drive profit: sales volume, sales price, product cost, and so on. A profit model provides the framework for understanding and analyzing profit performance. A good profit model also serves as the platform and the point of departure for mapping out profit strategies for the coming period.

Likewise, business managers need a model, or blueprint, in planning cash flow from operating activities. Managers should definitely forecast the amount of cash they will generate during the coming year from making profit. They need a reliable estimate of this source of cash flow in order to plan for other sources of cash flow they will need during the coming year — to provide the money for replacing and expanding the long-term operating (fixed) assets of the business and to make cash distributions from profit to owners. Managers need a model, or map if you prefer that provides a clear trail of how the sales and expenses of the business drive its assets and liabilities, which in turn drive the cash flow from operating activities.

Most business managers see the advantages of budgeting profit for the coming year; you don't have to twist their arms to convince them. At the same time, many business mangers do not carry through and do not budget changes in assets and liabilities during the coming year, which means they can't budget cash flow from operating activities. All their budget effort is focused on profit, and they leave cash flows and financial condition unattended. This is a dangerous strategy when the business is in a tight cash position. The business should not simply assume that its cash flow from operating activities would be adequate to its needs during the coming year.

Generally, a business should prepare all three budgeted financial statements:

- ✔ **Budgeted income statement (profit report):** A profit analysis model, such as the one shown in Book V Chapter 1's Figure 1-1, highlights the critical variables that drive profit. Remember that this model separates *variable* and *fixed* expenses and focuses on *sales volume*, *margin per unit*, and other factors that determine profit performance. These are the key factors that must be improved to enhance profit performance in the coming period. The highly condensed basic profit model provides a useful frame of reference for preparing the much more detailed, comprehensive profit budget.

- ✔ **Budgeted balance sheet:** The key connections and ratios between sales revenue and expenses and their corresponding assets and liabilities are the elements in the model for the budgeted balance sheet. These vital connections are explained throughout Book II Chapter 2. The budgeted changes in operating assets and liabilities provide the information needed for budgeting cash flows during the coming year.

- ✔ **Budgeted statement of cash flows:** The budgeted changes during the coming year in the assets and liabilities used in making profit (conducting operating activities) determine *cash flow from operating activities* for the coming year. In contrast, the cash flows of *investing* and *financing* activities depend on the managers' strategic decisions regarding capital expenditures that will be made during the coming year, how much new capital will be raised from debt and from owners' sources of capital, and the business's policy regarding cash distributions from profit.

In short, budgeting requires good working models of making profit, financial condition (assets and liabilities), and cash flow. Budgeting provides a strong incentive for business managers to develop financial models that help them make strategic decisions, exercise control, and do better planning.

Planning reasons for budgeting

One purpose of budgeting is to force managers to create a definite and detailed financial plan for the coming period. To construct a budget, managers have to establish explicit financial objectives for the coming year and identify exactly what has to be done to accomplish these financial objectives. Budgeted financial statements and their supporting schedules provide clear destination points — the financial flight plan for a business.

Book V

Accounting and Managing Your Business

The process of putting together a budget directs attention to the specific things that you must do to achieve your profit objectives and optimize your assets and capital. Basically, budgets are a form of planning that push managers to answer the question, "How are we going to get there from here?"

Budgeting can also yield other important planning-related benefits:

✔ **Budgeting encourages a business to articulate its vision, strategy, and goals.** A business needs a clearly stated strategy guided by an overarching vision, and it should have definite and explicit goals. It is not enough for business managers to have strategies and goals in their heads. Developing budgeted financial statements forces managers to be explicit and definite about the objectives of the business, as well as to formulate realistic plans for achieving the business objectives.

✔ **Budgeting imposes discipline and deadlines on the planning process.** Busy managers have trouble finding enough time for lunch, let alone planning for the upcoming financial period. Budgeting pushes managers to set aside time to prepare a detailed plan that serves as a road map for the business. Good planning results in a concrete course of action that details how a company plans to achieve its financial objectives.

Control reasons for budgeting

Many people have the mistaken notion that the purpose of budgeting is to rein in managers and employees, who otherwise would spend money like drunken sailors. Budgeting should not put the business's managers in a financial strait jacket. Tying the hands of managers is not the purpose of budgeting. Having said this, however, it's true that budgets serve a management control function. *Management control,* first and foremost, means achieving the financial goals and objectives of the business, which requires comparing actual performance against some sort of benchmarks and holding individual managers responsible for keeping the business on schedule in reaching its financial objectives.

The board of directors of a corporation focuses its attention on the *master budget* for the whole business: the budgeted income statement, balance sheet, and cash flow statement for the business for the coming year. The chief executive officer (CEO) of the business focuses on the master budget as well, but the CEO must also look at how each manager in the organization is doing on his or her part of the master budget. As you move down the organization chart of a business, managers have narrower responsibilities — say, for the business's northeastern territory or for one major product line. A master budget consists of different segments that follow the business's organizational structure. In other words, the master budget is put together from many pieces, one for each separate organizational unit of the business. For example, the manager of one of the company's far-flung warehouses has a separate budget for expenses and inventory levels for his or her bailiwick.

By using budget targets as benchmarks against which actual performance is compared, managers can closely monitor progress toward (or deviations from) the budget goals and timetable. You use a budget plan like a navigation chart to keep your business on course. Significant variations from the budget raise red flags, in which case you can determine that performance is off course or that the budget needs to be revised because of unexpected developments.

For management control, a budgeted profit report is divided into months or quarters for the coming year. The budgeted balance sheet and budgeted cash flow statement may also be put on a monthly or quarterly basis. The business should not wait too long to compare budgeted sales revenue and expenses against actual performance (or to compare actual cash flows and asset levels against the budget). You need to take prompt action when problems arise, such as a divergence between budgeted expenses and actual expenses.

Profit is the main thing to pay attention to, but accounts receivable and inventory can also get out of control (become too high relative to actual sales revenue and cost of goods sold expense), causing cash flow problems. A business cannot afford to ignore its balance sheet and cash flow numbers until the end of the year.

Additional Benefits of Budgeting

Budgeting has advantages and ramifications that go beyond the financial dimension and have more to do with business management in general. Consider the following:

- ✔ **Budgeting forces managers to do better forecasting.** Managers should be constantly scanning the business environment to spot changes that will impact the business. Vague generalizations about what the future may hold for the business are not good enough for assembling a budget. Managers are forced to put their predictions into definite and concrete forecasts. For example, a business newsletter listed the following costs that a business has to (or should) forecast:

   - Wages and salaries

   - Insurance (health, business owner policies, workers' compensation)

   - Energy costs

- Postage and shipping costs
- Interest rates
- Travel and entertainment
- Technology (software, hardware, and consultants)
- Legal fees, rents, and audits

✔ **Budgeting motivates managers and employees by providing useful yardsticks for evaluating performance.** The budgeting process can have a good motivational impact by involving managers in the budgeting process (especially in setting goals and objectives) and by providing incentives to managers to strive for and achieve the business's goals and objectives. Budgets provide useful information for superiors to evaluate the performance of managers and can be used to reward good results. Employees may be equally motivated by budgets. For example, budgets supply baseline financial information for incentive compensation plans. And the profit plan (budget) for the year can be used to award year-end bonuses according to whether designated goals were achieved.

✔ **Budgeting can assist in the communication between different levels of management.** Putting plans and expectations in black and white in budgeted financial statements — including definite numbers for forecasts and goals — minimizes confusion and creates a kind of common language. As you know, the "failure to communicate" lament is common in many business organizations. Well-crafted budgets can definitely help the communication process.

✔ **Budgeting is essential in writing a business plan.** New and emerging businesses need to present a convincing business plan when raising capital. Because these businesses may have little or no history, the managers and owners must demonstrate convincingly that the company has a clear strategy and a realistic plan to make profit. A coherent, realistic budget forecast is an essential component of a business plan. Venture capital sources definitely want to see the budgeted financial statements of a business.

In larger businesses, budgets are typically used to hold managers accountable for their areas of responsibility in the organization; actual results are compared against budgeted goals and timetables, and variances are highlighted. Managers do not mind taking credit for *favorable* variances, when actual comes in better than budget. But beating the budget for the period does not always indicate outstanding performance. A favorable variance could be the result of gaming the budget in the first place, so that the budgeted benchmarks can be easily achieved.

Likewise, *unfavorable* variances have to be interpreted carefully. If a manager's budgeted goals and targets are fair and reasonable, the manager should be held responsible. The manager should carefully analyze what went wrong and what needs to be improved. Stern action may be called for, but the higher ups should recognize that the budget benchmarks may not be entirely fair; in particular, they should make allowances for unexpected developments that occur after the budget goals and targets are established (such as a hurricane or tornado, or the bankruptcy of a major customer). When managers perceive the budgeted goals and targets to be arbitrarily imposed by superiors and not realistic, serious motivational problems can arise.

Is Budgeting Worth Its Costs?

As you have undoubtedly heard, there's no such thing as a free lunch. Budgeting has its costs, which managers should take into account before rushing into (or continuing with) a full-scale budgeting process. Whether or not to engage in budgeting is a prime example of how managers make tough decisions: comparing costs versus benefits. Budgeting has many benefits, but managers have to weigh these against the costs of budgeting. Costs don't mean just the monetary out-of-pocket costs. The costs of budgeting are in several different dimensions.

Budgeting is not without several serious problems on the practical level. Budgeting looks good in theory, but in actual practice things are not so rosy. Here are some concerns to consider:

- ✓ Budgeting takes time, and the one thing all business managers will tell you is that they never have enough time for all the things they should do. The question always is: What else could managers do with their time if budgeting were eliminated or scaled down?

- ✓ Budgeting done from the top down (from headquarters down to the lower levels of managers) can stifle innovation and discourage managers from taking the initiative when they should.

- ✓ Unrealistic budget goals can demotivate managers rather than motivate them.

- ✓ Managers may *game* the budget, which means they play the budget as a game in which they worry first and foremost about how they will be affected by the budget rather than what's best for the business.

- ✓ There have been cases in which managers resorted to accounting fraud to make their budget numbers.

There has always been grumbling about budgeting. A well-known adage in the advertising profession is that half of a company's advertising cost is wasted; the problem is that managers don't know which half. Likewise, you could argue that half the cost of budgeting is wasted; although it's difficult to pinpoint which particular aspects of budgeting are not cost effective.

"Freed from the Budget," by Russ Banham, from the September 1, 2012 issue of *CFO* magazine, offers several reasons for not budgeting, including the following:

- ✔ Budgeting prevents rapid response to unpredictable events
- ✔ Budgeting stifles initiative and innovations
- ✔ Budgeting protects non value-adding costs
- ✔ Budgeting demotivates people

The article makes a good case against budgeting, but in my mind it doesn't provide a very convincing answer to the question: If not budgeting, then what? Quite clearly business managers must plan and control. The trick is how to carry out these tasks in the most effective and efficient manner.

Realizing That Not Everyone Budgets

Most of what this chapter has said so far can be likened to a commercial for budgeting — emphasizing the reasons for and advantages of budgeting by a business. So every business does budgeting, right? Nope. Smaller businesses generally do little or no budgeting — and even many larger businesses avoid budgeting, at least in a formal and comprehensive manner. The reasons are many, and mostly practical in nature.

Avoiding budgeting

Some businesses are in relatively mature stages of their life cycle or operate in a mature and stable industry. These companies do not have to plan for any major changes or discontinuities. Next year will be a great deal like last year. The benefits of going through a formal budgeting process do not seem worth the time and cost.

At the other extreme, a business may be in an uncertain environment, where attempting to predict the future seems pointless. A business may lack the expertise and experience to prepare budgeted financial statements, and it may not be willing to pay the cost for a CPA or outside consultant to help.

But what if your business applies for a loan? The lender will demand to see a well-thought-out budget in your business plan, right? Not necessarily. Many banks do not expect a business to include a set of budgeted financial statements in the loan request package. Of course, they do demand to see the latest financial statements of the business. Few smaller business clients prepare budgeted financial statements.

Relying on internal accounting reports

Although many businesses do not prepare budgets, they still establish fairly specific goals and performance objectives that serve as good benchmarks for management control. Every business — whether it does budgeting or not — should design internal accounting reports that provide the information managers need in running a business. Obviously, managers should keep close tabs on what's going on throughout the business. One definition of management control is "watching everything."

Even in a business that doesn't do budgeting, managers depend on regular profit reports, balance sheets, and cash flow statements. These key internal financial statements should provide detailed management control information. These feedback reports are also used for looking ahead and thinking about the future. Other specialized accounting reports may be needed as well.

Making reports useful for management control

Most business managers, in my experience, would tell you that the accounting reports they get are reasonably good for management control. Their accounting reports provide the detailed information they need for keeping a close watch on the 1,001 details of the business (or their particular sphere of responsibility in the business organization).

Criticisms about internal accounting reports include the following:

- They contain too much information.
- All the information is flat, as if each piece of information is equally relevant.

Managers have only so much time to read the accounting reports coming to them. Managers probably have a valid beef on this score. Ideally, significant deviations and problems should be highlighted in the accounting reports they receive — but separating the important from the not-so-important is easier said than done.

Making reports useful for decision making

If you were to ask a cross-section of business managers how useful their accounting reports are for *making decisions,* you would get a different answer than how good the accounting reports are for management control. Management decision-making is a whole different animal than management control.

Business managers make many decisions affecting profit: setting sales prices, buying products, determining wages and salaries, hiring independent contractors, and purchasing fixed assets, for example. Managers should carefully analyze how their actions would impact profit before reaching final decisions. Managers need internal profit reports that serve as good profit models — that make clear the critical variables that affect profit. (Figure 2-1 in the next section presents an example.) Well-designed management profit reports are absolutely essential for helping managers make good decisions.

Keep in mind that almost all business decisions involve non-financial and non-quantifiable factors that go beyond the information included in accounting reports. For example, the accounting department of a business can calculate the cost savings of a wage cut, or the elimination of overtime hours by employees, or a change in the retirement plan for employees — and the manager would certainly look at this data. But such decisions must consider many other factors, such as effects on employee morale and productivity, the possibility of the union going on strike, legal issues, and so on. In short, accounting reports provide only part of the information needed for business decisions, though an essential part for sure.

Making reports clear and straightforward

Needless to say, the internal accounting reports to managers should be clear and straightforward. The manner of presentation and means of communication should get the manager's attention, and a manager should not have to call the accounting department for explanations.

Designing useful management accounting reports is a challenging task. Within one business organization, an accounting report may have to be somewhat different from one profit center to the next. Standardizing accounting reports may seem like a good idea but may not be in the best interests of the various managers throughout the business — who have different responsibilities and different problems to deal with.

Many management accounting reports could be improved — substantially! Accounting systems pay so much attention to the demands of preparing external financial statements and tax returns that managers' needs for good internal reports are often overlooked or ignored. The accounting reports in many businesses do not speak to the managers receiving them; the reports are voluminous and technical and are not focused on the most urgent and important problems facing the managers. Designing good internal accounting reports for managers is a challenging task, to be sure. But every business should take a hard look at its internal management accounting reports and identify what should be improved.

Watching Budgeting in Action

Suppose you're the general manager of one of a large company's several divisions, which is a major profit center of the business. (Book V Chapter 1 discusses profit centers.) You have broad authority to run this division, as well as the responsibility for meeting the financial expectations for your division. To be more specific, your profit responsibility is to produce a satisfactory annual operating profit, which is the amount of earnings before interest and income tax (EBIT). (Interest and income tax expenses are handled at the headquarters level in the organization.)

The CEO has made clear to you that she expects your division to increase EBIT during the coming year by 10 percent, or $256,000 to be exact. In fact, she has asked you to prepare a budgeted profit report showing your plan of action for increasing your division's EBIT by this target amount. She also has asked you to prepare a summary for the budgeted cash flow from operating activities based on your profit plan for the coming year.

Keeping an eye on sales mix

Most businesses, or the major divisions of a large business, sell a mix of several different products. General Motors, for example, sells many makes and models of autos and light trucks, to say nothing about its other products. The next time you visit your local hardware store, take the time to look at the number of products on the shelves. The assortment of products sold by a business and the quantities sold of each that make up its total sales revenue is referred to as its *sales mix*. As a general rule, certain products have higher profit margins than others. Some products may have extremely low profit margins, so they are called *loss leaders*.

The marketing strategy for loss leaders is to use them as magnets, so customers buy your higher profit margin products along with the loss leaders. Shifting the sales mix to a higher proportion of higher profit margin products has the effect of increasing the average profit margin on all products sold. (A shift to lower profit margin products would have the opposite effect, of course.) Budgeting sales revenue and expenses for the coming year must include any planned shifts in the company's sales mix.

Figure 2-1 presents the P&L report of your division for the year just ended. Note that fixed operating expenses are separated from the two variable operating expenses. (Your actual reports may include more detailed information about sales and expenses.) To keep number crunching to a minimum, I assume that you sell only one product in this example. Most businesses sell a range of products, not just one. So, they have to apply profit analysis to each product, department, product line, or other grouping of the company's sources of profit. See the sidebar "Keeping an eye on sales mix."

	Year Just Ended	
Sales volume	260,000	units
	Per Unit	Totals
Sales revenue	$100.00	$26,000,000
Cost of goods sold	$55.00	$14,300,000
Gross margin	$45.00	$11,700,000
Revenue-driven expenses	$8.00	$2,080,000
Volume-driven expenses	$5.00	$1,300,000
Margin	$32.00	$8,320,000
Fixed expenses		$5,720,000
Operating profit		$2,600,000

© John Wiley & Sons, Inc.

Figure 2-1: P&L report for the year just ended.

Developing your profit improvement strategy and profit budget

Being an experienced manager, you know the importance of protecting your unit margins. Your division sold 260,000 units in the year just ended (refer to Figure 2-1). Your margin per unit was $32. If all your costs were to remain the same next year (you wish!), you could sell 8,000 more units to reach your $256,000 profit improvement goal:

$256,000 additional margin needed ÷ $32 margin per unit = 8,000 additional units

The relatively small increase in your sales volume (8,000 additional units ÷ 260,000 units = 3.1 percent) should not increase your fixed expenses — unless you're already operating at full capacity and would have to increase warehouse space and delivery capacity to take on even a small increase in sales volume. But realistically, some or most of your costs will probably increase next year.

Take this one step at a time. First, look at your *fixed expenses* for the coming year. You and your managers, with the assistance of your trusty accounting staff, have analyzed your fixed expenses line by line for the coming year. Some of these fixed expenses will actually be reduced or eliminated next year. But the large majority of these costs will continue next year, and most are subject to inflation. Based on careful studies and estimates, you and your staff forecast total fixed operating expenses for next year will be $6,006,000, which is $286,000 more than the year just ended.

Fortunately, you think that your volume-driven variable expenses should not increase next year. These are mainly transportation costs, and the shipping industry is in a very competitive, hold-the-price-down mode of operations that should last through the coming year. The cost per unit shipped should not increase.

You have decided to hold the revenue-driven operating expenses at 8 percent of sales revenue during the coming year, the same as for the year just ended. These are sales commissions, and you have already announced to your sales staff that their sales commission percentage will remain the same during the coming year. On the other hand, your purchasing manager has told you to plan on a 4 percent product cost increase next year — from $55 per unit to $57.20 per unit, or an increase of $2.20 per unit.

Summing up to this point, your total fixed expenses will increase $286,000 next year, and the $2.20 forecast product cost will drop your margin per unit from $32.00 to $29.80 if your sales price does not increase. One way to achieve your profit goal next year would be to load all the needed increase on sales volume and keep sales price the same. (This strategy may or may not be a good one, but it serves as a good point of departure.)

So, what would your sales volume have to be next year? Remember: You want to increase profit $256,000 (orders from on high), and your fixed expenses will increase $286,000 next year. So, your margin goal for next year is determined as follows:

$8,320,000 margin for year just ended + $286,000 fixed expenses increase + $256,000 profit improvement goal = $8,862,000 margin goal

Without bumping sales price, your margin would be only $29.80 per unit next year. At this margin per unit you will have to sell over 297,000 units:

$8,862,000 total margin goal ÷ $29.80 margin per unit = 297,383 units sales volume

Compared with the 260,000 units sales volume in the year just ended, you would have to increase sales by more than 37,000 units, or more than 14 percent.

You and your sales manager conclude that sales volume cannot be increased 14 percent. You'll have to raise the sales price to compensate for the increase in product cost and to help cover the fixed cost increases. After much discussion, you and your sales manager decide to increase the sales price 3 percent, from $100 to $103. Based on the 3 percent sales price increase and the forecast product cost increase, your unit margin next year would be as follows:

Budgeted Unit Margin Next Year

Sales price	$103.00
Product cost	(57.20)
Revenue-driven operating expenses (@ 8.0%)	(8.24)
Volume-driven operating expenses per unit	(5.00)
Equals: Margin per unit	$32.56

At the budgeted $32.56 margin per unit, you determine the sales volume needed next year to reach your profit goal as follows:

$8,862,000 total margin goal next year ÷ $32.56 margin per unit = 272,174 units sales volume

This sales volume is about 5 percent higher than last year (12,174 additional units over the 260,000 sales volume last year = about a 5 percent increase).

You decide to go with the 3 percent sales price increase combined with the 5 percent sales volume growth as your official budget plan. Accordingly, you forward your budgeted profit report for the coming year to the CEO. Figure 2-2 summarizes this profit budget for the coming year, with comparative figures for the year just ended.

The main page of your budgeted profit report is supplemented with appropriate schedules to provide additional detail about sales by types of customers and other relevant information. Also, your budgeted profit plan is broken down into quarters (perhaps months) to provide benchmarks for comparing actual performance during the year against your budgeted targets and timetable.

	Actual for Year Just Ended		Budgeted for Coming Year	
Sales volume	260,000 units		272,170 units	
	Per Unit	Totals	Per Unit	Totals
Sales revenue	$100.00	$26,000,000	$103.00	$28,033,968
Cost of goods sold	$55.00	$14,300,000	$57.20	$15,568,378
Gross margin	$45.00	$11,700,000	$45.80	$12,465,590
Revenue-driven expenses	$8.00	$2,080,000	$8.24	$2,242,718
Volume-driven expenses	$5.00	$1,300,000	$5.00	$1,360,872
Margin	$32.00	$8,320,000	$32.56	$8,862,000
Fixed expenses		$5,720,000		$6,006,000
Operating profit		$2,600,000		$2,856,000

Figure 2-2: Budgeted profit report for coming year.

© John Wiley & Sons, Inc.

Budgeting cash flow for the coming year

The budgeted profit plan (refer to Figure 2-2) is the main focus of attention, but the CEO also requests that all divisions present a *budgeted cash flow from operating activities* for the coming year.

The profit you're responsible for as general manager of the division is the amount of operating earnings before interest and income tax (EBIT).

Increases in accounts receivable, inventory, and prepaid expenses *hurt* cash flow from operating activities, and increases in accounts payable and accrued liabilities *help* cash flow. In reading the budgeted profit report for the coming year (refer to Figure 2-2), you see that virtually every budgeted figure for the coming year is higher than the figure for the year just ended. Therefore, your operating assets and liabilities will increase at the higher sales revenue and expense levels next year — unless you can implement changes to prevent the increases.

For example, sales revenue increases from $26,000,000 to the budgeted $28,033,968 next year (refer to Figure 2-2) — an increase of $2,033,968. Your accounts receivable balance was five weeks of annual sales last year. Do you plan to tighten up the credit terms offered to customers next year — a year in which you will raise the sales price and also plan to increase sales volume? Probably not. More likely, you will attempt to keep your accounts receivable balance at five weeks of annual sales.

Assume that you decide to offer your customers the same credit terms next year. Thus, the increase in sales revenue will cause accounts receivable to increase by $195,574:

$5/52 \times \$2,033,968$ sales revenue increase $= \$195,574$ accounts receivable increase

Last year, inventory was 13 weeks of annual cost of goods sold expense. You may be in the process of implementing inventory reduction techniques. If you really expect to reduce the average time inventory will be held in stock before being sold, you should inform your accounting staff so that they can include this key change in the balance sheet and cash flow models. Otherwise, they will assume that the past ratios for these vital connections will continue next year.

Assuming your inventory holding period remains the same, your inventory balance will increase more than $317,000:

$13/52 \times \$1,268,378$ cost of goods sold expense increase $= \$317,055$ inventory increase

Figure 2-3 presents a brief summary of your budgeted cash flow from operating activities based on the information given for this example and using your historical ratios for short-term assets and liabilities driven by sales and expenses. *Note:* Increases in accrued interest payable and income tax payable are not included in your budgeted cash flow. Your profit responsibility ends at the operating profit line, or earnings before interest and income tax expenses.

Figure 2-3: Budgeted cash flow from operating activities for the coming year.

Budgeted Profit (See Figure 2-2)	$2,856,000
Accounts Receivable Increase	(195,574)
Inventory Increase	(317,095)
Prepaid Expenses Increase	(26,226)
Depreciation Expense	835,000
Accounts Payable Increase	34,968
Accrued Expenses Payable Increase	52,453
Budgeted Cash Flow From Operating Activities	$3,239,526

© John Wiley & Sons, Inc.

You submit this budgeted cash flow from operating activities (see Figure 2-3) to headquarters. Top management expects you to control the increases in your operating assets and liabilities so that the actual cash flow generated

Book V

Accounting and Managing Your Business

by your division next year comes in on target. The cash flow of your division (perhaps minus a small amount needed to increase the working cash balance held by your division) will be transferred to the central treasury of the business. Headquarters will be planning on you generating about $3.2 million cash flow during the coming year.

Considering Capital Expenditures and Other Cash Needs

This chapter focuses on profit budgeting for the coming year and budgeting the cash flow from that profit. These are the two hardcore components of business budgeting, but not the whole story. Another key element of the budgeting process is to prepare a *capital expenditures budget* for your division that goes to top management for review and approval. A business has to take a hard look at its long-term operating assets — in particular, the capacity, condition, and efficiency of these resources — and decide whether it needs to expand and modernize its property, plant, and equipment.

In most cases, a business needs to invest substantial sums of money in purchasing new fixed assets or retrofitting and upgrading its old fixed assets. These long-term investments require major cash outlays. So, each division of a business prepares a formal list of the fixed assets to be purchased, constructed, and upgraded. The money for these major outlays comes from the central treasury of the business. Accordingly, the overall capital expenditures budget goes to the highest levels in the organization for review and final approval. The chief financial officer, the CEO, and the board of directors of the business go over a capital expenditure budget request with a fine-toothed comb (or at least they *should*).

A major factor in analyzing capital expenditures is the *cost of capital*, or the return on investment (ROI) that a business must earn. Cost of capital refers to the time value of money, and is measured based on interest rates and return on equity (ROE) expectations. A company's cost of capital depends on its mix of debt and equity and the respective costs of these two capital determinants. The cost of capital is used in *capital budgeting* analysis (another term for capital expenditures analysis), which is beyond the scope of this book. It involves calculating the internal rate of return (IRR) and present value (PV) of the future cash flows from an investment of capital.

Business budgeting versus government budgeting: Only the name is the same

Business and government budgeting are more different than alike. Government budgeting is preoccupied with allocating scarce resources among many competing demands. From federal agencies down to local school districts, government entities have only so much revenue available. They have to make difficult choices regarding how to spend their limited tax revenue.

Formal budgeting is legally required for almost all government entities. First, a budget request is submitted. After money is appropriated, the budget document becomes legally binding on the government agency. Government budgets are legal strait jackets; the government entity

has to stay within the amounts appropriated for each expenditure category. Any changes from the established budgets need formal approval and are difficult to get through the system.

A business is not legally required to use budgeting. A business can implement and use its budget as it pleases, and it can even abandon its budget in midstream. Unlike the government, the revenue of a business is not constrained; a business can do many things to increase sales revenue. A business can pass its costs to its customers in the sales prices it charges. In contrast, government has to raise taxes to spend more (except for federal deficit spending, of course).

At the company-wide level, the financial officers merge the profit and cash flow budgets of all profit centers and cost centers of the business. (A *cost center* is an organizational unit that does not generate revenue, such as the legal and accounting departments.) The budgets submitted by one or more of the divisions may be returned for revision before final approval is given. One concern is whether the collective cash flow total from all the units provides enough money for the capital expenditures that will be made during the coming year — and to meet the other demands for cash, such as for cash distributions from profit. The business may have to raise more capital from debt or equity sources during the coming year to close the gap between cash flow from operating activities and its needs for cash. This is a central topic in the field of business finance and beyond the coverage of this book.

Chapter 3

Cost Accounting

* *

In This Chapter

▶ Measuring costs: The second-most important thing accountants do

▶ Recognizing the different needs for cost information

▶ Determining the right costs for different purposes

▶ Assembling the product cost of manufacturers

▶ Padding profit by producing too many products

* *

Measuring costs is the second most important thing accountants do, right after measuring profit. (Well, the Internal Revenue Service might think that measuring taxable income is the most important.) But really, can measuring a cost be very complicated? You just take numbers off a purchase invoice and call it a day, right? Not if your business manufactures the products you sell, that's for sure! This chapter demonstrates that a cost — any cost — is not as obvious and clear-cut as you may think. Yet, obviously, costs are extremely important to businesses and other organizations.

Consider an example close to home: Suppose you just returned from the grocery store with several items in the bag. What's the cost of the loaf of bread you bought? Should you include the sales tax? Should you include the cost of gas you used driving to the store? Should you include some amount of depreciation expense on your car? Suppose you returned some aluminum cans for recycling while you were at the grocery store, and you were paid a small amount for the cans. Should you subtract this amount against the total cost of your purchases? Or should you subtract the amount directly against the cost of only the sodas in aluminum cans that you bought? And, is cost the *before-tax* cost? In other words, is your cost equal to the amount of income you had to earn before income tax so that you had enough after-tax income to buy the items? And, what about the time you spent shopping? Your time could have been used for other endeavors.

You get the point.

These questions about the cost of your groceries are interesting (or maybe not). But you don't really have to come up with definite answers for such questions in managing your personal financial affairs. Individuals don't have to keep cost records of their personal expenditures, other than what's needed for their annual income tax returns. In contrast, businesses must carefully record all their costs correctly so that profit can be determined each period, and so that managers have the information they need to make decisions and to make a profit.

Looking Down the Road to the Destination of Costs

All businesses that sell products must know their *product costs* — in other words, the costs of each and every item they sell. Companies that manufacture the products they sell — as opposed to distributors and retailers of products — have many problems in figuring out their product costs. Two examples of manufactured products are a new Cadillac just rolling off the assembly line at General Motors and a copy of this book, *Bookkeeping All-In-One For Dummies,* hot off the printing presses.

Most production (manufacturing) processes are fairly complex, so product cost accounting for manufacturers is likewise fairly complex; every step in the production process has to be tracked carefully from start to finish. Many manufacturing costs cannot be directly matched with particular products; these are called *indirect costs.* To arrive at the *full cost* of each product manufactured, accountants devise methods for allocating indirect production costs to specific products. Surprisingly, established accounting standards in the United States, called *generally accepted accounting principles* (GAAP), provide little authoritative guidance for measuring product cost. Therefore, manufacturing businesses have more than a little leeway regarding how to determine their product costs. Even businesses in the same industry — Ford versus General Motors, for example — may use different product cost accounting methods.

Accountants determine many other costs, in addition to product costs:

- The costs of departments, regional distribution centers, cost centers, and other organizational units of the business
- The cost of the retirement plan for the company's employees
- The cost of marketing programs and advertising campaigns
- The cost of restructuring the business or the cost of a major recall of products sold by the business, when necessary

A common refrain among accountants is "different costs for different purposes." True enough, but at its core, cost accounting serves two broad purposes: measuring profit and providing relevant information to managers for planning, control, and decision-making.

Book V

Accounting and Managing Your Business

People may be inclined to take cost numbers for granted, as if they were handed down on stone tablets. The phrase *actual cost* often gets tossed around without a clear definition. An actual cost depends entirely on the particular methods used to measure the cost. These cost measurement methods have more in common with the scores from judges in an ice skating competition than the times clocked in a Formula One auto race. Many arbitrary choices are behind every cost number you see. There's no one-size-fits-all definition of cost, and there's no one correct and best-in-all-circumstances method of measuring cost.

The conundrum is that, in spite of the inherent ambiguity in determining costs, you do need exact amounts for costs. To understand the income statement and balance sheet that managers use in making their decisions, they should understand the choices an accountant has to make in measuring costs. Some cost accounting methods result in conservative profit numbers; other methods boost profit, at least in the short run. Book II Chapter 8 discusses the choices among different accounting methods that produce financial statements with a conservative or liberal hue.

This chapter covers cost concepts and cost measurement methods that apply to all businesses, as well as basic product cost accounting of manufacturers. It discusses how a manufacturer could be fooling around with its production output to manipulate product cost for the purpose of artificially boosting its profit figure. (Service businesses encounter their own problems in allocating their operating costs for assessing the profitability of their separate sales revenue sources.)

Are Costs Really That Important?

Without good cost information, a business operates in the dark. Cost data is needed for the following purposes:

✔ **Setting sales prices:** The common method for setting sales prices (known as *cost-plus* or *markup on cost*) starts with cost and then adds a certain percentage. If you don't know exactly how much a product costs, you can't be as shrewd and competitive in your pricing as you need to be. Even if sales prices are dictated by other forces and not set by managers, managers need to compare sales prices against product costs and other costs that should be matched against each sales revenue source.

✔ **Formulating a legal defense against charges of predatory pricing practices:** Many states have laws prohibiting businesses from selling below cost except in certain circumstances. And a business can be sued under federal law for charging artificially low prices intended to drive its competitors out of business. Be prepared to prove that your lower pricing is based on lower costs and not on some illegitimate purpose.

✔ **Measuring gross margin:** Investors and managers judge business performance by the bottom-line profit figure. This profit figure depends on the *gross margin* figure you get when you subtract your cost of goods sold expense from your sales revenue. Gross margin (also called *gross profit*) is the first profit line in the income statement (for example, see Figure 3-1 later in this chapter). If gross margin is wrong, bottom-line net income is wrong — no two ways about it. The cost of goods sold expense depends on having correct product costs (see "Assembling the Product Cost of Manufacturers" later in this chapter).

✔ **Valuing assets:** The balance sheet reports cost values for many (though not all) assets. To understand the balance sheet you should understand the cost basis of its inventory and certain other assets. See Book II Chapter 4 for more on the balance sheet (also called the *statement of financial condition*).

✔ **Making optimal choices:** You often must choose one alternative over others in making business decisions. The best alternative depends heavily on cost factors, and you have to be careful to distinguish *relevant* costs from *irrelevant* costs, as described in the section "Relevant versus irrelevant costs," later in this chapter.

In most situations, the historic book value recorded for a fixed asset is an *irrelevant* cost. Say book value is $35,000 for a machine used in the manufacturing operations of the business. This is the amount of original cost that has not yet been charged to depreciation expense since it was acquired, and it may seem quite relevant. However, in deciding between keeping the old machine or replacing it with a newer, more efficient machine, the *disposable value* of the old machine is the relevant amount, not the undepreciated cost balance of the asset.

Suppose the old machine has an estimated $20,000 salvage value at this time; this is the relevant cost for the alternative of keeping it for use in the future — not the $35,000 book value that hasn't been depreciated yet. To keep using it, the business forgoes the $20,000 it could get by selling the asset, and this $20,000 is the relevant cost in this decision situation. Making decisions involves looking forward at the future cash flows of each alternative — not looking backward at historical-based cost values.

Accounting versus economic costs

Accountants focus mainly on *actual costs* (though they disagree regarding how exactly to measure these costs). Actual costs are rooted in the actual, or historical, transactions and operations of a business. Accountants also determine *budgeted costs* for businesses that prepare budgets (see Book V Chapter 2), and they develop *standard costs* that serve as yardsticks to compare with the actual costs of a business.

Other concepts of cost are found in economic theory. You'll encounter a variety of economic cost terms while reading *The Wall Street Journal,* as well as in many business discussions and deliberations. Don't reveal your ignorance of the following cost terms:

- **Opportunity cost:** The amount of income (or other measurable benefit) given up when you follow a better course of action. For example, say that you quit your $50,000 job, invest $200,000 you saved up, and start a new business. You earn $80,000 profit in your new business for the year. Suppose also that you would have earned 5 percent on the $200,000 (a total of $10,000) if you'd kept the money in whatever investment you took it from. So you gave up a $50,000 salary and $10,000 in investment income with your course of action; your opportunity cost is $60,000. Subtract that figure from what your actual course of action netted you — $80,000 — and you end up with a "real" economic profit of $20,000. Your income is $20,000 better by starting your new business, according to economic theory.

- **Marginal cost:** The *incremental,* out-of-pocket outlay required for taking a particular course of action. Generally speaking,

it's the same thing as a *variable* cost (see "Fixed versus variable costs," later in this chapter). Marginal costs are important, but in actual practice managers must recover fixed (or nonmarginal) costs as well as marginal costs through sales revenue in order to remain in business for any extent of time. Marginal costs are most relevant for analyzing one-time ventures, which don't last over the long term.

- **Replacement cost:** The estimated amount it would take today to purchase an asset that the business already owns. The longer ago an asset was acquired, the more likely its current replacement cost is higher than its original cost. Economists are of the opinion that current replacement costs are relevant in making rational economic decisions. For insuring assets against fire, theft, and natural catastrophes, the current replacement costs of the assets are clearly relevant. Other than for insurance, however, replacement costs are not on the front burners of decision-making — except in situations in which one alternative being seriously considered actually involves replacing assets.

- **Imputed cost:** An ideal, or hypothetical, cost number that is used as a benchmark against which actual costs are compared. Two examples are *standard costs* and the *cost of capital.* Standard costs are set in advance for the manufacture of products during the coming period, and then actual costs are compared against standard costs to identify significant variances. The cost of capital is the weighted average of the interest rate on debt capital and a target rate

(continued)

(continued)

of return that should be earned on equity capital. The *economic value added* (EVA) method compares a business's cost of capital against its actual return on capital, to determine whether the business did better or worse than the benchmark.

For the most part, these types of cost aren't reflected in financial reports. They're mentioned here to familiarize you with terms you're likely to see in the financial press and hear on financial talk shows. Business managers toss these terms around a lot.

Becoming More Familiar with Costs

The following sections explain important cost distinctions that managers should understand in making decisions and exercising control. Also, these cost distinctions help managers better appreciate the cost figures that accountants attach to products that are manufactured or purchased by the business.

Retailers (such as Walmart or Costco) purchase products in a condition ready for sale to their customers — although the products have to be removed from shipping containers, and the retailer does do a little work making the products presentable for sale and putting the products on display. Manufacturers don't have it so easy; their product costs have to be "manufactured" in the sense that the accountants have to accumulate various production costs and compute the cost per unit for every product manufactured. The upcoming section "Assembling the Product Cost of Manufacturers" focuses on the special cost concerns of manufacturers.

The importance of correct product costs can't be overstated (for businesses that sell products, of course). The total cost of goods (products) sold is the first, and usually the largest, expense deducted from sales revenue in measuring profit. The bottom-line profit amount reported in a business's income statement depends heavily on whether its product costs have been measured properly during that period. Also, keep in mind that product cost is the value for the inventory asset reported in the balance sheet of a business.

Direct versus indirect costs

You might say that the starting point for any sort of cost analysis, and particularly for accounting for the product costs of manufacturers, is to clearly distinguish between *direct* and *indirect* costs. Direct costs are easy to match with a process or product, whereas indirect costs are more distant and have to be allocated to a process or product. Here are more details:

- **Direct costs:** Can be clearly attributed to one product or product line, or one source of sales revenue, or one organizational unit of the business, or one specific operation in a process. An example of a direct cost in the book publishing industry is the cost of the paper that a book is printed on; this cost can be squarely attached to one particular step or operation in the book production process.

- **Indirect costs:** Are far removed from and cannot be naturally attached to specific products, organizational units, or activities. A book publisher's telephone and Internet bills are costs of doing business, but they can't be tied down to just one step in the book editorial and production process. The salary of the purchasing officer who selects the paper for all the books is another example of a cost that is indirect to the production of particular books.

Each business must determine methods of allocating indirect costs to different products, sources of sales revenue, revenue and cost centers, and other organizational units. Most allocation methods are far from perfect and, in the final analysis, end up being arbitrary to one degree or another. Business managers should always keep an eye on the allocation methods used for indirect costs and take the cost figures produced by these methods with a grain of salt.

Fixed versus variable costs

If your business sells 100 more units of a certain item, some of your costs increase accordingly, but others don't budge one bit. This distinction between *variable* and *fixed* costs is crucial:

- **Variable costs:** Increase and decrease in proportion to changes in sales or production level. Variable costs generally remain the same per unit of product, or per unit of activity. Additional units manufactured or sold cause variable costs to increase in concert. Fewer units manufactured or sold result in variable costs going down in concert.

- **Fixed costs:** Remain the same over a relatively broad range of sales volume or production output. Fixed costs are like a dead weight on the business. Its total fixed costs for the period are a hurdle it must overcome by selling enough units at high enough margins per unit in order to avoid a loss and move into the profit zone. (Book V Chapter 1 explains the *break-even point*, which is the level of sales needed to cover fixed costs for the period.)

Note: The distinction between variable and fixed costs is at the heart of understanding, analyzing, and budgeting profit, explained in Book V Chapters 1 and 2.

Relevant versus irrelevant costs

Not every cost is important to every decision a manager needs to make; hence, the distinction between relevant and irrelevant costs:

- **Relevant costs:** Costs that should be considered and included in your analysis when deciding on a future course of action. Relevant costs are *future* costs — costs that you would incur, or bring upon yourself, depending on which course of action you take. For example, say that you want to increase the number of books that your business produces next year in order to increase your sales revenue, but the cost of paper has just shot up. Should you take the cost of paper into consideration? Absolutely — that cost will affect your bottom-line profit and may negate any increase in sales volume that you experience (unless you increase the sales price). The cost of paper is a relevant cost.

- **Irrelevant (or sunk) costs:** Costs that should be disregarded when deciding on a future course of action; if brought into the analysis, these costs could cause you to make the wrong decision. An irrelevant cost is a vestige of the past — that money is gone. For this reason, irrelevant costs are also called *sunk costs*. For example, suppose that your supervisor tells you to expect a slew of new hires next week. All your staff members use computers now, but you have a bunch of typewriters gathering dust in the supply room. Should you consider the cost paid for those typewriters in your decision to buy computers for all the new hires? Absolutely not — that cost should have been written off and is no match for the cost you'd pay in productivity (and morale) for new employees who are forced to use typewriters.

Generally speaking, most variable costs are relevant because they depend on which alternative is selected. Fixed costs are irrelevant assuming that the decision at hand does not involve doing anything that would change these stationary costs. However, a decision alternative being considered might involve a change in fixed costs, such as moving out of the present building used by the business, downsizing the number of employees on fixed salaries, spending less on advertising (generally a fixed cost), and so on. Any cost, fixed or variable that would be different for a particular course of action being analyzed is relevant for that alternative.

Furthermore, keep in mind that fixed costs can provide a useful gauge of a business's *capacity* — how much building space it has, how many machine-hours are available for use, how many hours of labor can be worked, and so on. Managers have to figure out the best way to utilize these capacities. For example, suppose your retail business pays an annual building rent of $200,000, which is a fixed cost (unless the rental contract with the landlord also has a rent escalation clause based on your sales revenue). The rent, which gives the business the legal right to occupy the building, provides 15,000 square feet of retail and storage space. You should figure out which sales mix of products will generate the highest total *margin* — equal to total sales revenue less total variable costs of making the sales, including the costs of the goods sold and all variable costs driven by sales revenue and sales volume.

Actual, budgeted, and standard costs

The actual costs a business incurs may differ (though we hope not too unfavorably) from its budgeted and standard costs:

- ✔ **Actual costs:** Costs based on actual transactions and operations during the period just ended, or going back to earlier periods. Financial statement accounting is mainly (though not entirely) based on a business's actual transactions and operations; the basic approach to determining annual profit is to record the financial effects of actual transactions and allocate the historical costs to the periods benefited by the costs. But keep in mind that accountants can use more than one method for recording actual costs. Your actual cost may be a little (or a lot) different than my actual cost. For instance, a business selling products can chose to use the First-in, First-out method (FIFO), or the Last-in, First-out method (LIFO). The resulting numbers for cost of goods sold expense and inventory cost can be quite different.

- ✔ **Budgeted costs:** Future costs, for transactions and operations expected to take place over the coming period, based on forecasts and established goals. Fixed costs are budgeted differently than variable costs. For example, if sales volume is forecast to increase by 10 percent, variable costs will definitely increase accordingly, but fixed costs may or may not need to be increased to accommodate the volume increase. Book V Chapter 2 explains the budgeting process and budgeted financial statements.

- ✔ **Standard costs:** Costs, primarily in the area of manufacturing, that are carefully engineered based on detailed analysis of operations and forecast costs for each component or step in an operation. Developing standard costs for variable production costs is relatively straightforward because most are direct costs. In contrast, most fixed costs are indirect, and standard costs for fixed costs are necessarily based on more arbitrary methods (see "Direct versus indirect costs," earlier in this chapter). *Note:* Some variable costs are indirect and have to be allocated to specific products in order to come up with a full (total) standard cost of the product.

Product versus period costs

Some costs are linked to particular products, and others are not:

- **Product costs:** Costs attached directly or allocated to particular products. The cost is recorded in the inventory asset account and stays in that asset account until the product is sold, at which time the cost goes into the cost of goods sold expense account. (See Book II Chapter 2 for more about these accounts; also, see Book II Chapter 8 for alternative methods for selecting which product costs are first charged to the cost of goods sold expense.)

   For example, the cost of a new Ford Taurus sitting on a car dealer's showroom floor is a product cost. The dealer keeps the cost in the inventory asset account until you buy the car, at which point the dealer charges the cost to the cost of goods sold expense.

- **Period costs:** Costs that are *not* attached to particular products. These costs do not spend time in the "waiting room" of inventory. Period costs are recorded as expenses immediately; unlike product costs, period costs don't pass through the inventory account first. Advertising costs, for example, are accounted for as period costs and recorded immediately in an expense account. Also, research and development costs are treated as period costs (with some exceptions).

Separating product costs and period costs is particularly important for manufacturing businesses, as shown in the following section.

Assembling the Product Cost of Manufacturers

Businesses that manufacture products have several cost problems to deal with that retailers and distributors don't have. The term *manufacture* is being used here in the broadest sense: Automobile makers assemble cars, beer companies brew beer, automobile gasoline companies refine oil, DuPont makes products through chemical synthesis, and so on. Retailers (also called *merchandisers*) and distributors, on the other hand, buy products in a condition ready for resale to the end consumer. For example, Levi Strauss manufactures clothing, and several retailers buy from Levi Strauss and sell the clothes to the public. The following sections describe costs unique to manufacturers.

Minding manufacturing costs

Manufacturing costs consist of four basic types:

- **Raw materials (also called *direct* materials):** What a manufacturer buys from other companies to use in the production of its own products. For example, General Motors buys tires from Goodyear (or other tire manufacturers) that then become part of GM's cars.

- **Direct labor:** Those employees who work on the production line.

- **Variable overhead:** Indirect production costs that increase or decrease as the quantity produced increases or decreases. An example is the cost of electricity that runs the production equipment: Generally you pay for the electricity for the whole plant, not machine by machine, so you can't attach this cost to one particular part of the process. When you increase or decrease the use of those machines, the electricity cost increases or decreases accordingly. (In contrast, the monthly utility bill for a company's office and sales space probably is fixed for all practical purposes.)

- **Fixed overhead:** Indirect production costs that do *not* increase or decrease as the quantity produced increases or decreases. These fixed costs remain the same over a fairly broad range of production output levels (see "Fixed versus variable costs," earlier in this chapter). Three significant examples of fixed manufacturing costs are:

  - Salaries for certain production employees who don't work directly on the production line, such as vice presidents, safety inspectors, security guards, accountants, and shipping and receiving workers.

  - Depreciation of production buildings, equipment, and other manufacturing fixed assets.

  - Occupancy costs, such as building insurance, property taxes, and heating and lighting charges.

Figure 3-1 presents an example for a manufacturer, including the top part of its annual income statement (down to the gross margin line), annual sales volume (generally not disclosed in external financial reports), the summary of manufacturing costs and production output for the year, and the cost components making up the $760 product cost, which equals the total manufacturing costs *per unit*. A business may manufacture 100 or 1,000 different products, or even more, and it must compile a summary of manufacturing costs and production output and determine the product cost of every product. To keep the example easy to follow (but still realistic), Figure 3-1 presents a scenario for a one-product manufacturer. The multiproduct manufacturer has additional accounting problems (not discussed here). This example exposes the fundamental accounting problems and methods of all manufacturers.

In Figure 3-1, notice in particular that the company's cost of goods sold expense is based on the $760 product cost (or total manufacturing costs per unit). This product cost is determined from the company's manufacturing costs and production output for the period. Product cost includes both the variable costs of manufacture and a calculated amount based on total fixed manufacturing costs for the period divided by total production output for the period.

Income Statement For Year (to Gross Margin Line)

Sales Volume   110,000   Units

	Per Unit	Totals
Sales Revenue	$1,400	$154,000,000
Cost of Goods Sold Expense	($760)	($83,600,000)
Gross Margin	$640	$70,400,000

Manufacturing Costs Summary For Year

Production Capacity   150,000   Units
Actual Output   120,000   Units

Production Cost Components	Per Unit	Totals
Raw Materials	$215	$25,800,000
Direct Labor	$125	$15,000,000
Variable Manufacturing Overhead Costs	$70	$8,400,000
Total Variable Manufacturing Costs	$410	$49,200,000
Fixed Manufacturing Overhead Costs	$350	$42,000,000
Total Manufacturing Costs	$760	$91,200,000
To 10,000 Units Inventory Increase		($7,600,000)
To 110,000 Units Sold (see above)		$83,600,000

Figure 3-1: Manufacturing costs example.

The information in the manufacturing costs summary is highly confidential and for management eyes only. Competitors would love to know this information. A company may enjoy a significant cost advantage over its competitors and definitely does not want its cost data to get into their hands.

Classifying costs properly

Two vexing issues rear their ugly heads in determining product cost for a manufacturer:

✔ **Drawing a bright line between manufacturing costs and non-manufacturing operating costs:** The key difference here is that manufacturing costs are categorized as product costs, whereas non-manufacturing operating costs are categorized as period costs (refer to "Product versus period costs," earlier in this chapter). In calculating product costs, you include only manufacturing costs and not other costs. Remember that period costs are recorded right away as expenses. Here are some examples of each type of cost:

- Wages paid to production line workers are a clear-cut example of a manufacturing cost.

- Salaries paid to salespeople are a marketing cost and are not part of product cost; marketing costs are treated as period costs, which means they are recorded immediately to expense of the period.

- Depreciation on production equipment is a manufacturing cost, but depreciation on the warehouse in which products are stored after being manufactured is a period cost.

- Moving the raw materials and partially completed products through the production process is a manufacturing cost, but transporting the finished products from the warehouse to customers is a period cost.

The accumulation of direct and indirect production costs starts at the beginning of the manufacturing process and stops at the end of the production line. In other words, product cost stops at the end of the production line — every cost up to that point should be included as a manufacturing cost.

If you misclassify some manufacturing costs as operating costs (non-manufacturing expenses), your product cost calculation will be too low (see the following section, "Calculating product cost"). Also, the Internal Revenue Service may come knocking at your door if it suspects that you deliberately (or even innocently) misclassified manufacturing costs as non-manufacturing costs in order to minimize your taxable income.

The IRS has its own ideas regarding production versus period costs that may not match the financial statements. These rules are found in IRC §263A and apply to businesses with sales over $10,000,000.

✔ **Allocating indirect costs among different products:** Indirect manufacturing costs must be allocated among the products produced during the period. The full product cost includes both direct and indirect manufacturing costs. Creating a completely satisfactory allocation method is difficult; the process ends up being somewhat arbitrary, but it must be done to determine product cost. Managers should understand how indirect manufacturing costs are allocated among products (and, for that matter, how indirect non-manufacturing costs are allocated among organizational units and profit centers). Managers should also keep in mind that every allocation method is arbitrary and that a different allocation method may be just as convincing. (See the sidebar "Allocating indirect costs is as simple as ABC — not!")

Allocating indirect costs is as simple as ABC — not!

Accountants for manufacturers have developed many methods for allocating indirect overhead costs, most of which are based on a common denominator of production activity, such as direct labor hours or machine hours. A different method has received a lot of press recently: *activity-based costing* (ABC).

With the ABC method, you identify each supporting activity in the production process and collect costs into a separate pool for each identified activity. Then you develop a *measure* for each activity — for example, the measure for the engineering department may be hours, and the measure for the maintenance department may be square feet. You use the activity measures as *cost drivers* to allocate costs to products.

The idea is that the engineering department doesn't come cheap; including the cost of their slide rules and pocket protectors, as well as their salaries and benefits, the total cost per

hour for those engineers could be $200 or more. The logic of the ABC cost-allocation method is that the engineering cost per hour should be allocated on the basis of the number of hours (the immediate cause, or driver of the cost) that is required by each product. So if Product A needs 200 hours of the engineering department's time and Product B is a simple product that needs only 20 hours of engineering, you allocate ten times as much of the engineering cost to Product A. In similar fashion, suppose the cost of the maintenance department is $20 per square foot per year. If Product C uses twice as much floor space as Product D, it would be charged with twice as much maintenance cost.

The ABC method has received much praise for being better than traditional allocation methods, especially for management decision-making. But keep in mind that this method still requires rather arbitrary definitions of cost drivers, and having too many different cost drivers, each with its own pool of costs, is not practical.

Cost allocation always involves arbitrary methods. Managers should be aware of which methods are being used and should challenge a method if they think that it's misleading and should be replaced with a better (though still somewhat arbitrary) method. Cost allocation essentially boils down to a "my arbitrary method is better than your arbitrary method" argument.

Calculating product cost

The basic equation for calculating product cost is as follows (using the example of the manufacturer in Figure 3-1):

$91,200,000 total manufacturing costs ÷ 120,000 units production output = $760 product cost per unit

Looks pretty straightforward, doesn't it? Well, the equation itself may be simple, but the accuracy of the results depends directly on the accuracy of your manufacturing cost numbers. The business example in this chapter manufactures just one product. Even so, a single manufacturing process can be fairly complex, with hundreds or even thousands of steps and operations. In the real world, where businesses produce multiple products, your accounting systems must be very complex and extraordinarily detailed to keep accurate track of all direct and indirect (allocated) manufacturing costs.

In the example, the business manufactured 120,000 units and sold 110,000 units during the year, and its product cost per unit is $760. The 110,000 total units sold during the year is multiplied by the $760 product cost to compute the $83.6 million cost of goods sold expense, which is deducted against the company's revenue from selling 110,000 units during the year. The company's total manufacturing costs for the year were $91.2 million, which is $7.6 million more than the cost of goods sold expense. The remainder of the total annual manufacturing costs is recorded as an increase in the company's inventory asset account, to recognize that 10,000 units manufactured this year are awaiting sale in the future. In Figure 3-1, note that the $760 product cost per unit is applied both to the 110,000 units sold and to the 10,000 units added to inventory.

Note: The product cost per unit for the example business is determined for the entire year. In actual practice, manufacturers calculate their product costs monthly or quarterly. The computation process is the same, but the frequency of doing the computation varies from business to business. Product costs likely will vary each successive period the costs are determined. Because the product costs vary from period to period, the business must choose which cost of goods sold and inventory cost method to use. (If product cost happened to remain absolutely flat and constant period to period, the different methods would yield the same results.) Book II Chapter 8 explains the alternative accounting methods for determining cost of goods sold expense and inventory cost value.

Examining fixed manufacturing costs and production capacity

Product cost consists of two distinct components: *variable* manufacturing costs and *fixed* manufacturing costs. In Figure 3-1, note that the company's variable manufacturing costs are $410 per unit and its fixed manufacturing costs are $350 per unit. Now, what if the business had manufactured ten more units? Its total variable manufacturing costs would have been $4,100 higher. The actual number of units produced drives variable costs, so even one more unit would have caused the variable costs to increase. But the company's total fixed costs would have been the same if it had produced ten more units, or 10,000 more units for that matter. Variable manufacturing costs are bought on a per-unit basis, as it were, whereas fixed manufacturing costs are bought in bulk for the whole period.

Fixed manufacturing costs are needed to provide *production capacity* — the people and physical resources needed to manufacture products — for the period. After the business has the production plant and people in place for the year, its fixed manufacturing costs cannot be easily scaled down. The business is stuck with these costs over the short run. It has to make the best use it can from its production capacity.

Production capacity is a critical concept for business managers to stay focused on. You need to plan your production capacity well ahead of time because you need plenty of lead-time to assemble the right people, equipment, land, and buildings. When you have the necessary production capacity in place, you want to make sure that you're making optimal use of that capacity. The fixed costs of production capacity remain the same even as production output increases or decreases, so you may as well make optimal use of the capacity provided by those fixed costs. For example, you're recording the same depreciation amount on your machinery regardless of how you actually use those machines, so you should be sure to optimize the use of those machines (within limits, of course — overworking the machines to the point where they break down won't do you much good).

The burden rate

The fixed cost component of product cost is called the *burden rate*. In our manufacturing example, the burden rate is computed as follows (see Figure 3-1 for data):

$42,000,000 fixed manufacturing costs for period ÷ 120,000 units production output for period = $350 burden rate

Note that the burden rate depends on the number divided into total fixed manufacturing costs for the period — that is, the production output for the period.

Now, here's an important twist on the example: Suppose the company had manufactured only 110,000 units during the period — equal exactly to the quantity sold during the year. Its variable manufacturing cost per unit would have been the same, or $410 per unit. But its burden rate would have been $381.82 per unit (computed by dividing the $42 million total fixed manufacturing costs by the 110,000 units production output). Each unit sold, therefore, would have cost $31.82 more than in the Figure 3-1 example simply because the company produced fewer units. It would have fewer units of output over which to spread its fixed manufacturing costs. The burden rate is $381.82 at the 110,000 output level, but only $350 at the 120,000 output level, or $31.82 higher.

If only 110,000 units were produced, the company's product cost would have been $791.82 ($410 variable costs, plus the $381.82 burden rate). The company's cost of goods sold, therefore, would have been $3.5 million higher for the year ($31.82 higher product cost × 110,000 units sold). This rather significant increase in its cost of goods sold expense is caused by the company producing fewer units, even though it produced all the units that it needed for sales during the year. The same total amount of fixed manufacturing costs is spread over fewer units of production output.

Idle capacity

The production capacity of the business example in Figure 3-1 is 150,000 units for the year. However, this business produced only 120,000 units during the year, which is 30,000 units fewer than it could have. In other words, it operated at 80 percent of production capacity, which results in 20 percent *idle capacity*:

120,000 units output ÷ 150,000 units capacity = 80% utilization, or 20% idle capacity

This rate of idle capacity isn't unusual — the average U.S. manufacturing plant normally operates at 80 to 85 percent of its production capacity.

The actual costs/actual output method and when not to use it

The product cost calculation for the business example shown in Figure 3-1 is based on the *actual cost/actual output method,* in which you take your actual costs — which may have been higher or lower than the budgeted costs for the year — and divide by the actual output for the year.

The actual costs/actual output method is appropriate in most situations. However, this method is not appropriate and would have to be modified in two extreme situations:

✔ **Manufacturing costs are grossly excessive or wasteful due to inefficient production operations:** For example, suppose that the business represented in Figure 3-1 had to throw away $1.2 million of raw materials during the year. The $1.2 million should be removed from the calculation of the raw material cost per unit. Instead, you treat it as a period cost — meaning that you record it directly into expense.

Then the cost of goods sold expense would be based on $750 per unit instead of $760, which lowers this expense by $1.1 million (based on the 110,000 units sold). But you still have to record the $1.2 million expense for wasted raw materials, so EBIT would be $100,000 lower.

✔ **Production output is significantly less than normal capacity utilization:** Suppose that the Figure 3-1 business produced only 75,000 units during the year but still sold 110,000 units because it was working off a large inventory carryover from the year before. Then its production output would be 50 percent instead of 80 percent of capacity. In a sense, the business wasted half of its production capacity, and you can argue that half of its fixed manufacturing costs should be charged directly to expense on the income statement and not included in the calculation of product cost.

The effects of increasing inventory

Looking back at the numbers shown in Figure 3-1, the company's cost of goods sold benefited from the fact that it produced 10,000 more units than it sold during the year. These 10,000 units absorbed $3.5 million of its total fixed manufacturing costs for the year, and until the units are sold this $3.5 million stays in the inventory asset account (along with the variable manufacturing costs, of course). It's entirely possible that the higher production level was justified — to have more units on hand for sales growth next year. But production output can get out of hand, as discussed in the following section, "Puffing Profit by Excessive Production."

Managers (and investors as well) should understand the inventory increase effects caused by manufacturing more units than are sold during the year. In the example shown in Figure 3-1, the cost of goods sold expense escaped $3.5 million of fixed manufacturing costs because the company produced

10,000 more units than it sold during the year, thus pushing down the burden rate. The company's cost of goods sold expense would have been $3.5 million higher if it had produced just the number of units it sold during the year. The lower output level would have increased cost of goods sold expense and would have caused a $3.5 million drop in gross margin.

Puffing Profit by Excessive Production

Whenever production output is higher than sales volume, be on guard. Excessive production can puff up the profit figure. How? Until a product is sold, the product cost goes in the inventory asset account rather than in the cost of goods sold expense account, meaning that the product cost is counted as a *positive* number (an asset) rather than a *negative* number (an expense). Fixed manufacturing overhead cost is included in product cost, which means that this cost component goes into inventory and is held there until the products are sold later. In short, when you overproduce, more of your total of fixed manufacturing costs for the period is moved to the inventory asset account and less is moved into cost of goods sold expense for the year.

You need to judge whether an inventory increase is justified. Be aware that an unjustified increase may be evidence of profit manipulation or just good old-fashioned management bungling. Either way, the day of reckoning will come when the products are sold and the cost of inventory becomes cost of goods sold expense — at which point the cost impacts the bottom line.

Shifting fixed manufacturing costs to the future

The business represented in Figure 3-1 manufactured 10,000 more units than it sold during the year. With variable manufacturing costs at $410 per unit, the business expended $4.1 million more in variable manufacturing costs than it would have if it had produced only the 110,000 units needed for its sales volume. In other words, if the business had produced 10,000 fewer units, its variable manufacturing costs would have been $4.1 million less — that's the nature of variable costs. In contrast, if the company had manufactured 10,000 fewer units, its *fixed* manufacturing costs would not have been any less — that's the nature of fixed costs.

Of its $42 million total fixed manufacturing costs for the year, only $38.5 million ended up in the cost of goods sold expense for the year ($350 burden rate × 110,000 units sold). The other $3.5 million ended up in the inventory asset account ($350 burden rate × 10,000 units inventory increase). The $3.5 million of fixed manufacturing costs that are absorbed by inventory is shifted to the future. This amount will not be expensed (charged to cost of goods sold expense) until the products are sold sometime in the future.

Shifting part of the fixed manufacturing cost for the year to the future may seem to be accounting slight of hand. It has been argued that the entire amount of fixed manufacturing costs should be expensed in the year that these costs are recorded. (Only variable manufacturing costs would be included in product cost for units going into the increase in inventory.) Established accounting standards require that *full* product cost (variable plus fixed manufacturing costs) be used for recording an increase in inventory. This is referred to as *absorption accounting* because fixed manufacturing costs are absorbed, or included in product cost.

In the example shown in Figure 3-1, the 10,000 units increase of inventory includes $3,500,000 of the company's total fixed manufacturing costs for the year:

$350 burden rate × 10,000 units inventory increase = $3,500,000 fixed manufacturing costs included in inventory increase

Are you comfortable with this effect? The $3,500,000 escapes being charged to cost of goods expense for the time being. It sits in inventory until the products are sold in a later period. This results from using the full cost (absorption) accounting method for fixed manufacturing overhead costs. Now, it may occur to you that an unscrupulous manager could take advantage of this effect to manipulate gross profit for the period.

There's (probably) no hanky-panky in the example shown in Figure 3-1. Producing 10,000 more units than sales volume during the year looks — on the face of it — to be reasonable and not out of the ordinary. Yet at the same time, it is naïve to ignore that the business did help its pretax profit to the amount of $3.5 million by producing 10,000 more units than it sold. If the business had produced only 110,000 units, equal to its sales volume for the year, all its fixed manufacturing costs for the year would have gone into cost of goods sold expense. The expense would have been $3.5 million higher, and operating earnings would have been that much lower.

Cranking up production output

Now consider a more suspicious example. Suppose that the business manufactured 150,000 units during the year and increased its inventory by 40,000 units. It may be a legitimate move if the business is anticipating a big jump in sales next year. On the other hand, an inventory increase of 40,000 units in a year in which only 110,000 units were sold may be the result of a serious over-production mistake, and the larger inventory may not be needed next year.

Figure 3-2 shows what happens to production costs and — more importantly — to the profit at the higher production output level. The additional 30,000 units (over and above the 120,000 units manufactured by the business in the original example) cost $410 per unit. (The precise cost may be a little higher than $410 per unit because as you start crowding production capacity, some variable costs per unit may increase a little.) The business would need $12.3 million more for the additional 30,000 units of production output:

> $410 variable manufacturing cost per unit × 30,000 additional units produced = $12,300,000 additional variable manufacturing costs invested in inventory

Income Statement For Year (to Gross Margin Line)

Sales Volume   110,000   Units

	Per Unit	Totals
Sales Revenue	$1,400	$154,000,000
Cost of Goods Sold Expense	($690)	($75,900,000)
Gross Margin	$710	$78,100,000

Manufacturing Costs Summary For Year

Production Capacity   150,000   Units
Actual Output   150,000   Units

Production Cost Components	Per Unit	Totals
Raw Materials	$215	$32,250,000
Direct Labor	$125	$18,750,000
Variable Manufacturing Overhead Costs	$70	$10,500,000
Total Variable Manufacturing Costs	$410	$61,500,000
Fixed Manufacturing Overhead Costs	$280	$42,000,000
Total Manufacturing Costs	$690	$103,500,000
To 40,000 Units Inventory Increase		($27,600,000)
To 110,000 Units Sold (see above)		$75,900,000

Figure 3-2: Example of when production output greatly exceeds sales volume.

© John Wiley & Sons

Again, its fixed manufacturing costs would not have increased, given the nature of fixed costs. Fixed costs stay put until capacity is hit. Sales volume, in this scenario, also remains the same.

But check out the business's gross margin in Figure 3-2: $78.1 million, compared with $70.4 million in Figure 3-1 — a $7.7 million higher amount, even though sales volume and sales prices remain the same. Whoa! What's going on here? How can cost of goods sold expense be less? The business sells 110,000 units in both scenarios. And variable manufacturing costs are $410 per unit in both cases.

The culprit is the burden rate component of product cost. In the original Figure 3-1 example, total fixed manufacturing costs are spread over 120,000 units of output, giving a $350 burden rate per unit. In the Figure 3-2 example, total fixed manufacturing costs are spread over 150,000 units of output, giving a much lower $280 burden rate, or $70 per unit less. The $70 lower burden rate multiplied by the 110,000 units sold results in a $7.7 million lower cost of goods sold expense for the period, a higher pretax profit of the same amount, and a much improved bottom-line net income.

Being careful when production output is out of kilter with sales volume

In the highly suspect example shown in Figure 3-2, the business produced 150,000 units (full capacity). As a result, its inventory asset includes an additional $7.7 million of the company's fixed manufacturing costs for the year as compared with the original example in Figure 3-1. Its cost of goods sold expense for the year escaped this cost (for the time being). But get this: Its inventory increased 40,000 units, which is quite a large increase compared with the annual sales of 110,000 during the year just ended. Who was responsible for the decision to go full blast and produce up to production capacity? Do the managers really expect sales to jump up enough next year to justify the much larger inventory level? If they prove to be right, they'll look brilliant. But if the output level was a mistake and sales do not go up next year . . . they'll have you-know-what to pay next year, even though profit looks good this year. An experienced business manager knows to be on guard when inventory takes such a big jump.

Summing up, the cost of goods sold expense of a manufacturer, and thus its operating profit, is sensitive to a difference between its sales volume and production output during the year. Manufacturing businesses do not generally discuss or explain in their external financial reports to creditors and owners why production output is different than sales volume for the year. Financial report readers are pretty much on their own in interpreting the reasons for and the effects of under- or over-producing products relative to actual sales volume for the year. Keep alert and keep in mind the profit impact caused by a major disparity between a manufacturer's production output and sale levels for the year.

Chapter 4

Filing and Paying Business Taxes

In This Chapter

▶ Sorting out business legal structures

▶ Filing sole proprietor taxes

▶ Reporting taxes on partnerships

▶ Filing taxes for corporations

▶ Reporting and paying sales taxes

*P*aying taxes and reporting income for your company are very important jobs, and how you complete these tasks properly depends on your business's legal structure. From sole proprietorships to corporations and everything in between, this chapter briefly reviews business types and explains how to handle taxes for each type. You also get some instruction on collecting and transmitting sales taxes on the products your company sells.

Finding the Right Business Type

Business type and tax preparation and reporting go hand in hand. If you work as a bookkeeper for a small business, you need to know the business's legal structure before you can proceed with reporting and paying income taxes on the business income. Not all businesses have the same legal structure, so they don't all pay income taxes on the profits they make in the same way.

But before you get into the subject of tax procedures, you need to understand the various business structures you may encounter as a bookkeeper. This section outlines each type of business. You can find out how these structures pay taxes in separate sections that follow later in the chapter. This is just a recap for purposes of tax discussion — Book II Chapter 3 covers these business structures in more detail.

Sole proprietorship

The simplest legal structure for a business is the *sole proprietorship,* a business that's owned by one individual. Most new businesses with only one owner start out as sole proprietorships. (If an unincorporated business has only one owner, the IRS automatically considers it a sole proprietorship.) Some never change their statuses, but others grow by adding partners and becoming partnerships. Some add lots of staff and want to protect themselves from lawsuits, so they become Limited Liability Companies (LLCs). Those seeking the greatest protection from individual lawsuits, whether they have employees or are simply single-owner companies without employees, become corporations.

Partnership

The IRS considers any unincorporated business owned by more than one person a *partnership.* The partnership is the most flexible type of business structure involving more than one owner. Each partner in the business is equally liable for the activities of the business. This structure is slightly more complicated than a sole proprietorship (see the preceding section), and partners should work out certain key issues before the business opens its doors, including the following:

- How the partners will divide the profits
- How each partner can sell his or her share of the business if he or she so chooses
- What will happen to each partner's share if a partner becomes sick or dies
- How the partnership will be dissolved if one of the partners wants out

Partners in a partnership don't always have to share equal risks. A partnership may have two different types of partners: general and limited. The general partner runs the day-to-day business and is held personally responsible for all activities of the business, no matter how much he or she has personally invested in the business. Limited partners, on the other hand, are passive owners of the business and not involved in its day-to-day operations. If a claim is filed against the business, the limited partners can only be held personally liable for the amount of money that matches how much they individually invested in the business.

Limited Liability Companies (LLCs)

The *Limited Liability Company,* or LLC, is a structure that provides owners of partnerships and sole proprietorships with some protection from being held personally liable for their businesses' activities. This business structure is somewhere between a sole proprietorship or partnership and a corporation: The business ownership and IRS tax rules are similar to those of a sole proprietorship or partnership, but like a corporation, if the business is sued, the owners aren't held personally liable.

LLCs are state entities, so the level of legal protection given to a company's owners depends on the rules of the state in which the LLC was formed. Most states give LLC owners the same protection from lawsuits as the federal government gives corporation owners. However, these LLC protections haven't been tested in court to date, so no one knows for certain whether they will hold up in the courtroom. (For more on the LLC, see the sidebar "Growth of the LLC.")

Corporations

If your business faces a great risk of being sued, the safest business structure for you is the *corporation.* Courts in the United States have clearly determined that a corporation is a separate legal entity and that its owners' personal assets are protected from claims against the corporation. Essentially, an owner or shareholder in a corporation can't be sued or face collections because of actions taken by the corporation. This veil of protection is the reason many small business owners choose to incorporate even though it involves a lot of expense (both for lawyers and accountants) and government paperwork.

Growth of the LLC

LLCs are relatively new to the world of business structures. They didn't become popular until the mid-1990s, when most states approved the LLC as a business structure.

Many law firms and accounting firms are set up as LLCs. More and more small business owners are choosing this structure rather than a corporation because the LLC's easier and cheaper to maintain (as in a lot less government paperwork plus less legal and accounting fees), yet it still provides personal protection from legal entanglements.

For more information on LLCs, check out *Limited Liability Companies For Dummies,* 2nd Edition, by Jennifer Reuting (John Wiley & Sons, 2014).

In a corporation, each share of stock represents a portion of ownership, and profits must be split based on stock ownership. You don't have to sell stock on the public stock markets in order to be a corporation, though. In fact, most corporations are private entities that sell their stock privately among friends and investors.

If you're a small business owner who wants to incorporate, first you must form a *board of directors* (see the sidebar "Roles and responsibilities of the corporate board"). Boards can be made up of owners of the company as well as nonowners. You can even have your spouse and children on the board — those board meetings would undoubtedly be interesting.

Tackling Tax Reporting for Sole Proprietors

The federal government doesn't consider sole proprietorships to be individual legal entities, so they're not taxed as such. Instead, sole proprietors report any business earnings on their individual tax returns — that's the only financial reporting they must do.

Most sole proprietors file their business tax obligations as part of their individual 1040 tax return by using the additional two-page form Schedule C, Profit or Loss from Business. You can download the latest version of Schedule C at www.irs.gov/pub/irs-pdf/f1040sc.pdf.

Sole proprietors must also pay the so-called *self-employment tax* — which means paying both the employee and the employer sides of Social Security and Medicare. That's a total of 15.3%, or *double* what an employee would normally pay, and it is a bummer for sole proprietors. Table 4-1 shows the drastic difference in these types of tax obligations for sole proprietors.

Table 4-1	Comparison of Tax Obligations for Sole Proprietors	
Type of Tax	*Amount Taken from Employees*	*Amount Paid by Sole Proprietors*
Social Security	6.2%	12.4%
Medicare	1.45%	2.9%

Social Security and Medicare taxes are based on the net profit of the small business, not the gross profit, which means that you calculate the tax after you've subtracted all costs and expenses from your revenue. To help you figure out the tax amounts you owe on behalf of your business, use IRS form Schedule SE, Self-Employment Tax. On the first page of this form, you report your income sources and on the second page, you calculate the tax due. You can find a copy of Schedule SE included with this book or download the most current version at www.irs.gov/pub/irs-pdf/f1040sse.pdf.

As the bookkeeper for a sole proprietor, you're probably responsible for pulling together the Income, Cost of Goods Sold, and Expense information needed for this form. In most cases, you then hand off this information to the business's accountant to fill out all the required forms.

As a sole proprietor, you can choose to file as a corporation even if you aren't legally incorporated. You may want to do so because corporations have more allowable deductions and you can pay yourself a salary, but it requires a lot of extra paperwork, and your accountant's fees will be much higher if you decide to file as a corporation. However, because corporations pay taxes on the separate legal entity, this option may not make sense for your business. Talk with your accountant to determine the best tax structure for your business.

If you do decide to report your business income as a separate corporate entity, you must file Form 8832, Entity Classification Election with the IRS. This form reclassifies the business, a step that's necessary because the IRS automatically classifies a business owned by one person as a sole proprietorship. You can download the most current version of the form at www.irs.gov/pub/irs-pdf/f8832.pdf.

Filing Tax Forms for Partnerships

If your unincorporated business is structured as a partnership (meaning it has more than one owner), it doesn't pay taxes. Instead, all money earned by the business is split up among the partners.

As a bookkeeper for a partnership, you need to collect the data necessary to file an information schedule called Schedule K-1 (Form 1065), Partner's Share of Income, Deductions, Credits, etc. for each partner. The company's accountant will most likely complete the Schedule K-1 forms. The entire information filing for the company is called Form 1065, U.S. Return of Partnership Income, which you can find online at www.irs.gov/pub/irs-pdf/f1065.pdf.

Any partner receiving a Schedule K-1 must report the recorded income on his or her personal tax return — Form 1040 — by adding an additional form called Schedule E, Supplemental Income and Loss. (Schedule E is used to report income from more than just partnership arrangements; it also has sections for real estate rental and royalties, estates and trusts, and mortgage investments.) You can find the most current version of this form online at www.irs.gov/pub/irs-pdf/f1040se.pdf.

Unless you're involved in a real estate rental business, you most likely only need to fill out page 2 of Schedule E. Pay particular attention to Part II, Income or Loss From Partnerships and S Corporations. In this section, you report your income or loss as passive or nonpassive income, a distinction that your accountant can help you sort out.

Paying Corporate Taxes

Corporations come in two varieties, S corporations and C corporations; as you may expect, each has unique tax requirements and practices. In fact, not all corporations even file tax returns. Some smaller corporations are designated as S corporations and pass their earnings on to their stockholders.

Check with your accountant to determine whether incorporating your business makes sense for you. Tax savings isn't the only issue you have to think about; operating a corporation also increases administrative, legal, and accounting costs. Be sure that you understand all the costs before incorporating.

Reporting for an S corporation

An *S corporation* must have fewer than 100 stockholders. It functions like a partnership but gives owners more legal protection from lawsuits than traditional partnerships do. Essentially, an S corporation is treated as a partnership for tax purposes, but its tax forms are a bit more complicated than a partnership's: All income and losses are passed on to the owners of the S corporation and reported on each owner's tax return, and owners also report their income and expenses on Schedule E (see the earlier section "Filing Tax Forms for Partnerships" for more on this form).

Reporting for a C corporation

The type of corporation that's considered a separate legal entity for tax purposes is the *C corporation*. A C corporation is a legal entity that has been formed specifically for the purpose of running a business.

The biggest disadvantage of structuring your company as a C corporation is that your profits are taxed twice — as a corporate entity and again on dividends paid to stockholders. If you're the owner of a C corporation, you can be taxed twice, but you can also pay yourself a salary and therefore reduce the earnings of the corporation. Corporate taxation is very complicated, with lots of forms to be filled out, so there's not enough room here to go into great detail here about how to file corporate taxes. However, Table 4-2 shows you the tax rates C corporations are subject to.

Table 4-2	C Corporation Tax Rates
Taxable Income	*C Corporation Tax Rate*
$0–$50,000	15%
$50,001–$75,000	25%
$75,001–$100,000	34%
$100,001–$335,000	39%
$335,001–$10,000,000	34%
$10,000,001–$15,000,000	35%
$15,000,001–$18,333,333	38%
Over $18,333,333	35%

You may think that C corporation tax rates look a lot higher than personal tax rates, but in reality, many corporations *don't pay any tax at all* — or pay taxes at much lower rates than you do. As a corporation, you have plenty of deductions and tax loopholes to use to reduce your tax bites. So even though you, the business owner, may be taxed twice on the small part of your income that's paid in dividends, you're more likely to pay less taxes overall.

Taking Care of Sales Taxes Obligations

Even more complicated than paying income taxes is keeping up-to-date on local and state tax rates and paying your business's share of those taxes to the government entities. Because tax rates vary from county to county, and even city to city in some states, managing sales taxes can be very time-consuming.

Things get messy when you sell products in multiple locations. For each location, you must collect from customers the appropriate tax for that area, keep track of all taxes collected, and pay those taxes to the appropriate government entities when due. In many states, you have to collect and pay local (for the city or county governments) and state taxes.

An excellent website for data about state and local tax requirements is the Tax and Accounting Sites Directory at www.taxsites.com/state.html. This site has links for state and local tax information for every state.

States require you to file an application to collect and report taxes even before you start doing business in that state. Be sure that you contact the departments of revenue in the states you plan to operate stores before you start selling and collecting sales tax.

All sales taxes collected from your customers are paid when you send in the Sales and Use Tax Return for your state — you must have the cash available to pay this tax when the forms are due. Any money you collected from customers during the month should be kept in an account called Accrued Sales Taxes, which is actually a Liability account on your balance sheet because it's money owed to a governmental entity.

Chapter 5

Prepping the Books for a New Accounting Cycle

*I*n bookkeeping, an *accounting period* or *cycle* can be one month, a quarter, or a year (or any other division of time that makes business sense). At the end of every accounting period, certain accounts need to be closed, while others remain open.

Just as adding accounts to your bookkeeping system at the beginning of a year is best (so you don't have to move information from one account to another), waiting until the end of the year to delete any accounts you no longer need is also a smart idea. With this approach, you start each year fresh with only the accounts you need to best manage your business's financial activities.

This chapter explains the accounts that must be closed and restarted with a zero balance in the next accounting cycle (see Book I Chapter 1 for more detail about the accounting cycle), such as Revenues and Costs of Goods Sold. It also reviews the accounts that continue from one accounting cycle to the next, such as Assets and Liabilities. In addition, it covers the process of closing the books at year-end and beginning a new accounting cycle for the next year.

Finalizing the General Ledger

After you complete your accounting work for the accounting cycle in which your business operates, you need to reexamine your General Ledger.

(Flip to Book I Chapter 3 for an introduction to the General Ledger.) Some accounts in the General Ledger need to be zeroed out so that they start the new accounting cycle with no detail from the previous cycle, whereas other accounts continue to accumulate detail from one cycle to the next. When you break down the General Ledger, the balance sheet accounts carry forward into the next accounting cycle, and the income statement accounts start with a zero balance.

Zeroing out income statement accounts

When you're sure that you've made all needed corrections and adjustments to your accounts and you have your cycle-end numbers, you can zero out all General Ledger accounts listed on the income statement — that's Revenues, Cost of Goods Sold, and Expenses. Because the income statement reflects the activities of an accounting period, these accounts always start with a zero balance at the beginning of an accounting cycle.

If you use a computerized accounting system, you may not actually have to zero out the income statement accounts. For example, QuickBooks adjusts your Income and Expenses accounts at cycle-end to zero them out so you start with a zero net income, but it maintains the data in an archive so you're always able to access it. You can set your closing date on the Company Preferences tab of the Preferences box (see Figure 5-1). To control who can make changes to prior year accounts, you should also set a password (see Figure 5-2) for editing closed accounts.

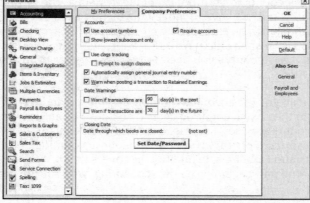

Figure 5-1:
Click on Date/ Password to set up the closing date in QuickBooks.

Image courtesy of Intuit

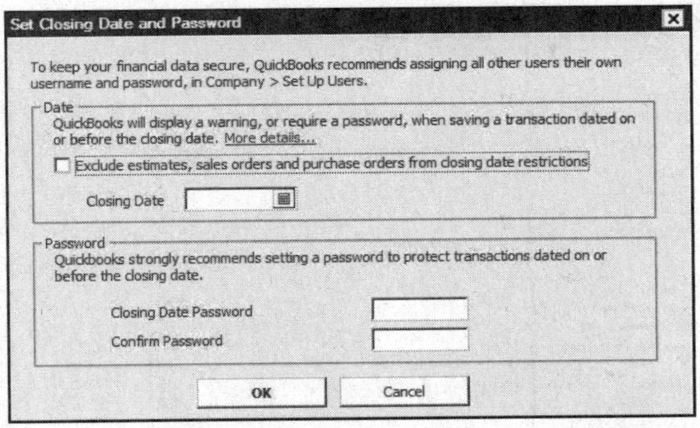

Figure 5-2: Set a password for controlling data in closed accounts.

> **Set Closing Date and Password** ☒
>
> To keep your financial data secure, QuickBooks recommends assigning all other users their own username and password, in Company > Set Up Users.
>
> ┌─ Date ──
> │ QuickBooks will display a warning, or require a password, when saving a transaction dated on
> │ or before the closing date. More details...
> │
> │ ☐ Exclude estimates, sales orders and purchase orders from closing date restrictions
> │
> │ Closing Date [   ] 🗒
> └──
>
> ┌─ Password ──
> │ Quickbooks strongly recommends setting a password to protect transactions dated on or
> │ before the closing date.
> │
> │ Closing Date Password   [   ]
> │ Confirm Password   [   ]
> └──
>
>   [OK   ]   [Cancel]

Image courtesy of Intuit

Carrying over balance sheet accounts

Unlike income statement accounts, you never zero out the accounts listed on a balance sheet — that's Assets, Liabilities, and Equity. Instead, you note your ending balances for each of these accounts so you can prepare a balance sheet, and you carry forward the data in the accounts into the next accounting period. The balance sheet just gives you a snapshot of the financial state of your company as of a particular date in time. From one accounting cycle to the next, your assets and (unfortunately) liabilities remain, and you also need to maintain the information about how much equity your investors have put into the company.

Conducting Special Year-End Bookkeeping Tasks

Before you start the process of closing the books for the year, print a summary of your account information from your computerized accounting system. If you make an error while closing the books, you can always use this printout to backtrack and fix any problems.

QuickBooks provides a Year-End Guide Checklist (see Figure 5-3) to help you keep track of all the year-end activities you need to do. The checklist also includes links to help screens that explain how to do all the year-end closing tasks. You can check off each task as you complete it and save the check marks to keep track of your progress during the closing process.

Figure 5-3:
Quick-
Books's
Year-End
Guide
Checklist
walks you
through
year-end
tasks.

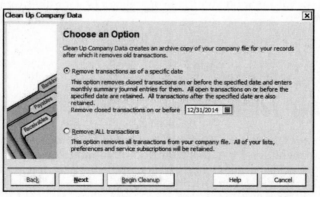

Image courtesy of Intuit

After you complete all your year-end tasks, you can condense and back
up all your accounting data for the year being closed. Most computerized
accounting systems have a process for condensing and archiving data.
For example, QuickBooks's Clean Up Company Data wizard guides you
through the process (see Figure 5-4).

Figure 5-4:
Quick-
Books's
Clean Up
Company
Data wizard
simplifies
condensing
and backing
up your
data.

Image courtesy of Intuit

Checking customer accounts

As you prepare your books for the end of an accounting cycle, review your
customer accounts. Unless it's the end of the year, you don't close the

Accounts Receivable account, and when you start a new accounting cycle, you certainly want to carry over any balance still due from customers.

Reviewing customer accounts for possible bad-debt expenses before closing your books at the end of the accounting cycle is a good idea. (Book III Chapter 2 talks about bad debt in greater detail.) Now is the time to be more critical of past-due accounts. You can use any bad debt to reduce your tax bite, so if you believe that a customer isn't likely to make good on a past-due account, write off the loss.

Assessing vendor accounts

The end of an accounting period is the perfect time to review your vendor accounts to be sure they're all paid in full and ready for the new cycle. Also, make sure you've entered into your vendor accounts any bills that reflect business activity in the period being closed; otherwise, expenses from the period may not show up in the appropriate year-end financial statements.

Review any outstanding purchase orders to be sure that your vendor accounts aren't missing orders that have been completed but not yet billed by the vendor. For example, if you received inventory on December 23 but the vendor won't bill for that inventory until January, you should record the bill in December to reflect the receipt of that inventory during that tax year.

Deleting accounts

The closing process at the end of an accounting year is a good time to assess all your open accounts and verify that you still need them. If an account has no transactions in it, you're free to delete it at any time. However, you should wait until the end of the year to delete any accounts that you don't think you'll need in the next year. If you're assessing accounts at the end of an accounting period that isn't also the end of the year, just make a list of the accounts to be deleted and wait for the year-end.

If you use a computerized accounting system, be aware that deleting an account deletes all past transactions in that account as well. So if you want to delete an account at the end of the year, you should mark the account as inactive instead so that you don't lose the information but new transactions can't be entered into the account inadvertently.

Starting the Cycle Anew

You certainly don't want to close the doors of your business as you prepare all your year-end reports, such as the financial statements and governmental reports — after all, that can be a two- to three-month process. So you need to continue making entries for the new year as you close the books for the previous year.

If you do the books manually, you probably need easy access to two sets of books: the current year and the previous year. In a manual bookkeeping system, you just start new journal pages for each of the active accounts. If you have some accounts that aren't very active, rather than start a new page, you can leave some space for adjustments or corrections, draw a line, and start the transactions for the new year on the same page.

If you keep your books by using a computerized accounting system, you can zero out the necessary accounts to start the new year while leaving the data for the previous year in the password-protected, closed accounts. You can still make changes to those closed accounts, but access is limited to people who know the password — most likely you, your accountant, and your book-keeping manager.

Part of closing out your books is starting new files for each of your accounts. Most businesses keep two years of data, the current year and the previous year, in the on-site office files and put older files into storage. As you start a new year, box up your two-year-old files for storage and use the newly empty drawers for the new year's new files. For example, suppose you're creating files for 2015. Keep the 2014 files easily accessible in file cabinet drawers in your office, but box up the 2013 files for storage. Then keep your 2014 files in the drawers where the 2013 files had been.

There's no hard and fast rule about file storage. You may find that you need to access some files regularly and therefore don't want to put them in storage. No problem. Pull out any files related to ongoing activity and keep them in the office so you don't have to run to the storage area every time you need the files. For example, if you have an ongoing legal case, you should keep any files related to that matter out of storage and easily accessible.

Index

• C •

• O •

• P •

• *R* •

Notes

Notes

Notes

Notes

Notes

Notes

Notes

About the Authors

Lita Epstein earned her MBA from Emory University's Goizueta Business School. She enjoys helping people develop good financial, investing, and tax planning skills.

While getting her MBA, Lita worked as a teaching assistant for the financial accounting department and ran the accounting lab. After completing her MBA, she managed finances for a small nonprofit organization and for the facilities management section of a large medical clinic.

She designs and teaches online courses on topics such as accounting and bookkeeping and starting your own business. She's written more than 35 books, including *Bookkeeping For Dummies, Reading Financial Reports for Dummies, Trading For Dummies, The Business Owner's Guide to Reading and Understanding Financial Statements,* and *Financial Decision Making.*

Lita was the content director for a financial services website MostChoice. com and managed the Web site Investing for Women. As a congressional press secretary, Lita gained firsthand knowledge about how to work within and around the federal bureaucracy, which gives her great insight into how government programs work. In the past, Lita has been a daily newspaper reporter, magazine editor, and fundraiser for the international activities of former President Jimmy Carter through The Carter Center.

John A. Tracy (Boulder, Colorado) is Professor of Accounting, Emeritus, at the University of Colorado in Boulder. Before his long tenure at Boulder, he was on the business faculty for four years at the University of California in Berkeley. Early in his career he was a staff accountant with Ernst & Young. John is the author of several books on accounting and finance, including *How To Read a Financial Report, The Fast Forward MBA in Finance*, and *Cash Flow For Dummies* and *Small Business Financial Management Kit For Dummies* with his son, Tage C. Tracy. John received his BSC degree from Creighton University. He earned his MBA and PhD degrees at the University of Wisconsin in Madison. He is a CPA (inactive status) in Colorado.

Publisher's Acknowledgments

Acquisitions Editor: Stacy Kennedy

Project Editor: Corbin Collins
                     Susan Hobbs

Copy Editor: Susan Hobbs

Technical Editor: Carla DeWitt

Art Coordinator: Alicia B. South

Production Editor: Kinson Raja

Project Manager: Jennifer Ehrlich

Cover Image: Getty Images/mark wragg

Apple & Mac

iPad For Dummies,
6th Edition
978-1-118-72306-7

iPhone For Dummies,
7th Edition
978-1-118-69083-3

Macs All-in-One
For Dummies, 4th Edition
978-1-118-82210-4

OS X Mavericks
For Dummies
978-1-118-69188-5

Blogging & Social Media

Facebook For Dummies,
5th Edition
978-1-118-63312-0

Social Media Engagement
For Dummies
978-1-118-53019-1

WordPress For Dummies,
6th Edition
978-1-118-79161-5

Business

Stock Investing
For Dummies, 4th Edition
978-1-118-37678-2

Investing For Dummies,
6th Edition
978-0-470-90545-6

Personal Finance

Personal Finance
For Dummies, 7th Edition
978-1-118-11785-9

QuickBooks 2014
For Dummies
978-1-118-72005-9

Small Business Marketing
Kit For Dummies,
3rd Edition
978-1-118-31183-7

Careers

Job Interviews
For Dummies, 4th Edition
978-1-118-11290-8

Job Searching with Social
Media For Dummies,
2nd Edition
978-1-118-67856-5

Personal Branding
For Dummies
978-1-118-11792-7

Resumes For Dummies,
6th Edition
978-0-470-87361-8

Starting an Etsy Business
For Dummies, 2nd Edition
978-1-118-59024-9

Diet & Nutrition

Belly Fat Diet For Dummies
978-1-118-34585-6

Mediterranean Diet

Mediterranean Diet
For Dummies
978-1-118-71525-3

Nutrition For Dummies,
5th Edition
978-0-470-93231-5

Digital Photography

Digital SLR Photography
All-in-One For Dummies,
2nd Edition
978-1-118-59082-9

Digital SLR Video &
Filmmaking For Dummies
978-1-118-36598-4

Photoshop Elements 12
For Dummies
978-1-118-72714-0

Gardening

Herb Gardening
For Dummies, 2nd Edition
978-0-470-61778-6

Gardening with Free-Range
Chickens For Dummies
978-1-118-54754-0

Health

Boosting Your Immunity
For Dummies
978-1-118-40200-9

Diabetes

Diabetes For Dummies,
4th Edition
978-1-118-29447-5

Living Paleo For Dummies
978-1-118-29405-5

Big Data

Big Data For Dummies
978-1-118-50422-2

Data Visualization
For Dummies
978-1-118-50289-1

Hadoop For Dummies
978-1-118-60755-8

Language &
Foreign Language

500 Spanish Verbs
For Dummies
978-1-118-02382-2

English Grammar
For Dummies, 2nd Edition
978-0-470-54664-2

French All-in-One
For Dummies
978-1-118-22815-9

German Essentials
For Dummies
978-1-118-18422-6

Italian For Dummies,
2nd Edition
978-1-118-00465-4

Available in print and e-book formats.

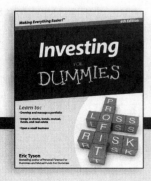

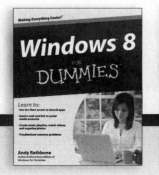

Available wherever books are sold. **For more information or to order direct visit www.dummies.com**

Math & Science

Algebra I For Dummies, 2nd Edition
978-0-470-55964-2

Anatomy and Physiology For Dummies, 2nd Edition
978-0-470-92326-9

Astronomy For Dummies, 3rd Edition
978-1-118-37697-3

Biology For Dummies, 2nd Edition
978-0-470-59875-7

Chemistry For Dummies, 2nd Edition
978-1-118-00730-3

1001 Algebra II Practice Problems For Dummies
978-1-118-44662-1

Microsoft Office

Excel 2013 For Dummies
978-1-118-51012-4

Office 2013 All-in-One For Dummies
978-1-118-51636-2

PowerPoint 2013 For Dummies
978-1-118-50253-2

Word 2013 For Dummies
978-1-118-49123-2

Music

Blues Harmonica For Dummies
978-1-118-25269-7

Guitar For Dummies, 3rd Edition
978-1-118-11554-1

iPod & iTunes For Dummies, 10th Edition
978-1-118-50864-0

Programming

Beginning Programming with C For Dummies
978-1-118-73763-7

Excel VBA Programming For Dummies, 3rd Edition
978-1-118-49037-2

Java For Dummies, 6th Edition
978-1-118-40780-6

Religion & Inspiration

The Bible For Dummies
978-0-7645-5296-0

Buddhism For Dummies, 2nd Edition
978-1-118-02379-2

Catholicism For Dummies, 2nd Edition
978-1-118-07778-8

Self-Help & Relationships

Beating Sugar Addiction For Dummies
978-1-118-54645-1

Meditation For Dummies, 3rd Edition
978-1-118-29144-3

Seniors

Laptops For Seniors For Dummies, 3rd Edition
978-1-118-71105-7

Computers For Seniors For Dummies, 3rd Edition
978-1-118-11553-4

iPad For Seniors For Dummies, 6th Edition
978-1-118-72826-0

Social Security For Dummies
978-1-118-20573-0

Smartphones & Tablets

Android Phones For Dummies, 2nd Edition
978-1-118-72030-1

Nexus Tablets For Dummies
978-1-118-77243-0

Samsung Galaxy S 4 For Dummies
978-1-118-64222-1

Samsung Galaxy Tabs For Dummies
978-1-118-77294-2

Test Prep

ACT For Dummies, 5th Edition
978-1-118-01259-8

ASVAB For Dummies, 3rd Edition
978-0-470-63760-9

GRE For Dummies, 7th Edition
978-0-470-88921-3

Officer Candidate Tests For Dummies
978-0-470-59876-4

Physician's Assistant Exam For Dummies
978-1-118-11556-5

Series 7 Exam For Dummie
978-0-470-09932-2

Windows 8

Windows 8.1 All-in-One For Dummies
978-1-118-82087-2

Windows 8.1 For Dummies
978-1-118-82121-3

Windows 8.1 For Dummies, Book + DVD Bundle
978-1-118-82107-7

Available in print and e-book formats.

Available wherever books are sold. **For more information or to order direct visit www.dummies.com**